The American Impasse

PITT SERIES IN POLICY AND
INSTITUTIONAL STUDIES

THE AMERICAN IMPASSE

U.S. Domestic and Foreign Policy after the Cold War

MICHAEL MINKENBERG and
HERBERT DITTGEN, Editors

University of Pittsburgh Press

Published by the University of Pittsburgh Press, Pittsburgh, Pa., 15260
Copyright © 1996, University of Pittsburgh Press
Manufactured in the United States of America
Printed on acid-free paper
Library of Congress Cataloging-in-Publication Data
The American impasse : U.S. domestic and foreign policy after the cold war / Michael
Minkenberg and Herbert Dittgen, editors.
    p. cm. — (Pitt series in policy and institutional studies)
    Includes bibliographical references and index.
    ISBN 0-8229-3945-2 (cloth : alk. paper). — ISBN 0-8229-5612-8 (pbk.)
    1. United States—Politics and government—1989–   . 2. Post-communism-United States.
I. Minkenberg, Michael, 1959–   . II. Dittgen, Herbert, 1956–   . III. Series.
JK271.A5735   1996
320.973'09'049—dc20

96-3225
                                                                                          CIP
A CIP catalogue record for this book is available from the British Library.
Eurospan, London

CONTENTS

Preface *vii*

Introduction *ix*

1 American Impasse: The Ideological Dimension at Era's End *1*
THEODORE J. LOWI

PART I Polity: The Institutions of Government

2 The Post–Cold War President *15*
BERT A. ROCKMAN

3 U.S. Executive Branch Politics in a Changing World *33*
JOEL D. ABERBACH

4 Stability and Change in the Post–Cold War Congress *58*
JAMES A. THURBER

5 President and Congress: From Divided Government
to Post–Cold War Gridlock? *76*
TOBIAS DÜRR

6 Federalism, Recent Foreign Policy, and the Present
Plight of the System *96*
DAVID B. WALKER

PART II Politics: Political Ideologies and the Party

7 The End of Conservatism? Public Opinion and the
American Electorate in the 1990s *125*
MICHAEL MINKENBERG

8 The American Parties after the Cold War:
A Comparative Perspective *157*
PETER LÖSCHE

PART III   **Policies: Challenges and Responses**

9   The Domestic and International Sources
of U.S. Deficits   *177*
PAUL E. PETERSON

10   Social Welfare: Policy Dynamics Emerging from
State-Federal Government Interaction   *198*
ADRIENNE HÉRITIER

11   Ideological Continuities and Discontinuities
in American Public Education: Parameters of a New
Consensus   *215*
HEINZ-DIETER MEYER

12   The Foreign Policy Impasse:
In Search of a New Doctrine   *238*
HERBERT DITTGEN

13   American Trade Policy after the End of the Cold War   *264*
ANDREAS FALKE

14   U.S. Immigration Policy after the Cold War   *298*
DEMETRIOS G. PAPADEMETRIOU

Contributors   323

Index   327

PREFACE

The Fourth of July is usually a day not of sober analysis but of patriotic speeches. James Russell Lowell, American poet and U.S. ambassador in London, chose to talk about patriotism itself at his Fourth of July speech in 1883: "Now the Fourth of July has several times been alluded to, and I believe it is generally thought on that anniversary the spirit of a certain bird known to heraldic ornithologists—and I believe to them alone—as the spread eagle, enters into every American's breast, and compels him, whether he will or no, to pour forth a flood of national self-laudation." And to make sure that he not be understood as unpatriotic, he added: "I ask you, is there any other people who have confined their national self-laudation to one day in the year?"

With this critical distance, American and German political scientists gathered in Göttingen on Independence Day 1993 and undertook a comprehensive examination of American politics after the end of the East-West conflict. The papers given at this Second European-American Conference at the Center for European and North American Studies at the Georg-August Universität Göttingen are now available in this volume.

This rather apatriotic, that is, international, conference was made possible by a grant from the Fritz Thyssen Stiftung. The editors would like to thank the *Stiftung* for its generous and unbureaucratic support. In Göttingen, Peter Lösche contributed substantially to making the conference a success by his tireless efforts. Theodore Lowi helped out the editors with invaluable advice whenever they ran into problems. Special thanks also to Paul Denig of the Amerikahaus in Hannover, Frank Gress of the University of Frankfurt, Carl-Ludwig Holtfrerich of the John F. Kennedy Institute at the Free University of Berlin, Manfred Knapp of the University of the Armed Forces in Hamburg, Ernst Kuper of the University of Göttingen, Martin Seelaib-Kaier of the University of Bremen, Kurt L. Shell of the University of Frankfurt/Main, Bernhard Welschke of the Federal Association of German Industry, and Jürgen Wilzewski of the University of Frankfurt/Main. All have commented on the conference papers and thereby contributed substantially to this volume. In Göttingen the staff members of the Center for European and North American Studies deserve our thanks for their help in organizing the meetings.

Finally, the editors would like to express their satisfaction that after ten years of friendship and crossing paths in Washington, D.C., Berlin, and Göttingen, they have managed to realize a common book project.

INTRODUCTION

This volume focuses on the contrast between rapid changes in the global system and the immobility in American policy. The end of communist regimes in Eastern Europe and the USSR produced strikingly little enthusiasm in the United States. The sense of domestic crisis displaced feelings of triumph about the end of communism with a general theory of decline of America's internal strength and international competitiveness. The budget deficit, the crisis of urban America, the decline of the education system, and America's economic standing vis-à-vis Japan and the European Community, to name just a few examples, dominated the public discourse in mass media as well as academic literature. For over forty years the global challenge of American-Soviet relations permeated U.S. numerous aspects of domestic politics, and much energy was absorbed by the military and ideological threat. It seems that the end of the East-West conflict freed this energy and redirected it at the inner self of the country. It produced a somewhat painful soul-searching process rather than a (relieved) rethinking of America's role in a dramatically changing world.

The military victory in the Gulf War, in a historically spectacular alliance with the Western partners as well as the Soviet Union and the Arab states, led to a rather short-lived sense of triumph which only temporarily swept aside the crisis atmosphere. This was President Bush's bitter experience. His widespread public support, especially his impressive approval ratings during and after the Gulf War, soon dropped to record lows in the months to follow. The first presidential elections after the cold war produced a domestically inspired Democratic administration rather than reaffirming the incumbent Republican president who oversaw the collapse of communism and the triumph of the West. In that, the 1992 presidential elections were a most telling indicator of the shifting American priorities in this age of global transitions. This shift was only reinforced by the 1994 elections, despite the very different message they seemed to send.

The criticism that American political institutions and elites fail to respond appropriately to international or domestic challenges is as old as the

Republic itself. But never before has the contrast between a radically changing international context and a rather static or inflexible approach in confronting this situation domestically been sharper than in the early 1990s.

What are the reasons for this stalemate? One might point out institutional factors, such as the built-in confrontation between president and Congress, intensified by a long period of "divided government" with opposing parties leading the two top institutions. Another set of issues involves the often deplored declining quality of political leadership in contemporary America. This was evident in the presidency of George Bush, whose main interest was foreign policy and who failed to inspire domestic reforms. Add to this the theorem that, especially in America, "all politics is local," and the discrepancy becomes even more pronounced. Finally, the interplay of increasing complexities and dynamism in domestic and international politics and rising expectations of government, which almost necessarily led to an image of failure of leadership and growing cynicism, may come to mind.

In response, Bill Clinton promised to focus on domestic policies. He would end the institutional confrontation and divided government; he would initiate long-overdue national debates and serious reforms in crucial political matters such as health care; he would be a leader of another caliber who would overcome the "brain-dead politics" of Washington and restore confidence in the American government. By the time of the midterm elections of 1994, it had become clear that Clinton was not able to meet the expectations. Divided government had ended but not the confrontation between Congress and the president. Clinton developed a vigorous reform effort but failed to build the coalitions necessary to carry through the major initiatives. Despite some success in legislation, he did not emerge as a strong leader in the public eye.

Whereas the epochal transitions of 1989 had a profound immediate impact on the countries and regions involved, that is, Eastern and Central Europe, their effects on America's role in the world and its domestic arena are only slowly unfolding and recognizable. The same holds true for the degree to which American institutions and politics were shaped by the East-West conflict. For example, one could argue that the adjustment to a bipolar world in international relations after World War II intensified a bipolarization of domestic politics in which anticommunism—often coupled with the opposition to liberalism, communism's alleged "soft" version—figured prominently in the American public discourse. But only a postcommunist world can reveal the true level of this penetration, with the international source and reference point of the anticommunist impulse gone.

It is this nexus of international and domestic aspects of American politics, its changes and continuities, in particular its gradually unfolding asynchronous nature, that is at the center of the questions that are addressed in this volume. The contributions revolve around two basic questions: First, in a retrospective view, What effect did the cold war have on American institutions and American politics? Clearly, after the end of the cold war, it should be easier to answer this question than before. Second, as a prospective undertaking, How does American politics evolve after the cold war? Are the political institutions of the United States capable of meeting the new domestic and international challenges, and how do they respond? The underlying perspective tries to account for the increasing interdependence of domestic and foreign policies; hence a strict analytical separation of the two areas is hardly justifiable. The editors are well aware that it is still too early to find clear-cut answers to these questions. And some essays will only strengthen the view that (American) institutions are particularly inflexible in responding to new global challenges and, despite the radical sea changes under way, most politics is still local.

The contributions to this volume are grouped according to the main dimensions of American government. The general theme that provides the horizon for the subsequent contributions is stated in Theodore J. Lowi's opening chapter. It places institutional, political, and policy changes (or lack thereof) in a broad, historical perspective. His concern is "in the realm of the subjective, in the world of reasons rather than causes. In brief, in the realm of the ideological." Lowi argues that the collapse of the statist liberal ideology of the New Deal has opened opportunities for other, older, ideologies to return and compete for "national hegemony." Among these he identifies nineteenth-century free market liberalism, the traditional conservatism of the religious right on a nationwide scale, and the ideology of nationhood and ethnicity. The current American impasse results from the challenges these ideologies pose for liberal democracy by each of them negating national government and promoting nonnegotiable identities and truths. The cold war order deeply penetrated the American ideology and conditioned the hegemony of New Deal liberalism. But the latter did not fall with the Berlin Wall. Rather, the collapse of the New Deal liberal hegemony and the new threats to liberal democracy precede the collapse of the cold war order. With the external threat removed, America finds her true enemy within. Following Lowi's piece is a series of contributions which focus on the American polity.

Polity: The Institutions of Government

The essays in the first part address the question of how the international order and its transformation have (or have not) affected key institutions. For example, the cold war, the global conflict with an ideological opponent, contributed significantly to a concentration of power in the presidency. The emergence of a "national security state" multiplied the responsibilities of the executive and led to a drastic expansion of the bureaucracy. At the same time its numerous powers resulted in a fragmentation of the administration. In consequence, one might expect a similarly massive impact of the end of the cold war on the executive, bureaucracy, and other components of the national security state. But the authors in this section provide little evidence for such an externally inspired change in the major institutions and, instead, stress the overall impression of continuity or domestically generated changes.

Bert Rockman looks into the presidency and begins his essay (chap. 2) with the assumption that the cold war provided a powerful filter through which presidents, presidential candidates, and the presidency were evaluated by the public. He maintains that with the end of the cold war, international issues and foreign policy areas have changed in salience, if not in quality, and both Bush and Clinton adjusted by cutting defense spending. But despite the striking differences between Bush and Clinton in style and outlook, Rockman finds that in the context of the changing international order, both post–cold war presidents have behaved rather similarly in (not) addressing major national security and foreign policy concerns, in particular their lack of coherence in defining the "national interest" and America's role and involvement in the new environment.

In a similar vein, Joel Aberbach elaborates (chap. 3) the predominance of continuities in the executive branch. He points out that the end of the cold war has brought about a fierce debate on military policy which accompanied the loss of a clear rationale for foreign policy. But he sees its main effects in a sharpening of already existing conflicts and tensions over government programs and their administrators, as a result of economic and budgetary, that is, domestic, constraints.

Likewise, James Thurber argues (chap. 4) that Congress has been affected very little by the international order. He demonstrates that Congress has been very stable in the post–World War II era but changed dramatically in the last twenty years. But he adds that neither the cold war arms buildup between 1947 and 1989 nor the collapse of the Soviet empire after 1989 had a measurable direct impact on congressional stability and change. The major changes in Congress in the recent past include a variety of areas such as change in membership and staff, reforms of committees, leadership, and the budget, and changes in ethics and management. These, Thurber maintains, were driven by pressures from inside and outside Congress, such as individual members or an angry electorate, but not from outside the United States.

Among the peculiarities of American governmental institutions are the multiple separation of powers and the relationships between different government branches and levels. These include the relationship between the executive and legislative branches, especially the experience of divided government, and the interaction between the federal and state levels. With the end of the cold war occurring during the Bush administration and the transition to a Democratic administration, one might expect an end to a cold war–induced partisanship in the divided government and an opening up of new forms of some bipartisan decision making.

Tobias Dürr argues (chap. 5) that gridlock is not uniquely linked to divided government. He points out the mixed legislative results of the Democratic single-party government under Clinton and the electorate's ending of "unified government" in 1994 after only two years of Democratic dominance in both the executive and the legislature. The 1994 elections also illustrate that divided government is hardly a reaction to the cold war order and its related polarities but is an inherently domestic institutional arrangement. Dürr suggests that far from reflecting institutional polarization and divided government in the face of national security issues, gridlock is better understood as a result of a mismatch between political problems and the institutions designed to handle them.

As with the "horizontal separation of powers," the "vertical separation" between federal and state powers shows little impact of the changing international environment. As David Walker demonstrates (chap. 6), the efforts of the Reagan administration, in a particularly confrontational phase of the cold war, to reduce the federal role in the political system by means of deregulation and program cuts was, albeit ambivalently, continued for the most part during the Bush administration and, with modifications, even in the Clinton years. The 1994 elections provide a new impulse to attack the federal government, but these attacks, as is already outlined in the Lowi chapter, derive from the ideological reconfiguration of the domestic arena rather than the rearrangement of the international order. This becomes even clearer when considering the realm of politics.

Politics: Political Ideologies and the Party

Political ideologies, public opinion, and the American party system were substantially shaped by the cold war and in particular the struggle against communism—domestically and internationally. Although there are indications that after the old bipolarity of East versus West or totalitarianism versus liberal democracy, new (bi)polarities emerge that will structure domestic discourse and conflicts, the evidence again points at domestic rather than international sources for these shifts.

Michael Minkenberg's essay (chap. 7) demonstrates that the "cold war schema" as a political paradigm and cultural predisposition has indeed structured partisan conflicts and lent ideological meaning to the dividing lines in the American electorate after World War II. However, while the dominant international factors of the cold war era have not changed much over forty years, there has been a significant reconfiguration among the parties, among voters, and in public opinion over the last twenty-five years. A new cleavage and a realignment trend, Minkenberg argues, contribute to ideological polarization between the major parties, increasing support for the Republican Party among formerly Democratic constituents, and a shift to the right of the Republican Party under the growing influence of the religious right. The realignment of the religiously conservative segments of the electorate with the Republican Party signals a "Europeanization" of the American party system in which the parties become ideologically more homogeneous and divide the religious and secular forces along a left-right partisan axis. These trends shaped the 1992 and 1994 elections, which, as contradictory as they may seem, are thus complementary expressions of common, underlying developments: a continuation of the conservative era beyond Ronald Reagan and the cold war.

The theme of convergence between American and European, more specifically, German, party systems is developed further in Peter Lösche's contribution (chap. 8). Lösche argues that whereas the American parties, beginning with party reforms in the early 1970s, have developed centralizing tendencies in organization and financial control, German mass parties have introduced new forms of internal grassroots democracy and decentralized into a stage of "loosely coupled anarchy." Among the sources of these trends is the influence of the cold war order on Western national party systems in terms of a pressure for internal discipline and integration. But Lösche emphasizes a more crucial role for other factors such as common social and cultural shifts, which include the expansion of educational opportunities, the restructuring of the labor markets, a value change among younger generations, and the increasing role of mass media. The end of the cold war certainly reduces the pressures on parties to conform and rearranges the role of national security issues for parties and their voters in both the United States and Germany. But the other trends will not be stopped by it even if more fragmentation is a likely outcome in post–cold war party systems.

Policies: Challenges and Responses

The cold war also largely determined the parameters for almost all policy areas. The impact of the cold war and its end on the most important policy areas such as the budget, social policy, public education, foreign policy, trade policy, and immigration are discussed in the third part of the book.

It is almost conventional wisdom that the cold war engaged the United

States in a costly military competition that eventually resulted in enormous budget deficits. Paul E. Peterson impressively challenges this view (chap. 9) by showing that budget deficits in the United States cannot be blamed on the cold war. On the contrary, if there is any connection between the two events at all, it was the relaxation in tensions between the two great superpowers which induced deficit policies in the United States. An important consequence of his finding is that the end of the cold war will not put an end to deficits if the intellectual and institutional order of the eighties continues.

Poverty represents a persistent and challenging problem for American society. Little progress has been made since President Johnson announced his War on Poverty in the sixties. On the contrary, in the eighties social disparities in the United States have deepened. Therefore one could have expected that the end of the cold war would release political and financial resources for a new antipoverty policy. But as Adrienne Héritier shows (chap. 10), the end of the cold war had a negative rather than a positive effect in that the large-scale layoffs by enterprises producing for the military sector have contributed to the rise of poverty. Moreover, the shrinking of the military has closed an important avenue of upward mobility, in particular for young underclass blacks. Héretier focuses on an aspect that is particularly striking to the foreign observer: the dynamics of social welfare policy making inherent in the federal structure.

Like economic wealth, the American school system is characterized by extremes: the best universities of the world and a poor general education. Heinz-Dieter Meyer's contribution (chap. 11) is an attempt to tie the difficulties the United States encounters in maintaining a world-class system of public education to some of the ideological strains and tensions running through the nation's cultural fabric. During the cold war, such divisions were likely to be attributed to the opposing forces of global ideological competition. With the erosion of this competition, one may, for the first time, identify the ideological fault lines running through the very heart of Western educational ideology and practice. But the outcome of American educational reform is still uncertain.

American foreign policy is naturally most immediately affected by the end of the cold war, or so it seems. Foreign policy in the cold war era, understood as the struggle with communism and the global containment of Soviet influence, had dominated the political agenda and almost all other political areas for almost half a century. Herbert Dittgen argues (chap. 12) that the end of the cold war necessitates a radically changed orientation of American foreign policy. This holds true not only for setting foreign policy objectives but—and this is the crucial point—also for the political process, the functioning of the political institutions, and the attainment of political legitimacy for the conduct of foreign policy. He begins by comparing the validity of the two main theoretical foreign policy strands—realism and liberalism—after the end of the cold war. He argues that even though power politics has not become obsolete, the view of liberal internationalism has become most convincing. Liberalism lies also at the heart of President Clinton's foreign policy. The implementation of his foreign policy doctrine, that is, the enlargement of democracy on a global scale, has been inconsistent. This weakness results from the liberal vision's lack of priorities without a clear enemy and its proclivity for military crusades in the name of democracy. After the cold war the main problem is, however, to develop a consistent foreign policy with clear priorities under the conditions of increasing international and domestic political fragmentation. These priorities have to be set by the president.

With the cold war and its obsession with military security ending, a new mania seems to occur: trade and economic competitiveness. Indeed, one can argue that the United States has entered an era in which foreign policy and national security increasingly revolve around commercial interests. Trade policy becomes essential to resolving the new conflicts within the interdependence of global economic linkages. Andreas Falke points out (chap. 13) that in the context of the East-West conflict, American trade policy was subordinated to a general strategy of strengthening America's allies economically. U.S. trade policy was previously integrated into an all-embracing security policy based on the concept of containing communism. With the end of the military threat, an accelerated paradigm shift takes place from "free trade" to "fair trade." This shift is occurring gradually and has not yet come to an end.

According to public opinion polls, the three biggest foreign policy problems facing the United States after the cold war are the nation getting involved in other countries' affairs, the waste of and by foreign aid, and immigration. This new salience of immigration is highlighted by the populistic political debate in California about the costs to the social infrastructure of undocumented immigrants. But more generally, the movement for restricting immigration is an expression of a new nationalism after the external enemy has disappeared. In the last chapter (chap. 14), Demetrios Papademetriou points out that the immigration discussion in the United States has always been driven by domestic considerations. There have been various adaptations to refugee situations and narrow immigration programs that respond to specific foreign and security policy concerns, but their overall impact was only marginal. This analysis remains valid beyond the end of the cold war. Overall, U.S. immigration policy has retained the conceptual framework that existed during the cold war. It was the issue of "international competitiveness" that played the critical role in shaping the first U.S. immigration legislation after the cold war, the 1990 Immigration Act. Papademetriou concludes that the trend toward focusing more fully on global economic competition in defining the overall approach to immigration is likely to continue.

All in all, the contributions to this volume show the very limited effects of the end of the cold war on processes and structures of American politics. Political institutions, political thought and behavior, and the capacities for problem solving have met the external forces of change with inflexibility. Whereas the institutions adjusted rapidly and flexibly to the challenges of the cold war as it unfolded, the possibilities of institutional reform after the cold war seem very constrained. In contrast, significant changes are taking place in the American public and the party system. But they are a result of internal social processes rather than a response to the epochal international transformation. Accordingly, among the various policy areas, it is domestic and particularly social policies that are characterized by a serious reform effort and a large degree of responsiveness to new pressures.

It is still uncertain which direction the United States will take in its everlasting search for new goals and purposes. At present, domestic reforms dominate the agenda. The disappearance of the old parameters of the cold war, however, has led to a widespread sense of uncertainty about America's identity and role in the world. Or, in John Updike's words in *Rabbit at Rest:* "Without the Cold War, what's the point of being an American?" An answer to this question will not be found soon.

The American Impasse

ONE

AMERICAN IMPASSE

The Ideological Dimension at Era's End

THEODORE J. LOWI

The cold war is over and we won. Why do we feel so bad? It is most appropriate that a conference on post–cold war American politics was held on the Fourth of July 1993, four thousand miles from Washington—just enough distance to provide some perspective. And the theme of the conference was strikingly appropriate:

> This conference will focus on the contrast between the rapid changes in the global system and the immobility in American policy. The end of Communist regimes in Eastern Europe and the USSR produced strikingly little enthusiasm in the U.S. The sense of domestic crisis displaced feelings of triumph about the end of Communism with a general theory of decline of America's internal strength and international competitiveness.

That is the phenomenon to be explained, and if we can explain it, we may perhaps learn how to do something about it.

The most popular term of reference in the United States for the American problem is *gridlock*, borrowed from the uniquely modern experience of a traffic jam that seems interminable. A more appropriate term may be *impasse* because it conveys the impression that things may actually be moving but getting nowhere, as though down a street that turns out to be a dead end. The evidence seems to be sufficient to convince most Americans that there is in fact a crisis of gridlock or impasse. The evidence includes the mounting annual deficits, which seem unresponsive to changes in the economy. It includes the fact that no new programs have been enacted and no old and outdated programs have been terminated. The evidence also includes chronic unemployment and underemployment despite efforts at all levels to the contrary—the sustained 1993–1994 recovery is called a "jobless recovery." A further piece of evidence is the seven increases during

1

1994 in Federal Reserve interest rates aimed at cooling down the genuine sustained economic growth, in fear that growth might be inflationary.

The election of Bill Clinton in 1992, ending years of "divided government," gave encouragement that the dead end street had been opened up; and the first session of Congress under President Clinton seemed to confirm the hope that the impasse was over, the gridlock was broken. Although slow to make all of his senior appointments and embarrassed at the very outset by being forced prematurely to confront the issue of gays in the military, President Clinton seemed then to do everything right. He put through Congress the most impressive volume of successful legislation since the 1960s, and his "batting average"—measured by the percentage of presidentially favored bills that were passed in Congress—was 86 percent, the highest first-session average since Eisenhower's 89 percent in 1953. (Kennedy's 1961 batting average was 81 percent; Carter's first-year average was 75 percent.) Moreover, in the process Clinton managed to cut the size of the annual deficit for the first time in well over a decade.

Yet not only did the sense of impasse persist, but also there were indications of political pathology far more serious—tending toward a sense of governmental incapacity. These were sure signs of illegitimacy. These messages had been passed out from elites to the masses as a political tactic all during the 1980s, but they were bouncing back toward elites with such force that elites themselves were being convinced by their own messages. Academic as well as journalistic publications were rife with such concepts as decline, dealignment, de-industrialization, decadence, distrust, and all seemed to come into focus around the question posed by one of the most prominent authors in this genre, "Why Americans hate politics."[1] And feelings turned increasingly toward actions, all strongly symbolic of mass voter frustration. A spontaneous movement for term limits was successful in over twenty states. After the 1994 election this became a very serious move to make term limits a new constitutional amendment, providing for only two six-year terms for senators and six two-year terms for members of the House. Another amendment strongly symbolic of the distrust of national politics was the balanced budget amendment, which required not only annual balanced budgets but also a three-fifths vote on any spending measure that would unbalance the budget and a three-fifths vote on any new taxes. Proposals for devolution of national government programs to the states were coming from a variety of sources, and there was an irresistible movement for placing a general freeze on all new regulations. In some ways far more ominous, there was a spreading tendency to demonize leaders, including elected representatives; there was a frenzied attack on all incumbents. Demonization was especially intense between opposing leaders.

The most dramatic representation of this, of course, was the congressional revolution of 1994. This was a disaster for all incumbents, and that mainly meant Democrats. For the first time in forty-two years, the Republicans gained control of the entire Congress—House as well as Senate. And they did it without the help of a victorious presidential candidate with long coattails. In many ways the 1994 Republican triumph overshadowed the clean sweep of Eisenhower in 1952. This was the biggest and sweetest Republican victory since 1946. In the Senate, Republicans moved from a 44-seat minority to a 53-seat majority. Making this even sweeter was the switch of two senators and three House members after the election from the Democratic to the Republican Party.[2] In the House, Republicans moved from a 178-seat minority to a 230-seat majority—9 more than the absolute majority of 218 votes. And the victory went deeper than that: Republicans came out of the 1994 election with a gain of 10 governorships, from 20 to 30, and with control of 17 state legislatures, more than double the previous 8. This has tremendous bearing on the 1996 presidential election, and the Democrats are the first to recognize it. All of this was brought home even more traumatically by the number of leading figures in the Democratic party suffering defeat: Governor Mario Cuomo of New York, the former chair of the House of Ways and Means Committee, Dan Rostenkowski, the House Judiciary Committee chair, Jack Brooks, three-term Senator Jim Sasser of Tennessee, and, most shocking of all, House Speaker Thomas Foley, the first sitting Speaker to be defeated for reelection to his own congressional seat since 1860.

Given these stark realities, intellectuals have not been far behind with explanations. Some of these will be found in the chapters to follow, including such objective evidence as the decline of the party system, the presidency, Congress, the federal system, the twenty-year intrusion of political action committees, the decline in voter turnout and concomitant increases in ticket splitting, divided government, and so on. Although I am sympathetic to these approaches, my own effort will be in the realm of the subjective, in the world of reasons rather than causes—in brief, in the realm of the ideological. It is my hope that this will also help provide a context for the causal analyses to come.[3]

I have identified three relatively recent ideological influences on American political life. These are not new ideologies but are revivals of old and established ones that have returned to the competition for national hegemony in the vacuum left by the collapse of the ideology that had been hegemonic for so long—the statist liberalism of the New Deal (which I will refer to as new liberalism). Let me first identify the three and then take each one for separate assessment:

1. the resurgence of old, nineteenth-century free market liberalism, erroneously labeled conservatism, "old liberalism," to be distinguished from the "new liberalism" of the New Deal;
2. the mobilization on a national scale of genuine conservatism; and
3. the rekindling of nationhood as a belief system—in the United States as well as worldwide.

The Revival of Old Liberalism

Twenty-five years ago, I anticipated "the end of liberalism,"[4] meaning the end of new or statist liberalism, but at the time I did not have much of an idea of what ideological force or forces would rise to replace it. The collapse of the New Deal political coalition created a great ideological vacuum, and that brought on an ideological realignment without an electoral realignment. The first ideology to gain advantage from this realignment was a form of liberalism itself: classic, nineteenth-century, Smithian, laissez-faire liberalism. Until the late 1960s, radical laissez-faire liberals—called libertarians by this time—such as Milton Friedman could hardly get a national forum. Yet, within just a few years, they were highly sought after and began to win their share of Nobel economics awards.

In so many ways this is a strange turn of events because nineteenth-century liberalism had been so thoroughly discredited by the Depression. Not only did the Democrats saddle Hoover with responsibility for that disaster, but Roosevelt even appropriated the liberal label, despite Hoover's strenuous effort to retain it. By the end of the 1930s, Hoover had given up his effort to retain the liberal label, claiming that Republicans should not seek to keep the label because it had been spoiled by the socialism in the Democratic Party. He advised that the Republican Party accept and try to be comfortable with the conservative label, despite its disadvantages. Conservatism stuck, even though it is a complete misnomer.[5] As the years went by, the New Deal brand of statist liberalism went into decline, the conservative label became more popular, and ultimately liberalism became stigmatized as a socialist, therefore foreign, doctrine. At one point, President Reagan referred to liberalism as so far left as to have left the country altogether. President Bush and associates further stigmatized liberalism by suggesting that liberals were "card-carrying" members of some kind of cult that could only be designated as "the L-word."[6]

The character of the influence of this resurgent old liberalism can be best epitomized by another remark of Ronald Reagan, early in his administration, that "government is the problem, not the solution." Reagan's victories coupled with Reagan's own prose established convincingly with millions of Americans that, with this bastardized and highly radicalized version of Adam Smith, we could virtually close the doors on the national government and get along a whole lot better. Reagan himself obviously did not believe that. Despite all his ravings and rantings, he did not seek the termination of a single major New Deal program, and he embraced government as long as it was in military uniform. But majorities of the American people took his discourse to heart.

Since the 1960s there had been what Lipset and Schneider have called "the confidence gap" in the United States.[7] But the libertarian critique beginning in the 1970s brought that lack of confidence into focus on government, specifically the national government. And it was not merely antagonism to the policies of the New Deal. The policies, and the intensifying allegations of wasteful implementation of those policies, were simply evidence that the positive state created by the New Deal had itself become illegitimate. Demands for political reform, such as those identified earlier, as well as widespread demands for forms of direct democracy, such as referendums, were evidence of the increasing reluctance of Americans to permit important social issues to be settled by normal government and political routines. Taken in its pure radical form, all liberalism is deeply antagonistic to democracy. "Liberal democracy" in this context is an oxymoron; radical liberalism is not democratic but *anarchic*. The great contribution of the progressivism that became New Deal liberalism was to adapt liberalism to democracy by finding an escape clause in liberalism that could justify state intervention. That escape clause can be put as follows: Government intervention can be justified when it is aimed at conduct deemed injurious in its consequences. Much of the strength of the New Deal arose out of this revision of liberalism. But it was also the source of its decadence and collapse as it became easier and easier to convince the Congresses of the late 1960s and early 1970s that any and every potential injury justified government intervention.

By the 1980s the reaction was so strong against New Deal liberalism that it became not only increasingly difficult to prove that some particular injury warranted new government action but in fact even embarrassing to suggest the possibility. But what is important here is not the specifics of policy decisions but the attitude toward government itself. Beginning even with President Carter, the effort to downsize the national government was accompanied by the spread and intensification of antigovernment rhetoric, particularly anti-Congress rhetoric. Congress bashing reached new levels of intensity, contributing to an unprecedentedly low rating of Congress in the opinion polls.[8] All of this contributes mightily to the sense that no new options are available to the national government to meet its domestic or its international obligations. As we shall see, the bottom line was negation of national government itself—the new antistatism.

Mobilization of genuine American conservatism

Since a genuine conservatism was emerging coincidentally with the revival of old liberalism (or libertarianism), it was perhaps natural to confuse the two, especially because of the mislabeling of libertarianism as conservatism. Yet two public philosophies could hardly be farther apart. American conservatism is a combination of the Bible and Edmund Burke. Liberalism (whether the nineteenth-century libertarian brand or the New Deal brand) is deeply individualistic, instrumental, and basically antagonistic to the imposition of moral principles onto public discourse; in contrast, genuine conservatism virtually reverses those positions, putting morality first and accepting individualism only with the proviso "properly understood." And whereas liberalism is against government in principle, conservatives are statists, quite strongly progovernment, unless and until the substance of a government action is contrary to conservative principles.[9]

Both of the major American political parties are liberal parties with a conservative wing. But the conservative wings of both had generally been content to remain minority wings because the concerns of conservatism had never been with the national government at all but with the state governments. Thanks to American federalism, the national government was always the home of liberalism while the state governments have been the home of conservatism. With certain significant exceptions, conservative leaders had traditionally not bothered much with Washington or with the national parties because, for conservatives, that would have been a waste of time. Conservatives are historically concerned with such public issues as marriage and sexual morality; family and custody and estates; property and crimes against property; personal conduct and crimes against persons; the content of public education; and all matters affecting public order, including the status of women and the right of women to deal with their own bodies.

Until the late 1960s, Washington was simply not relevant to most genuine conservatives. As a matter of fact, most conservatives, especially the Southern conservatives in the Democratic Party, were quite happy with the New Deal of the 1930s because capitalism itself is problematic to conservatives, and a national government capable of competing with capitalism could be a good thing. Russell Kirk, dean of American conservatives, gave the best characterization in an essay published early in the Reagan era: "To talk of forming a league or coalition between [conservatives and libertarians] is like advocating a union of ice and fire. . . . The libertarian [for example] takes the state for the great oppressor. But the conservative finds that the state is ordained by God."[10] The expansion of what came to be called social policies and social regulation in the 1960s wedged the conservatives out of the Democratic Party and riveted the attention of all conservatives, Democratic and Republican, on the activities of the national government. Thus one cannot say that a conservative movement was founded in the 1960s. Conservatism is as old as liberalism. One can say that conservatism was nationalized in the 1960s and became a national movement under the leadership of Moral Majority ministers, such as Jerry Falwell and Pat Robertson, and conservative entrepreneurs, such as Richard Viguerie and Paul Weyrich. They all came together around Ronald Reagan.

The winning Reagan coalition was obviously as contradictory as was the New Deal coalition. But with a difference. Roosevelt's was a coalition of interests. Reagan's coalition possessed some of that, but in addition, it was a coalition requiring a concordance. In other words, it was much less a patronage coalition of the New Deal type and much more of a coalition of ideologies, unique in U.S. experience. It was made possible by the fact that the libertarians (who, it should be repeated, made up the majority—the mainstream—of the Republican Party) could agree with the genuine conservatives on one very important thing: that the national government is an evil force. To the libertarians this was an extension of their general principle that all government is evil. They could make common cause with the conservatives because conservatives had come to the conclusion that the social policies of the post-1968 national government had to be opposed. The conservatives were even willing to keep the welfare state as long as it was decentralized and put within the powers of the state governments. Along with that, they sought to restore most of the powers that the Supreme Court had taken away from the states. That is, they were statists, as long as the state in question was the state government. In the short run, being against national government was a sufficient agreement to enable libertarians and conservatives to make common cause.

This brings us directly to the post–cold war American impasse: the only thing that the Reagan coalition could agree upon was just that, *negation of the national government.* For both the libertarians and the nationally mobilized conservatives, *liberal democracy was the problem.* The collapse of the cold war and the Soviet Union as an all-encompassing enemy simply made this opposition to liberal democracy (i.e., new liberalism) more explicit and out in the open. As long as there was a cold war, we could diminish or suppress liberal democracy in the name of national security. Once there was no longer a national security argument, liberal democracy had to be suppressed or opposed or reformed or constrained in other terms, with more direct arguments. Whatever triumph there was in the collapse of the Soviet empire, it was not democracy over communism; it was the market economy over state-centered socialist economies. Actually, the market economy would prove to be quite compatible with a whole variety of political systems, and the global market could be pursued consistently along with opposition or indifference to a liberal democratic state.

Rekindling nationhood as ideology

On principle, virtually everyone welcomes the end of armed suppression of minorities and the prospect of self-determination for all peoples. However, there are many dimensions of this phenomenon, and all of them are problematic. One dimension is of special relevance for the impasse in the United States today, and that is one I will concentrate on: the mobilization of nationhood and its variant, ethnic spirit, in the United States in the context of the globalization of market competition.

Nationhood (including ethnicity) and the market are contradictory. Nationhood is culturally specific, attached to land and blood, arising out of the sense of common past and common destiny. The market is universalistic, having no past or future, except by contract. It needs neither culture nor knowledge—only information, for purposes of instant communication. It needs no loyalty except to the bottom line and no responsibility except of the fiduciary kind. Although the globalization of markets is enormously productive, it leads to the interpenetration of cultures, causing friction.

This is a new kind of bipolarity. The bipolarity to which we had become accustomed is external bipolarity, between West and East, maintained by mutual assured destruction. The new type is internal bipolarity, wherein each country is struggling to make its own hard policy choices of how to maintain a balance between the cultural particularities of nationhood (sometimes called community) and the economic universalisms of the market.

This is a worldwide problem to which the United States is not immune. It is as though the raising of the Iron Curtain enabled us to see our own problems more clearly.

The assault of global competition on communities has led to a retreat by Americans from our commitment to enough redistribution to resist the Marxian axiom that the rich get richer and the poor get poorer. It has led to a retreat from the brief but successful campaign to extend civil rights to minorities and other low-status groups. It has produced status panic in response to new immigration, even though it is small compared to the great waves of the nineteenth and early twentieth centuries. At the same time, there has been a mobilization of the pride of these same minorities and ethnic groups, the revival, in effect, of nationhood as a belief system. And the demands of these minorities to use government affirmative action, not only to promote the right of full participation in the market and in politics but to compensate for past deprivations, has mobilized the antagonism of older and higher-status groups that feel the remedy will come at their expense.

There are several consequences of this kind of rekindling, but the most important and the most relevant here is the impact, once again, on liberal democracy. Negation. When self-determination goes beyond ethnic solidarity and becomes an all-encompassing belief in its own superiority and its right to autonomous existence, some form of "ethnic cleansing" is likely to take place, albeit rarely in the violent form of the Serbs against the Bosnian Muslims. In these circumstances, the only democracy possible is the hyphenated kind—such as Islamic democracy or Hebrew democracy or Christian democracy or Slavic democracy. But such qualified democracies either are completely homogeneous or are oxymorons. When an ethnic group exists within a country of many ethnic groups, ethnicity must be trivialized or democracy negated. There must be relativist multiculturalism or culture war.

In the United States there are precedents bearing on the impact of revived nationhood on liberal democracy. In 1798 the Napoleonic Wars and the refugees to the United States produced a reaction in Congress in the form of the Alien and Sedition Acts, providing the national government with the extraordinary powers to arrest and deport foreigners deemed un-American. Note the linkage: Alien *and* Sedition. The law provided not only that "dangerous" aliens could be expelled or imprisoned at the discretion of the president. It also provided that any American citizen would be guilty of a crime if he or she were involved in any combination or conspiracy against any actions of the government or conspired to encourage insurrection or riot, or engaged in any writing, publishing, or speaking that was of "a false, scandalous and malicious nature" against the government or any of its officers.[11] In other words, issues of nationality tended to trump ordinary politics. Once more: negation of liberal democracy.

Another precedent is the 1850s movement of the nativist Know-Nothing Party, which elected many governors and legislators on a program of putting an end to immigration. This was, among other things, a reaction against the abolitionist movement, and it helped bring down what little was left by then of the facade of representative government. Negation.

The aftermath of World War I produced a floodtide of national self-determination comparable to that of today. It also produced massive pressures to immigrate to the United States, along with historic levels of good works on the part of the United States (led by Herbert Hoover) to provide aid and comfort to war-ravaged peoples in Europe. The nationhood of that time, encouraged in our foreign policies and in the eloquent rhetoric of such people as Woodrow Wilson, also produced an extraordinary nativist reaction at home. Unsurprisingly, it produced America's first restrictive immigration laws. It also produced some of the most severe restraints and attacks on American civil liberties—the Red Scare, the vicious attacks on anarchists, attacks on free press and speech, the return of the Ku Klux Klan, the outlawing of the teaching of evolution. And so on, toward more negation.

The post–World War II period offers another confirming case. Once again, vast and restrictive revisions of American immigration law were incorporated in the same statute with some of the most restrictive assaults on freedom of speech since the 1798 Alien and Sedition Acts. McCarthyism itself was an aspect of this, and there may never have been a time in the history of the United States in which it took more courage to speak freely and to engage vigorously in the political process.

Again today we see another precedent aborning. Along with enhanced ethnic solidarity and mutual hostility, there is an unusual amount of public religiosity in American politics. The solidarity of blacks as an ethnic group has always had a religious element. But in recent years there has been a reaction to black and other ethnic minority solidarity in the mobilization of working-class and lower-middle-class whites; and this is itself an ethnic type of mobilization even though these people have long ago lost any kind of tie to a mother country. The demand by the recently formed Christian Coalition, headed by Pat Robertson, for a "Christian nation" and the more moderate demand for a nation and a government based on Christian principles is, if it continues to intensify, another threat to liberal democracy.[12]

Liberal Democracy—an Endangered Species?

As the prospect of total human annihilation faded, the demands on political institutions intensified, and democratic institutions were more severely tested just when the ideal of democracy was on the verge of universal triumph.

I do not believe this is a paradox or the figment of a runaway academic imagination. America is the beacon, but it is also the test case. Most of American history confirms the observation made by Gaetano Mosca toward the end of his life, after enduring more than two decades of fascism:

> Fifty years ago [I] sought to lay bare some of the untruths . . . of the representative system, and some of the defects of parliamentarism. Today advancing years have made [me] more cautious. . . . Specialization in the various political functions . . . and reciprocal control between bureaucratic and elective elements are two of the outstanding characteristics of the modern representative state. These traits make it possible to regard that state as the most complex and delicate type of political organization that has so far been seen in world history. From that point of view, and from others as

well, it may also be claimed that there is an almost perfect harmony between the present political system and the level of civilization that has been attained in the century that saw it come into being and grow to maturity.[13]

An appropriate response to Mosca's observation is one attributed to the American author Tom Wolfe: "The specter of fascism is constantly hovering over America but always seems to land in Europe." Next time, providence may not be watching over drunkards and Americans, as the old saying goes.

Fascism arose out of the breakdown of liberal solutions to governance: Liberal democracy offers a solution to the class warfare of the Left and to the tyranny also inherent in the moral discourse of the Right because liberal democracy removes morality from public discourse, making compromise, displacement, side payments, diversities, and other instrumental behaviors possible. And liberal democracy offers, in the same spirit, a solution to the tyranny inherent in nationhood, because liberal democracy recognizes only political identity, and this artificially produces political homogeneity, whereas nationality politics, like moral politics, requires moral, cultural, or biological homogeneity. You can have a Christian republic, an Anglican republic, an Islamic or Hebrew republic only so long as all citizens are Christian, Anglican, Islamic, or Jewish. But as soon as a minority of residents is not of that particular moral or biological category, the morality or the biology must disappear from public discourse, or tyranny becomes unavoidable.

Given the delicacy of which Mosca spoke—that is, given the susceptibility of even the most enlightened nations to ideologies based on greed, morality, or nationality—liberal democracy ought to be a rare specimen in world history, perhaps an extinct or even mythical creature. At this point in time, there is a conspiracy of all three of these ideological forces against the few liberal democracies still in existence. These three ideologies are not necessarily in self-conscious opposition to democracy itself, but they are antagonistic to the ability of this democracy to take actions that can continually renew the capacity of its citizens to entrust their claims, their values and their national identities to the crude and slow and uneven workings of a nonviolent political process, so rare "in the history of the human condition . . . [as] to be valued almost as a pearl beyond price."[14]

I conclude with a line from a famous American comic strip character: "We have met the enemy, and he is us."

Notes

1. E. J. Dionne, *Why Americans Hate Politics* (New York: Simon & Schuster, 1991).
2. These were Senators Richard Shelby of Alabama and Ben Nighthorse Campbell of Colorado; and Billy Tauzin, Louisiana, Nathan Deal, Georgia, and Greg Laughlin, Texas. A fourth, Mike Parker, Mississippi, was expected to switch also.

3. See also chap. 7.

4. Theodore J. Lowi, *The End of Liberalism: Ideology, Policy and the Crisis of Authority* (New York: W. W. Norton, 1969; 2d ed. 1979).

5. The best account is in David Greer, *Shaping Political Consciousness: The Language of Politics in America from McKinley to Reagan* (Ithaca, N.Y.: Cornell University Press, 1987).

6. For more on the stigmatization of liberalism by Reagan and Bush, see Gerald Pomper, "The Presidential Nomination," in Pomper, ed., *The Election of 1988* (Chatham, N.J.: Chatham House, 1989), 33–71.

7. S. M. Lipset and William Schneider, *The Confidence Gap: Business, Labor, and Government in the Public Mind* (New York: Free Press, 1983).

8. For figures on the 1960s and 1970s, see ibid., chap. 2; for the most recent figures, see Gordon Black and Benjamin Black, *The Politics of American Discontent* (New York: John Wiley, 1994), chap. 4.

9. For more on this distinction, see Theodore J. Lowi, *The End of the Republican Era* (Norman: University of Oklahoma Press, 1995).

10. Russell Kirk, "Libertarians, the Chirping Sectories," *Modern Age,* fall 1981, 545.

11. Officially, there were three relevant acts passed by Congress in 1798: the Alien Act, the Alien Enemies Act, and the Sedition Act, of which the last was the most infamous. The quotation is from the text of the Sedition Act.

12. See chap. 7.

13. Gaetano Mosca, *The Ruling Class* (New York: McGraw-Hill, 1939), 389, 491.

14. Bernard Crick, *In Defense of Politics* (Baltimore: Penguin Books, 1964), 17.

Part I

POLITY

THE INSTITUTIONS OF GOVERNMENT

TWO

THE POST–COLD WAR PRESIDENT

BERT A. ROCKMAN

The cold war was a pervasive institution in American public life. It was the fundamental schematic through which most foreign policy activity and opinion was filtered. It provided a significant source of political cleavage among attentive publics and elites. Increasingly, it also illuminated differences between the political parties, at least rhetorically. Presidential campaigns highlighted candidates' strengths and weaknesses as cold warriors. It helped to be perceived as firm but not fanatical. Goldwater lost in 1964 partly because he was regarded as too extreme and hence too dangerous a cold warrior. Reagan won in 1980 in spite of the perception that he was a cold war extremist. If it was bad form to be a cold war fanatic, it was equally fatal to be perceived as being insufficiently committed to the tenets of the cold war. McGovern in 1972 was regarded as too dovish. By 1980 so was Carter. And in 1988 the Democratic candidate, Michael Dukakis, made an ill-fated visit inside a battle tank which the Republicans joyfully used to ridicule his posture on defense in a now famous campaign advertisement. The advertisement showed Dukakis looking somewhat goofy with a tanker's helmet and jacket on while the visuals showed the tank spinning around aimlessly. In sum, the cold war was one of the most centrally defining features of the American political and governmental landscape.

In view of the powerful hold of the cold war on American public life, how have American institutions and particularly the presidency coped with its absence? If this seems a strange question, it is not dissimilar from asking how Germany has coped with the disappearance both of the Berlin Wall and ultimately of the former German Democratic Republic itself. Desirable outcomes may leave us quite unprepared—at least in the short run—to deal with their consequences.

The time of adjustment has been brief. Its duration depends upon whether one dates it from the end of the Soviet Union at the most recent point or at the earliest from Gorbachev's posture made clear by 1987 of seeking an end to the arms race. Not only has the adjustment time been relatively short, but it also arose unexpectedly. The demise of the cold war provided a dramatic case of punctuated equilibrium in which a reality that had been so stable for so long underwent a seemingly sudden and dramatic shift. Signs of the demise of the cold war should have been apparent. After all, in 1988 perestroika and glasnost were in full sail, liberalization in Poland and Hungary had reached extraordinary proportions, and the Soviets seemed clearly to be suing for peace on Atlantic Alliance terms. Yet a good part of the American presidential campaign of 1988 played to Bush's perceived strengths and firmness as a decision maker on national security policy and Dukakis's commensurate weaknesses. The background music continued to be the cold war.

A turn of events of epic proportions is often assumed to exert powerful effects on institutions, policy, and the behavior of presidential administrations. When shifts are both massive and sudden, the resulting behavior tends toward disorientation. American policy makers continue to grope toward a new American role in the world in the presence of more severely limiting conditions than existed in the 1950s and 1960s. That role is limited by both experiences and conditions. The Vietnam experience deters military interventions in areas (such as Bosnia) that lack the terrain and clear lines conducive to U.S. military doctrines, that is, the concentration of massive firepower. The relative decline of American economic fortunes in combination with the elimination of a Soviet threat makes assistance a difficult sell to a skeptical public. Pro-assistance politicians (who would hardly identify themselves as such) always skated on thin ice. The absence of threat and the presence of stagnant income growth turn thoughts inward toward domestic matters, and that seems initially to have coincided just perfectly with the agenda of the incumbent president, Mr. Clinton, whose hands-on style of leadership is far more noticeable on domestic than foreign policy matters.[1] Ironically though, since the election of 1994 the isolationist and nativist demands pressed in the Republicans' Contract with America have turned Bill Clinton's attention more to protecting his own leverage in foreign policy. The need to do this is made compelling by virtue of the fact that until the 1996 presidential election, all Clinton has left is foreign policy.

I begin in this chapter, therefore, with a discussion of the interplay between this changed agenda, the continuing demand for U.S. involvement in the world, and the narrowed degrees of freedom accorded the president to navigate in world affairs. A second focal point is that the end of the cold war has changed the international issue set and, having done so, also has produced certain institutional winners and losers. I then look at how the two presidents who could appropriately be called post–cold war presidents, Bush and Clinton, have reacted to the end of the cold war and whether either has generated an American strategy for dealing with the post–cold war world. Finally, I assess how the post–cold war environment has affected the U.S. presidency.

The End of the Cold War—Transforming an Agenda

The immediate reaction to the fall of the Berlin Wall and the end of the Soviet empire was euphoric—at least outside the military-industrial complex. As with most such states of mind, the euphoria did not last long. It may, however, have lasted longer in the United States than it did in Europe and especially in the countries (or former countries in the case of the German Democratic Republic) liberated from communist rule where the immediacy of the problems of economic backwardness and transformation were stunningly apparent. In the United States, by contrast, distance from these problems prompted talk about peace dividends from the inevitable cutback of large defense expenditures. Later, the seemingly complete and relatively costless (for the United States) military victory in the Gulf War in early 1991 provided another euphoric rush that was destined not to last long—at least long enough to save George Bush from electoral defeat in 1992.

One thing at least was clear, and it was that the cold war was gone as an issue. Presidents who found the cold war to be a useful political life preserver would have to look elsewhere for issues. Presumably, those who found that the cold war interfered with what they wished to achieve on the domestic front would no longer have that impediment. Domestic policy matters were now to become central. Politically, of course, they always were, but presidents, especially Republican presidents, often found domestic issues either intractable, routine, or politically costly to deal with. Generally speaking, Republican presidents, having a more limited view of the role of the state than Democratic presidents have had, find a government response or policy to a problem something they prefer to avoid unless the problem concerns one of the traditional functions of the state, such as the criminal justice system, defense, diplomacy, or finance. The immediate consequence for the Republicans was that they were to some extent disadvantaged in this new environment. The cold war not only provided a compass that most Republicans could use to sort out priorities and direction in foreign policy but also provided a rationale for avoiding initiating costly domestic programs. Obviously, however, the Republicans have since adjusted well to the changed conditions with their anti-welfare, small government, pro-gun, and old-time religion themes.

Democrats, on the other hand, felt the end of the cold war to be liberating from the standpoint of the issues to which they hoped to turn their attention. The issues on which Bill Clinton rode to victory in 1992 were focused on macroeconomic performance and social insecurity. And indeed the foremost legislative proposals of the Clinton administration in its first two years revolved precisely around these issues: an effort to reduce the federal deficit by raising taxes and cutting expenditures and an effort to universalize health care coverage and control its costs. It is fair to say in retrospect that these proposals were both major and contentious. In addition, the Clinton administration came to Washington with the intention of a major reworking of industrial-government relations. It had, in short, an inexhaustible if not always feasible policy agenda. In the circumstances, it preferred to have minimal interference from outside events over which it had no control but which could threaten to derail the stature of the president domestically. By the end of his first two years, of course, Clinton's neglect of foreign policy helped derail both his stature and his presidency so that, realistically, his domestic policy aspirations are at best on hold, while those of his opponents are at center stage.

International events are always in some measure unpredictable. A foreign policy is supposed to make responses to those unpredictable events reasonably predictable. In the case of the cold war, policy was relatively predictable, and even events seemed somewhat contained by the structures of cold war antagonism. The problem for any president in the post–cold war era, ironically, is to define a policy in an environment that holds fewer structural constraints on the use of American power but substantial domestic political constraints on its exercise. The world is abuzz with conflicts, but nothing seems attached to an overriding, dominant conflict between the United States and a perceived mortal enemy. Thus questions about the extent, ways, and duration of U.S. involvement have hardly been posed, much less answered. One thing is certain: there is limited public tolerance for American soldiers being brought home in body bags. The end of the cold war and the presence of a Democratic president have made it a lot easier for Republicans to oppose U.S. interventions around the world. Moreover, peacekeeping problems are abundantly complex and their politics little understood. If the open-ended U.S. intervention in Vietnam was known by its opponents as "the big muddy," there are now numerous little muddies around to swallow up a president's prospects for policy success and political stature. As a foreign policy official in the Clinton administration put it:

> Every one of these situations involves a lot of imponderables. It's not easy to define our national interests, to decide when to intervene, to see all the consequences of intervention, to know when to declare victory and end

the intervention. And there's no upside. You win, and nobody in the general public cares much, you lose American lives and the country demands that you pull your horns in.[2]

A low-risk strategy of noninterventionism may produce high-risk results. It certainly is likely to lead to a president being pilloried by opinion leaders, especially in the prestige media. On the other hand, a high-risk political strategy without a willingness to bear the consequences of the intervention will lead to political opposition and public inconstancy at the first signs of U.S. casualties, as the episode in Somalia suggests. There is little to be gained here and much to be lost, whether a president has a substantial domestic agenda to attend to or not. Moreover, a policy once enunciated becomes a statement of "will do's" and "won't do's." Such clarity can sometimes have disastrous effects. The statement by Dean Acheson, the U.S. secretary of state, shortly before the onset of the Korean War excluding the Korean peninsula from a zone of U.S. security interests possibly prompted the North Koreans to invade the South in 1950.

Even trade issues have had some partial cold war structuring to them. John F. Kennedy could speak of a world of interdependence in his July 4, 1962, address in Philadelphia. The interdependence was designed to strengthen the capitalist forces in the world—or what was then generously referred to as the free world. Communist systems lay outside that realm of interdependence. Today, however, except for a few despotic Asian states, there is no communism, and even those regimes are merely trying to become despotic Asian capitalist states governed through the apparatus of a Communist Party. As a consequence, the European Community or Japan or, above all, the newly industrializing countries (NICs) can be viewed as adversaries as readily as allies.

Undoubtedly, Clinton's presidency in its first two years was motivated by two imperatives: (1) to protect the domestic agenda from events that might endanger it and (2) within bounds, to seek to generate a just order in world affairs. With regard to the former, it is fair to say that Clinton learned that foreign policy could not save his presidency but could sink it. Regarding the latter, however, Clinton seems, like Jimmy Carter before him, to be inspired by the professed democratic ideals of Woodrow Wilson. Clinton's inspiration, however, is tempered by a heavy dose of sobriety with regard both to the substantial political constraints operating on him at home concerning the contested use of force abroad and to the possibilities of effectively changing the status of forces on the ground at the site of an intervention. President Clinton's national security adviser, Anthony Lake, described Mr. Clinton as a "pragmatic neo-Wilsonian" in foreign policy. In elaborating that concept, Mr. Lake was quoted as saying:

A policy needs a clear goal and I think our goal in this era is to expand democracy and take advantage of the democratic tide running in the world. I believe that you best promote general goals not through absolute doctrines but through a determined pragmatism that can give substance to the general principles. Principles without pragmatism is posturing, and pragmatism without principles becomes rudderless opportunism.[3]

Thomas Friedman, the *New York Times* reporter by whom Mr. Lake was interviewed, noted in the same article that Lake's effort to find a third way between "a merciless balance of power view of the world . . . [and] a foreign policy of rampant moralism" may, in many instances, be for naught. That is Mr. Clinton's dilemma. A foreign policy based upon cold, if narrowly defined, self-interest will be unlikely to find much worth contesting in the world, no matter how tragic and disconcerting the events are. Alternatively, a moralistic foreign policy will not want for possibilities to intervene. The cold war limited those possibilities for intervention in two ways: (1) communist police states kept the lid on ethnic and nationalistic antagonisms so that they did not lead to armed civil strife and thus create new areas of possible intervention; and, more important, (2) the potential of a Soviet counter to an American intervention (as well as a likely veto in the UN Security Council) made the opportunities for a successful intervention outside the U.S. sphere of influence formidably difficult.

In sum, Mr. Clinton has inherited a world without landmarks but not without landmines. He has a compelling interest to not venture too far. But Democratic presidents cannot afford to look unconcerned or uncompassionate, given their constituencies and the ideas that Democratic leaders hold. Unfortunately, concern and compassion are the handmaidens of intervention, and intervention frequently carries with it better prospects for policy and political failure than for their success.

The Changing Issue Set—Winners and Losers

Clearly the biggest change produced by the end of the cold war is the change from a focus on military security in a bipolar world to a world with no clear focus at all. In this new world, nationalisms and ethnic unrest seethe, producing low-grade conflagrations with disproportionately high civilian casualties. This world, as with the years prior to World War I, is a world of uncertain boundaries and internal unrest. The period of state consolidation has given way to nationalist dissolution. This too resembles the world at the onset of World War I. Peacekeeping operations—largely a misnomer—have expanded with the rising number of conflicts. What is central about such conflicts for Europe and the United States is that for the first time in many decades, some are being played out on European terrain. When these conflicts grow bloody enough and become prominent in the media, they induce tension between the United States and Europe over responsibilities for mediation or even military intervention. Without a cold war demonology, the United States will tend to resist active ground involvement in such conflicts.

The framework of the cold war as seen at least through American policy makers' eyes was all-encompassing. Civil wars and regional conflicts came to be defined in cold war terms—who was backing whom? Now internal conflicts and regional conflicts largely will be left to be settled by themselves or through UN mediation when the permanent Security Council members agree about the potential dangers of spreading conflict. In reality, most such conflicts will be played out locally and settled through force—when they are settled at all. If anything, a form of international social Darwinism seems to be the real new world order.

The *new world order* was a phrase that President Bush came to use during the buildup to the Persian Gulf War of 1991. The conception underlying it was that the UN Security Council and other major actors such as Germany and Japan would help organize a global peace and keep it. The case for the new world order was predicated on the notion that future conflicts might resemble the Iraqi invasion of Kuwait, in which a clear aggressor could be punished for a violation of accepted international boundaries. It appears, however, that the Persian Gulf conflict was more aberrant than typical. The conflicts within various of the southern republics of the former Soviet Union and, of course, in the Balkans are more common, less readily definable or bounded, and, ultimately, more difficult to control. Although, from time to time, American columnists fire off salvos about intervening in such circumstances, as occasionally do members of Congress, there is little taste for it. For a number of reasons, including both the failure in Vietnam and the success in the Gulf, the military, especially the army and marine corps, have achieved an effective veto power over the deployment of American ground troops. Despite the lessened importance of the military and the downsizing of the defense budget as a result of the end of the cold war, it may be difficult to say that the military's role in influencing policy decisions has declined. It has changed, and perhaps even become more influential. As a general matter, the air force possibly excepted, the U.S. military chiefs are singularly unanxious to engage their forces on behalf of unclear missions on unfamiliar turf with uncertain support to indefinite conclusions. They know what it takes, and that knowledge sobers thoughts. Moreover, with the downscaling of the forces, the military chiefs may no longer have what it takes.

As military issues have receded from center stage, economic issues have grown more important to the United States in the post–cold war world.

They were becoming so anyway, but a decline in wages amid perceptions of unfairness in gaining access to markets (particularly with regard to Japan) or in dealing with subsidized imports has heightened these issues for American policy makers. American policy making has been structurally designed to allow members of Congress to articulate publicly threats against trading partners perceived to be unfair while, in the end, giving great deference to executive authority, as the North American Free Trade Agreement (NAFTA) and General Agreement on Trade and Tariffs (GATT) reflected. They were certainly matters of intense controversy in the United States as various interests sought to calibrate their losses or gains from the agreement. Labor unions and environmentalists generally spearheaded opposition but, in the end, lost out to a business-government consensus on reducing trade barriers and entry costs into markets. Similarly, human rights concerns, while given voice, so far have taken a back seat to the less voiced but seemingly more compelling concerns about not losing opportunities to enter the vast and booming Chinese market.

A whole series of international negotiations of both a bilateral and a multilateral nature dealing with matters as varied as intellectual property rights, copyright and patent laws, and loans and investments have come to play a relatively larger role in the now less salient sphere of foreign policy in the United States. Of course, these issues were always there, but so was the cold war. Typically, when in conflict, the strategic concerns of the cold war tended to overshadow the stuff of commercial transactions. When Henry Kissinger was national security adviser to the president and later secretary of state, he was widely reputed to find the issues of international commerce to be the trivia of international affairs and to be therefore the province of small minds such as those belonging to economists. It is a good thing for Kissinger that he was secretary of state in more interesting times because the assortment on his plate would look different now than it did two decades ago. This by no means implies that the meat and potatoes of Kissinger's day are absent; it does mean that they are a relatively smaller portion of the foreign policy menu.

In addition to issues of international trade and commerce, those dealing with assistance packages for economic restructuring in Russia and, to a lesser extent, other former Soviet republics assumed a relatively greater degree of prominence on the platter of U.S. foreign policy during the Bush administration and the first part of the Clinton administration. Now, however, bailing out the Mexican peso has taken greater priority, and the Republican Contract with America promises to cut assistance to Russia further.

Moreover, global issues involving the regulation of public goods such as the environment also have attained a relatively more prominent role. Again, it needs to be emphasized that such issues always have been there.

What has changed is their relative salience. Because of the absence of the cold war, such issues become a larger part of the foreign policy diet. It is a foreign policy less focused on throw weights than on trade deficits and international or bilateral regulatory regimes. From a presidential standpoint, there are few dramatic announcements to be made, little to stir patriotic passion, and therefore little to be politically gained and much to be lost (the conflict with Iraq aside) in dealing with foreign policy problems. That is because these problems now often look like domestic problems and bring with them a diverse array of constituencies inside and outside the country's territorial boundaries.[4]

High diplomacy has not vanished with the end of the cold war. In fact, it is possible that the demands on it have magnified as the possibility of cutting deals in areas once torn by East-West conflict becomes more realistic. It is difficult to imagine, for instance, reaching a settlement in the Middle East in the midst of the cold war when the United States was aligned with Israel and the conservative Arab kingdoms and the Soviets with the confrontation states and the Palestine Liberation Organization (PLO). The absence of the Soviet lever creates incentives for the PLO (and perhaps even confrontation states such as Syria) to seek a settlement, though, to be sure, not only do the terms of finalizing that settlement remain to be negotiated but the settlement itself remains fragile.

Nor have potential regional threats disappeared. A North Korean nuclear threat would have powerful consequences not only for the Korean peninsula but also for Japan. It has been handled delicately but without finality, and it has been dependent on the unusual personal diplomacy of former President Jimmy Carter. The balancing act between the Iraqi and Iranian regimes apparently will be required for some time; the consequences of leaning too far in either direction became apparent when Saddam Hussein invaded Kuwait in 1990. Needless to say, the Balkans remain a powerful challenge and also a testament to the negative as well as positive externalities of the end of European communism.

In sum, the changing mix of issues includes plenty of the old kinds of security conflict, but few of these pose a direct threat to American security. Consequently, fewer of these conflicts will become central or compelling issues for U.S. foreign policy unless they directly threaten U.S. allies. From that standpoint, the Korean peninsula is a potentially bigger problem for the United States than is the raging war in the Balkans. For the most part, American foreign policy concerns may now more resemble those of the European states than has been the recent tradition. Global concerns will be overshadowed by regional concerns or those involving direct threats. Thus Haiti is more salient than Somalia because its refugee problem threatens U.S. borders. Consequently, immigration restraints (perhaps the most important reason for NAFTA and for supporting the peso), the regulation of public goods, import limits or, conversely, gaining market opportunities, and assistance needs are more likely to comprise the bulk of the U.S. foreign policy issue basket.

This mix of issues alters the comparative importance of the foreign policy actors. Relatively, the traditional national security apparatus is declining somewhat while the middle- and low-brow trade, commercial, and financial agencies of government are ascending. Similarly, the president's comparative advantage in the decision-making process is reduced because he has now lost what once seemed to be the invincible shield of national security. Decisions now have to be vetted, justified, and often shared with other political actors. Naturally, this means that Congress, already an important actor, will be more so. It also means that committees other than Foreign Affairs and Armed Services are likely to play a larger and more direct role in foreign policy issues. It certainly means that interest groups will be abundantly active and effects on constituencies will be important considerations in the congressional policy-making role. To be sure, the changes here are within a relatively narrow range. The cold war brought a heightened demand for military expenditures involving both procurement and basing. The American system with its independent legislature, powerful committee influences within that legislature, and representation based on geographic and political units will hardly fail to subject the massive procurement and basing expenditures generated by the cold war to political tests of local impact. Any set of expenditures that recently had driven about 6½ percent of gross domestic product is likely to beget impressive political pressures. In the end, therefore, the changing mix of issues will bring some alteration to decision making and to the composition of the organizational actors involved, but the change mostly reinforces a tendency to place a pork-barrel value on goods that create local economic activity.

Finally, while the military is likely to be an overall loser in a post–cold war world, its role has to be internally differentiated. Cold war military budgets, especially during the Reagan years, were particularly kind to naval and air forces and their doctrines. The demise of the cold war makes their doctrines relatively less important and their role somewhat more marginal. Alternatively, if the issue is whether to intervene in a small-scale conflagration of the sort discussed earlier, mobile ground forces become more important. And, as I noted, both the negative experience of Vietnam and the positive experience in the Persian Gulf have given the military the power to define its legitimate use, especially in regard to the introduction of ground forces. The Weinberger doctrine of "get it all but don't use it" that emerged during the Reagan administration (in which Caspar Weinberger served as secretary of defense) is now confined mostly to the second part of the doctrine since obviously the defense budget is in secular decline. Vietnam defined the conditions for failure—unclear goals, uncertain lines, terrain and foliage inadequate to optimizing U.S. military power. The Gulf defined the conditions for success—clear goals, definable lines, and optimal conditions for U.S. military power. More situations in the world involve conditions resembling those of Vietnam than those of the Gulf. Hence the military, especially the ground command, is now perceived to be worldlier, wiser, and more cautious than are civilian decision makers. As a consequence it would be inadvisable politically for any American president to cut against the grain of military advice. In this sense the military has gained a near de facto veto over its deployment, especially with an incumbent president who has no military experience and, indeed, has needed to have good relations with his top military commanders to provide him with legitimacy on defense matters.

From Confusion to More Confusion—Bush and Clinton as Post–Cold War Presidents

In Ronald Reagan's second term of office, the end of the cold war could be seen. By the end of George Bush's first year in office, virtually all of the states in the Soviet sphere of influence shed their communist governments. Two years later, the Soviet Union itself went out of existence. A mere five or six years before, none of these events seemed possible, much less plausible. By the time Bill Clinton came to office, the new reality was old news and presumably there would be greater opportunity to adjust to the changed conditions.

Bush and Clinton seem to have at least one thing in common. At some point in their education they each attended Yale University. There may be others, but for the most part the differences between Bush and Clinton are more striking than their similarities. For one thing, they are a generation apart. Bush came of age during World War II, and the cold war followed shortly thereafter. Clinton came of age during the Vietnam War and also "the age of Aquarius" (a song and symbol from the 1968 antiwar musical "Hair"). For another, they are of different political dispositions. Clinton is anxious to do. He has (or at least had) a very large domestic policy agenda and, like Jimmy Carter, wants to be intimately acquainted with its details. Bush, alternatively, is a man of genuinely conservative disposition. For want of a better concept, *anti-doing* defined his policy agenda. Bush frequently was accused of a lack of vision. In fact, his vision was that, unless proven otherwise, the status quo is preferable to the alternatives. Bush largely was a reactor to events, seeing little need for initiative, the major exception being the stimulation of Middle East peace negotiations. Whatever Clinton's thinking about foreign policy, it is clear that his first priority has been his domestic agenda. After the 1994 election, he appears to be finding his second priority more worthy of his attention.

Bush lived for foreign policy. Domestic matters seemed to bore him. This seems to be a condition, as I have noted, that generally characterizes Republican presidents (Reagan being a major exception), the reason being that, on the whole, Republican presidents are rarely interested in starting expensive new programs or in using government to actively intervene in domestic social or economic matters. Such matters, in any event, are heavily driven by Congress, bureaucratic agencies, and interest groups. There are opportunities for a president to lead here, but the costs in persistence, bargaining trade-offs, and detailed knowledge are high while the immediate payoffs and photo opportunities are limited in comparison with significant breakthroughs in foreign affairs.

Clinton seems to believe, however, that foreign policy and domestic policy are part of a web that makes it difficult if not impossible for them to be disentangled. Nonetheless, the beginning point for Clinton is domestic policy. A domestic agenda designed (in Clinton's view, of course) to strengthen the country's internal capabilities is necessary to allow it to project its interests abroad. This, in fact, was a theme common to more than one Democratic candidate running for president in 1992. From this perspective, foreign policy is designed to improve the domestic economic and social welfare of the United States. Without this improvement, there are powerful limits to the role that the United States can play in the world.[5] The paradox is this: for Clinton, an excessive focus on foreign policy burns up domestic policy capital, and without sound domestic policies, foreign policy capabilities are weakened.

Among Republican presidents generally, and for Bush particularly, foreign policy is what the country needs a president for. Bush had spent a significant part of his long public career in the foreign policy–national security arena as UN ambassador, director of the Central Intelligence Agency, and ambassador to China. His relentless style of getting to know other leaders (widely reported from his UN days) made him comfortable in his dealings with a variety of national leaders.

Clinton, by way of contrast, was the governor of a small and rather provincial state, though he is a man of more than casual knowledge about the world. What Clinton wants is often vague or ambiguous. But he does seem to have a model of what he does not want to be. What he does not want to be is Lyndon Johnson, whose programs of social reform floundered in the morass of Vietnam. For Clinton, then, the key is to stick with his domestic agenda by not repeating Johnson's mistake and getting overly committed to any unpredictable military involvements. While Clinton was campaigning for the presidency, of course, he criticized Bush for seeming to be callous toward the fate of Haitian refugees and of the Bosnian Muslim community. The reality has been that Clinton's policies, despite halting movements toward alternatives, are ultimately nearly indistinguishable from Bush's. Only when the Haitian refugee problem got out of hand did Clinton move to oust the military government there—a path eased for him once again by the peripatetic former President Carter.

Thus, despite the differences in style and outlook between the two post–cold war presidents, there seem to be relatively few differences in the policies of the two presidencies in the post–cold war era as they groped for a new American role in the world. The differences, such as they are, seem to be defined by their parties and the differences in party constituents. Bush preferred markets to political harmonization between trading partners. Labor unions are not a Republican constituency. Nor are groups pushing for increased regulatory activity. Nor are human rights advocacy groups. The last group places pressure on Democratic presidents to intervene, but usually through nonmilitary means. On trade, as in the domestic economy itself, Clinton believes partially in the invisible hand but also in the guiding one. In the end, Clinton had to carry with him at least some of those of his political allies who were skeptical of the reputed benefits of an unmanaged international trading system. He also needed in the first two years to placate at least symbolically those advocacy groups and opinion leaders who want U.S. policy to right the world's injustices with or without (and mostly without) the use of military force. Now he needs to fend off the "America-firsters," who want more defense but neither intervention nor assistance.

Understandably, both Bush and Clinton cut defense spending. But Clinton's proposed cuts ran deeper. Again, party differences are important here. Republicans have been kinder to the Pentagon mainly because they saw it as the bulwark against the Soviet threat. Democrats tend to look at the defense budget as a source of largesse for domestic programs or for deficit reduction. There has been, of course, a dramatic decrease in strategic weaponry and other weapons that were designed to combat a Soviet advance through Europe. But it is not clear that a new military strategy has evolved or precisely how the United States seeks to organize and project its force structure. Success in the Persian Gulf, achieved heavily by armored units that had been stationed for NATO forces in Germany, feeds the emphasis on high technology conventional arms. But for the most part, these armored units are being heavily cut back. While the Republican Contract wants to stoke money into the "star wars" of Ronald Reagan's dreams against some as yet undefined intercontinental or, perhaps, intergalactic threat, the question of what force structure is necessary against what possible adversaries certainly has yet to be seriously debated in any public way.

One thing, though, is crystal clear: in the post–cold war world, there will be a powerful reluctance to commit forces that are likely to suffer significant casualties. As the events in Bosnia suggest, the United States will watch and it will implore, but it will not fight, at least on the ground. Eventually, the United States may even cease imploring, merely hoping that a less bloody equilibrium can be achieved without significant spillover effects elsewhere in the Balkans. In spite, therefore, of Bush's Realpolitik and Clinton's "pragmatic neo-Wilsonianism," in the present circumstances and with past American experience in situations of limited hostilities, Bush and Clinton have largely behaved similarly. The difference between them is that Bush likely would have arrived at his conclusion at the outset whereas Clinton reaches it by fits and starts, hoping to produce a U.S. influence on the outcome without a commensurate willingness to pay the price for that influence.

Neither President Bush nor President Clinton has articulated a coherent post–cold war policy, especially one that defines the terms of involvement. Without such a policy having been articulated, however, one seems to have evolved. The much discussed background comments of Peter Tarnoff, U.S. undersecretary of state, seemed to sum up the inevitable condition of U.S. policy leadership despite being quickly disavowed by Secretary of State Warren Christopher. The unofficial version in this case seems to speak more soundly and forthrightly than the official one. Tarnoff's message boils down to this: There are profound limits to American power in the world which, in any event, is declining; expect less from us.[6]

That message is correct not only because the facts underlying it are but also because the rationale for external commitments has drastically weakened. That is the legacy of the end of the cold war. No one should expect the United States to disappear as an important world actor. But it will be more likely to measure its international involvement in terms of its domestic payoff. There will be no return to what is popularly conceived of as isolationism, but there will be no return to unbridled Wilsonism (or even Reaganism) either. National interest, however imperfectly marked, is apt to be a more predictable guide to American foreign policy behavior in the post–cold war world than any ideological mission. The present lack of coherence in policy, therefore, principally reflects both the absence of a clearly antagonistic set of ideas in the world and the inherent ambiguities underlying the concept of "national interest." The new Republican majority in Congress, moreover, has amended the Tarnoff doctrine in effect to read: expect nothing from us.

The Post–Cold War Era and Its Impact on the U.S. Presidency

Foreign policy has saved no president but possibly ruined several. In spite of its allure, particularly for Republican presidents, it is no panacea for any president's fortunes. To a considerable extent during the time of the cold war, a president's short-term appeal often rested on things the Soviets or its allies were perceived to do rather than things the United States did. Crises often provided a modest to sizable but typically short-term rally effect behind the incumbent president. When the Soviets invaded Afghanistan, for example, President Carter's popularity rose from very low levels. That was enough to help him win a number of Democratic primaries in 1980 but not enough to arrest the ultimate long-term political decline of his presidency.

The cold war provided a framework for policy—and later a fulcrum for contentions about policy. It never provided a political escape valve for presidents to rescue their fortunes beyond the short run, however. Unless a foreign policy intervention was brief, relatively costless, and regarded as an unconditional success, partisan and other political conflict always surrounded the choices presidents made even in the most intense days of the cold war. Politics, in other words, always surrounded policy, and later it came to surround the concept of the cold war itself long before communism expired in the Soviet Union. The controversial war in Vietnam began to produce partisan political fault lines after Richard Nixon assumed custody of it. By the Reagan years, the partisan fault lines were as wide as they had ever been.[7] One interpretation was that persistent divisions came about in the United States which essentially revolved around a pro- and antidetente view of the cold war. Another interpretation, however, stressed a widened band of differences between the parties in general that manifested itself around security policy issues.[8]

If this second interpretation is the more valid one, then the end of the cold war will have affected the presidency itself relatively little while it will have affected the universe of policy options much more. To state this a bit differently, foreign policy is likely to remain contentious in the absence of overwhelming congressional majorities within a unified government, whatever those policies may be, because the parties are more likely to oppose each other almost regardless of what the policies are. The efforts of the then Senate minority leader, Robert Dole, in 1994 to constrain a possible American military intervention in Haiti to enforce a UN-sponsored agreement is indicative. It is hard to imagine Senator Dole proposing to so constrain a president of his own party.

Policies, of course, are more unpredictable because the world is more unpredictable. Hence the real effect of the end of the cold war is policy confusion. Its effect on the institution of the presidency or any president's political prowess is apt to be relatively slight. For the fact is that presidents were being regularly contested for dominance in foreign policy making by Congress. Of course, presidents retain the power of initiative, and from that standpoint Congress is less involved in foreign policy making up front. Institutionally, that is likely to continue. Congressional monitoring, signaling, and reaction, however, shape the boundaries of where presidents may expect to go—at least in their next venture. Although there are legal landmarks and certainly political ones that serve to widen and narrow the president's discretion in foreign affairs, presidents are often granted leeway because Congress cannot or chooses not to stop them in advance of an intervention.[9] The test of congressional involvement typically is based on whether the executive action succeeds or fails. None of this is fundamentally new.

The end of the cold war will not end the perpetual struggle between the executive and legislative branches of the U.S. government for control over foreign policy. That is because the cold war did not begin that struggle, nor did it give presidents uninhibited authority to do as they wished. The salience of threat did help achieve a significant measure of consensus in the 1950s, but that was because consensus-minded and relatively bipartisan political leaders such as President Eisenhower, Senate Majority Leader Lyndon Johnson and Speaker of the House Sam Rayburn helped override dissenting (often isolationist) opinion in the Congress. The issue, however, is not how the end of the cold war will shape the presidency but, rather, how presidents will help shape the post–cold war world. So far, neither of the two presidents who have had to operate in the post–cold war atmosphere has successfully given definition to an American role in this new environment. The absence of definition is explained by the ambiguity of the circumstances. But without an operating demonology, circumstances are always ambiguous. What was unique about the cold war was that it reduced the normal ambiguity that resides in the interpretation of international events and America's interests, if any, in influencing them.

The new, more chaotic setting awaits some strategic definitions of what lies in the realm of the desirable and the doable. The Bush administration focused like a laser only on the latter, consistently with its conception of the world but not necessarily with certain conceptions of public morality articulated by elements of the leadership class. The Clinton administration seems continually to struggle with how much of the desirable is really doable, and it seems to struggle out loud while trying to shape a policy in the midst of reacting to a problem. The challenge for U.S. presidents will lie in assessing and balancing the enormous political risks attendant on trying to influence world affairs and the even larger risks of doing little or nothing to shape matters of strategic importance for a civilized world order. Between doing nothing and doing everything, there is much to do. What should be done will require a strategic guideline cloaked with a necessary degree of operational ambiguity. The strategic guideline may already have been articulated by Undersecretary Tarnoff, but it subsequently has been supplanted by other doctrines of the moment. It is not yet clear whether that strategic guideline is in process of evolution within the Clinton administration or whether it consists largely of ad hoc reactions to events that the Clinton administration would like to influence in principle but which it will not bear the risks of doing so in practice.

In any event, it is now evident that a new reality has come to Washington, perhaps for a moment, perhaps for longer. That reality is manifesting itself in cutting the obligations of the federal government in general and those of foreign policy in particular. The post–cold war period began by looking like the period before World War I. From an American perspective that is increasingly isolationist, the post–cold war period now is looking like the period between the two world wars.

Notes

I am grateful for the hospitality and support provided by the Centre for European Studies, Nuffield College, Oxford.

1. According to one account, Clinton's foreign policy advisers have urged him to become more engaged in foreign policy. Apparently, unlike his predecessors, he does not hold regular meetings with his national security adviser. See Elaine Sciolino, "3 Players Seek a Director for Foreign Policy Story," *New York Times*, Nov. 8, 1993.

2. R. W. Apple, Jr., "Policing a Global Village," *New York Times*, Oct. 13, 1993.

3. Thomas L. Friedman, "Clinton's Foreign Policy: Top Adviser Speaks Up," *New York Times*, Oct. 31, 1993.

4. See especially Robert D. Putnam, "Diplomacy and Domestic Politics: The Logic of Two Level Games," *International Organization* 42 (Summer 1988): 427–60; Bert A. Rockman, "Presidents, Opinion, and Institutional Leadership," in David A. Deese, ed., *The New Politics of American Foreign Policy* (New York: St. Martin's Press, 1993), 59–73.

5. John T. Judis, "The Foreign Unpolicy," *New Republic*, July 12, 1993, 16–20.

6. Joshua Muravchik, "Forsaking Bosnia, Clinton Signals U.S. Retreat," *Wall Street Journal*, June 10, 1993.

7. See George C. Edwards III, "The Two Presidencies: A Reevaluation," *American Politics Quarterly* 14 (1986): 247–63. Moreover, David Rohde observes that "the persistence of partisan conflicts into the Bush administration serves to demonstrate that the sharp disagreements of the previous eight years were not simply the consequence of typically extreme ideological views on the part of the president." See David W. Rohde, "Partisan Leadership and Congressional Assertiveness in Foreign and Defense Policy," in Deese, *New Politics of American Foreign Policy*, 99.

8. Rohde, "Partisan Leadership."

9. Matthew McCubbins notes, for example, that Congress grants discretion in relation to the uncertain nature of the activities it wishes to control and the costs

incurred in trying to exercise the control. The more uncertain the nature of the activity—and foreign affairs fits perfectly here—the more Congress is likely to respond in post hoc fashion. In other words, Congress will be outcome-oriented rather than procedurally oriented in its evaluation of the executive. See Matthew D. McCubbins, "The Legislative Design of Regulatory Structure," *American Journal of Political Science* 29 (1985): 721–48.

THREE

U.S. EXECUTIVE BRANCH POLITICS IN A CHANGING WORLD

JOEL D. ABERBACH

The Executive Branch before the End of the Cold War

Background: Growing Tensions in the Executive Branch

A large bureaucracy has now become a seemingly permanent feature of the U.S. government, but this is actually a relatively recent phenomenon. As James Q. Wilson notes: "During its first 150 years, the American republic was not thought to have a 'bureaucracy' and thus it would have been meaningless to refer to the 'problems' of a 'bureaucratic state'" (Wilson 1975: 77).

The executive branch bureaucracy the United States has today started to take shape in the late nineteenth and early twentieth centuries, but its current dimensions come in large part from the myriad programs and agencies created in the New Deal, World War II, and Great Society periods. Since most of these agencies were created under Democratic presidents and with heavy Democratic support, there was a built-in basis for tension between the executive branch agencies and elected and appointed officials when and if assertive, "conservative" (in the modern American usage of that term) Republicans ever got control of the government. That happened in the latter years of the Nixon administration and most particularly in the Reagan administration. (Eisenhower was a consolidator who did not challenge the major premises of the New Deal or the administrators of its agencies.) The period prior to the end of the cold war thus also featured an acrimonious debate about the mission and shape of the executive branch in the United States.

In addition to this ideological debate, there was also an increase in tension between the president and Congress in the years during and following the Vietnam War. While every student of U.S. government is aware of the built-in rivalry between the branches, President Johnson's deceptive behavior during the controversial Vietnam conflict heightened suspicion between the branches. This was made worse by President Nixon's conduct of the war and by his "administrative presidency" strategy of bypassing the Congress (see below). It was then reinforced by the almost equally aggressive and often deceptive presidential practices under the Reagan administration. The bureaucracy was inevitably a player in many of the dramas of these administrations and many times a victim as well. It is not too surprising, then, that coincident with the end of the cold war, there was spirited discussion within the political elite about the nature and future of the public service (Volcker Commission 1989).

One consequence of the tensions in the world following World War II was the growth of a "national security state" in the United States to fight the cold war and, if necessary, a hot war. The cold war provided the United States with a clear goal: defending what came to be known as the free world. There was general consensus in the country on the goal, if not always on the means to the agreed-upon end. The national security state featured a large peacetime military, a large intelligence apparatus, and a complex set of foreign alliances—all unprecedented for the United States. The end of the cold war eliminated the goal of containing communism and left large questions about how to reconfigure the agencies of the security state.

The United States entered the cold war as the most prosperous state in the world. It had a vigorous economy and a government well positioned to pursue domestic programs at the same time that it built up the nation's military forces and intelligence arms. The United States was able to provide significant aid to rebuild the devastated economies of Western Europe. It paid for many of the military and development programs in the noncommunist world.

The years after the Vietnam War, however, have been marked by increasing tensions over resources. Federal spending, driven mainly by entitlements and at times by the military, went from an annual average of 19.0 percent of gross national product in the 1960s, to 20.5 percent in the 1970s, to an annual average of 23.1 percent in the 1980s (Shapiro 1993: 26). This increase in spending occurred more and more through borrowing. In the 1950s the average annual share of federal spending met through borrowing was 2.5 percent. This increased to 4.4 percent in the 1960s, to 11.1 percent in the 1970s, and reached 17.7 percent in the decade of the 1980s. The figures for the early 1990s average 19.0 percent (Shapiro 1993: 45). The Reagan and Bush years saw the gross federal government debt grow from $909 billion in fiscal year 1980 to $4,003 billion in fiscal year 1992 (U.S. House).

There were, in short, growing government deficits and futile attempts to deal with them. This was particularly the case during the Reagan administration, which combined supply side attempts to cap taxes with an effort (perhaps successful) to spend the Soviet Union into the ground militarily even if domestic expenditures remained uncapped. The result is that at the end of the cold war, the United States stands as the world's preeminent military power, but its government is also swimming in debt and faced with serious questions about the efficacy of its institutions, personnel, and programs.

Tension over Control of Policy and Administration

The Administrative Presidency[1]

When Richard Nixon was inaugurated as president of the United States in 1969, he faced a difficult situation. He had won the election with only 43 percent of the vote (George Wallace, a third-party candidate, did quite well in the election), and he faced a Congress controlled by the opposition Democratic party. He was widely hated by Democratic liberals for his behavior during the post–World War II communist scare. They strongly suspected that his sometimes enigmatic views on domestic policy (there were periodic "new" Nixons during his career) masked a consistently reactionary bent. Whatever his actual beliefs, Nixon came into office during a period of policy innovations, some of which he supported, even if tepidly. New safety and health regulations were enacted early in his first term, for example, and the Environmental Protection Agency was established in 1970 through an administration reorganization plan.

Be that as it may, "the Nixon administration [certainly] came to power suspicious of the existing bureaucracy. The tone of the administration's rhetoric stressed the philosophy of decentralization and substantial curtailment of some of the directions undertaken in the previous eight years of Democratic rule. . . . Suspicious of the responsiveness and loyalty of the administrators, the Nixon administration's litmus test of loyalty often went beyond even the partisan affiliations of the administrators to rather exacting ideological standards of loyalty" (Aberbach and Rockman 1976: 457).

The administration's early relations with the bureaucracy and the Congress were not marked by unrelieved hostility. Using the same basic approach as his predecessors, Nixon initially appointed cabinet members "to represent the major interests in the inner councils of government" (Nathan 1983: 30), and he allowed cabinet members to choose the subcabinet officials who would serve in their departments. He developed his own legislative proposals for Congress to consider, but as I noted above, signed legislation favored by liberals on regulatory and environmental matters.

However, after a year or two Nixon decided that this approach would not enable him either to control decision making in the executive branch or lead Congress to enact legislation that would make fundamental changes in the programs Democrats had created during their years in control of the presidency. He therefore developed what Richard Nathan labeled the "administrative presidency" strategy, a strategy he intended to implement fully in his second term. The strategy had four basic elements: (1) filling high-level positions in the administrative agencies with Nixon loyalists who would do what they were told; (2) using the president's reorganization authority to change or even eliminate programs that the White House opposed and Congress wished to continue in their traditional modes of operation; (3) writing administrative regulations in a manner designed to achieve the president's objectives no matter what the views of the majority in Congress or the intent of the relevant statutes; and (4) impounding funds duly appropriated by the Congress in order to undermine or eliminate programs not wanted by the president.

Nixon was not able to carry out his experiment in control because of Watergate. But the Reagan administration, which was strongly influenced by the experiences of Nixon, set out to learn from Nixon's failures. "The Nixon experience, then, was more than just a historical aberration. It was a school for many who followed; its lessons were assimilated and applied with telling effect in the Reagan period" (Aberbach 1991b: 225).

Nixon himself commented tellingly about what he considered an inadequate appointments strategy in his first term and about his plans for the second.

> I regretted that during the first term we had done a very poor job in the most basic business of every new administration of either party: we had failed to fill all the key posts in the departments and agencies with people who were loyal to the President and his programs. Without this kind of leadership in the appointive positions, there is no way for a President to make any major impact on the bureaucracy. That this was especially true of a Republican President was confirmed a few years later by a study reported in the *American Political Science Review*. Researchers Joel Aberbach and Bert Rockman found that in 1970 only 17 percent of the top career bureaucrats in the executive branch were Republican; 47 percent were Democrats and 36 percent were independents who "more frequently resemble Democrats than Republicans." The authors of this study confirmed that the frustration we felt with the bureaucracy was based on solid reasons: "Our findings document a career bureaucracy with very little Republican representation but even more pointedly portray a social service bureaucracy dominated by administrators ideologically hostile to many of the directions pursued by the Nixon administration in the realm of social

policy." . . . I was determined that we would not fail in this area again, and on the morning after my re-election I called for the resignation of every non-career employee in the executive branch. (Nixon 1978: 768)

When Ronald Reagan became president, he enjoyed many advantages Nixon did not have. He was elected by a majority of the voters. He carried in a Republican Senate and had a more conservative House of Representatives than had existed in the previous Congress. His message was unabashedly conservative, and people in Washington believed that the election results confirmed his claim to a mandate to forge a "new beginning." Most important, as I noted above, Reagan's advisers had learned their lesson well from the experiences of the Nixon administration. They devised a recruitment and selection system designed to populate the appointive positions of the executive branch with people who would carry out the tenets of "Reaganism," not just because of loyalty to the man but because they believed in the philosophy he espoused. This meant, of course, that they had to have a relatively clear philosophy—a factor that set them off from the more traditional and pragmatic Nixon administration.

The success of the Reagan administration in this regard can be seen in tables 3.1 and 3.2, which present data Bert A. Rockman and I collected for a study of the changing federal executive in the United States. The tables show the political party affiliations of top-level federal executives in the Nixon, Reagan, and Bush administrations broken down by their job status (table 3.1) and also present data on the views top executives held on the role government should play in the economy, both in the aggregate and broken down by a variety of factors such as party affiliation, agency type, and job status (table 3.2). The job status categories for senior career executives are complicated by a change in the civil service laws which was enacted in 1978 and will be explained below. For the moment it is enough to say that the "Supergrade Career" sample in 1970 was drawn from top career officials who reported to political appointees. The "CA-I" samples in 1986–1987 and 1991–1992 also consist of top civil servants who reported to political appointees (and are thus analogous to those in the 1970 Supergrade Career sample), while the "CA-II" samples in those years were drawn from senior-level civil servants who reported to other civil servants.

A look at these data is very revealing. The lopsidedly Democratic top civil service of the Nixon years—one inherited from a period of almost unbroken Democratic control—has given way to one that is more balanced. In fact, where Democrats outnumbered Republicans almost three to one among supergrade career civil servants in 1970, the comparable Career I civil servants were more Republican than Democratic in 1986–1987, and that finding is reinforced by a similar (and slightly more pronounced) pat-

Table 3.1 Party Affiliation by Job Status and Year

(in percentages)

Formal Job Designation[b]	Party Affiliation[a]					Totals[c]	(N)
	Republican		Independent		Democrat		
1970							
High political appointee	81		6		13	100	(16)
(PAS designation)		65		11		25	
Middle-level appointee (NEA, Schedule C designation)	59		12		29	100	(41)
Supergrade career	17		36		47	100	(58)
			Gamma=.58				(N=115)
1986–1987							
High political appointee	94		6		0	100	(18)
(PAS designation)		97		3		0	
Middle-level appointee (SES-NA)	98		2		0	100	(44)
Career I (SES-CA-I)	45		17		38	100	(64)
Career II (SES-CA-II)	27		19		54	100	(63)
			Gamma=.74				(N=189)
		(Gamma=.91 excluding CA-IIs; N=126)					
1991–1992							
High political appointee	100		0		0	100	(21)
(PAS designation)		100		0		0	
Middle-level appointee (SES-NA)	100		0		0	100	(24)
Career I (SES-CA-I)	42		27		31	100	(52)
Career II (SES-CA-II)	42		19		40	100	(53)
			Gamma=.64				(N=150)
		(Gamma=1.00 excluding CA-IIs; N=97)					

Source: Reprinted by permission of the *Journal of Politics*.

[a]Party affiliation was measured by asking the administrators whether they normally vote for one party or the other. Those who said that they did not normally vote for one party or the other were coded as Independents.

[b]Because of the small number of PAS-designated appointees in our samples, hereafter analyses involving the job status variable will collapse political appointees into a single category. PAS indicates a Presidential appointment, by and with the advice and consent of the Senate. NEA stands for Noncareer Executive Assignment. SES-NA indicates a noncareer appointment in the Senior Executive Service. Supergrade career civil servants held ranks GS 16–18. Other terms are defined in the text.

[c]Totals may not equal 100% because of rounding.

tern in 1991–1992 under the Bush administration. The data for the political appointees also indicate great changes. Whereas the traditional appointment system Nixon used in his first term gave him an administration whose appointees were only two-thirds Republican, the method used by Reagan and then by Bush yielded virtually all Republican appointees.

The political views of these high-level officials are perhaps even more significant than their party affiliations. As table 3.2 indicates, the views of top government officials in 1986–1987 on the role of government in the nation's economy were quite a bit to the right of the views of officials who held office in 1970. Even more revealing is that all officials were more to the right—Democrats as well as Republicans, career officials as well as political appointees. The "kinder, gentler"—and, it appears, more ideologically indifferent—Bush administration in office in 1991–1992 had officials who were clearly to the right of those in the Nixon administration but not, on average, so far to the right as those in the Reagan administration.

It is easy to understand how an administration could work its will to get the type of political appointee that it wanted, but the situation with respect to career civil servants is more complex. As Bert Rockman and I said in an earlier paper about the data on party affiliation in table 3.1:

> Although the data available to us now do not permit us to distinguish between explanations for the growing Republicanism of senior civil servants, it seems reasonable to infer that one of the causes rests in the longevity of Republican control of the executive branch. When a party controls the executive branch (or, in parliamentary systems, a government) for a long enough period of time, the top bureaucrats tend to look more and more like their political masters. The causes are diverse and hardly mutually exclusive. Just to mention a couple, the administration is in a position to manipulate at least some of the choices of personnel even within the career ranks. And the career bureaucrats themselves have incentives to retire or stay depending upon the incompatibility or compatibility of their perspectives and those of the presidential administration in power. (Aberbach and Rockman 1992: 6)

Clearly, the attention that the Reagan administration gave to selecting top officials paid off. They managed to appoint a set of political appointees much in tune with their political philosophy and to secure a set of career officials who, if not as conservative as they would have liked, were much more to their taste than the career officials the Nixon administration had to work with.

Civil Service Reform

Ironically, one way that the Reagan administration was able to work its will was to take advantage of the provisions of the Civil Service Reform Act of 1978, enacted under the Democratic presidency of Jimmy Carter. Coming on the heels of the disastrous experience of the Nixon administration, the reform was designed to make the civil service more responsive to political executives as well as to create an elite corps of generalist civil servants. The

Table 3.2 Role of Government in the Nation's Economy by Year, Party Affiliation, Agency, and Job Status
(in percentages)

	Strongly Supports Active Government (Left)	Sum of Left and Left-Center	Supports, with Reservations, Active Govt. (Left-Center)	Pro/Con Views, Balance of Pos. and Neg. (Center)	Opposes, with Reservations, Active Govt. (Right-Center)	Sum of Right and Right-Center	Strongly Opposes Active Govt. (Right)	Totals^a	(N)
Marginal distributions									
1970	28	52	24	32	15	16	1	100	(115)
1986–1987	4	22	18	26	39	52	13	100	(197)
1991–1992	9	35	26	20	36	45	9	100	(149)
Party Affiliation									
1970									
Republican	7	32	25	43	25	25	0	100	(44)
Independent	36	50	14	41	5	10	5	101	(22)
Democrat	46	77	31	13	10	10	0	100	(39)
				Gamma=−.50					
1986–1987									
Republican	5	10	5	20	48	71	23	101	(106)
Independent	0	24	24	32	44	44	0	100	(25)
Democrat	5	43	38	36	20	21	2	101	(56)
				Gamma=−.62					
1991–1992									
Republican	5	19	14	20	49	62	13	101	(87)
Independent	17	38	21	21	29	42	13	101	(24)
Democrat	16	70	54	19	11	11	0	101	(37)
				Gamma=−.56					
Agency									
1970									
Social services	39	60	21	30	9	9	0	99	(33)
Other	23	49	26	33	17	18	1	100	(82)
				Gamma=.27					

								Total	(N)
1986–1987									
Social services	4	24	20	28	39	48	9	100	(46)
Other	4	21	17	26	38	53	15	100	(151)
Gamma=.10									
1991–1992									
Social services	16	40	24	24	26	37	11	101	(38)
Other	7	34	27	17	40	49	9	99	(111)
Gamma=.15									
Job Status									
1970									
Political appointees (pooled)	17	40	23	42	19	19	0	101	(53)
Career supergrades	37	63	26	24	11	13	2	100	(62)
Gamma=−.35									
1986–1987									
Political appointees (pooled)	2	7	5	19	45	74	29	100	(62)
Career I (SES-CA II)	3	21	18	28	42	51	9	100	(67)
Career II (SES-CA II)	7	36	29	31	29	32	3	99	(68)
Gamma=−.50									
1991–1992									
Political appointees (pooled)	2	13	11	18	51	69	18	100	(45)
Career I (SES-CA II)	12	35	23	27	31	39	8	101	(52)
Career II (SES-CA II)	14	54	40	14	29	33	4	101	(52)
Gamma=−.42									

Source: Reprinted by permission of the *Journal of Politics*.

Note: The role of government in the nation's economy item read as follows: It is argued by some people that government must play a greater role in the nation's economic affairs, while others say that decisions in this area should be left to the private sector. On the whole, which of these positions comes closest to yours? (*Probe*: How strongly do you feel about this?)

[a] Totals may not equal 100% because of rounding.

Table 3.3 Party Affiliation by Agency, Job Status, and Year
(career executives only, in percentages)

	Party Affiliation				
Job Status	*Republican*	*Independent*	*Democrat*	*Totals[a]*	*(N)*
1986–1987					
Career I					
Social service agencies (ED, HHS, HUD)[b]	67	—	33	100	(12)
Other agencies	40	21	39	100	(52)
		Gamma=.32			
Career II					
Social service agencies (ED, HHS, HUD)	12	12	77	101	(17)
Other agencies	33	22	46	101	(46)
		Gamma=−.55			
1991–1992					
Career I					
Social service agencies (ED, HHS, HUD)	33	28	39	100	(18)
Other agencies	47	27	27	101	(34)
		Gamma=−.25			
Career II					
Social service agencies (ED, HHS, HUD)	36	18	46	100	(11)
Other agencies	43	19	38	100	(42)
		Gamma=−.13			

Source: Reprinted by permission of the *Journal of Politics*.
[a]Totals may not equal 100% because of rounding.
[b]ED=Department of Education. HHS=Department of Health and Human Services.
HUD=Department of Housing and Urban Development.

latter had been a goal for some time of many who wished to reform the U.S. civil service.

One of the most important provisions of the act was that members of the new corps—called the Senior Executive Service—were to have rank in the person rather than in the position as was previously the case. This meant that individuals could be moved about within a broad band of positions re-served for members of the Senior Executive Service without fear of charges of "adverse action." In other words, an administration now had the option to decide which civil servants in an agency will be at the top of a hierarchy and report to a political appointee (Career I in our sample) and which will be lower in the hierarchy and report to other civil servants (Career II in our sample).

Table 3.3 shows just what can be accomplished by a determined administration using the provisions of the act. Under the Nixon administration, Democrats were especially prominent in the social service agencies of the U.S. government (Aberbach and Rockman 1976). By contrast, under Reagan the proportion of Democrats in these agencies looked much like the proportion in other agencies (Aberbach and Rockman 1990). But, for our purposes, of greater interest is the way in which the Reagan administration—which targeted these agencies for special attention since they represented what the Reaganites most despised about the programs of the New Deal and Great Society—apparently manipulated career civil service personnel to put the people it wanted in top career positions. While 77 percent of the career officials in the Career II positions in the social service agencies under Reagan were Democrats, only 33 percent of the Career I executives professed an affiliation with the same party. There was, in fact, a clear majority of Republicans in the Career I positions. This pattern virtually disappears in the Bush administration, where there was apparently much less concern about the political views of career executives.

The small numbers of respondents in the social service entries in table 3.3 make one cautious about overinterpreting the data, but there is a discernible pattern in the findings in these tables. Nixon, who lacked political support and who used exceptionally crude methods despite his weak position, failed in his efforts to undo the missions and personnel of agencies built up over the years by Democratic administrations. Reagan, who had a stronger political position, a clearer sense of mission, and better tools to work with (the provisions of the Civil Service Reform Act), and who came to office in a period of clear Republican dominance of the presidency, was able to impact government, especially the personnel at the top of the agencies, much more effectively. Bush, who had few policy passions and provided relatively little direction to government in comparison to Reagan, continued in the Reagan tradition of selecting only Republicans for noncareer positions, but his appointees were slightly more moderate than Reagan's, and his administration seemed to show less interest in the political views of top career civil servants.

Congressional Oversight

The last twenty years of the cold war witnessed a phenomenal increase in the amount of congressional oversight of policy and administration. A recent study I did documented the hearing and meeting activity of congressional committees for the first six months of each odd-numbered year from 1961 to 1983 (Aberbach 1990). This period covers the relatively quiescent years of the early to mid 1960s and the turbulent period that followed marked by often intense congressional conflict with the president and significant internal reforms within the Congress.

The numbers speak for themselves. Congressional committees (in total) devoted an average of 149 days to oversight during the first six months of each year in the period from 1961 to 1965. The average increased to 192 in the years from 1967 to 1971. The number of days of committee oversight rose to 290 in 1973 and reached a high of 587 in 1983. To summarize the data succinctly, the average number of days of oversight activity of congressional committees in the years after 1975 was more than three times the 1961–1965 average.

"Oversight . . . started to climb in 1967 when tension between President Johnson and Congress heightened and then took off in the seventies as the struggle between President Nixon and Congress intensified and as Congress, ever more conscious of real and potential threats to its influence over the executive branch and of public discontent with government, made significant internal changes to encourage oversight" (Aberbach, forthcoming). Congressional oversight of policy and administration continued at a high level during the clashes between Reagan's strongly assertive and conservative Republican administration and the decidedly more liberal Democratic Congress. I have no data on what transpired with respect to oversight during the Bush administration, but I believe that the pattern loosely resembled what we have just seen with respect to the civil service—a somewhat less tense relationship, but continued watchfulness by the Congress.

Volcker Commission Worries

The tensions within the American government which started in the 1960s increasingly troubled those in what some would call the Washington establishment. They were especially concerned about the impact on the civil service of years of denunciation that started with Nixon, continued into the Carter administration as part of its effort to build support for the Civil Service Reform Act, and reached a crescendo under Ronald Reagan, who regularly denounced the civil service of the executive branch as a part of what he perceived to be the problem of government in the United States.

In its introduction, the commission's report said: "Commission members saw three main threats to the health of the public service: public attitudes, political leadership, and internal management systems. These threats were seen as eroding the ability of the government to function effectively at the same time that demands on government were growing" (Volcker Commission 1989: xviii). The commission recommended a series of steps to end what some have called the quiet crisis in the government service. These included strengthening the relationship between career civil servants and political appointees by building a spirit of partnership between them and reducing the number of political appointees so that there would be more room near the top for civil servants. The commission also lavishly praised

President Bush for his statements during the 1988 presidential campaign about the value of public service and his decision to make an address to a meeting of senior career executives after his inauguration in which he commended the career service.

An analysis of data from the changing federal executive study led me to the following conclusions about the commission's report:

> The Volcker Commission's report presented a picture of a "dangerously eroded" public service facing a "quiet crisis." Data from studies of top federal executives done in 1970 and 1986–87 [relevant data on the Bush administration were—and are—not yet prepared for a full analysis of issues raised by the commission] indicate that whatever crisis may exist, it is quiet, not only because few people, even in the elite, are interested in the public service, but because the nature of the problem, assuming one's values lead one to call it a problem, is quite subtle. There is *no evidence*, despite an apparent increase in retirement rates, that the senior civil service has slipped in experience or quality over the years. There is *evidence* of effective political manipulation in filling top career SES positions, and of effective steps by the Reagan administration to diminish the role and influence of civil servants in the policy process. While the morale of those who chose to stay in the career SES has not slipped too far as of 1986–87, it was down somewhat. If the decrease in morale is part of a trend, it could represent a major problem in the future. . . .
>
> It appears that the Bush administration has done many of the things that the Volcker Commission recommended, and it is likely that it has increased somewhat the role and morale of the senior civil service while deemphasizing partisan and ideological influences in determining assignments and advancement. That is a relatively easy thing for a moderate, equilibrium oriented administration like Bush's to accomplish. The question is whether one can expect other types of presidencies to follow suit. (Aberbach 1991a: 417)

The termination of the cold war came at the end of an often turbulent two decades of tension and change in American government. The roles of the bureaucracy, of the Congress, and of the federal government itself were all challenged and in many ways altered by what transpired during these years. Although the cold war ended during a relatively placid and directionless administration, the problems of the period prior to the Bush administration reflected fundamental challenges to the status quo established during the period of Democratic dominance of the presidency which ended in 1968.

Edward Lynch, in a critical review of the report of the Volcker Commission, put the matter quite well.

> The Commission [report] . . . ignores the political questions at the heart of the disputes about the roles of appointees in the public service. Rather than attempt to relate concerns about numbers of political appointees to the surrounding political environment, it proceeds as if "nonpolitical" administration was still possible, even as it concedes that it is not. The Commission somehow concludes that government would work better if the institutional memory and specialized knowledge of career civil servants made a greater impact. But the restrictions on political appointees that it proposes can only impair the effectiveness of a president who might want to eliminate programs that no longer serve the public interest. The Commission has provided a classic example of a team of horses deciding upon directions for the coachman. (Lynch 1990: 128)

The cold war, in short, ended during a quiet period in what has been an on-and-off-again struggle, sometimes principled and often simply nasty, of more than two decades to remake the fundamental premises of American government. Civil servants who were identified with the Democratic regimes of the New Deal and the Great Society, which built many of the institutional structures of the executive branch—the bureaus and agencies designed to administer the programs established from the thirties to the sixties and even in the first years of the Nixon administration—were often targets in this struggle. Whatever else might be said, at the end of the 1980s the senior civil service was a more Republican and less liberal group than the top executives Richard Nixon found when he assumed the presidency.

The Executive Branch after the End of the Cold War

The Post–Cold War Bureaucracy

George Bush, president of the United States in 1989 when the cold war ended, fine-tuned some of Ronald Reagan's changes, but in general he was much more moderate and decidedly less hostile to the career civil service.

As part of our longitudinal study of top federal executives in the United States, Bert Rockman and I conducted round-table discussions with political appointees in the Bush administration to discuss our preliminary findings and to get a better sense of how to interpret them.

One thing that intrigued us was that senior civil servants who served during the Bush administration tended to report that the quality of Bush administration political appointees was superior to that of political appointees in the Reagan administration. We asked the Bush appointees why they thought civil servants saw them in this favorable light. The answers were informative. A Department of Labor official said the following:

Civil servants prefer competence to ideology. . . . If you are really there to make a change in a fairly dramatic way, I think the civil servants will rate you bad. There is an important value in government: stability and sameness. It is something that makes us a non–South American republic. But, on the other hand, when the political will is to make the change, you need certain kinds of people who will not be rated as high by civil servants.

But, I mean, I guess if I was President Reagan, I would say "good; that is what I wanted." And if I was President Bush I would say "good; that is what I wanted." Because 1981 is very different from 1989. In 1989 we wanted stability, and marginal adjustment, and competence. In 1981, we said, "Hey, let's make changes."

So I think that says more about the standards of judgment of civil servants than it does about the quality of the people [in the two administrations]. (Brookings Institution 1992: 50)

Another appointee, who served at the Department of Transportation, made what might be a particularly telling statement about the main role of administrators in the Bush administration: "My old boss said that essentially his job was to keep George Bush out of trouble" (Brookings Institution 1992: 39). It is hard to imagine a Reagan appointee in a domestic agency making the same sort of statement.

In short, Bush's appointees were at least somewhat more moderate than Reagan's, and they were clearly more comfortable working with top civil servants and made fewer efforts to move them about or manipulate them than had been the case during the Reagan years. Their goal was consolidation, not further radical change. At the end of Bush's administration, he left the new president, Bill Clinton, a less liberal top civil service than the one Lyndon Johnson had bequeathed to Richard Nixon, but a more liberal one than Reagan's. That should not be too uncomfortable for at least one version of Bill Clinton.

Bill Clinton ran as a "different kind of Democrat," which was code for a more moderate Democrat than many in the electorate identified with the party's usual nominees for president. Clinton promised to reinvigorate the economy, make needed investments in human and physical capital, solve the nation's emerging health care crisis, and deal with the deficit problem. Clinton saw America's economic competitiveness and vigor as the keys to its strength in the post–cold war world. His famous campaign headquarters sign—saying "It's the economy, stupid!"—was supposed to be a symbol for his main focus on the issue that most troubled the electorate—economic drift and stagnation.

Defining Clinton's political views became a sport after his emergence as a major candidate. It was clear to all that Clinton had "policy ambitions galore," as *National Journal* columnist Burt Solomon put it, but it was another matter how they fit together and what his priorities truly were. Solomon interviewed a number of people and noted the following:

> To Elaine C. Kamarck, a senior fellow at the Progressive Policy Institute in Washington, a home to some key Clinton advisers, Clinton counts as a liberal, which she defines as believing in an activist government. But at the Urban Institute, senior fellow Isabel V. Sawhill regards him as "genuinely a moderate-to-conservative Democrat in terms of his values." . . . [In short,] a persistent political ambiguity has exacerbated the blurry picture the voters have of Clinton. . . .
>
> If what he's trying to do proves unpopular, "he'll rethink it," said [Gloria] Cabe, who was a top aide on his gubernatorial staff and has been handling congressional relations for Clinton's campaign. "He's very pragmatic." . . .
>
> If you ask Clinton's advisers if he'd cull priorities from his pile of domestic proposals, they'll tell you that he learned the dangers of doing too much too soon during his first, failed term as governor. Then if you ask what his priorities as President would be, they'll offer a list that doesn't quit.
>
> "Clinton gives a sense that everything is important," an adviser explained. (*National Journal*, Oct. 24, 1992: 2411–12)

Clinton promised a more diverse administration than Bush's but distanced himself from militants. "During the entire campaign, Clinton's most famous moment on civil rights was not an uplifting speech to a black audience but the deliberate, skillful orchestrated rebuke of rap singer Sister Souljah at an event in June sponsored by [Jesse] Jackson" (*National Journal*, Dec. 12, 1992: 2825).

In many ways this was classic Clinton. In the same article, reporter W. John Moore noted, "Clinton has been portrayed by some supporters and in some news accounts as an ardent backer of affirmative action programs. But he ducked the issue throughout the campaign." And "from the New Hampshire primary to election night, Clinton delivered much the same message, praising diversity, vowing an economic transformation and promising 'full participation, full partnership' in his presidency to black and white audiences alike. But he avoided addressing such issues as affirmative action, civil rights enforcement, and race-specific remedies for discrimination" (*National Journal*, Dec. 12, 1992: 2826, 2824).

As was noted above, "from the beginning of his campaign, a central feature of Clinton's foreign policy message was that America must be strong at home economically before it can be a force for good in the world. Clinton emphasized trade and competitiveness issues, putting them on a par with foreign policy" (*National Journal,* Jan. 9, 1993: 63).

This emphasis paralleled the language in a report prepared for the Bush administration under the direction of Undersecretary of State John W. Rogers. Called *State 2000: A New Model for Managing Foreign Affairs,* the report stressed that with the Soviet threat gone as the major factor defining U.S. national interest, driving its policy, and determining the organization of its national security and foreign policy organizations, the United States "must renew our economy if we are to compete in an increasingly interdependent world." The report stressed support for the "worldwide movement toward democracy and market economies," the need to "confront global issues such as the environment," and the need to "redefine our national security" in light of the troublesome legacies of the cold war and the rise of "new opportunities for multilateral cooperation" (*State 2000,* 1992: 3).

Overall, then, Clinton's foreign policy thinking apparently paralleled the type of thinking already in evidence in parts of George Bush's State Department (although Clinton characteristically declined for a time to commit his administration to the North American Free Trade Agreement (NAFTA), negotiated by Bush but opposed by some Democrats). On the domestic front, candidate Clinton was by any account more liberal than Bush—no matter how vague or slippery some of his views may have been—but overall it is fair to say that his moderate-appearing views probably did not sit too badly with the generally moderate top civil service he was inheriting from Bush.

The Early Clinton Record

Appointments

Bill Clinton's experiences in his initial few months of appointing officials to the executive branch were difficult.

Drawing in part on the model of recent Republican presidents, Clinton appointed a director of personnel "to coordinate sub-Cabinet appointments with Mr. Clinton's Cabinet choices. In so doing, he seemed to be following the example of recent Republican Presidents, who closely controlled appointments below the rank of Cabinet secretary. By contrast, the last Democratic President, Jimmy Carter, allowed his department heads to choose most deputies, who then often pursued policies at odds with White House views—so much so that one senior Carter aide once joked about calling his memoirs: 'Present at the Confusion' " (*New York Times,* Nov. 18, 1992).

As the months went by, there was grumbling about the slow pace of appointments from "cabinet officers and others in the Clinton Administration [who] are expressing frustration with the time-consuming efforts by the White House to add diversity and otherwise influence selections for top Government posts" (*New York Times*, Feb. 25, 1993). The administration experienced several embarrassing flaps over Social Security payments for domestic workers hired by some early nominees whose names had to be withdrawn, and checking to prevent a recurrence of this embarrassment took added time. But the main problems were said to be the desire to have a diverse set of appointees and the active role in the process played by Bill and Hillary Clinton and the White House personnel director in passing judgment on departmental recommendations.

One embarrassing story in the *Los Angeles Times* was entitled "Pace of Clinton Appointments Not E-G-Gs-actly Swift" (May 12, 1993). The story, which actually indicated that Clinton was no slower than his immediate predecessors in filling positions, stressed that ethnicity, gender, and geography were included as qualifications for top posts at the insistence of the president. It also stressed that "Clinton and his wife, Hillary, are personally signing off on most choices—a factor that has caused added delay, especially in view of the President's propensity to take his time and to change his mind on such matters, officials said."

There was even a discomfiting leak that Henry G. Cisneros, Clinton's secretary of housing and urban development and of Latino origin, "had been told that his list of proposed nominees included the names of too many New Yorkers" (*New York Times*, Feb. 25, 1993). And then there was a not unexpected sort of conflict when one plays the politics of numbers in appointments: the National Hispanic Leadership Agenda criticized the White House for choosing Latinos for only 5 percent of the top appointive jobs when nearly 10 percent of the American population is self-identified as Latino. The White House countered that 7.9 percent of its top-level appointees were Latinos (*Los Angeles Times*, May 18, 1993).

Clinton also had trouble with the appointment of Lani Guinier to be head of the Justice Department's civil rights division. Guinier had written articles arguing "that majority rule is often insufficient to guarantee blacks their fair share in the political process" and suggesting remedies to overcome the problem (*New York Times*, June 3, 1993). After a tremendous uproar in which Guinier's support evaporated amid charges that she was a "quota queen," Clinton withdrew her nomination. He claimed that he had not previously read her writings and that when he did, he found that they did not represent his views. The withdrawal of the nomination was widely regarded not only as a pragmatic step, since it was very unlikely to get through the Senate, but also as an attempt by the president to reclaim the center as part of an effort to get his economic package passed by the Congress. Supporters such as Al From, president of the Democratic Leadership Council, a self-proclaimed organization of centrist Democrats, which Clinton had chaired before his nomination, praised Clinton's decision.

> Three years ago, as chairman of the Democratic Leadership Council, Gov. Bill Clinton signed a declaration of principles with his plank: We believe the promise of America is equal opportunity, not equal outcomes.
>
> In the defining speech of his candidacy, at Georgetown University in October 1991, he promised a new convenant in which "it is the responsibility of every American . . . to fight back against the politics of divisions and bring this country together."
>
> In her writings, Ms. Guinier has emphasized the divisions among Americans, raising questions about the legitimacy of majority rule and asserting that "racism excludes minorities from ever becoming part of the governing coalition."
>
> When the President read her writing, he concluded that her views and his did not mesh and as a matter of conscience pulled back her nomination. Her backers assert that she is the victim of a misinformation campaign. That is wrong: the problem was her views could not pass muster with many Democrats, including the President. (*New York Times*, June 5, 1993)

When one looks at the early results, it appears that—events such as the Guinier controversy and the symbolically wrenching but ideologically clouded debate over gays in the military aside—Clinton actually fashioned a rather moderate administration. The clearest symbol of this was his decision to appoint David Gergen, a former adviser to George Bush and Ronald Reagan, and widely regarded as a pragmatist and moderate, to a post in the White House. But even before this, a revealing analysis of Clinton's top-tier appointees indicated that his cabinet, while "more diverse in background than any in history," was "hardly a mosaic of America." What the author meant was that "none is strident in ideology or anything but pragmatic," "most attended elite colleges," and in general they were "raised in comfort." In fact, the analyst claims, "in Clinton's first wave of appointees, a higher proportion of the blacks and Hispanics were raised in comfort than of the whites" (Burt Solomon, "Clinton's Gang," *National Journal*, Jan. 16, 1993: 116–19).

Policy

Clinton's early policy actions represented a pragmatic response to the problems the country faced and the political pressures that had been built up by Ross Perot. The version of Clinton's budget plan eventually passed by the

Congress raised taxes on the wealthy, but "virtually all that is left of Clinton's original 'vision for change' is a grim determination to chop the deficit. His short-term economic stimulus plan has been defeated, and his long-term agenda for increasing government investment in such things as public works, job training and national service has been gutted" (*Los Angeles Times,* June 25, 1993). The administration's health care reform effort eventually failed amid charges that it entailed a "big government" response to the nation's health care problems, but it is fair to say that Clinton charted a characteristically "centrist course . . . when [he] decided to propose an ideological hybrid, a market-based system of health care marbled by the sorts of federal interventions that congressional liberals like" (*National Journal,* Sept. 4, 1993: 2152).

After Fall 1994

The foregoing was written in June 1993 when the Clinton administration was less than a year old and few people imagined that the 1994 congressional election would so change the landscape of American politics. Rather than fill in events from June on, I will draw a broad sketch of how things have changed (or, in many areas, not changed) and what the changes that have occurred mean for the executive branch bureaucracy.

First, the general pattern of the Clinton administration was clear in mid-1993, and little occurred afterward that would change more than the details in the essay. Clinton continued to stress diversity in his appointments. However, the most notable thing about his appointees was their diversity, not their policy views. This pattern extended to the judiciary also. As David O'Brien notes, while nearly 60 percent of Clinton's judicial appointees were women or minorities, "the great irony is that Clinton has not sought out liberal nominees. On the contrary. A quest for diversity and a more representative judiciary have basically replaced ideology as Clinton's guiding principle" (*Los Angeles Times,* Feb. 5, 1995). Clinton's administration, in short, was most distinctive in demographic terms, but his appointees gave little evidence that he had a coherent policy thrust in mind for his administration. Bert Rockman has described Clinton as having "an uncertain political identity" (Rockman, forthcoming). It's a good description, despite the pillorying the administration has experienced from its opponents as an advocate of "big government."

Second, the administration launched its "reinventing government" initiative with a report issued in September 1993. The initiative (labeled the National Performance Review, or NPR for short) calls for a government that works better and costs less. No one could reasonably dispute that it would be good for any organization to achieve these two goals, but the devil, as always, is in the details. The report lays out four "key principles" for reaching the goals. It calls for the federal government to cut red tape, put customers first (satisfy those who receive government services), empower employees to get results (decentralize authority to those on the "front lines"), and cut back to basics (Gore 1993: xxxviii–xl).

It will be some time before one can render a definitive judgment on this complex initiative, but Donald Kettl argues persuasively that NPR implicitly supports "the need to transfer power from Congress to the executive branch" and explicitly argues for a transfer of power within the bureaucracy "from top-level to lower-level officials" (Kettl 1994: 22). These are matters, as I noted earlier in the chapter, which have been sources of controversy for some time. Congress is not likely to surrender such authority to the executive branch easily, and what it actually means for democratic accountability to put customers first and empower lower-level employees—when neither customers nor employees have been elected by anyone—ought to be very carefully considered.

Third, and quite clearly as a result of the end of the cold war, Clinton administration officials have continued to put less emphasis on military policy and more on domestic policy, particularly economic growth and trade policy. Early signs of activity in these regards could be seen in the Clinton administration's creation of a National Economic Council in the White House, the pledge, certainly fulfilled, made by the Secretary of Commerce Ronald Brown that the Commerce Department "would be a major player in the Clinton Administration's efforts to reinvigorate the U.S. economy and to make the nation more competitive in the global marketplace" (*National Journal,* Dec. 19, 1992: 2896), the vigorous push to approve NAFTA, and in President Clinton's touting of investment in human as well as physical capital.

The so-called new world order has turned out to be more a "new world disorder." The world has gone from one in which there was basically an ordered struggle between the superpowers to one marked by outbreaks of virulent ethnic and religious strife. What to do is unclear, but policy makers such as Undersecretary of State Peter Tarnoff have signaled that U.S. strategists recognize that with its current economic problems and debt, the United States no longer has the resources, the leverage, or the inclination to play world policeman in the post–cold war disputes that have broken out all over the world. (The Clinton administration distanced itself from Tarnoff's remarks when he made them, but tellingly it left him on the job.)

Administration foreign and defense policy have been sources of difficulty and confusion. The Clinton administration's "1993 Bottom-Up Review plan for military forces and spending is already under heated fire from all sides as being both underfinanced and understrength to meet the goal of waging two near-simultaneous regional conflicts" (*National Journal,* Feb. 4, 1995: 276). The one thing that has already happened, and is unlikely to be affected much even by the Republican congressional victory in 1994, is the downsizing of the military. A recent *National Journal* article contained data showing a drop of 33 percent in U.S. army divisions (from 18 to 12) and a decline in active air force fighter wings from 24 to 13.4 in the period between fiscal years 1990 and 1994 (Sept. 17, 1994: 2129). And informed opinion indicates that, no matter what preferences the new Republican majority may have, there is simply not enough money available to "re-Reaganize" military spending. What will happen, however—indeed what has already happened—is that "congressional Republicans can make their views strongly felt on such issues laid out in the Republicans' [Contract with America] as restricting American involvement in U.N. peacekeeping missions" (*National Journal,* Feb. 4, 1995: 276).

The bottom line is that the military has gotten smaller and is unlikely soon to increase in size. More important, post–cold war America has yet to find its foreign policy footing. As Larry Berman and Emily O. Goldman say in the conclusion to their assessment of Clinton's foreign policy at midterm: "To project a coherent foreign policy package, the Clinton administration needs a paradigm to work from—at this point, that paradigm is still in the making" (Berman and Goldman, forthcoming). There is likely to be a good deal of turmoil surrounding American foreign policy in the immediate future as the nation's decision makers struggle to develop a coherent conception of the United States' role in the world.

Fourth, foreign policy, as well as other areas, was made more complex by the victory of the Republican party in the 1994 election. The implications for public policy are only now becoming clear. The Republicans are pushing for monumental changes in policy, using notions about administration as one way to achieve these goals. This is not the place to focus on their notions about changing policy in such areas as welfare, the environment, food stamps, and school lunches. The key point is that congressional Republicans, especially the leadership and its most ardent followers, hope to reduce many programs and eliminate others. The tool they often propose, adopted from earlier efforts by the Nixon and Reagan administrations, is to deliver funds to the states and localities in the form of block grants to achieve broadly specified ends. The grants enable the federal government more easily to limit spending (by combining numerous programs into one with a smaller appropriation than the previous total, or by capping what was previously an entitlement, such as food stamps) and take influence away from the federal bureaucracy by granting much greater authority over policy to the states. If adopted, these policy changes will profoundly affect the executive branch. More important, they will have a profound impact on who gets what in American society.

Concluding Comments

The end of the cold war has brought important changes to U.S. executive branch politics in the form of a strong debate about military policy and the loss of a clear organizing principle for foreign policy, but its main effect likely will be to sharpen already existing tensions brought on by stagnant middle-class real income, budget stringency, an economy in flux, and the continuing debate about the role of government programs and their administrators.

The victory of the Republicans in the 1994 congressional election certainly gives that party's more radical wing a major new platform for attacking traditional Democratic programs and policies, but most observers would not put the end of the cold war high on the list of factors causing the Republican triumph. What we know for sure is that the Republican victory has heightened the long-standing debate about the proper role of the federal government in American life. And, as I noted above, the Democrats are also struggling to find their own way through the morass of questions about the cost, performance, and effectiveness of government programs and services and the agencies that deliver them. The Clinton administration's reinventing government initiative, to cite the most prominent current example, raises questions about the way the government is organized and delivers services and about who should control policy. Although the nature of the debate about reinvention is more genteel in tone, the reinvention initiative is not necessarily less radical in its implications for the executive branch.

In short, the basic debate about what the federal government should do, how it should be staffed, and who should control it started before the end of the cold war and, after some muting following the end of the Reagan administration, continues today. But overall, it seems fair to say that the main problems of the U.S. government in the post–cold war era are not really centered in issues concerning the nature of the civil service or even of management—certainly the civil service, as a result of the 1978 reform, is more controllable than it was before and also more moderate and therefore probably more flexible. There are more fundamental, and still unresolved, debates. The existing organizations and personnel systems in the executive branch, in other words, may be part of the problem, but they are not in themselves central elements. The issues are more basic. Partially masked by the debate about government forms and processes is the crucial question: What kind of society do Americans want?

The Republicans in the House of Representatives have a plan (which they call the Contract with America), but it may be so mean spirited in its attack on lower-income citizens that it eventually falls of its own weight. The Clinton administration has what seems like a flawed plan for the "reinvention" of government and, for the moment, little else but some tepid counterpunching initiatives and the hope that the public gags on its opponents' proposals. Bill Clinton is said to have remarked, "Gosh, I miss the cold war." Sometimes one imagines that he might even have meant it just a bit. But the cold war is over, and the focus now more than ever is on the values Americans hold and not on the flawed and failed values of the nation's former communist adversaries.

Note

1. Portions of this section are adapted from Aberbach and Rockman 1995.

References

Aberbach, Joel D. 1990. *Keeping a Watchful Eye: The Politics of Congressional Oversight.* Washington, D.C.: Brookings Institution.
——. 1991a. "Public Service and Administrative Reform in the United States: The Volcker Commission and the Bush Administration." *International Review of Administrative Sciences* 57: 403–21.
——. 1991b. "The President and the Executive Branch." In Colin Campbell and Bert A. Rockman, eds., *The Bush Presidency: First Appraisals,* 223–47. Chatham, N.J.: Chatham House.
——. Forthcoming. "An Interpretive History of the U.S. Congress in the Twentieth Century." In Stanley Kutler, ed., *Encyclopedia of the United States in the Twentieth Century.* New York: Simon & Schuster.
Aberbach, Joel D., and Bert A. Rockman. 1976. "Clashing Beliefs in the Executive Branch: The Nixon Administration Bureaucracy." *American Political Science Review* 70: 456–68.
Aberbach, Joel D., and Bert A. Rockman. 1990. "The U.S. Federal Executive from Nixon to Reagan to Bush." Paper Presented to the Conference of Governance in an Era of Skepticism, Stockholm, Sept.
Aberbach, Joel D., and Bert A. Rockman. 1995. "The Political Views of U.S. Senior Federal Executives, 1970–1992," *Journal of Politics* 57: 838–52.
Aberbach, Joel D., and Bert A. Rockman, with Robert M. Copeland. 1990. "From Nixon's *Problem* to Reagan's *Achievement:* The Federal Executive Reexamined." In Larry Berman, ed., *Looking Back on the Reagan Presidency,* 175–94. Baltimore: Johns Hopkins University Press.
Berman, Larry, and Emily O. Goldman. Forthcoming. "Clinton's Foreign Policy at Mid-Term." In Colin Campbell and Bert A. Rockman, eds., *The Clinton Presidency: First Appraisals.* Chatham, N.J.: Chatham House.
Brookings Institution. 1992. Transcript of Round-Table Discussion with Federal Executives, May 27.
Gore, A. 1993. *Creating a Government That Works Better and Costs Less.* New York: Plume.
Kettl, Donald F. 1994. *Reinventing Government? Appraising the National Performance Review.* Washington, D.C.: Brookings Institution.

Lynch, Edward J. 1990. "Politics, Nonpartisanship, and the Public Service." *Public Interest* 98 (Winter): 118–32.

Nathan, Richard P. 1983. *The Administrative Presidency.* New York: Wiley.

National Commission on the Public Service (Volcker Commission). 1989. *Leadership for America: Rebuilding the Public Service.* Lexington, Mass.: Heath.

Nixon, Richard M. 1978. *RN: The Memoirs of Richard Nixon.* New York: Grosset & Dunlap.

Rockman, Bert A. Forthcoming. "Leadership Style and the Clinton Presidency." In Colin Campbell and Bert A. Rockman, eds., *The Clinton Presidency: First Appraisals.* Chatham, N.J.: Chatham House.

Shapiro, Robert J. 1993. "Enterprise Economics and the Federal Budget." In Will Marshall and Martin Schram, eds., *Mandate for Change,* 21–50. New York: Berkeley.

State 2000: A New Model for Managing Foreign Affairs. 1992. Report of the U.S. Department of State Management Task Force.

U.S. House of Representatives, Ways and Means Committee. n.d. Tables prepared by the staff.

Wilson, James Q. 1975. "The Rise of the Bureaucratic State." *Public Interest* 41 (Fall): 77–103.

FOUR

STABILITY AND CHANGE IN
THE POST–COLD WAR CONGRESS

JAMES A. THURBER

What has been the impact, if any, of the cold war and the dramatic changes in the international environment as a result of the demise of the Soviet Union and the Eastern European communist bloc on the organization and operation of Congress? This analysis will show that the cold war arms buildup (1947–1989) and the collapse of the Soviet Union (1989) has had little direct impact on congressional stability and change. However, change came spasmodically through new issues and new congressional membership. These issues, members, and events conspired to change congressional campaigns, the role of party leadership, the number and power of committees and subcommittees, norms and ethics, congressional staffing, media coverage of Congress, and the congressional budget process. None of these changes can be directly linked to the cold war or its passing, except for dramatic cuts in the congressional defense budget since 1990.

Although its original design establishing a powerful and decentralized representative bicameral legislative assembly persists, Congress continues through the post–cold war 1990s to change, to adapt to a dynamic political environment, as is shown by the dramatic congressional reforms after the 1994 election. The changes that occurred from 1968 to 1994, such as a more democratic and responsive Congress, growing member individualism, devolution of full committee power to independent subcommittees, dramatic reforms of the budget process, and seeming endless deadlock between Congress and the executive, were not directly linked to the dramatically altered post–cold war world. The centralization of power in the House and "nationalization" of the 1994 Republican campaign with the Contract with America occurred as a response not to a post–cold war world but to a variety of purely domestic economic and political factors.

To understand the sources of stability in Congress that prevent it from changing dramatically because of world events, such as the demise of the Soviet empire, it is necessary to describe its historical and constitutional roots and to explain why certain aspects of Congress remain the same and others have changed in recent years. To achieve these purposes, this chapter is organized around a brief discussion of the historical roots of Congress and more recently the sources of stability and change in the post–cold war Congress.

Historical Roots of Congressional Stability

The primary source of congressional stability during the post–cold war period is the constitutional design of Congress, which was initially based on five hundred years' experience with legislatures in Western Europe and Britain. The drafters of the Constitution were especially influenced by the British experience with Parliament. The framers designed a Congress that followed the long struggle toward representative and powerful legislatures in Great Britain and later in the colonies. James Madison, a major author of the Constitution, put the primary focus on Congress succinctly: "In republican government, the legislative authority necessarily predominates."[1]

The fifty-five delegates who gathered in Philadelphia in 1787 devoted most of their time at the Constitutional Convention to the provisions in Article I of the Constitution—the article establishing the Congress and setting forth its powers—which established the framework of Congress which exists in the post–cold war 1990s.[2] Article I of the Constitution vests "legislative powers herein granted" to a Congress consisting of two chambers, a Senate and a House of Representatives, and requires that bills be passed in identical form by both bodies and signed by the president before they can become law. Many of the basic principles establishing Congress come directly from the experience with legislatures in Europe, Britain, the colonies, and the failure of the Articles of Confederation. These principles include limited government, separation of power, checks and balances, and federalism.

Congress is designed to function in at least three ways: to legislate or make national laws, to represent the people of the United States, and to check and help control the power of the president and the executive branch of government. The framers created a powerful and democratic Congress. Most of the controversial compromises at the Constitutional Convention were about the powers Congress would hold; however, the general agreement that the United States would have a powerful national legislature was never seriously questioned. The framers' decisions resulted in a powerful but restrained legislature that has forced the U.S. government to struggle with the problem of disintegration for two hundred years. As James Madison argued in the *Federalist* papers numbers 10 and 51, Congress is designed to be powerful but limited.[3] Its power is limited by the judicial and executive branches of the federal government, by the states, and by the power of the people to organize and to put popular political pressure on the institution.

The framers authored a Constitution that deliberately fragments power between the national government and the states and among the executive, legislative, and judicial branches. They also divided legislative powers by creating two coequal houses, a bicameral Congress. Although divided, Congress was designed to be independent and powerful, checking the power of the executive and directly linking the people to government through popular, free periodic elections. The framers wanted an effective and powerful federal government, but they wanted to limit its power in order to protect personal and property rights. They were wary of excessive authority in an executive, for they had experienced the abuses of British monarchs and their colonial royal governors. They were also concerned with "elective despotism" or excessive legislative power, which they had experienced with their own state legislatures under the Articles of Confederation.

The U.S. Constitution makes clear that the principal functions of government are entrusted to Congress (e.g., to declare war, to authorize and appropriate funds for programs, to tax, to oversee the executive), but these powers are limited by the principles of checks and balances, separation of powers, and federalism. Consequently, in pursuing its constitutional functions of lawmaking, representation, and oversight, Congress is sure to clash with the president and other political actors. The realities of the post–cold war world have not changed these basic functions or the constitutional basis of congressional power.

Sources of Congressional Stability

How has the original constitutional design of Congress been maintained? How has it changed over time? Has the post–cold war period altered Congress? Three basic characteristics in the structure and organization of Congress help to explain the stability of the institution and the differences between the House and Senate during the post–cold war period and before: size, terms of office, and constituency.

The first Congress (1789–1791) served a population of 4 million in thirteen Atlantic coast states and consisted of twenty-six senators and sixty-five representatives. Congressional activities were limited to the passage of 108 laws that dealt with the creation of the new government and its relations with the states and with matters of defense and foreign affairs. Because of the size of both chambers, deliberations were guided by a few simple rules on the floors of the Senate and House. They conducted most of their deliberations on the floor in both chambers, but that soon shifted to temporary select committees and later to permanent standing committees, a stable feature of Congress.

The U.S. House of Representatives has always been larger than the Senate; today the House has 435 members and the Senate 100. House members have shorter terms of office (2 years) compared to their counterparts in the Senate (6 years). The constituencies of House members are much narrower and focused than the broad and more varied statewide constituencies of senators. These characteristics have not changed significantly over time, and they have generated several important differences that have remained constant between the House and Senate. Because of the large size of the House, there is a need for more structure and formality in the rules than in the smaller Senate. The House is more hierarchically organized and power less evenly distributed than in the Senate. The House uses a Rules Committee to control the flow of legislation to the floor. The Senate has no counterpart. Debate, amendments, and voting in the House are tightly controlled with the aim of expediting legislative business. The Senate has much more informal control over legislation coming to the floor. The Senate is more individualistic and personal than the House. Much of the Senate's business is handled by unanimous consent agreements between the majority and minority parties and informal norms rather than elaborate and more tightly controlled floor action in the House. The House uses a strict rule of germaneness and the Senate does not. All House amendments must pertain to the subject matter of the legislation under consideration on the floor. Senate rules rarely call for debate or amendments to be germane to the bill being considered.

The Senate is allowed unlimited debate (the filibuster), which cannot be employed by the House. Senate rule 22 protects minority rights by allowing an individual to speak without being stopped unless an extraordinary majority of sixty members votes to close debate. The Senate operates in a spirit of comity, respecting the prerogatives of all its members. Consequently, floor debate is more expeditious in the House than in the Senate. The flexibility of the Senate allows delay and even deadlock, checking the populist views of the House of Representatives, as has been shown with the Senate's reaction to the Contact with America in 1995.

Generally, House members fulfill the role of technical experts and the senators are less concerned with technical perfection of legislation and more involved in gaining general public support for policies. The House has a larger work force and its division of labor allows for policy specialization by its members. The Senate is smaller, with the same amount of work; thus senators do not usually specialize. They are compelled to become policy generalists. As a result of size and the policy generalist tendency, the Senate relies on personal and committee staff to a greater degree than the House.

Another difference between the House and the Senate is that power is distributed more evenly among the 100 senators than the 435 House members. Senators are more visible, have their floor amendments adopted more easily, have more immediate influence in committees and more success in scheduling their bills for consideration, and in general participate more widely than do House members. Although the House and the Senate have been covered by live television in recent years, there is less interest in the House by the media than in the Senate. The Senate is more prestigious and visible than the House. Generally these characteristics have remained relatively constant between the House and the Senate, although there have been significant changes within both bodies since passage of the Constitution.

Two other facts have helped to establish the stability of the two houses over the last 160 years and especially through post–cold war politics. First, there have been only two major parties controlling the House and Senate since 1828.[4] The Democrats have had primary control of both houses since 1932 (except in the Senate from 1947 to 1948; 1953 to 1954; 1981 to 1986; and after the historic 1994 congressional election).

The second major source of stability is the committee system, including standing committees. Committees and subcommittees are where the work of Congress gets done, and that has been the way the institution has worked for well over one hundred years. Committees gather information, consider alternatives, and draft and refine legislation. They monopolize the legislative workload. Committees were such a stable and important characteristic of Congress that in 1885, Woodrow Wilson wrote, "It is now, though a wide departure from the form of things, no great departure from the fact to describe ours as a government by the standing committees of Congress."[5] Over the years the most distinguishing characteristic of Congress is the predominant role played by the committee system. Since the early 1800s most of the business of Congress has been done in committees. The number of committees and their jurisdiction was relatively stable until the 1970s. From 1910 to the early 1970s, committees were powers unto themselves. Most committees and their chairmen had power to operate pretty much as they wished. The most important committees in the Senate are Appropriations and Finance. The most powerful committees in the House are Rules, Appropriations, and Ways and Means. The committees play a determining life-or-death role over legislation at every stage of the legislative process.

In sum, four important underlying factors establish a stable base of operation for the House and Senate through the reforms of the 1970s and through the post–cold war period in the mid-1990s: bicameralism, their size difference, their differing bases of representation (states versus districts), and their different terms of office. The House, larger, is more formal, is hierarchical, acts more quickly, and has more rigid rules. Power is unevenly distributed in the House. It is more impersonal and less prestigious than the Senate. Since the Senate has only one hundred members, it is less formal and less hierarchical, it moves more slowly, the rules are more flexible, and power is distributed more evenly. It is more personal and has greater prestige. Senators serve longer terms (6 years) than Representatives (2 years), which gives senators more freedom from constant campaigning. The bicameral structure of representation assures additional checks on the legislative process by making it less efficient and more responsive to the differences between the homogeneous House districts and the more heterogenous states. These characteristics have not changed significantly since the first Congress or since the end of the cold war.

Both institutions have the same responsibilities: legislating, oversight of the executive, and representation. Historically these responsibilities have not changed, but the way Congress has done its work has varied according to the political and economic environment of the times. Both the House and Senate have always used political parties to organize legislative work. Political parties have always been a feature of the congressional landscape, but they only emerged as a central feature of Congress in the late nineteenth century. The role of party has waxed and waned. Both bodies have always conducted business through a decentralized committee system. The committee system is at the heart of congressional work. The Senate and House have equal workloads, and from the 1970s to present, their workloads have been especially heavy.

Sources of Change in the Post–Cold War Congress

Although it is a relatively stable institution, as the size of Congress grew in the nineteenth and early twentieth centuries, and as the volume and complexity of problems facing Congress multiplied, it underwent several important changes. The structure of Congress is decentralized through its committee and subcommittee system. The post–cold war Congress is marked by a diffusion of power, a weak central core of authority, and little unity of command. Leadership is weak and divided among committee chairmen, subcommittee chairmen, and the party leaders.

Congress changed especially dramatically as a result of major reform in the 1970s and the transformational election of 1994. The changes of the 1970s and 1994 have had a significant impact on the legislative workload, rules and procedures, committees and subcommittees, staff bureaucracies, the seniority system, the budget process, leadership style, the role of party organization, constituency demands, oversight of the executive, the nature of decision making, and ethics during the post–cold war period.

What are the major post–cold war changes in Congress?[6] After years of relative stability (1970–1990), Congress seemed unable to overcome policy gridlock. It seemed unable to deal with several major issues facing society: the economy in general, crime and drug abuse, education, health care, and other major domestic issues. Scandal also scarred Congress with the "Keating Five," the House check "kiting" affair, and the post office fiasco. Public approval of Congress dropped dramatically in the polls to historic lows. Many members chose to retire, others were defeated, and still others pushed for reform. In 1992, Congress created a joint committee to examine its organization, operations, and procedures, but the Democrats failed to report significant reforms from the committee. It took the elections of 1992 and 1994 to bring change. The 1994 Republican sweep in the House and Senate brought profound changes in the committee system, management and administration, staffing, leadership, and legislative-executive relations and the speed with which legislation is considered, especially in the House. However, interviews with members of Congress and staff and an analysis of the post-1994 election reforms show that none of the changes is explicitly linked to the realities of the post–cold war world outside the United States. The 1995 changes were driven by pressures from outside Congress by an angry electorate demanding change in the way Congress worked and from inside Congress by members wanting to improve the workings and image of the institution.

Change in Membership

Change in its members is a primary source of change in Congress and is shown by the historic elections of 1992 and 1994. Over 90 percent of the members of the House and Senate are new since 1968. The 1992 elections produced 110 new House members (87 of whom returned in 1995) and eventually 14 new senators (only 1948 had a larger turnover of 118 House members). The 1994 contests added 86 new representatives and 11 new senators. This impressive turnover brought important changes to the Hill, especially in the House of Representatives. Many of the new House members owed their seats to retirements generated by redistricting and the House bank scandal. Most new members promised to reform Congress and to shake up the way Washington worked. Newly elected members are younger and more conservative on fiscal policy and social issues (e.g., support for the Contract with America). Very few of the new members campaigned on post–cold war defense and foreign policy issues. The plight of the post–cold war world was rarely an issue in a congressional campaign.

They are well informed, activist, and unwilling to wait to be heard, thus breaking many long-established norms of Capitol Hill. The 1970s, 1980s, and 1990s saw a reversal in the longtime trend of increased tenure of office. The number and proportion of veterans with service in World War II and Korea dropped steadily from the 1970s to present, while the number and proportion of junior members with no cold war military experience increased. If seniority characterized Congress in 1960 and 1970, "juniority" is a more appropriate term for the 1980s and 1990s. This change in membership helped to bring the impressive reforms in committees and subcommittees, leadership, staff and analytic capabilities, the congressional budget process, openness and speed of lawmaking, campaign finance, and the ethics of members.

Committee Reform and "Democratization" of Power

The 1970s brought a "democratization" of decision making to the House of Representatives which was a reality of post–cold war congressional politics until the reforms of 1995 brought a centralization of power in the Republican House of Representatives. The imperial presidency of the 1960s and 1970s (Watergate and the Vietnam War) brought major reforms to Congress in the early 1970s. After twenty years of relative stability and calm, major reform came again after the 1994 election.

In January 1969 the House Democratic caucus reestablished control over committee assignments by requiring that the Committee on Committees receive caucus approval of committee assignments before taking them to the House floor for pro forma approval. In 1973 further inroads on the seniority system occurred in the House when an automatic secret ballot was required on committee chairmen at the start of each Congress (this is also now the case in the Senate). At the beginning of the 94th Congress, three chairmen were defeated through this process. Also in 1985 the Democratic caucus removed the sitting Armed Services Committee chairman from his post, and Les Aspin (D., Wis.) was selected to replace him, although Representative Aspin was well down the list of senior Democrats. The power of committee chairmen was also limited through the election of subcommittee chairmen by the Democratic members of each committee in the House.

Committee majority caucuses were also given the right to organize each committee, and the "subcommittee bill of rights" was adopted in the House which allows subcommittees and subcommittee chairmen to have staff and budget and thus more power. These reforms helped to take power away from the "barons" (committee chairmen) and give it to the "baronets" (subcommittee chairman), thus decentralizing influence in the House from the early 1970s to 1994. Congressional government became subcommittee government until the dramatic transformation and centralization of the

House under the Republican leadership in 1994 and the reinstitution of a modified party government. The House also brought "sunshine" to committee meetings (as did the Senate) by requiring a separate roll call vote to close a committee meeting or hearing (first passed in 1973 and strengthened in 1975 and 1995).

Each House committee (except Rules and Budget) was required to establish at least four subcommittees, a change that had the consequence of spreading the power of the Ways and Means Committee (which had no subcommittees before this reform in 1973). In 1975 a revolution in committee rules and procedures came to the House in which the responsibilities of the Committee on Committees of the Ways and Means Committee were transferred to the Steering and Policy Committee, a caucus vote was required on Appropriations subcommittee chairmen, additional limitations were placed on the committee service of full committee chairmen, conference committees were opened, and minority staffing for each committee was expanded (to one-third of the its total staff). This was a major move to democratize the House.

The unsuccessful attempts of the Bolling-Hansen committees to reorganize the sizes, numbers, and jurisdictions of committees in the House in 1973–1974 were not repeated in the Senate in late 1976 and early 1977. Passage of Stevenson's committee reorganization brought new committee and subcommittee assignment limitations to the Senate, it "modernized" and realigned committee jurisdictions (especially energy, environment, and governmental affairs), it eliminated several committees, and it gave the leadership more power to refer bills and to monitor the "health" of the Senate committee system more effectively. The reform effort of 1993 attempted to revise the committee system.

The changes of the 1970s modified the House seniority system for selecting committee chairs, limited the number of chairs an individual could hold, devolved power to subcommittees, and revised the committee assignment process. The reforms democratized the House and made it more responsive during the post–cold war period; however, Republican members were profoundly dissatisfied with the committee system and pushed for new committee realignment after the 1994 congressional election. In 1995 the House Republicans reduced the number of committees and subcommittees, reduced the number of committee assignments, cut congressional staff, reduced the overlap of jurisdictions among committees, and centralized power with the leadership.

Democrats fought loudly and publicly for congressional reform in the 103rd Congress, but in the end nothing happened. The landslide victory of the Republicans in 1994 brought a radical overhaul to the House committee system. The Contract with America promised major reform, and the Republicans kept their promise. The first actions of the 104th Congress were to reduce the number of committees and subcommittees, reduce the number of committee assignments, ban proxy voting in committees, place term limits on committee chairs, and cut the staff by one-third. The seniority system was altered in the House when three chairs who were not the most senior were selected by the Speaker. Three committees (Post Office and Civil Service, District of Columbia, and Merchant Marine and Fisheries) were consolidated into the new Government Reform and Oversight Committee in the House. The first bill passed by the House and Senate and signed by President Clinton forced Congress to abide by federal employment laws. Approximately 20 percent of the Energy and Commerce Committee's jurisdiction was transferred to other committees. Committee statutory and investigative budgets were cut and consolidated. Republicans also promised to stop jointly referring bills to committees, a sure way to speed up the legislative process in the House. The Senate made no major changes after the 1994 election, preferring to continue the seniority system and highly decentralized power structure.

Leadership Reform

The dilemma of the post–cold war House and Senate is the struggle between centralization and decentralization of power. Individualism and independence on the part of members ran unchecked from the 1970s to the election of 1994. Until the 1970s committee chairs held power through the seniority system (i.e., tenure on each committee rather than election) and therefore were not subject to party control. The committee assignment reforms and secret ballot selection of committee chairs established in the 1970s led to an anomalous situation for party leaders. The Democratic leaders of the 1970s, 1980s, and early 1990s were stronger on paper, but in reality they were weak because of member individualism and the excessive strength of interest groups or "hyperpluralism."

The post–cold war decade has brought new leaders and personalities to all of the party positions in the House and the Senate. Party leadership in the Senate changed from Democratic to Republican in 1981, back to Democratic in 1987, and then back to Republican again in 1995. Change in leaders and their style was also accompanied by several major changes in the formal powers of the leadership (especially in the House). These include giving the Speaker the chairmanship of the House Democratic Steering and Policy Committee in 1974 that gave the authority to nominate committee chairs and make committee assignment nominations until the Republican takeover in 1995. The reforms also give the Speaker sole power to nominate the Democratic members and the chair of the Rules Committee so that they would be more responsive to the leadership. The Speaker was also given authority to nominate several members to the Steering and Policy Committee. On paper, these reforms gave the Democratic Speaker much more power than before the 1990s. In reality, he was much weaker than Speakers Rayburn, Cannon, and others.

The Democratic caucus in the House was also given more power to coordinate the legislative process. In January 1969 the rules of the caucus were changed so that monthly meetings were required and individual members were given the right to place matters before the caucus for debate and action. This reform, more than any other, set the groundwork for the major changes in the 1970s: the use of the caucus to pass reform measures.

The 1994 election helped the Republican leadership centralize decision making in the House through its control of the legislative agenda, committee assignments, selection of committee chairs, staff cuts, reduction in the number and size of committees, the imposition of term limits on chairs, the elimination of proxy voting, and jurisdictional realignment of committees. The consequences of these reforms for the House have been a new legislative process with fewer committee and subcommittee roadblocks and speedy action. The chairs lost power to block legislation. The freshmen and sophomore House Republicans were loyal to the Contract with America and the leadership. These reforms in the House allowed for more committee meetings, more days and hours in session, more votes, and more measures passed in an unprecedented amount of time. However, the breakneck speed of House lawmaking was checked by the Senate with its careful deliberation and oversight.

The Senate has been cautious in giving more power to the majority leaders, although through the style of leadership under Senators Byrd, Mitchell, Baker, and Dole, power and influence has increased for Senate majority leaders. After the 1994 election, the Senate was still fundamentally a decentralized, informal, deliberative legislative body.

However, central party leadership in both the House and Senate has often been suspect to most members in the 1980s and 1990s, and the decentralizing forces of member individualism and subcommittee power often predominate. Critics argue that there is a need in the post–cold war 1990s for stronger central congressional leadership to orchestrate the activities of the scattered committees and subcommittees, schedule consideration of bills, and provide better central services.

Staff and Analytic Capabilities

During the reform years of the 1970s, Congress improved its staffing and information-gathering capabilities, and these reforms continued into the 1990s. Congress gave its members and committees more staff and better access to information. In the mid-1990s, Congress employed around thirty thousand staff for committees, member's offices, and support agencies. Some eighteen thousand staff work for members, committees, and the leadership. Congress now has an expanded Congressional Research Service and an improved General Accounting Office. Congress created the Office of Technology Assessment in 1972 and the Congressional Budget Office in 1974, which improve its analytic support capabilities. There have also been recent impressive improvements in computing capacity and utilization by both the House (House Information System) and the Senate. These reforms expanded the capacity of Congress to do policy analysis and evaluation of presidential initiatives and department requests.

However, Congress has grown not one bureaucracy but many, clustered around centers of power. This growth has presumably improved the responsiveness and accountability of Congress, but some argue that it has reduced its efficiency. Efforts to impose a common framework on staff and the new congressional bureaucracy have generally failed. The attempt to reduce the size and power of staff is a common theme of Congress of the 1990s. The post–1994 election reforms of the House Republicans cut staff by one-third and significantly cut the budgets of committees and the congressional analytic support agencies as a result of promises in the Contract with America and a response to the public's lack of regard for Congress.

Budget Reform

The election of 1994 marked the twentieth anniversary of the passage of the historic Congressional Budget and Impoundment Control Act and still another round of major budget reforms. The focus of the congressional budget process has been transferred dramatically in the last twenty years from budgetary priority setting in the 1974 Budget Act (1974–1985) to deficit control in the Gramm-Rudman-Hollings Deficit Reduction Act (1985–1990), to spending control in the 1990 Budget Enforcement Act (BEA), the balanced budget amendment, and line item veto of the 1990s.

The budget reforms of 1974 were passed to recapture fiscal power from the president and to pursue both liberal and conservative policy objectives. The Congressional Budget and Impoundment Control Act of 1974 established two budget committees, a budget timetable, the Congressional Budget Office, and a tough procedure for controlling presidential impoundments (recissions and deferrals). The 1974 budget reform, the 1985 Gramm-Rudman-Hollings (GRH I) Deficit Reduction Act, and its 1987 amendments (GRH II) call for Congress to establish a budget with firm expenditure levels, project revenues, estimate surplus or deficit (which has existed for the last two decades), pass budgets on time, and show fiscal discipline. Congress has failed to meet these objectives.

Congress must do something that it never did before 1974; account for expenditures, revenues, and deficits in a single resolution rather than figuring out what has happened to the budget at the end of actions by the Appropriation committees. The budget impoundment control procedures give Congress new capabilities to counter the president's budget with its own analysis and priorities. However, the 1980s saw ever increasing budget deficits and an inability to pass budget and appropriation bills on time.

The most important post–cold war congressional reform is the BEA of 1990, which further centralizes budget power within Congress to make zero-sum choices; that is, trading visible reductions in one program for visible increases in another, or tax cuts for some in exchange for tax breaks for others. The most visible change was the elimination of fixed deficit targets as established in GRH I and II for other innovations such as pay-as-you-go provisions on taxes and spending, and categorical sequesters and major cuts (over 25%) in defense spending, the one major policy change in the BEA directly linked to the end of the cold war.[7] The substantial tax increases and spending cuts enacted by Congress in the 1990 BEA were continued in President Clinton's first budget, the Omnibus Budget Reconciliation Act of 1993. Both of these acts resulted in substantial cuts in defense and significant deficit reductions. The demand for budget reform was not over just because the deficit was declining. The balanced budget amendment, the Line Item Veto Act, and the Unfunded Mandates Reform Act were all part of the Republican-led budget reforms in 1995. However, Congress is still dominated by special interests, and tough money decisions, the Budget and Impoundment Control Act, GRH, the BEA, and other reforms have not given it enough new courage to deal with those tough post–cold war budget decisions.

Further change in budgetary decision making will come, if at all, from the American electorate. If voters wanted a balanced budget, Congress would pass a balanced budget wihout new procedures. Budgetary process reforms have not made up for the lack of political will on the part of members of Congress. Neither the American voters nor their elected officials have displayed the political courage to make revenues match outlays in all the post–cold war budgets. The basic instinct in Congress is to not accept constraints.

"Sunshine" Reforms

"Sunshine"—or openness, less secrecy and more accountability—was pushed upon Congress by "good government" organizations such as Common Cause in the 1970s and supported internally by those concerned about the poor public image of the institution in the 1990s. In response, Congress passed several major reforms from the 1970s to the mid-1990s that changed its visibility, efficiency, and public image. Television and radio coverage of

House committee hearings were authorized in 1970. House and Senate committee votes were recorded and made available to the public during the same year. In 1973 all House committee sessions were open to the public unless a separate roll call vote was taken to close the sessions. All Senate committee sessions were opened to the public in 1975. This had the effect of opening almost all committee sessions in both the House and Senate. In 1977 the House voted to require a full recorded roll call vote in the House to close conference committee hearings. In 1978 the House permitted continuous television coverage of floor sessions, and the Senate did the same in 1985.

In 1995 the Republicans further opened up the process in the House with internet access to legislative documents and speeches (i.e., "Thomas") and extensive televising of committees and subcommittee hearings and markups. The House restricted closed committee meetings to national security matters, required that committee reports include committee roll call votes, and mandated on-the-record floor votes on tax increase bills, all of which made legislators' actions more visible to outside observers. The Republicans also instituted fewer restrictive Rules Committee orders which limited the possibilities for presenting policy alternatives as amendments on the floor. Years of mainly closed rules from the Democratic Rules Committee had brought more debate and openness to the floor of the House on the part of the Republican leadership. These reforms initiated openness, which brought more accountability and permeability in the way Congress makes laws and oversees the executive. These reforms made it easier for the electorate to inform itself about the policy alternatives being debated by the parties.

Ethics and Management

The American electorate's traditional distrust of politicians and Congress turned into overt cynicism in the 1970s, and it has only increased during the post–cold war 1990s, as is shown by the massive turnover of members in the 1992 and 1994 elections. Politicians felt a backlash following Watergate, the Vietnam War, the corruption of Adam Clayton Powell and ABSCAM, and the way members collected money for election campaigns. Generally, voters felt members were beholden to special interests. Congress became keenly aware of the low esteem in which it was held in the public eye in the early 1970s, especially after Wilbur Mills's aquatic exhibitionism, Wayne Hays's affair with a nontyping typist, the questions about contributions made to representatives by the South Korean government, and the rapid growth of special interest campaign money. In response, Congress passed the campaign finance reforms of 1974, which limited individual and organizational contributions to congressional campaigns and required candidates to report the source and use of campaign funds. Members were also required to report earned income, dividends and interest, gifts, holdings in property and securities, and total debt. Congress addressed the issue of public cynicism with a new vigor by passing stricter codes of conduct (in 1977 and 1978), by establishing two new Ethics committees, and by limiting outside income (1985). It also studied its problems through a Commission on the Operation of the Senate, a Temporary Select Committee to Study the Senate Committee System, a Commission on Administrative Review of the House, and the 1993 Joint Committee on the Organization of Congress. But the cynicism about Congress continued unabated into the 1990s.

Although the intent of these reforms and study groups was to inhibit unethical behavior and restore public confidence in Congress, members are still concerned about the lack of public trust in their institution. The 1993 joint committee report calling for a new code of ethics and improved management of the institution and congressional reforms enacted by the 104th Congress are responses to public outrage about Congress. The reform efforts of the 1990s (term limits, ethics reforms, reorganization of the House management, campaign finance reform, and lobbying reforms) were driven by internal scandal (especially the House bank check "kiting," post office scandals, the Bob Packwood affair, and indictment of Dan Rostenkowski) and distrust by the American public of Congress rather than the realities of the international politics of the post–cold war period.

Conclusions

Congress has changed significantly during and since the end of the cold war, but not because of it. It has maintained its three essential functions: lawmaking, oversight, and representation, although they have been altered over time. It still firmly holds the power of the purse, as is shown by the post–cold war defense cuts; it oversees the executive and checks the power of the president, as is revealed by the battle over post–cold war foreign policy; it legislates new programs, although slowly (e.g., foreign aid to the former Soviet Union), and reviews old ones (e.g., the debate over UN and NATO support in the 1990s). Most important, Congress is still responsive (some think too much so) to political preferences and public pressure, as is exhibited by the 1994 election and the Contract with America. It is representative; in fact, it is significantly more responsive (especially to the hyperpluralism of well-organized groups and associations) in the 1990s. This is the stable core of Congress; however, the institution has also changed dramatically.

The reforms of the past three decades and those made in the post-1994 Congress have made the institution more representative and accountable, given it more tools to perform better oversight, and changed the way it makes laws and passes budgets. These changes have not come as a result of the end of the cold war or the dramatic change in the international environment, but they have had an impact on the president and Congress working together to figure out how to keep order in the post–cold war world. Pressure to check the power of the president (e.g., the 1973 War Powers Act and the Congressional Budget and Impoundment Control Act of 1974) brought reforms that helped Congress reclaim some of the power it had lost to the president during the previous decades. Internal pressure for more democratization brought decentralized power in Congress and helped to make the institution more inefficient and permeable, but it eventually brought centralization in the House in 1995.

With openness came more accountability and responsiveness at the price of efficiency and effectiveness as a lawmaking body. The overly partisan and individualistic House of the early 1970s to 1994 led to the centralized and more efficient Republican House of 1995 and beyond. Presidents, even of the same party, like President Clinton and the Democratic Congress of 1992–1993, find Congress harder to influence; it is more well informed and independent. Congressional party leaders find it more difficult to coordinate the legislative process (except in the post-1994 House of Representatives); it is more democratic and accountable to the electorate. The struggles in the cold war period between representativeness and efficiency, openness and accountability, Congress and the president, leadership and followership, and specific interests and the public good continue today as they did before the collapse of the Soviet Union and as they did two hundred years ago during the debates in Philadelphia. Observers have argued that the changes of the 1970s pushed Congress into a state of paralysis which was not the intent of the authors of the Constitution two hundred years ago.[8] Before the transformational election of 1994, they argued that Congress was so inefficient that it could no longer legislate and oversee as it was intended. The 1995 Republican House responded with the Contract with America and basic reforms in the leadership, committee system, and rules and procedures which spectacularly changed the way the House works.

Americans are highly critical of congressional inefficiency and deadlock and have called for major internal reforms, campaign finance reform, lobby registration reforms, and term limits on members. The Republicans responded with change. In survey after survey, Americans describe Congress as inefficient and complain of legislative deadlock. In a September 1992 *New York Times* poll, only 17 percent of those surveyed approved of the way Congress was handling its job. Additionally, presidential candidate Ross Perot and the passage of term limits on members of Congress in fifteen states in

1992 have sent a message to Congress to improve the way it does business. The House Republicans responded by cutting the number of committees and committee assignments, by increasing oversight of the executive, by reducing congressional staff by one-third, and by streamlining the legislative process in the House. However, the post-1994 election did not improve the miscommunication between the chambers and between the branches of government, lack of policy integration, excessive partisanship, and general public concern about the institution's ability to govern.

Congress has changed dramatically in the last twenty years, but it is likely to change even more dramatically in the next decade. In the post–cold war era, Congress faces issues that have changed significantly, and it must adapt to face those issues or it will lose the power to deal with them. It faces enormous scientific and technological complexity, in everything from arms control verification and assistance to countries in the former Soviet Union to environmental protection and telecommunication and trade policy. There is an array of issues that are both domestic and international and which no longer cut neatly across organizational lines. There are deep-seated problems that call for longer-term perspectives by members of Congress. In the past fifteen years, Congress has passed all of the thirteen appropriations bills only once. Since 1985 there have been three major budget reforms/agreements and new "quick fixes" in the mid-1990s, all attempting to control spending and entitlements, without overwhelming success. It is clear that Congress has not performed well in recent years and needs to adapt, to change even more than it did in the 1970s, 1980s, and early 1990s. Congress seems increasingly unable to tackle the main issues that Americans are concerned about, from jobs and crime to how we should react to the post–cold war world.

The pendulum of congressional change seems to be moving to correct these problems after the 1994 election with the Contract with America. The unintended consequences of the congressional reforms of 1995 will mean that change will continue into the next century. However, the major sources of stability—size, terms of office, constituency, party, bicameralism, separation of power, and the committee system—remain the predictable bedrock of the institution. They have not changed. The Congress of the post–cold war and the post-1994 election will be distinct from that of the 1780s, 1880s, and 1980s, but it is not clear in what ways. Unless there is a major constitutional crisis, which is unlikely, the constitutional design of Congress forces the institution to remain relatively stable, but it will continue to change with the new members (60% of the House since 1990), strong interest groups (hyperpluralism), weak political parties, and the uncertain post–cold war international environment.

Notes

1. Alexander Hamilton, James Madison, and John Jay, *The Federalist,* ed. Benjamin F. Wright (Cambridge: Harvard University Press), no. 51, 356.

2. For an excellent record of the convention, see Max Farrand, ed., *The Records of the Federal Convention of 1787,* 4 vols. (New Haven: Yale University Press, 1966).

3. See Hamilton, Madison, and Jay, *The Federalist,* nos. 10, 51.

4. See David W. Rhode, *Party Leaders in the Postreform House* (Chicago: University of Chicago Press, 1991).

5. Woodrow Wilson, *Congressional Government* (Boston: Houghton Mifflin, 1885), 55.

6. See Leroy N. Rieselbach, *Congressional Reform* (Washington, D.C.: Congressional Quarterly, 1994), on the reform of the 1970s; and James A. Thurber and Roger H. Davidson, eds., *Remaking Congress: Change and Stability in the 1990s* (Washington, D.C.: Congressional Quarterly, 1995), on the 1990s.

7. James A. Thurber, "New Rules for an Old Game: Zero-Sum Budgeting in the Postreform Congress," in Roger H. Davidson, ed., *The Postreform Congress* (New York: St. Martin's, 1992), 257–78; and James A. Thurber, "If the Game Is Too Hard, Change the Rules: Congressional Budget Reform in the 1990s," in Thurber and Davidson, *Remaking Congress,* 130–44.

8. See James L. Sundquist, *Congressional Reform and Effective Government* (Washington, D.C.: Brookings, 1986).

FIVE

FROM DIVIDED GOVERNMENT TO POST–COLD WAR GRIDLOCK?

TOBIAS DÜRR

O ne of the central themes of the 1992 election campaign was "grid-lock." The visibly deepening estrangement and alienation of the governed from their government, many observers agreed, was due largely to paralysis and stalemate in Washington. President George Bush and Congress, it was said, were unable to work together, rendering government unable to deal with the important issues of the day. "The president has seen few initiatives enacted and has wielded his veto to block dozens of bills," one journalist remarked shortly before the election. By the end of George Bush's presidency, his administration and Congress were "caught in monumental deadlock."[1] The allegation was not new. For years commentators had been describing American government as gridlocked, deadlocked, stalled, or incoherent. And most of them agreed that the main cause for this predicament was "divided government"—the control of the White House and one or both houses of Congress by opposing parties. Throughout the presidential campaign of 1992, George Bush and his challenger Bill Clinton shared this interpretation. Each called upon the electorate to end gridlock by voting a one-party government of either Republicans or Democrats into office. The voters obliged, though not in the way George Bush would have preferred. By electing Bill Clinton president while at the same time re-affirming the Democratic majorities in the Senate and in the House of Representatives, they equipped Washington with "unified government" after more than a decade of split party control of the presidency and the legislature. "For the first time in twelve years," the New Republic rejoiced shortly after Bill Clinton's victory at the polls, "we have an undivided government, and with it the opportunity to put to an end the legislative cold war that has crippled the country."[2]

But just as unified government did not by and of itself guarantee well-informed, timely, coherent, effective, and responsible public policy (to borrow Michael Mezey's standards for government performance)[3] during the presidency of Jimmy Carter, it did not automatically do so under President Clinton. In fact, if divided government alone had been the problem behind what Americans consider as gridlock, the electorate would hardly have ended unified government again in 1994 by sending Republican majorities to both houses of Congress after only two years of Democratic single-party government.

This is not to say that it makes no difference at all whether one party controls both the presidency and the Congress or not. Divided government certainly poses problems of governance. But if unified government is no safeguard against poor public policy either, it seems necessary to draw a clearer distinction between the adverse effects directly attributable to divided government and those caused by other obstacles standing in the way of smooth executive-legislative cooperation and, hence, a more satisfactory government performance.

It is interesting, moreover, that political scientists only recently "discovered" the phenomenon of divided government. In fact, they did so "just before unified party government returned to Washington," as Charles O. Jones mocked after the election of Bill Clinton.[4] This belated identification of divided government as a problem worth considering appears odd at first sight. After all, split party control of the executive and legislative branches has been the norm rather than the exception since World War II. If divided government were really such a serious problem, would it not have been noticed earlier? David Menefee-Libey accordingly suggests that "divided government is often a scapegoat, standing in as the target for our real frustrations with the nonperformance of the federal government."[5] But why should these "real frustrations" have grown? Is it purely by accident that the increased concern about the perceived effects of divided government in the early 1990s coincided with an unprecedented proliferation of policy problems, while at the same time the end of the cold war deprived Americans of an integrating sense of mission?

This chapter seeks to address these questions. It first discusses the implications of divided government for presidential-congressional relations. Then it attempts to assess the limitations even a single-party government faces in dealing with the problem of policy paralysis that has commonly, though perhaps not altogether correctly, been ascribed to divided government. Finally, the problem of executive-legislative gridlock will be considered in terms of the radically changed post–cold war environment.

Divided Government: The Problem?

When President Harry Truman's Democrats lost their majorities in both houses of Congress in the midterm elections of 1946, consternation was widespread. Considerable Democratic losses had been predicted, but few had foreseen a situation of divided government. The election results alarmed both the public and politicians. Democratic Senator J. William Fulbright even suggested that President Truman appoint a Republican secretary of state and subsequently resign. Since the vice presidency was vacant, the appointee would automatically have become president, thereby restoring unified government.[6] Without such a measure, the senator feared, the United States would become a "big helpless giant that is unable to make up its mind, unable to function."[7]

In the mid-1990s it takes some effort to see the situation through Fulbright's eyes. After the early return to the normalcy of divided government as a result of the 1994 midterm elections, the idea that anything but single-party control of both the presidency and the Congress should be considered a serious aberration seems out of place. Yet in 1946 the perspective was different. Since 1897 there had been no more than three cases of divided government, the most recent of them ending in 1933. Contemporaries looked back on an unprecedented era of unified control, unmatched even in the nineteenth century, when divided government had been frequent in the two periods 1840–1860 and 1874–1896.[8] In almost all of these cases, divided government had come as a result of midterm losses of unified control won at the preceding presidential election and had been ended again after only two years. Just once, in 1884, the winner of a two-way presidential race had failed to carry both houses of Congress.

In principle, this pattern still held for the period of split-party control caused by the midterm election of 1946, which lasted only until 1948, when President Harry Truman was reelected and the Democrats regained majorities in Congress. Republican President Dwight D. Eisenhower, too, during his first two years in the White House, could deal with a Congress dominated—if only marginally—by his own party. What has been called the "Era of Divided Government" began in earnest only when the Republicans lost their congressional majorities in 1954, for this was the last time before the "Republican revolution" of 1994 that a period of unified government ended as the result of a midterm election. For the next forty years, not a single period of divided government began at midterm any more. When Eisenhower was reelected in 1956, he became the first president in this century to be faced with a congressional majority of the opposite party at least in one house of Congress from the beginning of a presidential term. The same happened to all Republican presidents after him. Richard Nixon in 1968 and

1972, Ronald Reagan in 1980 and 1984, and George Bush in 1988 all confronted Democratic majorities among representatives or among representatives *and* senators upon inauguration, and Gerald Ford in 1974 inherited Nixon's second-term party split. Of the nine presidents elected between 1956 and 1988, only the three Democrats, John F. Kennedy in 1960, Lyndon B. Johnson in 1964, and Jimmy Carter in 1976, found Capitol Hill dominated by members of their own party. In all, American government was divided between Republican presidents and Democratic congressional majorities for twenty-six out of the thirty-eight years between 1955 and 1992. By the time the election of Bill Clinton temporarily ended divided government, it had been sixteen years since the American electorate had last voted a unified government into office.

This chapter is not about the electoral origins of divided government—the decline of party loyalty among voters and the increase in ticket splitting[9]—neither will it deal with premature views arguing that the 1992 election somehow ended the cold war era of divided government and ushered in a new post–cold war era of unified government. The most recent earlier period of unified government is today referred to as the "Carter interlude," and it cannot be ruled out that the condition of unified Democratic government during the first two years of the Clinton presidency will be seen as no more than just another interlude ten years hence.

As it turned out in 1994, the American electorate had not once and for all concluded in 1992 that "gridlock would end if one party ran the show."[10] "Voters have ended divided government in the 1992 balloting," Everett Carll Ladd rightly observed at the time. "There is no indication that they did anything to curb the conditions that have encouraged it."[11] Indeed, the 1992 contest did not bring about the long-awaited electoral realignment but proved to be a "deviating election." The Republicans did lose the presidency, but they lost it "as a result of short-term forces rather than in response to shifts in the structure of groups' political loyalties or a sea turn in the public's expectations about the proper course of public policy."[12] Ladd concluded that despite the election of Bill Clinton, "the distinctive parties and elections system that took form in stages from the mid-1960s through the mid-1980s remained in place in 1992, dictating many features of the competition."[13] The implication was, of course, that in terms of electoral alignment alone, the Republicans would stand a fair chance of regaining the presidency in 1996, thereby restoring divided government after four years. On the other hand, it has long been known that the president's party often loses ground in Congress in off-year elections,[14] and it was therefore considered possible that the Democrats might lose their majority in the Senate after only two years, or find the already slim vote margin in their favor reduced to such an extent that some form of de facto divided government would develop.[15]

Neither Ladd nor anybody else predicted a Republican takeover of both houses of Congress by 1994 until very shortly before the elections;[16] however, an early return of divided government was never to be ruled out completely, and critics of this condition had little reason to draw relief from its temporary disappearance. Their questions about the detrimental effects of split control of the presidency and the Congress on government performance continued to be relevant even before Newt Gingrich's Republicans stormed Capitol Hill, particularly since the new reality of Democratic party government offered a standard of comparison that made it possible to measure the consequences of divided government somewhat more precisely than before.

The theoretical foundations of what might be termed the "divided government causes gridlock" thesis have been set out most persuasively by James Sundquist.[17] With the Constitution designed by the framers above all to prevent partisan majorities from oppressing minorities, the resulting system of "separated institutions *sharing* powers"[18] has traditionally been an impediment to strong and effective government. In order to generate policy results collectively, the president, the Senate, and the House need to cooperate. This, however, is possible only to the extent that the three power centers can find some overarching principle that binds them together and concentrates their actions. That principle is party government: "When the same party controls all three of these power centers, the incentive to reach such agreement is powerful in spite of their institutional rivalries and jealousies," Sundquist argues. "The party *does* serve as the bridge or a web, in the metaphors of political science."[19] Conversely, when government is divided, the parties inevitably cease to integrate its fragmented branches: "Then, the president and Congress are motivated to try to discredit and defeat each other."[20]

> "If the president sends a proposal to Capitol Hill or takes a foreign policy stand, the opposition-controlled House or houses of Congress—unless they are overwhelmed by the president's popularity and standing in the country—simply *must* reject it. Otherwise they are saying the president is a wise and prudent leader. That would only strengthen him and his party for the next election, and how can the men and women of the congressional majority do that, when their whole object is to defeat him when that time arrives? By the same token, if the opposition party in control of Congress initiates a measure, the president has to veto it—or he is saying of his opponents that they are sound and statesmanlike, and so is building them up for the next election."[21]

Given these circumstances, each side's primary goal is not so much sensible public policy but scoring political points in what Hedrick Smith has called "the blame game."[22] For instance, while "some kind of budget" is necessarily concluded each year on a lowest common denominator basis, it reflects the views of neither side and does not seriously address the deficit. Meanwhile the president and the congressional majority blame each other for the lackluster results, leaving the public confused and uncertain whom to hold responsible, not least because neither side really *is* responsible. Likewise, the call for presidential leadership of Congress must necessarily come to naught when the two are engaged in this sort of trench warfare. As Sundquist writes, "The President is not the leader of the congressional majority. He is precisely the opposite—the leader of their opposition, the man they are most dedicated to discredit and defeat."[23]

These theoretical considerations seem to be borne out convincingly by data on the uneasy relationship between President Bush and Congress. According to *Congressional Quarterly*'s figures, in 1992, Bush won just 43 percent of the roll-call votes on which he took a stand—"the worst performance of any president at any point in his term since CQ began keeping score 39 years ago."[24] At the same time, partisanship in Congress reached "near-record levels."[25] In the House a majority of Democrats voted against a majority of Republicans on 64 percent of all recorded votes in 1992. This constituted a 9 percent increase from the 1991 figure of 55 percent and before had been matched only in 1987. In the Senate, 53 percent of the roll-call votes fell along party lines, the highest percentage in three decades except for 1990, when the number was 1 percent higher. Of course, 1992 was an election year, and both Bush's low success rate and partisanship in Congress must be evaluated in this context. On the other hand, that can be only part of the explanation. For his full term in office, George Bush's average success score was no more than 51.8 percent—compared, for instance, to Jimmy Carter's 76.6 percent or Ronald Reagan's 72.3 percent during his first term. Bush's success rate was clearly the "lowest of any first-term president since CQ began tracking this variable in 1953." Only Reagan's second-term score of 51.7 percent was slightly lower still. Similarly, a tendency toward stronger partisanship in Congress had been discernible for a number of years, predating the 1992 surge in party-line voting. In sum, there are multiple signs that the alleged blockade between the Republican presidency and a Congress dominated by Democrats actually *increased* in magnitude after James Sundquist lamented the baneful effects of divided government in 1988.

Budget Deficits and Divided Government

Prior to the election of Bill Clinton, the rapidly growing budget deficits and the apparent inability of the federal government to curb them, contributed more than anything else to the impression that divided government inevitably led to gridlock and stalemate.[26] As the *Economist* observed, "Federal spending is the prime example of an important issue where progress involves hard choices, and hence where blaming the opposing party is always safer than helping to make these."[27] It certainly appears suggestive, on the face of it, that of the fourteen years since World War II in which the federal deficit has exceeded 3 percent of gross national product, every one has come during a period of divided government—one under Truman in 1948, two under Ford in 1975 and 1976, and eleven under Reagan and Bush from 1982 through 1992. But correlations are not causes, as Paul E. Peterson rightly points out.[28] Rather than divided government, what triggered deficits were the popular 1981 tax cuts requested by President Reagan and enacted by a Republican Senate and a conservative majority in the House, in combination with the equally popular refusal of Congress to cut domestic programs. Indeed, to claim that budget deficits were *caused* by divided government would be to overlook the fact that the era of deficit politics of the eighties and nineties began precisely at a time when government was virtually unified by the popularity of Ronald Reagan.

On the other hand, while split party control of the presidency and Congress was not the root cause of deficit politics, it is certainly true that all attempts at deficit reduction between 1981 and 1992 were in one way or another subject to the logic of divided government. What seems significant, to begin with, is that it took several years before the president and Congress resolved that something needed to be done about the growing gap between revenues and expenditures, even though in principle almost everybody had long agreed that deficits constituted a serious problem. But substantial deficit reductions would have required sacrifices—cuts in entitlement programs or tax increases, or in all probability both—which for ideological reasons or out of fear of incurring the wrath of the electorate, neither the president nor congressional Democrats were willing to make. The device to get around this deadlock seemed to be the Gramm-Rudman-Hollings Deficit Reduction Act of 1985, which purported to solve the problem "automatically" by mandating a fixed reduction in the deficit over several years (bringing it down to zero, it was actually forecast, by 1993).[29] Should the annual deficit-cutting targets not be reached, across-the-board cuts would take place. The whole idea behind Gramm-Rudman-Hollings (GRH) was, of course, to enable politicians of both parties to avoid blame for the effects of their own actions. "The point is to leave no 'fingerprints' on difficult policy decisions—not 'look, ma, no hands' but rather 'who, me?' "[30] Even so, the conflicting interests of Republicans and Democrats made sure that GRH was never fully implemented in the following years. Whenever it seemed remotely likely that its provisions would have to be invoked, the president and Congress saw to it that they would not be.[31] As James Pfiffner put it, the requirements of GRH "only resulted in a plethora of budget gimmicks to achieve the appearance of deficit reduction, while the fiscal reality of huge deficits remained."[32] The GRH scheme thus became a metaphor for gridlock under divided government.[33]

The next attempt to tackle the budget deficit came in the form of the Budget Act of 1990. This measure, too, was defined by the dynamics of divided government, but in a different way than GRH. In 1990 a Republican administration and a Democratic Congress, in the face of soaring deficits, eventually managed to agree on a reduction package of significant proportions that also included a tax increase. Although doubts rightly persisted about whether the compromise really "lived up to its billing as the biggest, most honest attempt to reduce the deficit in U.S. history,"[34] the five-year $490 billion plan as such received generally good marks at the time of its passage. In this sense, then, it could be argued that the 1990 budget deal proved that divided government is indeed capable of producing meaningful policy results.[35]

Yet the cost at which this deal was struck must be taken into account. A solution was arrived at only after months of arduous haggling. The process involved the temporary shutdown of the Statue of Liberty and even the National Zoo. The public, once again unable to tell who exactly was responsible for the protracted stalemate that preceded the deal, reacted with anger and disgust. As a result, confidence in government as a whole—president and Congress alike—received yet another severe blow.[36] What is most interesting in terms of the effects of divided government, however, is the role of George Bush before, during, and after the 1990 budget battle. He had won the presidency not least by making his imprudent "read my lips" campaign pledge, which in itself was a by-product of divided government since, to make any sense at all, it relied on the existence of a Democratic majority in Congress supposedly bent on taxing and spending. Going back on that careless promise in 1990 certainly was a responsible and statesmanlike decision to make by comparison, yet given the blame-game dynamics of divided government, Bush incurred heavy political costs in doing so. First promising "no new taxes," then breaking that promise, and finally even apologizing for breaking it, as Bush did during the 1992 campaign, no doubt contributed greatly to his defeat at the polls. As Garry Wills remarked, the pledge "might have been his undoing whether he kept it or broke it—but it was fatal when he did both."[37] Whatever the 1990 compromise may have been worth in terms of deficit reduction, then, *politically* it turned out to be a monumental disaster for President Bush.

The Uses of Adversity?

As James Sundquist reminds us, "To rest a theoretical proposition on concrete examples from history is to invite debate on the merits of each exam-

ple and to call forth counterexamples."[38] But despite this "difficulty of arguing from cases,"[39] the circumstances surrounding the 1990 deal as well as its
long-term political effects seem to suggest that the passage of legislation
alone may not be the appropriate yardstick for the workability or unwork-
ability of divided government. Interestingly, David Mayhew takes an altogether different view. For him, the important point about the 1990 budget
compromise is not how it was reached and at what cost, but simply that in
the end "a five-year $490 billion plan did pass."[40] More generally, "the
question should be: Is the system capable of generating important legislation?"[41] The underlying assumption is, of course, that because of legislative
deadlock, less such "important legislation" should be enacted during periods of divided control than during periods of unified control. However,
having analyzed 267 relevant laws passed between 1946 and 1990, Mayhew concludes that "it does not seem to make all that much difference
whether party control of the American government happens to be unified
or divided."[42] "On average, about as many major laws passed per Congress
under divided control as under unified control."[43] Yet the mere fact that
legislation gets passed under divided government does not guarantee well-
informed, timely, coherent, effective, and responsible public policy or, in
short, good government in a procedural and substantive sense.[44] As Mayhew himself concedes, his work skirts "the separate and obviously important question of whether the American system of government, with its
separation-of-powers features, has been functioning adequately in recent
times."[45]

Surprisingly, perhaps, the received opinion that divided government is
detrimental to good government has been challenged even on this score.
While Mayhew stops well short of claiming that government functions better when control is divided—he argues only that there is "very little difference"—others have in fact suggested that in particular circumstances the
uses of adversity, as it were, do indeed exist. One important example usually
cited is the 1986 Tax Reform Act, which owed its passage, it is said, to the
fact that in a process of interparty competition, both Republican and Democratic leaders "first sought to win credit with the public for enacting reform
and later competed to avoid blame for killing it."[46] In this instance, then,
divided government arguably helped pass the legislation. But more recently
there seem to have been few, if any, memorable cases of this kind of productive bidding for political credit under divided control. During the Bush presidency, the Clean Air Act of 1990 may in fact have been the only example to
fit this pattern.[47]

As the further rise in party-line voting toward the end of the Bush years
indicates, bipartisan coalition building under the conditions of divided
control declined precisely at a time when the problems facing government—

from the deficit to America's undefined role in the post–cold war world—seemed to be proliferating. Conversely, the fact that, as a result of deteriorating executive-legislative relations, even the most conspicious policy problems increasingly remained unresolved further contributed to the already widespread impression that government was deadlocked. Gridlock and the perception thereof appeared to be mutually reinforcing. As the *Economist* concluded, by the end of 1992 "things really had got worse. And it was at least reasonable to believe that divided government deserved much of the blame."[48] On the whole, then, the experience of Bush years seems to make it harder than ever to challenge the assertion that divided government necessarily leads to "unhealthy, debilitating conflict between the institutions of government themselves."[49] At the same time, it is precisely the observation that, by all accounts, divided government produced particularly poor results in recent times as compared to earlier periods of divided control that calls into question the assumption that unified government alone can make all the difference. The mixed legislative results of the Democratic single-party government under President Clinton confirm this view. It seems that divided government was not the real problem after all.

Unified Government: The Solution?

"With great fanfare and immense hope, the people elect a president each four years. But then, most of the time these days, they given him a Congress a majority of whose members tried their best to beat him in the last election and who will do so again in the next," a despairing James Sundquist observed in 1988.[50] In 1992 the American people, for once, made sure that their new president and the congressional majority would belong to the same party. Thus Sundquist took heart.[51] But rightly so? Judging purely from historical precedents, a sustained and productive legislative relationship between the president and Congress is unlikely. In this century the exceptions were the administrations of Franklin D. Roosevelt, Lyndon B. Johnson, and Ronald Reagan. Even in these few cases, though, and even when presidents and congressional majorities belonged to the same party, cooperation was not sustained after early outbursts of activity.[52] So skepticism seemed justified with regard to the probability that everything would come out differently under Bill Clinton. But why is it so difficult for the president and Congress to come to a lasting arrangement? And why may it have become yet more difficult after the end of the cold war?

The Madison Curse?

One early skeptic came up with a compellingly simple answer. "Clinton is failing, he'll keep failing and it's not his fault. It's James Madison's," Mickey

Kaus flatly declared only five months after President Clinton had been sworn in.[53] That was a pretty grim prediction to make at the time, but indeed, as noted earlier, a unified party government changes nothing at all about the *constitutional* division of powers. Within a system deliberately designed by its framers to fragment power between the federal government and the states and among the executive, legislative, and judicial branches, the president and the two houses of Congress remain independent from each other even when the government is unified. More often than not, this has posed problems. In the words of Arthur Schlesinger, "A governing process based on the separation of powers among three supposedly equal and coordinate branches has an inherent tendency toward stalemate and inertia."[54] For any president, then, to deal with Congress means having to work together with two halves of a distinct institution, each of which is invested with constitutional powers and prerogatives in its own right and is determined to protect them.

Yet work together they must, in spite of everything. Under the U.S. Constitution, effective government becomes possible only to the extent that the legislative and the executive branches cooperate. Perhaps unjustifiedly in part, but not least because the executive branch alone is structurally capable of taking the initiative, the burden of responsibility for making that cooperation work is commonly placed not with Congress but with the presidency. Presidents are expected both to have "policy objectives" and to "lead" Congress, in order to achieve these goals. When interbranch relations become stalled during periods of divided government, presidents are likely to receive the bulk of the blame for lacking leadership or goals. Presidents, in turn, will invariably resort to complaining about the opposition on Capitol Hill but are unlikely to get very far with that tactic.[55] As Charles O. Jones remarks, "Even Republican Presidents are somehow expected to 'lead' Democratic Congresses."[56] George Bush found that out to his cost.

By contrast, presidents should find it much easier to supply the expected leadership when their party also has a majority in Congress. That, in any case, is the point made by James Sundquist. But unified government has pitfalls of its own. If the public and the media hold even Republican presidents accountable for their alleged failure to lead Democratic Congresses, then any president, whether Democratic or Republican, will find the situation even more difficult with a Congress dominated by his own party. In no circumstances will he remain unscathed, should presidential-congressional relations go sour. Jimmy Carter, the last Democrat in the Oval Office before Bill Clinton, quite intentionally, if unpolitically, interpreted his role as that of a *trustee*, an official entrusted to represent the public or national interest at large, downplaying electoral considerations and parochial concerns. According to Jones, "He appeared to have arrived in Washington prepared to teach that community some lessons about good government and doing the right thing."[57] This insistence on "doing what's right, not what is political," as well as Carter's unwillingness to mingle with the Washington establishment, may have been laudable from a moral point of view, but on the other hand his self-righteous attitude certainly did not help him in his relations with Congress, which quickly deteriorated beyond repair.[58] Predictably, the media and the public in 1980 evaluated the Carter years not so much in terms of the president's good intentions as in terms of the perceived gap between his lofty policy goals and the lack of leadership he had displayed in pursuing them.

Obviously Bill Clinton was no Jimmy Carter. But like Carter before him, he became president promising to tackle the big issues of the day. Like Carter, though probably not with quite the same conviction, Clinton frequently expressed contempt for within-the-Beltway politics. Returning to his antigridlock campaign theme of 1992 more than five months into his presidency, he proclaimed, "I was sent to the White House, I think, to take on brain-dead politics in Washington from either party—or from both."[59] Yet, like Carter, he could not evade being held accountable in the midterm elections of 1994 for his failure to provide the leadership of Congress which the public and the media expected of him.

Neither was it unimportant for congressional Democrats whether President Clinton would be considered the successful leader Jimmy Carter wasn't. "No Democrat," *Congressional Quarterly* observed just after Clinton's election, "wants to relive those days, where divisiveness between the two branches—both controlled by Democrats—helped sow the seeds for 12 years of Republican rule."[60] Indeed, by all accounts, fear of a rerun of the Carter experience haunted congressional Democrats in the early phases of the Clinton presidency and should have proved to be the strongest psychological incentive to their continued willingness to cooperate with the administration. The more tangible grounds for toeing the party line, however, probably stem from the nature of what has been called the postreform Congress.[61] The legislative branch of the American government has become more centralized, more hierarchical, and more partisan in recent years. Particularly in the House of Representatives, party organization and institutionalized party leadership have been strengthened, and party voting has been on the increase.[62] This revival of partisanship in Congress is due in part to the nationalization of the two parties, their growing ideological homogeneity, and the concurrent decline of the bipartisan conservative coalition.[63] But it also resulted from the persistence of divided government. To adapt Roger Davidson's words, as long as the White House and one or both chambers are in different parties' hands, there is an inevitable temptation to regard legislative products as partisan declarations.[64] This temptation became all but irresistible for congressional Democrats once they were reasonably confident of beating the increasingly unpopular George Bush in 1992.

But, of course, during the first two years of the Clinton presidency, the Democrats could no longer count on divided government to help them maintain the—certainly by American standards—high level of party unity they reached during the Reagan and Bush years. To the extent that additional cohesiveness is in fact attainable by way of clashing with unpopular presidents, congressional Republicans now held the high ground. Predictably, Senate Minority Leader Bob Dole tried hard to forge the Republic senators into a homogeneous political force, scoring his first success in April 1993 when all of the forty-three Senate Republicans, in a sustained filibuster, practically defeated the president's economic stimulus package. According to Senator John H. Chafee, the important lesson this episode taught Republicans was "that this has only come about because we stuck together, and that we will be nonplayers if we do not."[65] Predictably, President Clinton denounced Senate Republicans as upholders of gridlock and paralysis in the weeks following this early defeat, and Senate Republicans knew that excessive use of their right to filibuster could easily backfire.[66] Still, in principle at least, the potential for filibusters makes the Senate the one remaining locus of minority party leverage in presidential-congressional relations during periods of unified government. According to Robert Dole, "All this talk about gridlock is a joke. That's what the Founding Fathers had in mind when they created the Senate and said we could debate forever."[67] Arguably, then, the threat of divided government always was a reality to the extent that the Senate Republicans managed to team up against the Democrats.

Putting Presidents First?

But not only the Republican blocking minority in the Senate stood in the way of sustained and productive executive-legislative cooperation. As has already been indicated, it was also questionable whether the Democrats would be able to translate the relative cohesiveness they had achieved vis-à-vis Republican administrations into support for a president belonging to their own party. The Carter experience seemed to suggest above all that the congressional Democrats simply could not afford to desert President Clinton. After all, in 1980 it was largely Jimmy Carter's perceived failure that cost them 12 Senate seats and cut their 119-seat House majority in half.

Yet the link between President Clinton's fate and that of his fellow Democrats in Congress was not quite that unequivocal. In part the reasons once again lie in the institutional separation of the executive and legislative branches or, more specifically, in the different constituencies and terms of office of presidents and members of Congress. Senators and representatives do not support a president who belongs to their own party at all costs, because in some respects they depend on his success considerably less than he depends on them to help him push through his agenda. Whereas presidents are elected by and accountable to very broad electoral coalitions, senators and particularly representatives must remain responsive to much narrower constituency and interest group pressures in order to secure their reelection. Citizens, far from willing to reward their legislators for taking courageous but necessary policy decisions, tend to consider their members of Congress primarily as ombudsmen and evaluate them in terms of their record of constituency service and their personal characteristics.[68] "Today the continuity of congressional membership largely depends on members' ability to serve and benefit their customers," according to Michael Mezey.[69] And since elections are always just around the corner for members of the House and one-third of the senators, and deviations from the pattern of responsiveness to constituency concerns will therefore hardly remain unnoticed in the home districts and states, legislators do not usually feel that they can afford to consistently put the president first. If they did so in any circumstances, this would, in many cases, bring them into conflict with their voters and, hence, their own best interest.

For President Clinton the problem was compounded by the fact that his claim to a "mandate for change" stood on shaky ground from the start. As one early observer put it rather bluntly, "This is a 43 percent presidency."[70] More to the point, Bill Clinton's presidential coattails were not proportionate to his extensive policy agenda. While his party barely held on to its fifty-seven Senate seats in the November 1992 elections, it actually lost nine seats in the House. Moreover, in only five congressional districts did the new president receive a higher share of the votes than the winning House candidate did. While it is true that "mandates are not objective realities," as Thomas E. Mann reminds us,[71] President Clinton never had much leverage in appealing to Democratic members of Congress, at any rate not on the basis of his personal popularity among their constituents.[72]

Taken together, then, these factors help to explain why Bill Clinton could not count on the Democratic majority in Congress to support him in any circumstances. According to Tip O'Neill, "How am I going to protect myself?" was the question Democratic members of Congress began to ask themselves at some point during the Carter years.[73] By August 1994 the same question was being asked again.

Toward Post–Cold War Gridlock?

To be sure, unified government during the first two years of the Clinton administration was considerably less prone to legislative gridlock than the divided variety under Presidents Bush and Reagan. During his first year in office, Clinton failed to get his $16.3 billion economic stimulus package through Congress but eventually prevailed on all other major votes, including the administration's deficit reduction plan and the North American Free Trade Agreement. Clinton's 88 percent first-year success rate in Congress was as high as that of any president since Dwight Eisenhower, and it remained as high in 1994. He did not veto a single bill during the entire 103rd Congress.[74]

Most observers remained unimpressed. "Gridlock still seems to be the rule" in Washington, and "it doesn't matter which party controls the White House and Congress," were some of the typical complaints in 1993.[75] They could be heard well before the legislative collapse of the Clinton administration's effort in 1994 to reform the health care system.[76] In large part this view seemed to be due to the somewhat belated realization that the constitutional fragmentation of American government which, for that matter, made divided government possible in the first place did not go away just because government was unified for a change. Those who unwisely expected the immediate "change" that Bill Clinton had incessantly promised during his campaign were bound to be disappointed. The president's inexperience and recurring public relations blunders on the part of the administration no doubt played a role as well.

But, given the Clinton administration's *comparatively* smooth legislative start, all this still cannot quite account for the magnitude and persistence of public frustration with government and politics in general that eventually translated into the Republic victory in November 1994. Obviously there is a widespread notion that the real problem—the problem behind the problem of gridlock, as it were—must somehow run deeper. "Something has happened to the constitutional theory in recent years," writes Anthony Lewis. "Dealing wḯth urgent national necessities has become not just difficult but, we often feel, impossible."[77]

By contrast, Arthur Schlesinger some years ago warned against the "fallacy of self-pity that leads every generation to suppose that it is peculiarly persecuted by history." "Obviously," he wrote, with the imperturbability befitting a historian,

> the substantive problems of the 1970s and 1980s were not easy. But do we really face tougher problems than our forefathers did? Tougher problems than independence? slavery? the Civil War? the Great Depression? the Second World War? The substantive problems confronting contemporary Presidents are, nuclear weapons aside, relatively manageable compared to those that confronted Washington or Lincoln or Franklin Roosevelt.[78]

And, one is tempted to add, after the end of the cold war and global bipolarity, even the threat of thermonuclear war no longer persists as a realistic possibility. However, the important question is perhaps not so much how tough the contemporary problems are by historical comparison but whether the existing institutions and mechanisms of government correspond to the types of problems facing the nation. This may no longer be the case. Today's problems may not be tougher than those of earlier times, but in many respects they are *different* in ways that make the fragmented and far-flung political institutions appear outmoded and overloaded. "The American dilemma lies in a political process that is increasingly irrelevant to our policy problems," argues James Morone.[79] Contemporary challenges—the deficit, the economy, the infrastructure, industrial decline, global competition, health care, education, poverty, housing, violence, drugs, racial antagonism, immigration, the underclass, the cities, or the environment[80]—all seem to call for stronger, more coherent government that is designed to focus the national resources and to mobilize the public for common projects.[81]

But even the absence of a political center capable of acting more forcefully than can justly be expected from the executive and legislative branches of government today—no matter whether they are divided or unified—does not quite explain the rampant frustration with "brain-dead politics." Arguably, the problem facing the American government not only concerns poor institutional performance and excessive public expectations but ultimately boils down to something like a post–cold war crisis of national purpose.[82] As becomes fully apparent only in retrospect, the cold war and the concomitant threat of global communism had the invaluable side-effect of serving as an ordinating principle for American society and politics. The cold war instilled a sometimes ennobling sense of a national mission and for forty years was the central yardstick by which the American polity determined its policy priorities. In part at least, domestic goals were regularly defined *ex negativo* in terms of the global competition with the Soviet Union. This was true, for instance, when a commission appointed by President Truman stated the case for civil rights in the following manner:

> We cannot escape the fact that our civil rights record has been an issue of world politics. The world's press and radio are full of it. . . . Those with competing philosophies . . . have tried to prove our democracy an empty fraud and our nation a consistent oppressor of underprivileged people. This may seem ludicrous to Americans but . . . the United States is not so strong, the final triumph of the democratic ideal is not so inevitable that we can ignore what the world thinks of our record.[83]

While it is not clear whether the end of the cold war also constituted the "final triumph of the democratic ideal," it is certainly true that "competing philosophies" no longer present a serious threat to the concept of Western liberal democracy. But the reality of the cold war threat at the same time

provided an important point of focus for the American people and the fragmented American political system. After the cold war such an integrative
mechanism from without is no longer at hand. Unified control of both the
presidency and Congress by one party removes some of the obstacles to
more effective and coherent government. At the same time, the end of the
cold war has curbed the ability of presidents to arouse what James Patterson calls "a persistent popular yearning for bold presidential leadership,"
thereby shifting the balance of power toward Congress.[84] And, as the 1994
midterm elections proved quite convincingly, unified government is an abstract matter that cannot by itself produce the common goals and aspirations that would contribute to bridging the gap between the branches of
government and between the governed and their government.

In future all serious attempts at tackling the big post–cold war problems
facing the United States, most notably the deficit, will arguably necessitate
forceful and coherent government action involving the allocation of costs
rather than benefits. It is hard enough to see how America's fragmented
political institutions will cope with this challenge; it is even more difficult to
imagine how a new sense of national or, for that matter, communal purpose
could emerge from the current post–cold war disorientation. Health care
reform and the issue of universal health coverage did not turn out to be a
step in this direction, as Bill and Hillary Clinton had evidently hoped.[85]
Neither is it likely that Newt Gingrich and his Contract with America will
achieve this goal.[86] Yet unless some sense of common purpose takes hold of
American society again, the all-pervasive lamentation of "gridlock in Washington" is unlikely to stop, no matter who controls Capitol Hill and the
White House. Warren Rudman, the former senator, argues that the real
gridlock is "not so much between the Congress and the president, but between the government and its people, who have a totally erroneous perception of what the government is and what it does."[87] He may be right.

Notes

I am grateful to Herbert Dittgen for his support and encouragement during the
writing of this chapter, and I wish to thank Paul E. Peterson and Juergen Wilzewski
for their helpful comments on an earlier version.

1. Pamela Fessler, "Bush's Sway with Congress Hits Record Low in 1992," *Congressional Quarterly Weekly Report,* Oct. 17, 1992, 3247.

2. "Bill's Blue Pencil," *New Republic,* Dec. 14, 1992, 7.

3. See Michael Mezey, "The Legislature, the Executive, and Public Policy: The
Futile Quest for Congressional Power," in James A. Thurber, ed., *Divided Democracy:
Cooperation and Conflict between the President and Congress* (Washington, D.C.: Con-
gressional Quarterly Press, 1991), 99–122.

4. Charles O. Jones, "Noticing Divided Government" (review article), *Congress
and the Presidency* 19 (Autumn 1992): 193–95.

5. David Menefee-Libey, "Divided Government as Scapegoat," *Political Science and Politics,* Dec. 1991, 643–45.

6. See David McCullough, *Truman* (New York: Touchstone Books, 1993), 523.

7. Quoted in Gary W. Cox and Samuel Kernell, "Governing a Divided Era," in Gary W. Cox and Samuel Kernell, eds., *The Politics of Divided Government* (Boulder, Colo.: Westview Press, 1991), 1–2.

8. See Morris P. Fiorina, "An Era of Divided Government," *Political Science Quarterly* 107 (1992): 389; Charles H. Stewart III, "Lessons from the Post–Civil War Era," in Cox and Kernell, *The Politics of Divided Government,* 203–38.

9. See Gary C. Jacobson, *The Electoral Origins of Divided Government: Competition in U.S. House Elections, 1946–1988* (Boulder, Colo.: Westview Press, 1990).

10. "United We Stand, for the Moment," *Economist,* Apr. 3, 1993.

11. Everett Carll Ladd, "The 1992 Vote for President Clinton: Another Brittle Mandate?" *Political Science Quarterly* 108 (1993): 27.

12. Ibid., 2.

13. Ibid.

14. See, for instance, John E. Chubb and Paul E. Peterson, "American Political Institutions and the Problem of Governance," in Chubb and Peterson, eds., *Can the Government Govern?* (Washington, D.C.: Brookings, 1989), 33.

15. See for instance James A. Barnes, "In a Jam," *National Journal,* Sept. 25, 1993, 2297–2300.

16. See William F. Connelly Jr. and John J. Pitney Jr., "The Future of the House Republicans," *Political Science Quarterly* 109 (1994): 571–93.

17. See James L. Sundquist, "Needed: A Political Theory for the New Era of Coalition Government in the United States," *Political Science Quarterly* 103 (1988): 613–35.

18. Richard E. Neustadt, *Presidential Power and the Modern Presidents: The Politics of Leadership from Roosevelt to Reagan* (New York: Free Press, 1990), 29.

19. Sundquist, "Needed: A Political Theory," 629.

20. Ibid.

21. Ibid., 630.

22. Hedrick Smith, *The Power Game* (New York: Ballantine Books, 1989), chap. 17.

23. Sundquist, "Needed: A Political Theory," 630.

24. Phillip A. Davis, "Politics, Drop in Senate Support Put Bush's Ratings in Cellar," *Congressional Quarterly Weekly Report,* Dec. 19, 1992, 3841.

25. Holly Idelson, "Signs Point to Greater Loyalty on Both Sides of the Aisle," *Congressional Quarterly Weekly Report,* Dec. 19, 1992, 3849.

26. See Paul J. Quirk, "Domestic Policy: Divided Government and Cooperative Presidential Leadership," in Colin Campbell and Bert A. Rockman, eds., *The Bush Presidency: First Appraisals* (Chatham, N.J.: Chatham House, 1991), 76–77.

27. "United We Stand, for the Moment."

28. See chap. 9.

29. See James A. Thurber, "New Rules for an Old Game: Zero-Sum Budgeting in the Postreform Congress," in Roger H. Davidson, ed., *The Postreform Congress* (New York: St. Martin's Press, 1992), 263–66.

30. James P. Pfiffner, "Divided Government and the Problem of Governance," in Thurber, *Divided Democracy,* 51.

31. See Anthony King and Giles Alston, "Good Government and the Politics of High Exposure," in Campbell and Rockman, *The Bush Presidency,* 253.

32. Pfiffner, "Divided Government," 52.

33. Smith, *The Power Game,* 654.

34. Tom Morgenthau, "The Art of the Deal," *Newsweek,* Nov. 5, 1990, 29.

35. See David R. Mayhew, *Divided We Govern: Party Control, Lawmaking, and Investigations, 1946–1990* (New Haven: Yale University Press, 1991), 187–88.

36. See Barbara Sinclair, "Governing Unheroically (and Sometimes Unappetizingly): Bush and the 101st Congress," in Campbell and Rockman, *The Bush Presidency,* 155–84.

37. Garry Wills, "The End of Reaganism," *Newsweek,* Nov. 16, 1992, 74.

38. Sundquist, "Needed: A Political Theory," 627.

39. Ibid., 629.

40. Mayhew, *Divided We Govern,* 35. Also see Mayhew, "Divided Party Control: Does It Make a Difference," *PS: Political Science & Politics* 24 (1991): 637–40.

41. Mayhew, *Divided We Govern,* 35.

42. Ibid., 198.

43. Mayhew, "Divided Party Control," 639.

44. See King and Alston, "Good Government."

45. Mayhew, *Divided We Govern,* 198.

46. Timothy J. Conlan, Margaret T. Wrightson, and David R. Beam, *Taxing Choices: The Politics of Tax Reform* (Washington, D.C.: Congressional Quarterly Press, 1990), 237, quoted in Pfiffner, "Divided Government," 46. See also Fiorina, "An Era of Divided Government," 406; Quirk, "Domestic Policy," 71; Thurber, introduction, in Thurber, *Divided Democracy,* 6.

47. See Sinclair, "Governing Unheroically," 169.

48. "United We Stand, for the Moment."

49. Sundquist, "Needed: A Political Theory," 629.

50. Ibid., 630.

51. See his comments in James L. Sundquist, ed., *Beyond Gridlock: Prospects for Governance in the Clinton Years—and After* (Washington, D.C.: Brookings, 1993), 25–27.

52. See James P. Pfiffner, "The President and the Postreform Congress," in Davidson, *The Postreform Congress,* 230.

53. Mickey Kaus, "The Madison Curse," *New Republic,* May 31, 1993, 4.

54. Arthur Schlesinger Jr., *The Cycles of American History* (Harmondsworth: Penguin, 1989), 285.

55. See William Schneider, "Don't Complain: A Warning to Clinton," *National Journal,* Jan. 28, 1995, 266.

56. See Charles O. Jones, *The Trusteeship Presidency: Jimmy Carter and the United States Congress* (Baton Rouge: Louisiana State University Press, 1988), 78.

57. Ibid., 215.

58. See Pfiffner, "The President and the Postreform Congress," 231.

59. William Schneider, "The Trick Is in Finding What Works," *National Journal,* June 12, 1993, 1440.

60. Pamela Fessler, "Democrats Dress for Dance with New Administration," *Congressional Quarterly Weekly Report,* Nov. 14, 1992, 3617.

61. See Roger H. Davidson, "The Emergence of the Postreform Congress," in Davidson, *The Postreform Congress,* 3–23.

62. See David W. Rohde, "Electoral Forces, Political Agendas, and Partisanship in Congress," in Davidson, *The Postreform Congress,* 27–47.

63. See Andrew Taylor, "Southern Democrats May Score if Fading Alliance Dissolves," *Congressional Quarterly Weekly Report,* Dec. 19, 1992, 3845–48; Robert

Marshall Wells, "A Longtime Voting Bloc Falls with Southern Democrats," *Congressional Quarterly Weekly Report,* Dec. 31, 1994, 3627–29.

64. Davidson, "The Emergence of the Postreform Congress," 20.

65. Quoted in Chuck Alston, "The Minority Strikes Back," *Congressional Quarterly Weekly Report,* Apr. 10, 1993, 908.

66. See "Beyond Gridlock," *New Republic,* May 3, 1993, 7.

67. Fred Barnes, "King Robert," *New Republic,* Apr. 5, 1993, 28.

68. See Michael Mezey, "Congress within the U.S. Presidential System," in Thurber, *Divided Democracy,* 27.

69. Ibid.

70. Eleanor Clift, "The No Fear Factor: Congress Isn't Afraid to Challenge Clinton," *Newsweek,* May 31, 1993, 22.

71. Thomas E. Mann, "The Prospects for Ending Gridlock," in Sundquist, *Beyond Gridlock,* 13.

72. Richard E. Cohen, "What Coattails?" *National Journal,* May 29, 1993, 1285.

73. Quoted in Jones, *The Trusteeship Presidency,* 188.

74. See Janet Hook, "Clinton's Months of Missteps Give Way to Winning Streak," *Congressional Quarterly Weekly Report,* Nov. 27, 1993, 3243–45.

75. William Schneider, "Gridlock Still Seems to Be the Rule," *National Journal,* June 5, 1993, 1384. For other journalistic examples of this kind, see e.g., David S. Broder and Michael Weisskopf, "Again, Gridlock Grips a Capital Wary of Change," *International Herald Tribune,* June 14, 1993; Anthony Lewis, "Most Often Inertia Wins Out," *International Herald Tribune,* June 19–20, 1993; Kaus, "The Madison Curse"; Richard E. Cohen, "Some Unity," *National Journal,* Sept. 25, 1993, 2290–94.

76. For an analysis of Clinton's 1994 success rates in Congress, see Steve Langdon, "Clinton's High Victory Rate Conceals Disappointments," *Congressional Quarterly Weekly Report,* Dec. 31, 1994, 3619–23.

77. Lewis, "Most Often Inertia Wins Out."

78. Schlesinger, *The Cycles of American History,* 288.

79. James A. Morone, *The Democratic Wish: Popular Participation and the Limits of American Government* (New York: Basic Books, 1990), 329.

80. For a survey of the "American dilemma," see Paul Kennedy, *Preparing for the Twenty-First Century* (New York: Random House, 1993), chap. 13.

81. See Morone, *The Democratic Wish,* 330.

82. See John W. Jeffries, "The 'Quest for National Purpose' of 1960," *American Quarterly* 30 (1978): 451–70.

83. Quoted in Morone, *The Democratic Wish,* 196–97.

84. James Patterson, "Not So Fast, Newt: The Presidency Is Stronger Than You Think," *New Republic,* Jan. 23, 1995, 28.

85. See Joe Klein, "Facing Up to the Big Worry," *Newsweek,* Sept. 27, 1993, 28. For a pointedly critical view of the reception and adaptation of communitarian ideas, see Leon Wieseltier, "Total Quality Meaning," *New Republic,* July 19 and 26, 1993, 16–26.

86. For some skeptical evaluations, see James Fallows, "The Republican Promise," *New York Review of Books,* Jan. 12, 1995, 3–6; William Schneider, "Will the Republican 'Revolution' Work Out?" *National Journal,* Jan. 7, 1995, 54.

87. See Sundquist, *Beyond Gridlock?* 51; also see "United We Stand, for the Moment."

SIX

FEDERALISM, RECENT FOREIGN
POLICY, AND THE PRESENT PLIGHT
OF THE SYSTEM

DAVID B. WALKER

The period from the outbreak of the cold war in 1947 until the collapse of the Soviet empire in 1990 saw historic changes in American foreign relations. Several dramatic departures were observable: sustained leadership in world affairs, a steady commitment to countering an aggressive adversary by a general policy of "containment," and a willingness on the part of two generations of Americans to find the wherewithal required to enforce this policy. All this represented a break with the country's earlier neoisolationism, fear of foreign entanglements, and impatience with large outlays for defense, save in time of war.

This period also marked the consolidation of the New Deal domestic policy gains (1946–1960), the beginning and continuation of the most aggressive period of national liberal activism (1964–1978), and a reaction that produced a crude synthesis of the national policy interventionism of the 1960s and 1970s with the retrenchment trends of the 1980s and early 1990s. The adjective *crude* is emphasized here, for as we shall see, the number of conflicting current developments in the overall system of federal governance is so great that no synthesis, in fact, appears to have occurred. In addition, the most crucial challenge confronting the country—domestically and in international affairs—is the federal deficit, and its bloated condition is a direct product of fundamental disputes in the eighties over foreign policy against certain domestic goals. In short, the cold war's legacy is very much with us and it conditions nearly every aspect of American intergovernmental and foreign relations.

The Impact of Foreign Policy on Domestic Government

In terms of power politics and high policy, the leading American role during the cold war years was a major factor making for a greater centralization within the government system. Unlike the period following World War I, there was no return to a severely reduced federal role after World War II, although slashes in military spending and wartime grants-in-aid did occur in 1946 and early 1947. But as Soviet designs in the Balkans, Eastern Europe, and the West became more obvious, a series of interventionist American actions pushed foreign policy and defense outlays to peacetime highs (see table 6.1).

Fiscal Effects

Initially, more than half of the federal budget and well over one-third of all governmental expenditures during the Truman-Eisenhower years were earmarked for cold war purposes. It was during this period that the federal government's domestic role shrank, with only thirty permanent grant programs emerging from the pre-1932 and the Roosevelt years. Nearly one hundred additional grants were enacted between 1946 and 1960, most of which were small project grants. In constant dollar terms, state-local expenditures surpassed federal domestic outlays by 1954 ($27.2 billion versus $22.8 billion), and this continued throughout the 1960s.[1] Despite Truman's election in 1948 and Democratic Congresses in all but four of these fourteen years, domestic policy making was largely controlled or at least checked by the so-called conservative coalition all the way through until 1964.

As table 6.1 shows, defense and foreign policy outlays were reduced proportionately during the sixties, thanks to the economic recovery of Western Europe, the increased role played by other NATO members, and growing federal domestic outlays generated by the enactment of Lyndon Johnson's 210 new "Creative Federalism" programs. At the same time, Johnson's initial attempt to have "guns and butter" with the pickup in American involvement in Vietnam sowed the seeds of later fiscal and economic difficulties and necessitated budgetary restraint for some of his Great Society undertakings. As the figures suggest, the greatest cuts in defense came paradoxically under Nixon and Ford—with the assistance, of course, of solidly Democratic Congresses. The so-called peace dividend was shifted to expanding old and funding new domestic programs. The difference between total defense–foreign policy outlays and those for all federal grants was narrowest in these years (see table 6.1).

In response to Soviet interventions in a series of countries beyond its borders, a defense buildup began gradually in Carter's last two years and rose much more rapidly during Reagan's first five years. All this was prom-

Table 6.1 Defense and Foreign Affairs as a Percentage of Total Governmental and Federal Outlays, of Federal Grants, and of Personal Income, 1952–1990

	1952	1957	1962	1967	1972	1977	1982	1985	1986	1987	1990	1992
Total $ outlays (in millions)	48,187	47,500	55,172	74,638	79,258	105,596	204,275	288,736	312,183	319,084	344,069	351,684
% of total government outlays	48.3	37.9	31.3	29.0	19.9	15.5	16.6	18.3	18.4	17.6	15.5	14.1
% of federal total outlays	67.3	58.0	48.6	44.7	32.7	24.4	25.6	28.0	28.5	27.8	24.7	23.1
% of federal grant outlays	1,864	1,226	713.3	496.5	236	142.7	237.5	269.2	269.9	286.2	254.1	197.5
% of personal income	17.6	13.3	12.2	11.6	8.1	6.6	7.6	8.7	8.9	8.5	7.4	6.8

Sources: Adapted from Advisory Commission on Intergovernmental Relations, *Significant Features of Fiscal Federalism, vol 2,* M-180-11 (Washington, D.C., Sept. 1991), 102–03, 106–07; Advisory Commission on Intergovernmental Relations, *Significant Features of Fiscal Federalism, vol 2,* M-190-11 (Washington, D.C., Dec. 1994), 24, 30, 47, 50–51, 53, 55.

ised in Reagan's 1980 campaign, as were reduced domestic spending, tax cuts, and a balanced budget by 1984. The last promise bit the dust once leaders computed the extent of the costs to the Treasury of the Economic Recovery and Tax Act of 1981, the revenue shortfalls caused by the severe 1981–1982 recession, and the basic failure of Congress to follow through with the 1981 Omnibus Budget Reconciliation Act's future domestic spending cut scenario.

In effect, federal budget making in these years and the resulting $1.4 trillion added to the national debt (1982–1989) revolved around five sacred cows: entitlements, especially Social Security, which both Ronald Reagan and the Democrats sought to protect (but not Senate Republican leaders briefly in the early eighties); other social programs, defended by liberals and moderates of both parties; defense, protected by the president and the conservatives of both parties; no new or major tax hikes, vigorously advocated by the president, most Republicans, and some conservative Democrats (though Sen. Robert Dole [R., Kans.] engineered two tax hikes in 1982 and 1984); and interest on the debt, which began to soar in this period and which no one wanted to look at and everybody had to honor. In the final analysis, only the last "cow" was and is truly sacred, and the other four were all "touched," to lesser or greater degrees, by the budget jousting of the Reagan years, but not to the extent they should have been.

The Bush years added to the national budget scenario a seriously deteriorating economy, one major and one minor military engagement, and continued gridlock between the Congress and the White House. Until very recently, defense was a major issue in these budgetary battles. Put differently, the conflicting policy claims of the Department of Defense (DOD) and the State Department along with those of major domestic items (that is, entitlements, the "safety net" programs, the interest on the debt, and agriculture) along with the political failure to increase taxes significantly produced the fundamental policy challenge confronting the Clinton administration, the Congress, and the country. And the costs of concluding the cold war were very much a factor in the unfolding of this spectacularly shocking scenario of the "deadly deficit."

Clinton did confront the deficit dilemma head-on in the battle for his fiscal year (FY) 1994 budget and surpassed his predecessor's not insignificant 1990 struggle in this same troubled terrain. The Omnibus Budget Reconciliation Act of 1993 called for $250 billion in tax hikes over the next five years as well as $254.7 billion in program cuts, including some painful ones in defense. Meanwhile, there was indirect American involvement in Bosnia; direct action in Macedonia, Somalia, Haiti, South Korea; and the threat of having to cope with other brush fires. Hence there was an increase in defense outlays for FY 1994 and some for FY 1995. Moreover, the new

Republican 104th Congress was calling for even greater defense expenditures (including "star wars") but heavy cuts in foreign aid, while the president's FY 1996 budget calls only for a pay raise.

Domestic Programs and Politics

Domestic programs and politics were indirectly and sometimes directly affected individually by cold war events. At the outset of the fifties, Congress passed the affected aid program to provide grant funds to school districts having sizable numbers of children from military families, and this program still exists despite more than twenty years of efforts to scrap it. A civil defense grant came along about the same time, and this was one of the few direct federal-local links in those years. In the Eisenhower period the two most significant departures from the heavily incremental rate of grant growth were enacted: the massive 1956 interstate highway system legislation and the National Defense Education Act of 1958. Both were proposed to meet defense needs, the latter being a direct by-product of the Soviets' launching of Sputnik. By the end of the Eisenhower era, highways constituted the largest federal grant program. Throughout the more than four decades of the cold war, the DOD itself administered some grant programs, which by FY 1993 still numbered three.

During the sixties and seventies the need to promote domestic programs as a means of enhancing national defense faded. Johnson argued for his Great Society programs on their own merits,[2] though some of them did condition America's image abroad (e.g., civil rights, War on Poverty, and educational programs). As table 6.1 reveals, federal domestic and state-local spending soared throughout the 1960s and well into the 1970s. Even during the Vietnam years, defense spending declined as a proportion of total federal and of all government outlays. All this reflected the emergence of a new, more centralized, more liberal political system—but more about that later.

This raises the power political issue of the military-industrial complex that President Eisenhower warned of in his last State of the Union message. Although elements of such a complex have existed since the early forties and congressmen and senators from states with bases and defense-related industries seek to protect their military constituents and industries, defense cuts in 1946 and 1947 and during the mid-1970s demonstrated beyond a doubt the political capacity of a determined president and of countervailing forces in Congress to reduce DOD appropriations when the international and economic situations seemed to warrant it. Thus, until 1994, America was experiencing its third effort since World War II at downsizing the Pentagon, and the howls of spokespersons from hard-hit states such as California and Connecticut were deafening. These heavy cuts in DOD appropriations were a significant factor prolonging the recession in various areas, prompting some states—for example, Connecticut—to advance special favors if a company stayed and decided not to relocate to areas with cheaper labor.[3]

Summary Observations

What firm conclusions can be discerned from this all-too-brief assessment of the cold war's impact on American federalism. The firmest include:

- During the Truman, Eisenhower, and Kennedy years, the cold war produced a significant degree of centralization within the system without any real significant hike in national domestic responsibilities.
- It facilitated passage of certain grant programs in the fifties that otherwise probably would not have been enacted.
- It indirectly necessitated heavy systemic reliance on state and local governments in the fifties and even the sixties when federal grant programs expanded. (All those schools built for the baby boomers, for example, were financed by local and state governments.)
- It provided a very significant case study of a powerful pressure group–government agency–congressional committee collaboration and even collusion with even a territorial dimension to it, but its strength has waxed and waned, depending on foreign policy exigencies.

Less clear and not fully covered above are certain other questions:

- Would the federal domestic role have been larger in the forties and the fifties had there been no cold war? My guess, based on the conservative trends of the times, is not by much.
- Would race relations have become as significant as they were without integration in the military and the role of minority troops in Korea, not to mention Vietnam later? Probably not.
- All told, which were the more significant conditioners of the course of federalism from 1947 to 1990—foreign or domestic factors? As I have suggested above and will spell out below more clearly, both were important, but domestic factors were far more controlling.

Domestic Dynamics and the Transformation of Federalism

In terms of domestic federalism, the cold war period actually encompassed the last part of the earlier "cooperative federalism" era (1933–1960) and the present era of centralized and "permissive federalism"[4] that really began with Johnson but was ushered in by John Kennedy in 1961. First, when one gauges the health of a federal system—whether American, German, or Australian—experience teaches us that there must be some sort of significant territorial division of key domestic government functions, for this is a cardinal constitutional precept of federalism. Second, some special representational status must or ought to be assigned to constituent governments at the center either within (as with the German Federal Republic) or closely adjacent to the national decision-making process (as with Australia), since this representational arrangement also usually has a constitutional basis and is especially crucial in the twentieth century wherein powerful centralizing tendencies can combine to truncate the policy discretion of subnational governments. Yet a third factor to assess is the role of the institutions or processes assigned the always delicate task of authoritatively umpiring the interlevel jurisdictional disputes that inevitably arise in a federal system. In most cases, this is a high court, though with the Swiss, it is primarily a national referendum. Finally, there are the political bases of the system that may or may not reinforce the territorial foundations of a federation. Foreign relations obviously condition these formal underpinnings of federalism, but domestic developments clearly were much more crucial.

Cooperative Federalism

The postwar period witnessed the definition, the gradual expansion, and the culmination of cooperative federalism. In operational terms, the legacy of the New Deal to the national government were regulation, subsidizing, and providing modest grants-in-aid. Grants accounted for less than $1 billion in 1946, and over the next fourteen years the amounts increased to only a little over $7 billion by 1960. Four programs—all state oriented—dominated the package in that year; conditions, by current standards, were innocuous; nearly all funds (92%) went to the states, with "by-passing" occurring in only a few program areas; state aid to localities surpassed federal grants in dollar amounts; and federal aid represented only about 14 percent of combined state and local outlays. Only about four state agencies dealt heavily with federal administrative counterparts, and traditional agencies of city or county government possessed no such Washington connection. It was a simple, inexpensive, administratively easy, and nonthreatening system. It also reflected disproportionately rural, racist, and neoreactionary traits.

Judicially, the Supreme Court had assigned broad power to Congress as early as 1923 in the area of conditional spending power (that is, the basis of Congress's capacity to spend money for any purpose it wants by means of grants-in-aid and to attach any conditions to grants that it desires—all under the theory that they are contractual relations voluntarily entered into and susceptible to being withdrawn from if a federal stipulation proves onerous to a recipient government). Congress's commerce power was given broad latitude in most post-1938 cases. A beginning was made in extending some of the Bill of Rights to the states by including some of its provisions within the scope of the due process and equal protection clauses of the Fourteenth Amendment.[5] The high wall of "separate but equal" was lowered in crucial areas, most notably in public education with *Brown v. Board of Education of Topeka* (1954).[6]

The party system still was the old state and local-based one, with meager power at the center and some cohesion and authority in some state and local parties. It was confederative in structure, generally nonideological in principles, and heterogeneous in socioeconomic makeup. There was a strong interest group component to American politics, but economic and professional groups were the primary ones. There were only a few in the social welfare, programmatic, and moralistic categories, and these clearly were of tertiary importance.

All in all, it was a federal system whose tiers were roughly in balance. Centralization obviously had occurred thanks to the Depression, the cold war, and the federal government's expanded regulatory and subsidizing roles. But functionally, most domestic sources were handled and funded by state and local governments. In domestic fiscal and program terms, the national role was modest. This was partly because of the federal government's major foreign policy commitments, but more because of the ascendancy of the conservative coalition in Congress between 1939 and roughly 1964. Once southern Democrats and conservative and moderate Republicans agreed on a policy—as they frequently did—Congress generally adopted that course. In most instances, this merely meant relying on the capacity to use one or more of the procedural means then provided to protect the rights of minorities represented in Congress.

Creative Federalism: 1964–1968

Although the election of Kennedy and Johnson in 1960 ushered in a new era, it was not until Johnson's swearing in as president that it was really launched. With the tragedy that required that act, there came the enactment of the various Kennedy programs that had been bottled up in committees, along with dozens of new Johnson initiatives.

Johnson was probably the ablest Senate majority leader in this century and the last president to serve as the authoritative setter of the national agenda for most of his tenure. He carved out a new intergovernmental era—one that, despite mutations, stretches up to the present. It is the Johnson legacy, especially the entitlement portion thereof, with its various additions, that constitutes part of the national policy dilemma today. The extraordinary outpouring of legislation, especially during the 89th Congress; the

remarkable civil rights victories; the turning to poverty as a national issue when times were good, very good, for everyone else; the reliance on
the carrot (categorical grants) far more than on the stick (regulations) to
achieve his objectives; and Johnson's courageous and costly escalation of
the Vietnam War and the profound lesson that war taught us (that America's resources are finite and containment was a policy best defined in terms
of the periphery of the Soviet empire). But there was more, much more!
There were the halving of the poverty figures (1964–1980), marked decreases in infant morality, prolongation of life for the elderly,[7] the emergence of a sizable black middle class, and the political transformation of
Dixie. Take-home pay in real dollars soared in these years. Johnson's failure
to face up fully to the guns or butter issue was his chief and only major
shortcoming. Ultimately, it helped undercut these economic gains.

With Johnson, the demands of the cold (and hot) war and those of
domestic governance came into conflict. But they were not so clearly seen
at the time as they were later. National liberal activism reached its apex with
Johnson, and its results were not all on the negative side of the agenda. His
was a vision, after all, of a Great Society, with all government tiers contributing to the common greater good. Hence his obliviousness to jurisdictional
niceties, his hike in "by-passing" (see table 6.2), his resort to nonprofit
organizations, and his involvement with the private sector. A panoramic
principle of partnership emerged, one that unnerved traditional federalists
and could never be applied in other federal capitals such as Bonn/Berlin,
Ottawa, Berne, or Canberra.

Politically, the party system was in transition. The Democratic National
Committee and the convention committees had begun to hand down rules
to their state and local counterparts. Yet Johnson and most members of
Congress still acted as if significant political power rested at the subnational
levels. The state convention system dominated the delegate selection process through the sixties, but bosses of the old school had disappeared in most
areas. The ugly and divisive Democratic National Convention of 1968 put
the final nail in the coffin of the old confederative, decentralized party
system that dated back to 1828. It after all led to the "liberal reforms" of the
McGovern-Fraser Committee, and they helped launch a new political system, one that is still with us.

Judicially, the retirement of Justice Felix Frankfurter in 1962 marked
the beginning of a second phase in the history of the Warren court, one that
was much more activist, liberal, and complementary to many of Johnson's
domestic program goals. The court, in effect, "assumed a novel role as a
leader in the process of social change quite at odds with its traditional position as a defender of legalistic tradition and social continuity."[8] In its reapportionment, due process, prayer, and civil rights decisions, it asserted

national authority and protection against state power. Yet, in the process, the court helped contribute to the revitalization of the states.

Where stood federalism at the end of Johnson's administration? Somewhat more centralized than before, given the civil rights, regulatory, and categorical enactments—but with a massive reliance on subnational governments to implement all but a couple, notably Medicare, of Johnson's 210 new programs. Many states, however, were still in the throes of reapportionment and the civil rights revolution, and the same applied to thousands of localities. Johnson, in effect, placed his entire domestic career in the lap of state and local officials, many of whom were totally rooted in a repressive past. This along with the foreign policy nightmare of Vietnam presented him with a Hobson's choice.

Yet Johnson lived on in the Democratic Congresses of the seventies. As they confronted two Republican presidents and a moderate Democratic one, the response was to reenact, expand, and elaborate on Johnson's legislative legacy (see table 6.2). What they lacked was his ability to set an agenda, to be as cognizant of outlays as of revenues, and to rise above the growing pressure group power. The damage to federalism largely came after LBJ's tenure, not during it.

The Many Faces of Federalism: 1969–1980

The second phase of the current intergovernmental era began with the election of Richard Nixon and ended in the middle of Carter's tenure. During this phase various versions of federalism appeared: Nixon's "new federalism," Carter's "new partnership" approach, the bureaucratic "bamboo federalism," the congressional de facto form, and differing judicial conceptualizations. All this suggests divergences, debate, and—in some ways—deep concern about the future of federalism. And such was the case, especially with the last, for by the late seventies, observers ranging from John Gardner and Samuel H. Beer to the Advisory Commission on Intergovernmental Relations, and others, including this writer, found the system overloaded, dysfunctional, and on a doubtful course.

First, there was a steady continuation of the national activism of the Johnson years (see table 6.2). Nixon was no traditional conservative president. Far from it: he had perhaps the clearest conception of what the federal system should be of any president since Woodrow Wilson, one of his favorites. He sought greater devolution of authority over program decisions via block grants and general revenue sharing, greater administrative decentralization of relations between the federal headquarters and field offices (by reorganizing the latter into ten regions, each with a field headquarters and with sign-off authority conferred on federal field managers), greater deference to generalists and general governments at the subnational level (re-

Table 6.2 Intergovernmental Relations (IGR) Trends, 1960–1994

	1960 Total (FY 1960)	Great Society 1964–1968 (FY 1964–1969)	New Federalism 1969–1976 (FY 1970–1977)	New Partnership Federalism 1977–1980 (FY 1978–1981)	1980 Total (FY 1981)	Reagan Federalism 1981–1988 (FY 1982–1989)	Bush Era 1989–1992 (FY 1990–1993)	Clinton 1993–1994 (FY 1994–1995)
Number of grant programs	132	397 (FY 1967)	442 (FY 1975)	492 (FY 1978)	539	404–492	492–593 (FY 1989–1993)	640 (FY 1994)
Grant outlays in current dollars (billions)	7.0	10.2–20.2	24.1–68.4	77.9–94.8	94.8	88.2–122.0	135.4–193.7 (FY 1990–1993)	238.7 (FY 1995)
Grant outlays in constant 1987 dollars (billions)	29.1	39.7–65.8	73.6–124.3	131.4–121.5	121.5	106.5–112.2	119.7–155.0 (FY 1990–1993)	169.3 (FY 1994)
Federal aid as a % of state-local outlays	14.5	15.4–17.8	19.0–25.5	26.5–24.7	24.7	21.6–17.3	19.4–21.9 (FY 1990–1993)	N/A
Federal aid (current dollars) as a % of total federal outlays	7.6	8.6–11.0	12.3–16.7	17.8–14.0	14.0	11.8–10.7	10.8–13.8 (FY 1990–1993)	14.6 (FY 1994)
Grants for payments to individuals as a % of total federal aid	35.5	35.0–35.9	36.3–33.2	31.8–39.9	39.9	44.0–55.2	57.0–62.7	63.3 (FY 1994)

Form(s) of grants	% of aid bypassing the states	Major IGR regulations	Federal preemptions
100% categorical	8	2	189 (1959)
2 block grants, 3 target grants, rest categorical	12	7 (1961–1968)	47 (1960–1969)
5 block grants, GRS,[a] 2 target grants, 426 categoricals (1975)	24 (1974)	23 (1969–1976)	108 (1970–1979)
5 block grants, GRS, 492 categoricals	29 (1978)	5 (1976–1980)	
4 block grants, GRS, 534 categoricals	23.6	37 (1980)	344 (1980)
12 block grants, GRS, 396 categoricals (1982); 14 block grants, 478 categoricals (1989)	24.2–14.5 (1988)	21 (1981–1988)	100 (1980–1989)
15 block grants, 578 categoricals (FY 1993)	11.2 (FY 1992)	5 (1989–1993)	25 (1990–1991)
N/A	N/A	10 (1994–1995)	5 (1994–1995)

Sources: Adapted from Advisory Commission on Intergovernmental Relations; Significant Features of Fiscal Federalism 1985–86 Edition M-146, p. 19; 1989 Edition M-163-II, pp. 18–24; Walker, David B., Towards a Functioning Federalism, (1961), pp. 100–131; ACIR, A Catalog of Federal Grant-in-Aid Programs . . . Funded FY 1989, pp. 1–3, U.S. Bureau of the Census, Government Finances, 1988–1990 Editions. ACIR, Characteristics of Federal Grants-in-Aid Programs to State and Local Government M-183 (March 1992), p. 1; ACIR, Significant Features of Fiscal Federalism-Vol. 2-1993, M-185-II, p. 13; ACIR, *Significant Features of Fiscal Federalism.* Vol. 2-1994, M-190-II, p. 9. President's Budget FY 1995, p. 169.

flected in the eligibility provisions of General Revenue Sharing (GRS) and the block grants and in the early notification on grant rule changes begun under LBJ but fully operationalized under Nixon), and a better grant delivery system (witness the lengthy staff work on improving grant application procedures and forms with Circular A-102, the Joint Funding Simplification Act, and the planning and communicational provisions of Circular A-95). Some of this represents a continuation of Johnson staff efforts; some of it was quite new, especially the anticategorical, anticentralization, antifunctional government and antifederal administrator thrusts.[9] Moreover, Nixon was the first president to propose a serious reform of the welfare system (such as the Family Assistance Plan) and to assert active executive branch involvement with the environment, in competition with congressional protagonists such as Senators Edmund S. Muskie (D., Maine), Henry ("Scoop") Jackson (D., Wash.), and Representative John Blatnik (D., Minn.).

Yet the Nixon application of old-style public administration managerial approaches (such as the management circulars) and of newer, more surgical techniques (for example, mergers and no-strings GRS funds) did not achieve their goals. In some cases, Congress was obstinate, but the changes in the grant system itself suggested that the Nixon efforts amounted to not much more than a band-aid operation. But why? His efforts were vigorous and commitment was strong.

Take a look at a few of the more startling intergovernmental relations figures: (1) grant outlays nearly doubled in constant dollar terms between Johnson's last year and Ford's ($54.8 billion to $103.6 billion); (2) the number of new programs rose by more than fifty, despite mergers and blocking of more than sixty categoricals; (3) the "bypassing" proportion more than doubled, reaching the 24 percent level, and the number of subnational governments involved in at least one federal aid program soared to well over fifty thousand; and (4) federal aid as a proportion of state-local outlays rose from 18.0 percent in FY 1968 to 25.5 percent in Ford's last year (see table 6.2).

In short, the system seemed to be out of hand, and these trends continued during Carter's tenure, yet with a slight reduction in bypassing, a tapering off of the rate in grant-in-aid outlays, and a hike in DOD outlays occurring in his last two budgets (see table 6.2). But again, why this continued activism for eight of these ten years—especially with the advent of that strangest of all economic maladies, stagflation? There are five factors to be noted that add up to an answer.

1. Institutionally, Congress became the architect of IGR during most of the seventies. Between 1973 and 1975, it reformed its procedures to further pulverize what already was a highly decentralized power

structure (see chap. 9). In addition, its basic operational theory of federalism included incrementalism (to cope with problems, programs, and pressures in an ad hoc, piecemeal fashion starting from the point where you last left off), confrontation (with weakened presidents, sometimes amateurish political executives, and increasingly supplicant state and local spokespersons), procategorical (for example, the addition of 140 new categoricals between 1969 and 1980), and procondition (conditions in some grants took on the character of dictates, a trend new to this decade).[10]

2. Representationally, the number of pressure groups and lobbyists in Washington soared during the seventies. To the earlier economic and professional lobbies were added programmatic (seemingly one for every major program Congress had enacted since 1964), demographic, moralistic, citizen, single-issue, etc. lobbies. Moreover, the intergovernmental lobby also arrived, which included the National Governors' Association, National Conference of State Legislatures, Council of State Governments, National Association of Counties, National League of Cities, U.S. Conference of Mayors, and International City Management Association (as well as the people supporting specific programs, whether in transportation, welfare, health, or the environment). Since the national policy processes were exceptionally porous in this period (again, see chap. 9), the incentives to come to Washington were many; and the results were the dozens of project grants, categoricals, and conditions as well as outright regulations that Congress enacted.

3. Politically, a new system finally arrived with all its questionable results. Gone were state and local parties with control over their own nominations and frequently those of national officials and with authoritative voices in the nation's capital without any full-time lobbying organizations on the scene. In their place came strengthened national party organizations for the first time since 1824, even stronger political actors such as the media, pressure groups, political action committees, pollsters, and all the hangers-on who constitute an individual candidate's campaign organization. All these players were essentially centralizing in their thrusts; and the concomitant loss of a strong territorial basis for American politics has done damage to the system and to federalism.

4. In policy terms, the seventies were the decade in which the "new social regulation" was launched. Many of the regulations were used to further national (and interest group) goals in environmental protection, health and safety, nondiscrimination, equal access, working conditions, and other such areas, but they frequently were peremp-

tory in nature.[11] Only the changes during the 1970s in the political, representational, and congressional arenas, along with an aroused public opinion in some cases, can explain what would have been found totally unacceptable in the fifties. It was this new regulatory development that prompted criticisms that described the system as "more centralized," "cooptive," not "cooperative," and "overloaded" as the decade ended.

5. Finally, in the realm of judicial federalism, the Burger court proved to be no restorer of the ancient balance between the levels that some had thought it might be. Only with *National League of Cities v. Usery* (1976)[12] was a serious effort made to curb the Congress's use of its commerce power in regulating the wages and hours of state and local employees. But by 1980 it was clear that *Usery* was exceptional and its days were numbered.

The only counterweights to all these centralizing propensities in the system were (1) the national government's growing reliance on local and especially state governments to implement its domestic policies, even regulatory ones; and (2) the remarkable transformation experienced by nearly all of the states—politically, institutionally, programmatically, fiscally, and parentally (vis-à-vis the localities of America). National factors such as the reapportionment cases, the Voting Rights Act of 1966, and the many grant programs that thrust major new responsibilities on the states combined with pressures from below—from school districts, cities and towns, counties, and citizens (now fully enfranchised)—to help instigate a major revolution at the constituent level of American government. And in the Reagan years, this proved to be providential.

The Reagan-Bush Era: 1981–1992

The third phase of the contemporary intergovernmental period began with the swearing in of Ronald Reagan as president. Practically all of the centralizing trends discussed above were on his hit list. He favored a heavily reduced federal role in the federal system, hence a devolution of many grant programs, elimination or a serious softening of federal regulations on the private sector and the subnational governments, and slashing revenues and personnel for federal domestic programs. But he also called for dramatic hikes in defense outlays and engaged in several aggressive foreign policy initiatives. And these were costly and centralizing actions.

In domestic programs, Reagan and the Congress eliminated sixty-odd, mostly small grants with the 1981 Omnibus Budget Reconciliation Act, merged seventy-six more in nine block grants, and eliminated a few more later. Yet he ended up with a total of 492 at the end of his second term, though with outlays that were $15.2 billion in constant dollars below those for FY 1978 (see table 6.2). To be more specific, outlays for entitlements and safety net programs soared during the Reagan years, while nearly all grant programs of assistance to governments (especially local governments), not people, were cut, sometimes severely—as with federal-local grants.

As for regulations, very few were repealed outright, and several new social ones were signed into law (see table 6.2). Yet the process was significantly softened—if not forgotten in some cases—by a combination of appointing antiregulatory administrators, reducing personnel budgets, and issuing centripetal executive orders (e.g., E.O. 12291 and E.O. 12498) which established a regulatory review process that had a strong impact on the rate and content of new issuances. With his goal of reducing government activism generally (defense excepted, of course), Reagan was not successful. Federal expenditures rose from $615 billion in 1980 to $1,117.6 billion by 1988. Combined state-local outlays nearly doubled, soaring from $363.2 billion to $647.9 billion during the same period. In short, Reagan federalism achieved far more than most Washington observers in 1980 thought possible: a narrowing of the grant-in-aid package, a real reduction in its rate of growth and in its number of recipients, a curbing of regulatory issuances and implementation efforts, and a return to the traditional federal-state partnership approach. But none of this added up to a revolution.

Had Reagan's 1982 proposal to nationalize Medicaid and to devolve Aid to Families with Dependent Children, food stamps, and other grants, been adopted, there would have been a revolution in federalism. In the perilous area of public finance, however, he did achieve a revolution of sorts by chalking up with Congress a peacetime deficit record unequaled until that time (see chap. 9). The interest payments on that debt rose from 8.9 percent of total federal outlays in FY 1980 to nearly 15 percent (or $69 billion) by FY 1989. This and its continuing rise are the prime current conditioners of national public policy, prompting all sorts of federal actions that caused others funding headaches and which undercut a positive national role in various major domestic government matters and in certain foreign affairs (notably foreign aid, contributions to international agencies, etc.). This weakening of the federal role and the much greater responsibility assumed by the states (and localities, to a lesser degree) prompted many experts to conclude that the system was more decentralized in 1988 than in 1980. Yet the twenty-one new regulatory enactments, the ninety-one new preemptions, the continuing political centralization, the continuing centripetal judicial developments, and the beefing up of the DOD during this eight-year span were considered strong arguments that greater centralization had occurred.

The Bush years in some respects were part of the Reagan legacy. Certainly Bush's 1988 campaign reiterated Reaganite themes. The record, however, was more mixed. The deepest recession since the thirties produced a "deficit-driven federalism" at all levels whose national figures eclipsed Reagan's. Despite the famous November 1990 budget accord with its caps, cuts, and $137 billion in new revenues (over a five-year period), the number of federal grants rose to an all-time high of 593 by FY 1993, and in current dollar terms over $71 billion was added to the grant totals between FY 1990 and FY 1993. Some of this reflected Bush's personal program preferences for education, child health, and so on. Major new enactments were few, however; the Clean Air Act amendments of 1990 and the Intermodal Surface Transportation Efficiency Act of 1991 were the chief exceptions. Transcending all these actions was the $42 billion jump in Medicaid outlays from FY 1990 to FY 1993.

In the regulatory area, four new major social regulations were adopted and a new cooptive ethic dominated these unilateral, unfunded mandates—the extension of Medicaid's coverage was by far the most controversial. Like Reagan, Bush signed new social regulations, but by administrative means he blunted their real impact and in some cases thwarted any implementation, as with the much heralded Clean Air Act amendments. All told, however, Congress proved to be much more of a shaper of the course of intergovernmental relations from 1989 to 1992 than the president or his surrogates.

What emerges from the Reagan-Bush record is a series of contradictions such as:

- The governance system was retrenching, even as its activism picked up.
- The grant system was larger in numbers, in categoricals (despite the fifteen block grants), and in favoring the states, yet it represented a lesser proportion of state-local (especially local) outlays than it did in 1980.
- In the regulatory realm at both the state and federal levels, the number of new enactments gave no hint of any slowdown; but serious internal control methods were adopted in both the Reagan and Bush administrations to achieve the opposite effect, and forty-three states had enacted fiscal note legislation to help achieve a similar effect.
- The fifty state-local operating systems implemented most of the national government's domestic programs, had made various new educational and even, in some cases, welfare reform initiatives (see chap. 10) but were beset from 1989 to 1992 with serious "fend for yourself" and "deficit-driven federalism" pressures and had taken

courageous policy actions to cope with these challenges. Yet these governments were treated in the national political and the judicial arenas as second-class partners in the overall system.

- The federal judiciary, which was loaded with Reagan-Bush appointees, had enunciated some conservative doctrines narrowing the scope of federal preemptions, reducing the number and reach of section 1983 cases, and affording states more opportunities to appear as appellants. But with *Garcia v. San Antonio Metropolitan Transit Authority* (1985), *E.E.O.C. v. Wyoming* (1983), *South Dakota v. Dole* (1987), *South Carolina v. Baker* (1988), and *Rust v. Sullivan* (1991), the Supreme Court in the eighties and early nineties enunciated some of the most nationalist, anti–states' rights opinions relating to Congress's conditional spending and taxing powers ever handed down.[13]

- Finally, the states in the system never had been more representative, reformed, and responsible than they were then; but, their leaders never were accorded less influence in national party deliberations and their officials less deference before congressional or executive branch bodies.

Varying Approaches to Federalism: Clinton, the New Congress, and the States

Both the 1992 presidential and 1994 congressional elections had clear anti-federal program regulation and bureaucracy themes (even though new Washington initiatives were implicit in various campaign proposals). In 1992 the result was the selection of a new president bearing the label of a "New Democrat" (meaning more centrist) with a record of prior service as a leader of the National Governors' Association (especially in its many tilts with Washington, D.C.), as an active spokesman for the moderate Democratic Leadership Council, and as a six-term governor of Arkansas. Clinton's subsequent record, for the most part, was one of significant sensitivity to state and local concerns. The newly elected Republican 104th Congress clearly has downsizing, devolution, and deregulation among its goals; but, as will be noted, other objectives (a balanced budget amendment, tax cuts, and a very prescriptive approach to various program reform proposals) may well eclipse efforts to assist subnational governmental jurisdictions.

Like the Clinton election, the midterm elections gave rise to varying interpretations. Most agreed that it signified a shift to the right, but how far? Many contended that they signified "a huge scream from the gut about the arrogance of Washington, D.C."[14] But does this mean only a downsizing of the power, programs, and prescriptions of the national government? of all governments? Does this mean a shift of power and program to the states and localities or a complete shifting of them to the private sector? William Kristol, one of Speaker Gingrich's close advisers and articulate voice of the conservative right, asserted, "People want problems addressed in new ways. They want government cut back at all levels."[15] Not all Republicans simply want smaller government, not to mention Democrats. And no notice is given to the huge middle-class federal entitlements when downsizing, cutting, and budget balancing by the federal government are discussed. "Don't let them [the federal government] take away my Medicare," was one elector's cry, and hers was not a solo voice.

Multiple issues are being discussed, many with overt federalist implications. Some solutions involve the states and localities, and others entail further federal involvement. So we have a new phase in the recent record of a conflicted American federalism, but at least it is a phase where federalism is a prime focus of attention: it is New Federalism III (Nixon's was I and Reagan's was II).

In effect, the first phase of the New Federalism III started with President Clinton's federalism reforms. His various actions in personnel, program, procedure, and general performance until about May 1994 were viewed favorably at the state and local level. In appointments, Clinton's selection of two former governors and two ex-mayors as cabinet members and other former state and local officials to lesser posts was applauded by the intergovernmental community. In the important (but frequently overlooked) procedural field, Clinton, both on his own initiative and in line with Vice President Al Gore's National Performance Review (NPR) report took several positive though necessarily limited steps.

Clinton's broad goals for a better "partnership"[16] included curbing regulations, making intergovernmental procedures more cooperative, improving communications, and increasing the discretionary authority of state and local grant recipients. Thus in the regulatory realm, Executive Order 12866, issued in September 1993, required relevant agencies to begin planning for regulatory relief; a later addition to this order barred the issuance of unfunded executive agency mandates (of which there were very few). Agencies again would have a primary role in regulatory decision making, but centralized review was to be continued to assure that new regulations were in conformity with the president's priorities.[17] The follow-up Executive Order 12875 (Oct. 1993) set up a federal-state-local consultative process for IGR regulatory issuances. But the regulatory relief provided here was modest. To be effective, Congress should have enacted the legislation (H.R. 4771 and S.R. 993), which was supported by the president and which confronted the fact that Congress itself is the "mother of mandates." This, of course, did occur early in the new 104th Congress.

Pursuant to the Government Performance and Results Act of 1993, which was initiated by congressional members (notably Sen. William Roth [R., Del.]) but supported by the president, the Office of Management and Budget (OMB) launched a series of "performance measurement" experiments. OMB started with fifty-three pilot projects in twenty-one federal agencies and departments. The goal in each case was to have each project establish strategic plans, clearly define its mission, set goals, and establish performance standards against which to measure progress or success.[18] This legislation and these follow-up undertakings dovetailed neatly with President Al Gore's NPR effort, since performance measurements were a crucial foundation of the "reinventing government" crusade.

Vice President Al Gore's report on his NPR, issued on September 7, 1993, launched a major effort by the Clinton administration to revamp government organization and management.[19] Drawing heavily from David Osborne and Ted Gaebler's "Reinventing Government," the NPR report stipulated certain extrepreneurial precepts that should guide reform of the federal government: above all else, the government must put people first by better serving its customers, by empowering its employees, and by fostering excellence. These goals, in turn, would be achieved by creating a clear sense of agency mission, delegating authority and responsibility, substituting incentives for regulations, developing budget-based outcomes, and gauging success by customer satisfaction. *From Red Tape to Results: Creating a Government That Works Better and Costs Less* contained over eight hundred recommendations, some minor, some major. Some were procedural (e.g., streamlining procurement and biennial budgets); some related to personnel (e.g., slash the number of federal employees by over 252,000 over five years); and some involved management (e.g., cutting middle management, decreasing the size and management capacity of OMB, increasing the use of interagency committees, and decentralizing management authority to the lowest level possible). In addition to these proposals—all of which have indirect if not direct intergovernmental implications, the report also set forth a list of some reforms of federalism.

These included reducing the number of categoricals, facilitating federal interdepartmental and intergovernmental collaboration so that government credibility and a more "viable federal partnership" might be enhanced, and rethinking program rules and regulations to shift their focus to outcomes, not mere compliance.[20] More innovative was the recommendation that "rather than defining accountability by inputs, transactions, error rates, and failure to progress, the Federal government should hold state and local governments accountable for performance." Neat idea, but not easy to implement.

More specifically, the report called for six consequential proposals that would "empower state and local governments": (1) creating a cabinet-level enterprise board to oversee the community empowerment initiatives (which has been carried out); (2) reducing the number of unfunded federal mandates (noted above); (3) merging fifty-five categoricals into a broader "flexible grant"; (4) enhancing state and local flexibility in using the remaining grants; (5) permitting federal agencies to waive rules and regulations when they impede effective program results; and (6) deregulating the public housing program. Nearly all of these are commendable and seemingly simple proposals. But when first issued, they seemed to pay inadequate attention to Congress's role and that of pressure groups in this intergovernmental program and management field.

In his first-year report (September 1994), Vice President Gore highlighted an extraordinary array of "reinventing initiatives," many of which directly affected intergovernmental relations and the intergovernmental partners. In the "better delivery" area, for example, electronic grant payments were instituted with five states, with twenty-two more in the planning stages, and the Department of Health and Human Services (DHHS) is reviewing state requests for waivers in the Medicaid and Aid to Families with Dependent Children (AFDC) programs within 120 days.[21] In federal departments, Washington and field staff have been cut, but field offices have been restructured and given more authority. And in the area of expansion of recipient discretion, the new Education Flexibility Act is being implemented in a way that precludes the need for departmental approval of waivers of regulatory requirements, and DHHS has entered into an agreement with the state of Oregon and the city of Portland whereby certain federal requirements are eased and state benchmarks are accepted to measure the success of programs.[22]

The administrative merger of four health and human services within DHHS has also expanded state discretion, along with congressional passage of the NPR proposal that states and localities be given greater flexibility in school grants, child immunization, family support, and human services.[23] Enactment of the Local Empowerment and Flexibility Act of 1994 within the Omnibus Budget Reconciliation Act of 1993 enables certain pilot communities to integrate federal programs and their funds. In addition, the Higher Education Technical amendments of 1993 simplify institutional eligibility and certification for participation in federal student aid. These and dozens of other like actions underlie the empathy of the administration for state and local concerns, but the more reluctant stance of Congress on many of the NPR proposals requiring a legislative basis was a hindrance. (Notable exceptions include the overhaul of federal procurement, the first ever governmentwide buyout authority, and the legislation cited above that permits greater recipient discretion in school grants and three other aid programs.)[24]

Given such a brief period of implementation, much can be said about its more than respectable record of achievement—more so in the area of direct federal operations than in the intergovernmental area. The latter, after all, frequently requires congressional sanction, and Congress was not a focal point of NPR follow-up actions. Nevertheless, twenty-one NPR bills had been enacted by September 1, 1994, eleven others had passed both houses and were in conference; and ten more, containing forty-six NPR-supported provisions, had passed one house of Congress.

Given their thrust, NPR proposals might be expected to do well with the new Congress. But will they? The underlying thrusts of the vice president's (and the president's) efforts here relating to Washington is a downsized, better-directed, better-instructed, and dynamic (though smaller) national government. In the intergovernmental area, they are achieving a better, more flexible delivery system unburdened by unfunded mandates, a more open dialogue with the subnational governmental partners, better communication, and grant consolidations, waivers, and curbs on conditions to enhance recipient discretion. In their paternity, these precepts are both Johnsonian and Nixonian, with a mild dash of Osborne, whose forte is not intergovernmental administration. Both Johnson and Nixon sought a better delivery, a better dialogue, and a continual national role in less conditional grants.

The second part of the New Federalism III came with the November 8, 1994, triumph for the Republicans at the national and state levels. A few of the Clinton-Gore goals in intergovernmental relations (IGR) are acceptable to most Republicans, and some are even favored. But Republican leaders in Congress are after much more surgical operations. Not all of them bear directly on state and local governments, however. Like much else that was unusual about November 8, 1994, national issues loomed large in many of the contests, in part because of Rep. Newt Gingrich's clever plan of having practically all of Republican House candidates sign on to his ten-point Contract with America before election day. And the media as usual added to the nationalizing dynamics of election politics, which really began with the systematic Republican drive to obstruct nearly all of Clinton's legislative proposals from June 1994 on.

Whether the electorate was deeply aware of all the implications of the Contract with America is doubtful, but the advent of a Republican Congress must be interpreted generally as a vote for "smaller government, lower taxes, less power in Washington, and greater emphasis on individual responsibility and personal morality."[25] This hints of a realignment of power within our federal system. Yet this was not clearly spelled out during the campaign, and the Contract is still murky on this score. Its details and those of the less well-publicized seven-part Dole program focused heavily on fiscal items (a balanced budget amendment; a line item veto; tax cuts such as a

$500-per-child tax credit for middle-income families, a 50% cut in capital gains, elimination of the so-called marriage tax penalty, reauthorization of individual retirement accounts, and three types of tax relief for senior citizens), all to the tune of an estimated $220 billion over the next five years; as well as hikes in defense spending.[26] The only direct relief to state and local government in these areas was endorsement of the to give relief from measure unfunded mandates. This timely but not terribly drastic measure (it does not bar totally the enactment of such mandates; it excludes various types of mandates; and it is prospective, not retroactive) also was sanctioned by the president, his chief of staff, and the budget director.[27]

In four specific program areas (crime, welfare, children, and product safety liability), states and, to a somewhat lesser degree, localities are strongly affected, either directly or indirectly. The package of anticrime proposals includes beefed up "truth in sentencing," "good faith" exclusionary rule exemptions, effective death penalty provisions, and cuts in preventive local programs, with the savings going to more prison construction and more neighborhood policing. The president, most Democrats (especially in the Senate), a few Republican moderates, and many in the judicial and corrections fields will fight many of these "reforms" either because they conflict with last year's crime legislation or because the local proposals are patently political and fly in the face of all studies on this subject. The welfare reform plan calls for prohibiting AFDC benefits to children born to unwed mothers under age eighteen, cutting off such aid after two years—combined with work requirements, requiring that recipients report the identity of a child's father before they can receive benefits, merging ten nutrition programs (including the large food stamp grant) into a discretionary block grant with a cap, and placing lids on other social welfare programs.[28] Various of these provisions will be approved by the president, most Democrats, some Republican moderates, and several governors of both parties who want maximum program discretion by the state in any reform of public welfare.

The "family reinforcement" reform package calls for tougher enforcement of child support by establishing a nationwide tracking system to find delinquent fathers, a school voucher program to enhance parental choice in education, stronger laws against child pornography, and a tax credit for families caring for elderly parents.[29] While many of these proposals are popular and some have a good chance of passage, some Republican moderates will oppose the parental choice option, along with the public education lobby and several Democrats.

The "commonsense legal reform" cluster of proposals seeks to authorize judges to require losers in lawsuits to pay lawyers' fees for both sides and to limit the amount of noneconomic and punitive damage awards juries may impose in product liability as well as medical malpractice lawsuits.

Although these proposals have long been popular with most Republicans, most business interests, practically all of the medical community, and many Democrats oppose wholesale overhaul, as do trial lawyers (obviously) and some judicial officials. The platform advanced by Republican congressional leaders, then, seeks to make for a leaner and less activist national government by the imposition of caps, program cuts, budgetary and regulatory procedural constraints, and tax reductions. In a range of program areas, however, specific and detailed provisions are advanced that look as prescriptive, unilateral, and nationally intrusive as any of the liberal initiatives of the 1960s.

Although the House has passed a balanced budget amendment as of this writing, ratification by the needed thirty-eight state legislatures is in doubt (thirty-two are tending toward it), largely because the amendment does nothing actually to balance the national budget by the year 2002. Any serious attempt to achieve this end would inevitably hit the already reduced federal discretionary aid to states and localities and would necessitate the blocking of certain welfare and other social programs along with the caps. This in a few instances might eliminate a few entitlement programs, but not those of the extravagant middle-class variety. Cutting the latter will require real "profiles in courage" performances. States and localities also are beginning to worry about the fallout from enacting a balanced budget amendment for fear that it would further strengthen the "shift and shaft" (the governors' term) strategy of the Reagan-Bush years. Even without such a constitutional revision, these state and local worries would remain, given the GOP's general promise to achieve a reduced federal programmatic and regulatory role and its refusal to raise taxes.

This brings us to part three of New Federalism III and the quite different interpretation the governors, especially the thirty Republican chief executives (in particular the newly elected eleven) who have called for a wholesale devolution of power, programs, and discretion from Washington.[30] They wanted and got quick passage of the unfunded mandates bill. They want to see "maintenance of effort" requirements in grant programs scrapped because of their rigidity and cost. They want grant consolidation in various areas, but without significant slashing of funds, and they have already indicated that they want far more elbowroom in coping with welfare overhaul than contemplated by the new Speaker and other congressional Republicans.[31] They seek authority here to treat different parts of their individual states differently, and they want discretionary authority to experiment on their own—as several have done since 1981. They want to litigate more and to litigate successfully, thus giving some renewed clarity to the Tenth Amendment. These and other proposals were advanced in the "Williamsburg Resolve" adopted by the Republican governors at their celebrative conclave held two weeks after the election in the colonial capital of the Old Dominion.

Taking a much longer-range view of the future of the states in the federal system is Governor Michael A. Leavitt of Utah. Sensing a chance for more profound changes, given Congress's apparently deeply devolutionary mood, he called for a conference of states to meet in 1995. He wants a deep probe of the reforms needed to restore the states to their earlier powerful position within our federalism.[32] He is joined by Nebraska's Democratic Governor Ben Nelson in a drive to get all states aboard and has the blessing of the National Governors' Association and the National Conference of State Legislatures. Among the possible fundamental changes to be discussed is reviewing the second option stipulated in Article V of the Constitution for initiating constitutional amendments, namely by two-thirds of the states petitioning the Congress for a call for a convention to deliberate on a proposed amendment, and establishing a constitutional basis for the states to "sunset" a federal statute by a vote of two-thirds of the legislatures. These, indeed, are elemental constitutional issues, and they counter the centripetal thrusts of the Congress and the Supreme Court.[33]

In the current congressional battles over welfare and crime control, additional differences have erupted between and among the two branches of Congress, the White House, and the states (and localities in some cases). Republican Ways and Means members are hammering out a set of six block grants consolidating as many as three hundred welfare, child care, food and nutrition, and other related programs, while the chairwoman of the Senate Committee on Labor and Human Resources, Nancy Landon Kassebaum, favors a "big swap," with federalization of Medicaid and the states assuming full responsibility for AFDC, food stamps, and other social programs to make the exchange equal—a latter-day resurrection of Reagan's 1982 "Big Swap" proposal.[34] On February 11, 1995, the president warned the Republican Congress that he would veto any crime bill that repealed or undermined the commitment to put one hundred thousand new police officers on the street. The threat was in response to the GOP's rewriting of the anticrime measure enacted last year by rescinding the police hiring provisions and reallocating the monies in the proposed new Local Law Enforcement Block Grant Act of 1995, which would leave it largely to local officials to decide how the crime control funds would be spent.[35] With welfare reform, the president, DHHS, the Children's Defense Fund, and Republican and Democratic governors, among others, have weighed in to do battle with the GOP House proposal to hand over most control over welfare to the states by granting them block grants with few strings.[36] Both AFDC and food stamps (which now are entitlements) would—along with dozens of social welfare categoricals—be merged into blocks with caps placed on them. The reduction in funds, the absence of a federal protective role, lack of minimum standards, and silence regarding extra federal assistance in time of recession were among the chief criticisms made by the measure's opponents.

Clearly, the GOP road to reform will not be smooth. The Speaker will doubtless prevail generally in the House. But the Senate, with eleven of its twenty standing committees chaired by GOP moderates and a mere three-seat Republican majority, will experience delays, lengthy debate, and divisions. And the president must also be dealt with, though the Republican leaders at the moment claim he is "irrelevant"—a foolish stance for a party that is functioning in Madison's Washington, not John Major's London.

Conclusion

As the forces of centralization and devolution do battle in the months ahead, the chances are great of a return to gridlock on issues of momentous concern to the future of this democratic federal republic. For the most part, neither political reform nor judicial rethinking is part of this effort to overhaul federalism. And this suggests weaknesses, though positive balancing actions in the actual operations of our intergovernmental system are not to be denigrated.

The founders taught us that it is the presence of a few overriding desired goals, along with the capacity to strike compromises at the appropriate time, that leads to success. If narrow ideologies and factions, as well as the mischievous superficiality of the media, prevail, the opportunity of a lifetime will be lost. A return to the spirit of the founders' deliberations, then, is just as crucial as is a capacity to recapture their sense of vision, of history, of destiny. Both are required for true statecraft.

Notes

1. See Advisory Commission on Intergovernmental Relations, Fiscal Balance in the American Federal System, vol. I-A-31 (Washington, D.C., 1967), 140–42.

2. See Lyndon B. Johnson, "Speech to the New York Liberal Party," Oct. 15, 1964, Public Reports, 1350–51.

3. Hartford Courant, June 13, 1993.

4. Michael D. Reagan and John G. Sanzone, The New Federalism, 2d ed. (New York: Oxford University Press, 1981), 175. "Permissive federalism" means that states and localities have whatever power national governmental instrumentalities permit them to have.

5. See Harry N. Scheiber, "The Condition of American Federalism: An Historian's View," a study submitted by the Subcommittee on Intergovernmental Relations of the U.S. Senate Committee on Government Operations, 89th Congress, 2d Session, 15 Oct. 1966, 653.

6. 349 U.S. 294 (1954).

7. John Schwarz, *America's Hidden Success,* rev. ed. (New York: W. W. Norton, 1987), 17–70.

8. Alfred H. Kelly and Winfred A. Harbison, *The American Constitution: Its Origins and Development* (New York: W. W. Norton, 1976), 856.

9. David B. Walker, *Toward a Functioning Federalism* (Cambridge, Mass.: Winthrop Publishers, 1981), 105–06.

10. Ibid., 107–12.

11. See Donald F. Kettl, *The Regulation of American Federalism* (Baltimore: Johns Hopkins University Press, 1987); Advisory Commission on Intergovernmental Affairs, *Regulatory Federalism: Policy, Process, Impact, and Reform* (Washington, D.C., 1984).

12. 426 U.S. 833 (1976).

13. 469 U.S. 528 (1985), 460 U.S. 226 (1983), 483 U.S. 203 (1987), 111 S. Ct. 1759 (1991), 485 U.S. 505 (1988).

14. Rochell L. Stanfield, "The New Federalism," *National Journal,* Jan. 28, 1995, 226.

15. Ibid.

16. See "Clinton Calls for Partnership," *PA Times* 1 Mar. 1993, 20.

17. See Vice President Al Gore, *From Red Tape to Results—Creating a Government That Works Better and Costs Less, Report of the National Performance Review* (Washington, D.C., Sept. 10, 1993).

18. Stephen Barr, "Performance Measures Expand Their Horizons," *Washington Post,* Feb. 3, 1994.

19. Gore, *From Red Tape to Results.*

20. Ibid., 35–41.

21. Vice President Al Gore, *Creating a Government That Works Better and Costs Less: Status Report* (Washington, D.C.: Office of the Vice President, Sept. 1994), 5.

22. Ibid., 6; David Broder, "Resuscitating Federalism," *Washington Post National Weekly Edition,* Dec. 19–25, 1994, 4.

23. Broder, "Resuscitating Federalism," 5–6.

24. Ibid., 125–26.

25. "Republicans' Initial Promise: 100 Day Debate on 'Contract,'" *Congressional Quarterly,* Nov. 13, 1994, 3216–19.

26. Ibid.

27. See Advisory Commission on Intergovernmental Relations, *Draft Report by the U.S. Advisory Commission on Intergovernmental Mandates* (Washington, D.C., Dec. 30, 1994).

28. "Republicans' Initial Promise," 3217.

29. Ibid.

30. Dan Balz, "Governors Press Congress for Power to Manage Programs at State Level," *Washington Post,* Dec. 11, 1994; also see Jack W. Germond and Jules Witcover, "Governors Want Money, Not Strings," *National Journal,* Nov. 26, 1994, 7799.

31. Stanfield, "The New Federalism," 228–29.

32. Broder, "Resuscitating Federalism," 4.

33. "Lexington" and "Williamsburg's New Federalists," *Economist,* Nov. 26, 1994, 32.

34. Stanfield, "The New Federalism," 229.

35. Melissa Healey, "Clinton Fights for Hire of Police," *Hartford Courant,* Feb. 12, 1995.

36. "GOP Cautioned on Handling Welfare Burden to States," *Hartford Courant,* Jan. 14, 1995.

Part II

POLITICS

POLITICAL IDEOLOGIES
AND THE PARTY

THE END OF CONSERVATISM?

Public Opinion and the American Electorate in the 1990s

MICHAEL MINKENBERG

To many it seems to be more than a coincidence that the end of the cold war comes together with the end of a twelve-year-long occupation of the White House by the Republican Party. Depending on the perspective of the observer, one may look at either of these ends or at their combination as the end of an era, or even as the "end of history." On the other hand, various scholars agree that fundamental changes in American history and politics are homegrown, self-generated rather than induced by external factors. One can indeed argue that there has been a significant reconfiguration of American politics in the last twenty-five years whereas the dominant international factors as shaped by the cold war have not changed much for over forty years.

Therefore, instead of tracing directly the effects of international sea changes on the American public and electoral outcomes, this chapter tries to look at the "end of an era" thesis from the domestic angle and to account for the state of the American mind at the moment the cold war order was transformed into the new world disorder. The main goal of the chapter is to provide an assessment, in terms of U.S. public opinion trends and changes in the electorate, of whether the elections of the early 1990s signify an end to an era. Or, to put it differently, I want to show what did *not* end with the end of the Reagan-Bush era. One might interpret the vote for Clinton as a return to liberalism, old or new, and the final word in the "end of realignment" debate.[1] But there is evidence—even before the 1994 elections—that with the end of the Reagan-Bush regime, the era of conservatism—and Republicanism—has not ended at all.

These questions point to some hypotheses that will guide the arguments I make here. I maintain that the American electorate of the early 1990s is not returning to the liberalism that preceded the neoconservative era of the Reagan-Bush years. In consequence, partisan conflict is determined by a realignment trend benefiting the Republican Party and an increasing role for ideology on the right. My argument will be presented in three steps. First I will argue that a neoconservatism reflects a new cleavage based on value and cultural change. It is not simply the revival of traditional conservatism in the "old politics" sense—that is, opposition to the welfare state and to redistribution of income—but a new coalition of forces that see their common enemy in the postmaterialist new Left and its political agenda. Neoconservatism combines members of the old left who felt challenged by the new left with traditional conservative groups. This orientation is expressed by a heightened concern with sociocultural values and issues. The new (religious) right[2] radicalizes this neoconservative reaction and fuses its tenets with a populist, antiestablishment, and initially antiparty thrust.

There are two pieces of evidence for this proposition: public opinion data concerning trends in issue positions and patterns of liberalism and conservatism across segments of American society, and changes in the party system and the way people see political parties in the United States.

The second part of my argument documents major trends in public opinion at the national level.[3] The focus here is on the Reagan-Bush years, but for the sake of comparison, the time frame of this analysis ranges back to 1972. The database for the analysis is the general social surveys (GSS) of the National Opinion Research Council. The advantage of the GSS data for time series analysis is that they use identical wording of questions over time, which eliminates some spurious variations across the years.[4]

Finally I discuss the evidence from changes in the party system, in particular the ideological differences between the parties and the changing group alignments with the Democratic and Republican Parties. This will help to determine in which sense the Republican era has come to an end with the 1992 election. I will argue in particular that the changes discussed here show that the emergence of the "new politics" and the neoconservative reaction have contributed to a rearrangement of the U.S. party system in which the parties became ideologically more consistent while further departing from (rather than returning to) their traditional reflection of social cleavages that stem from the New Deal realignment. In particular, the emergence of the Republican Party as the party of economically *and* culturally conservative groups and ideologies contributes significantly to a "Europeanization" of the U.S. party system in which the party of the Right becomes the party of religion whereas the party of the Left becomes the more secular party.

The Current Cycle of American Politics:
From Old Politics to New Politics

The study of electoral changes in the United States or the delineation of political eras in American history is often based on the notion of cyclical developments. Two basic approaches to periodize American politics stand out: one based on electoral realignments and one defined by cycles that stem from nonpartisan factors such as economics or generations. Here I seek a combination of both. The roots of the recent changes in the United States are seen in generational replacement, long-run changes in the economy, in particular the rise of postindustrialism, in which class-based cleavages lose their salience, and the emergence of a new paradigm of politics that leads to dealignment and realignment trends.

The classic model of realignment defines political eras in the United States in terms of "party systems" generated by "critical elections" or "secular realignments."[5] These party systems are defined by durable regroupings of the electorate and major shifts in electoral majorities which lead to the replacement of one party as the majority party by another or to the emergence of new parties at the expense of older ones. This model tends to identify five party systems in American history since 1800, each lasting about thirty years or a generation. The last such realignment having occurred in the 1930s with the establishment of the New Deal party system, the model raises the expectation that the next realignment would come about in the 1960s. The 1968 election was, in fact, interpreted as the latest realigning election since—with the exception of Jimmy Carter's interregnum—it sent the Republican party back to the White House for five of the next six presidential terms. At the same time, however, the 1968 election failed to make the Republicans the new majority party in Congress and initiated instead a period of "divided government as a normal condition."[6] It also began a period of dealignment rather than realignment trends, with weakening party loyalties and a decline of political parties as the primary agents of mass mobilization.[7] Thus the debate on realignment has shifted from the question whether 1968, or 1980, was a realigning election to the issue of the usefulness of the concept itself.

For the purpose of this chapter, it seems helpful to combine the cyclical model suggested by Arthur Schlesinger with the concept of old and new politics[8] while retaining a redefined version of realignment that keeps its party-related meaning. This version replaces the emphasis on the majority status of parties in the electorate or in institutions with a stress on durable changes in partisan attachments which may or may not result in new electoral majorities. This approach is preferable because it allows us to use the realignment concept in analyses of two-party and multiparty systems alike.

It is furthermore closely tied to the notion that a party system translates social conflicts into political conflicts and is structured ideologically by the grouping of parties along the major conflict dimensions.[9] Sundquist provides a useful definition of *realignment* by confining the term to "those redistributions of party support, of whatever scale or pace, that reflect a change in the structure of the party conflict and hence the establishment of a new line of partisan conflict on a different axis within the electorate."[10]

Whether and how the fortunes of parties change in the course of voter realignment depends very much upon the actions of each party. A lack of responsiveness may lead to the emergence of new political movements and to intraparty tension so that regular party elites are challenged by movement activists and related party factions. If forces supporting the new issues gain control of one of the parties or succeed in influencing the party's agenda, groups that hold opposing views and feel more strongly about the new issue dimension than the old abandon their traditional party loyalties and either become detached or, if they feel their concerns are better represented by another party, realign themselves.

Another, related aspect of the realignment-dealignment process is fundamental demographic change, such as generational replacement. New issues arise as a result of generational conflicts and the different patterns of political socialization that are shaped by the historical context in which each generation grows up.[11] In the context of the cyclical model of American history, the idea of generational replacement and the model's emphasis on "moods" rather than the mechanics of a distinct party and electoral system also open up possibilities of comparing the U.S. eras to those of other Western nations. To the degree that generations, as a crucial unit for historical analysis, increasingly undergo similar experiences across countries (World War II, communism as an external threat, protest movements, international economic cycles, modern mass communication, etc.), it is plausible to assume that political eras become more alike in various countries and that "American exceptionalism" becomes increasingly a thing of the past. The following discussion argues, in fact, that the combined effects of generational changes and the emergence of new conflict dimensions in various Western democracies played an important role in the rise of the new politics: the new left movements and parties and their neoconservative reaction; and that the new politics era in the United States and in several Western European democracies bear similar characteristics.

Most important for shaping the new politics were the conditions of postwar economic prosperity and internal and international security (relative to the insecurity of great economic crises and wars) among the Western countries. These have provided conditions under which a value change occurred that has contributed to the decline of social class voting and tends

to neutralize political polarization based on social class.[12] Ronald Inglehart demonstrated that this phenomenon is largely attributable to inter-
generational changes. Considerable parts of younger age cohorts, having
been raised in an environment of material saturation and security, have
developed value priorities that emphasize postmaterial issues—such as a
less impersonal, cleaner, more cultured society, personal freedom and self-
actualization, and democratization of political, work, and community life—
over materialist issues—such as a stable economy, economic growth, fighting rising prices and crime, and maintaining the political order. Among the
postwar generation (those born after 1945), the postmaterialists were as
numerous as the materialists and were mostly found among students and
the better educated.

As a result of these interrelated individual and structural transforma-
tions, a new paradigm of politics emerged. The shift of class structure within
postindustrial society and the rise of a generation-specific postmaterialism
heralded a new cleavage that defined a new, value-based constellation of
conflict. The old politics cleavage is based on the conflict between the old
left coalitions, identified with the working class and labor unions, secular
groups and urban interests, and the old right coalitions, formed of business,
rural, middle-class, and in some countries church-related, interests. Old
politics issues are formed within the confines of the hitherto consensual
values of economic growth, public order, national security, and traditional
lifestyles. In contrast, the postmaterialist values of the new politics challenge the old politics consensus along a dimension of conflict about new
issues such as alternative lifestyles, environmental quality, minority rights,
social equality, and more political participation.[13] In structural terms, this
new politics is centered in the new social movements of the new left initially
organized outside the formal structure of political representation and its
opponents in established political parties, institutions, and the public. The
year 1968 stands out as a symbolic date marking this shift of political para-
digms in Western democracies and connecting the events in Berkeley and
Chicago with those in Paris and Berlin.

In the United States the political forum for the new left remained the
Democratic Party. The influence of the new left reached its first peak in the
nomination of George McGovern as Democratic candidate for president in
1972.[14] This election coincided with a low point in class-based voting.[15] In
contrast to the successful establishment of a new left party in Germany and
some other European democracies,[16] the American new left has continuously worked with or through the Democratic Party even after the 1972
debacle. With the nomination of Jimmy Carter in 1976, both old left, especially the Democratic South and the intraparty organization of the old
left, the Coalition for a Democratic Majority, and new left forces found a

compromise candidate. But four year later the insurgency of Ted Kennedy against the incumbent president in the Democratic nomination process and the criticism of Carter from the right by members of the Coalition for a Democratic Majority demonstrated the ongoing conflict between old and new forces within the party. During the 1980s the rise of Jesse Jackson mobilized the new left forces in nomination campaigns, although in 1984 they were also drawn to Gary Hart, McGovern's campaign manager of 1972. Overall, by the 1980s the new left found a more or less comfortable home in the Democratic Party, a fact that also became manifest in the growing liberalism of Democratic convention delegates and activists on new politics issues.[17]

While the new left is easily identified as the focal point of the postmaterialist value priorities of new social movements and their party-political allies, the same cannot be said for the neoconservative reaction. For although the point of departure for a definition of neoconservatism has been the same "value shift" that delineates the new left, not all social elements that have abjured the postmaterialist shift are equally neoconservative. The "materialist reaction" to the new left assumes neoconservative properties when people perceive a threat to their values and related status anxiety, and the resulting defense of both, in the face of the shifting social differentiation within postindustrial societies.[18] This defense of status leads people to support the existing regime as the legitimate bulwark of traditional values or even to use the regime to defend and advance these values and results in an ideological polarization of the new cleavage.

The neoconservative response to the rise of postmaterialism and the related agenda of the new left has been articulated by influential elites, by political movements, and in public opinion among Western mass publics. Although there are differences between the intellectual neoconservatism of cultural elites and the (fundamentalist) populism of new right movements and parties, they are united on a common conflict axis against their political foe. In fact, the novelty of this mounting conservative response does not lie in the issues of the underlying philosophy itself but in the fact that it is an alliance of traditionally liberal groups (in the old politics sense), both at the elite level and at the mass level, with traditionally conservative groups against the new challenge on the dimension of value-based conflict. The neoconservative reaction is characterized by an emphasis on the old politics agenda of economic growth, technological progress, and economic and national security and by a common concern with the "decline" of civic values, as well as with the vitality of a number of secondary virtues. These concerns lead to a critique of the "demand overload" of democracy and the "excesses" of the welfare state and welfare spending, an attack on the "counterculture" and alternative lifestyles, and an ideologically driven politics of power and interest that take on neonationalist overtones under the legitimating mantle of militant anticommunism.

In the United States, empirical evidence documents the emergence of the new conflict axis in the early seventies. A general increase in ideological polarization of the American mass public across several issue dimensions[19] was accompanied by intense conflicts over the "new social issues" (race discrimination, Vietnam, student protests, counterculture, law and order) between the postmaterialist new liberals on the one hand and the conservative reaction on the other.[20] Most prominent was a group of east coast intellectuals with a liberal or even radical biographical background who strongly reacted to the student protest movement of the sixties and to whom the term *neoconservatism* was first applied.[21] While still adhering to the principles of New Deal (i.e., old politics) liberalism, these neoconservatives rejected Great Society welfare statism and were rather conservative on social and cultural issues.

These shifts toward neoconservatism at by cultural elites and intellectuals have been accompanied by the emergence of new right movements and parties in several Western democracies. In the United States, the new right became politically relevant with the revival of nonmainline conservative and fundamentalist churches. Their religious and political leaders struggled for a "populist conservatism," that is, the reinstitution of religious, particularly Christian, values in public life, combined with a new emphasis on the free enterprise system and technological progress. Although the direct appeal of new right organizations such as the Moral Majority was limited to a small segment of the American public, they succeeded in mobilizing previously unpolitical parts of the electorate, such as fundamentalists of, usually, lower-class and rural background, and registering large numbers of new voters. Moreover, their stance on various sociocultural issues was shared by large parts of the public across class and party lines.[22]

By the mid-1980s the new right had even established a working alliance with neoconservative intellectuals and became ever more closely associated with the Republican Party.[23] As their new left counterparts did with the Democrats, the new right, after an initial phase of independence from both parties, used the Republican Party as their addressee and platform for national political action. Beginning with the 1976 Republican nomination campaign, the new right has succeeded in slowly taking over parts of the Republican Party at the levels both of ideology and platform and of personnel—that is, activists and candidates—by continuously fighting the established Republican leadership and forces of the old right. The nomination of Ronald Reagan as Republican presidential candidate documented most dramatically the conservative shift among Republican Party leaders and the advance of the new right.[24]

This concept of changing cleavage structures does not suggest that the old politics dimension disappears as a result of the new conflict axis but that its polarization decreases in the face of the polarization in the new cleavage. As to now, there is already empirical evidence that Western publics polarize more strongly on new politics issues than on old politics issues and that the left-right or liberal-conservative spectrum is being redefined.[25] In consequence, the established parties have suffered increased internal tensions and risk losing parts of their constituencies at either end of the new spectrum—if they do not adjust to the new pressures—or at the center—if they accommodate new politics concerns. The later parts of this chapter will discuss the scope and limits of the restructuring of the political spectrum in the United States in the 1980s and early 1990s and its impact on the electorate and the party system in order to determine whether the country is in the process of entering a new, post–new politics cycle in the 1990s.

The U.S. Public in the 1990s: Conservative Consolidation or Liberal Rebound?

As new and crosscutting issues such as Vietnam, race relations, and law and order emerged during the 1960s, the American electorate experienced a rise in consistency of issues and ideological polarization, and views of elites and the mass public became more consistent as well.[26] Because of the structural and individual changes I have outlined, the newly emerging conflict axis based on values and the new social issues contributed significantly to the restructuring of political thought among the electorate. It was above all the new politics ideologues who consistently and most frequently used the abstract concepts *liberal* and *conservative* to summarize their policy preferences.[27]

Most notably, in the seventies, contrary to previous decades, the term *conservative* became preferred over the term *liberal*.[28] Although the concepts are imprecise, research suggests that at the core of the concepts of liberal and conservative lies the symbolic meaning of "change vs. preservation of traditional values and institutions."[29] Hence the changes in ideological self-identification in the 1970s reflect a reaction to the changes in values and traditional institutions promoted by the protest movements and party factions of the new left. Under the New Deal, large-scale change was confined to the realm of government and the economy, and an "operational liberalism" as well as a liberal self-identification prevailed among most voters until the late sixties.[30] But the protest and mobilization cycle enhanced sociocultural change, and the term *liberal* lost its appeal since liberalism came to be linked to alternative lifestyles, cultural modernization, unconventional political behavior, and so forth.[31] The data on ideological self-identification

Table 7.1   Ideological and Issue Trends, 1972–1991, Nation

	Nixon/Ford	Carter	Reagan I	Reagan II	Bush
Ideological self-identification	0	6	9	8	6
Old politics: government spending on					
Welfare	31	47	26	22	18
Health	−59	−50	−53	−59	−69
New politics: law and order					
Spending on crime	63	63	67	64	67
Death penalty	33	42	53	53	56
New politics: racial integration					
Spending on blacks	−7	0	−11	−18	−21
School busing	62	62	55	43	32
New politics: women's issues					
Equal role	−35	−35	−52	−58	−62
Abortion	6	9	12	18	10
New politics: sociomoral issues					
School prayer	30	32	21	17	18
Homosexuality	57	57	57	61	59
Extramarital sex	70	73	75	80	82
Foreign policy					
Anticommunism	52	64	73	68	71
Spending on arms	−16	18	−7	−26	−24
(n)	(7,590)	(4,530)	(4,578)	(5,951)	(4,426)

Source: General Social Surveys, 1972–91.
Note: The data indicate the conservative bias for selected issue items. The percentage of liberal responses was subtracted from the percentage of conservative responses.

reveal that the trend of the seventies has stopped and consolidated in the 1980s (see table 7.1). Under Ronald Reagan's leadership, more people than ever were willing to summarize their political views as "conservative." The continuous downward trend for the "liberal" badge came to a halt in the mid-eighties, that is, at the time of Reagan's reelection.

In order to interpret these abstract ideological changes in any meaningful way, one must look at trends in various issue areas. For the following analysis I have selected a set of issues that broadly reflects the new politics agenda of the left and right (issues of law and order, racial integration, women's rights, sociomoral concerns) together with some old politics issues, those related to economic welfare and foreign policy. Since the general social surveys do not allow a good representation of these old politics issue areas, I will use secondary literature when necessary.

To summarize and structure such an enormous mass of data, I will apply the following procedure. First, each issue variable is coded into a liberal and a conservative response, and the conservative bias is measured by subtracting the percentage of liberal responses from the percentage of conservative responses. A value of 100 (-100) would indicate that all respondents with an opinion favor the conservative (liberal) response to the question; a value of 0 would mean that liberal and conservative responses cancel each other out, but it does not tell whether there is a strong polarization between liberal and conservative positions or a large moderate group. The second step involves aggregation of the data in time periods rather than showing a yearly account of the trends. The periods coincide with presidential administrations: Nixon-Ford (1972–1976), Carter (1977–1980), Reagan I (1981–1984), Reagan II (1985–1988), and Bush (1989–1991).[32]

The national trends in ideological change regarding selected issues over a twenty-year period are summarized in table 7.1. On welfare state issues, the American public took different positions regarding the problem of government spending. The conservative bias against more welfare spending prevailed throughout the entire period, but the trend underwent a significant reversal in the Reagan years, so that by the early 1990s it reached its lowest level since the Nixon-Ford era. Additional survey research shows that it was largely the Reagan administration's massive assault on social programs that produced the liberal rebound on this issue,[33] although this finding should not obscure the fact that in 1991 more Americans believed too much is spent on welfare (39.6%) than those who think too little is spent (23.5%). It would be incorrect, however, to interpret these figures as an outright rejection of social programs by a plurality of Americans. Since there is no one simple welfare program, one must distinguish between the negative connotations the word *welfare* might have in the public mind and support for specific programs. For instance, support for government spending went up when *welfare* was replaced by *assistance for the poor,* and large majorities of respondents in the mid-1980s showed no desire for spending cuts when asked about a series of specific programs such as Medicare, Social Security, Aid to Families with Dependent Children, and even food stamps.[34]

In contrast to this trend, the Reagan-Bush era is characterized by an ever increasing concern for the nation's health care that can be interpreted as an almost unanimous, yet abstract, liberal consensus on this issue (the question on spending on education produced almost exactly the same figures in the 1980s). Taken together, the figures on government spending reflect a continuing discrimination of "who should be helped"[35] between those deemed more worthy and those less worthy of public assistance. In other words, the American public continues to support basic welfare state arrangements on a large scale if the mass public or the "truly needy" are affected but rejects notions of (more) public spending when the principles of "recipient deservingness" and "program effectiveness"[36] are threatened and expansion of the welfare state violates basic capitalist and individualist values.[37] In all, extensive research on popular support for the American welfare state shows that not only did the welfare state survive the most massive onslaught in its history during the first years of the Reagan administration, but also in its present form it remained firmly embedded in the public mind.[38] In general, attitudes toward old politics issues regarding the economic welfare of the country and its political economy underwent little change in the 1970s and 1980s, in stark contrast to the massive changes that occurred between the New Deal and the Great Society years.

A closer look at a variety of new politics issues provides a different picture. As table 7.1 illustrates, law-and-order concerns are rather high on the agenda of many Americans, and the public expressed increasingly conservative positions. Unlike the case of welfare spending, the Reagan regime did not halt the concerns with the rising crime rate. Support for more spending to combat crime stayed very high throughout the 1980s, and support for the death penalty increased steadily. Whether this simply reflects the public's loss of faith in the idea of rehabilitation as a consequence of the state of prisons and the criminal justice system in the United States is doubtful.[39] It could also be the expression of growing rigidity in dealing with the perceived threats of crime and the increasing exposure to it in the mass media.

Issues of minorities' and women's rights show rather ambivalent trends. On the one hand, some of the most clear-cut liberal trends in the United States since World War II have been the decline of outright racism and the growing acceptance of women's equality in public life and the workplace. This is illustrated by the two indicators chosen here, support for spending on blacks and acceptance of an equal role for women, as well as by widespread research.[40]

These broad trends, however, hide a more complex reality, as attitudes on more specific items show. School busing—a hotly debated instrument to achieve racial integration—became more accepted over the 1980s, but in 1991 it was still opposed by almost two-thirds of the American public. The abortion issue is usually seen as an indicator for a long-lasting liberal trend.[41] The data in table 7.1 diverge from this view because the variable is coded in a way that excludes extreme qualifiers such as termination of pregnancies caused by rape and incest, terminations indicated by the risk of severe birth defects, and protection of the mother's health. While the public does indeed display increasingly proabortion attitudes in conjunction with these premises, the view of abortion as a matter of a woman's choice regardless of the circumstances is highly controversial. In no other question under consideration was the proportion of respondents in the middle category as small as in this case (8–12% in each year), and in no other question was the public polarized into two similarly large opposing camps. The trend line shows a slight conservative edge in the years following the Supreme Court's decision in *Roe v. Wade*. From then on, opposition to a prochoice position increased steadily until it reached its peak in Reagan's second term (the highest mark being 55.4% in 1987). After that, it slid back slightly, although it did not return to the level of the 1970s. The complexity of the abortion issue, with its mixed religious-moral, political-ideological, class, race, and gender aspects,[42] makes it difficult to interpret this trend, but the figures make it clear that abortion is one of the most controversial issues on the agenda of the 1980s and early 1990s.[43]

Conservatism also prevails with regard to sociomoral issues, which, like abortion, are key elements of the new right's ideology. Throughout the 1970s large numbers of Americans disapproved of the Supreme Court's ruling on "the Lord's Prayer or Bible verses in public schools" (the actual question wording in the GSS). Support for the freedom to hold prayers in public school and thus to transgress the principle of separation of church and state dropped somewhat in the 1980s to a level of around 60 percent, but the figures indicate a consolidation of the public's view rather than a liberalizing trend. This finding correlates with evidence showing similarly stable support among a majority of Americans for other traditional values such as loyalty to the American flag, rejection of pornography, and legalization of marijuana.[44] When it comes to lifestyle issues such as disapproval of homosexuality or extramarital sex (both can be interpreted as indicators of support for traditional "family values"), Americans are overwhelmingly conservative. Acceptance of homosexuality actually declined in the late 1980s and early 1990s, while rejection of extramarital sexual relations has grown in an almost linear fashion since the days of the permissive counterculture. These and other data on sexual matters defy the notion of a "sexual revolution" in America in the wake of the 1960s. Rather, the 1980s witnessed a return to or reaffirmation of traditional lifestyles and sexual mores with a few exceptions (support for sex education in schools, toleration of premarital sex), and there is no sign that after the Republican era in the White House the public is becoming less traditional again.[45]

In the realm of foreign policy and international relations, the public's views have undergone more fluctuations than in domestic affairs, and it is even debatable whether foreign policy orientations follow patterns and cycles that reflect or extend domestic patterns.[46] There is widespread agreement among scholars that with the Vietnam War and its political repercussions in the United States, the foreign policy consensus that was established when the cold war unfolded and which implied an internationalist position on a global scale broke into various approaches among American leaders and the mass public alike.[47] To the degree that the Vietnam War was a catalyst for the emergence of the protest movement cycle not just in the United States but in other Western democracies as well, one can assume some congruence between the post-Vietnam era in international relations and the new politics era in domestic affairs. Indeed, new politics liberals redefined U.S. involvement in global affairs in cooperative and human rights terms, replacing the emphasis on the cold war by the emphasis on the North-South conflict, economic interdependence, and the preservation of peace through nonmilitary means.[48] In reaction to this approach and to world events such as the Soviet Union's military buildup in the 1970s and its growing involvement in developing countries, a neoconservative foreign policy agenda formed that combined moralism, globalism, criticism of detente, and support for a massive military buildup.

This agenda and the activism of its most ardent carriers among neoconservative intellectuals, new right ideologues, and the first Reagan administration served to revive the cold war consensus as well as a sense of national identity and pride rooted in anticommunism and the belief in American superiority to the "evil empire." However, this reactivation did not carry over into substantial and lasting shifts in policy preferences. Table 7.1 demonstrates that, as in the case of concern for law and order and support for traditional lifestyles, anticommunism—the sine qua non of American conservatism[49]—was shared by very large and increasing parts of the U.S. public over the last twenty years. The figures presented here support the view that the "cold war schema" as a cultural predisposition[50] does not react immediately to changes in world affairs. While the Soviet empire crumbled and the Soviet Union and Gorbachev received more favorable ratings by the U.S. public in the late 1980s and early 1990s,[51] the overwhelming rejection of communism persisted. In a divergent trend, support for defense spending dropped significantly throughout the 1980s, after soaring in the late 1970s, and the public's view on arms control and other policy areas vis-à-vis the Soviet Union became less confrontational but remained cautious.[52] Despite the loss of the global adversary in the post–cold war era, however, the cold war schema and the attachment to internationalist policies and commitments will not disappear as quickly as did the cold war.[53]

So far, the discussion of national public opinion trends provides an aggregate summary of changing as well as stable orientations among the U.S. mass public. In a separate analysis, variations of these opinion trends across selected subgroups, as derived from the cleavage structures of the United States (race, class, region, and religion) and differences in age and education, were examined (data not shown). Overall, these trends signify a persistence in issue polarization in which the cleavage structures defined by the old politics of the New Deal are reinforced by most of the new politics issues.

Most notable is the persistent clash of views on issues of racial integration between blacks and the white South, although blacks share some of the white South's traditionalism in values and lifestyle issues. To what extent these similarities reflect a common cultural heritage of the patriarchic and traditionalist Old South remains a matter of controversy.[54] Some observers point out that for blacks, particularly in the South, tradition and religiosity have always been a way to reaffirm their identity and build a power base for the fight against oppression and racism.[55] While a persistent conservatism in several sociomoral issues sets southern Protestants, Catholics, and fundamentalists apart from the decidedly more liberal nonreligious whites and Jews (with the other groups in between), it is in particular the abortion issue that in the transition from the Reagan II years to the Bush years moved the Catholic working and middle class and the southern middle class farther to the right, thus pulling closer to the considerably conservative southern working class in this issue. These shifts clearly diverge from the national trend and, with other examples from the data presented here, suggest that the concept of "parallel publics" based on unidimensionally defined groups (groups of different age, income levels, education levels, etc.)[56] does not provide sufficient evidence on how attitudes are changing in various segments of the American public. How these issue polarizations between subgroups translate into the American party system and to what extent the cleavage structures of the New Deal system are still meaningful in the 1990s will be answered below.

The American Electorate and the Party System: More Choice, Less Echo

The American electorate and party system of the 1990s are undergoing a restructuring of electoral coalitions and a growing interparty polarization. The rise of the new politics and the rearrangement of the political spectrum in America, as I discussed in the previous two sections, have complicated political alliances and contributed to dealignment and realignment trends that have permanently altered the electoral underpinnings of the American party system.

The growing polarization between the Democratic and the Republican Parties is most visible at the level of party elites and activists. Because of its inherent heterogeneity, the New Deal Democratic coalition was very vulnerable to the emergence of new issues and the new politics cleavage in the 1960s. Throughout the 1970s and 1980s, party regulars were challenged by new left movements and activists who found their issues not being represented appropriately in the party's ideology. The nomination struggles of the 1970s and 1980s point at the ongoing tensions in the Democratic Party, as, for example, the ideological profile of Democratic convention delegates shows.[57] Regardless of the presidential candidates and their ideological profiles, Democratic activists and delegates were predominantly liberal in self-identification, in their support for women's issues and opposition to increased defense spending, but continuously split into opposing groups regarding abortion, school busing, and economic policies. However, intra-party conflicts were softened by the fact that after 1972 no major effort was made to mobilize conservative Democrats on the race issue—in part because those conservatives concerned with the race issue and ready to be mobilized on it could find a comfortable alternative with the Republican Party.

In contrast to the Democrats, the Republicans underwent an ideological purification due to the activism of the new right in the 1980s and early 1990s. During the 1980s the new right entered a stage that some observers have interpreted as the demise of the movement.[58] The disarray of the movement became obvious in 1988, when Jerry Falwell chose from the beginning to endorse the "heir" of the Reagan era, George Bush, while another religious leader of the new right, Pat Robertson, waged an unsuccessful nomination campaign that quickly faltered.

Despite the limits encountered by the new right in the 1980s, it would be shortsighted to conclude that it had become a phenomenon of the past. Not only did the new right become more sophisticated and more "secular" as well—replacing some extreme positions on religious and moral values with a more moderate rhetoric and adding new organizations[59]—but also it readjusted its strategies, which focus increasingly on local and regional levels. On election day in November 1992, for example, fundamentalist Christian candidates won about 40 percent of the five hundred races for seats on school boards, city councils, state legislatures, etcetera.[60]

Finally, and most important, the new right continues to play a crucial role in the Republican Party. Despite Pat Robertson's meager performance in the 1988 Republican primaries, his candidacy was influential in mobilizing grass-roots conservative support and sending a message that helped determine the tenor of the Republican Party convention. The overall theme of the party gathering was conservatism, and the effort to make an ideological appeal rather than to run on the Reagan presidency's record was reflected in Bush's choice for his vice presidential candidate, Dan Quayle, as well as in the platform drafting, which echoed the new right's 1980 and 1984 triumphs on taxes, abortion, school prayer, defense spending, and strategic defense.[61]

These tendencies were replicated in the 1992 nomination period. This time, George Bush was challenged by two candidates from the far right: the one, David Duke, from the extreme right with ties to the Ku Klux Klan, the other, Pat Buchanan, an ultraconservative with professional experience as a

TV talk show host and a speechwriter for Nixon and Reagan. Buchanan scored one-third of the primary vote in several states but failed to damage Bush seriously. He did, however, manage to undermine David Duke by taking a hard-line position on welfare, law and order, and immigration. These positions and his ultranationalist, racist, and religious appeals won him support especially among those Republicans who were looking for a right-wing alternative to the incumbent president and who made up sections of the new right constituency.[62]

In order to secure his nomination, Bush handed the convention over to the organizers from the new right and their allies in the party. The theme was "family values," and the TV public learned from Buchanan in the prominent opening-night speech that "a religious war [is] going on for the soul of America," from speeches by Pat Robertson, Ronald Reagan, and Dan and Marilyn Quayle that the Republicans seemed ready to launch a big government offensive in this "cultural war" against liberalism in all its facets—feminism, pornography, blacks, atheists, drug users, socialism, and Democrats.[63] These themes found their way into the platform-drafting process, which was heavily dominated by the new right. Phyllis Schlafly, Pat Robertson, and others saw to it that the 1992 Republican platform exceeded all other Republican platforms as a true expression of new right ideology.[64]

The extent to which these ideological shifts at the level of party activists and nomination struggles are reflected in the party rank and file is illustrated in tables 7.2 and 7.3. These trends, issue positions among Democratic and Republican identifiers in the American public, reveal a rather high degree of readiness among Republicans to adopt the conservative label while Democrats increasingly diverge from the Republicans as well as the general public in identifying themselves as liberals. In accordance with the traditional differences in socioeconomic and welfare state issues, Democrats and Republicans continued to polarize with regard to spending on health and, more strongly, welfare. Under Reagan, the differences concerning welfare spending increased, possibly reflecting the partisan clashes over his program to cut welfare spending. Another area of interparty differences were race-related issues, particularly school busing, and the death penalty.

Regarding sociomoral and women's issues, the trends in the 1980s reveal some interesting shifts. Democrats and Republicans alike shared the view that women should have an equal role in society, but they differed increasingly on the abortion issue. Whereas in the early 1970s the Democrats were more conservative than the general public in this issue and the Republicans more liberal, this relationship was reversed by the early 1990s. A similar trend took place with regard to the tolerance of homosexuals, although here both partisan groups started at about the same level in the Nixon-Ford era. These issues document the reconfiguration of the ideologi-

Table 7.2   Ideological and Issue Trends, 1972–1991, Democrats

	Nixon/Ford	Carter	Reagan I	Reagan II	Bush
Ideological self-identification	−10 (−10)	−4 (−10)	−3 (−12)	−12 (−20)	−15 (−21)
Old politics: government spending on					
Welfare	20 (−11)	40 (−7)	13 (−13)	9 (−13)	1 (−17)
Health	−64 (−5)	−59 (−9)	−60 (−7)	−67 (−8)	−77 (−8)
New politics: law and order					
Spending on crime	65 (2)	67 (4)	70 (3)	68 (4)	73 (6)
Death penalty	28 (−5)	37 (−5)	43 (−10)	48 (−15)	53 (−13)
New politics: racial integration					
Spending on blacks	−15 (−8)	−8 (−8)	−23 (−12)	−30 (−12)	−35 (−14)
School busing	49 (−13)	56 (−6)	44 (−11)	32 (−11)	20 (−12)
New politics: women's issues					
Equal role	−29 (6)	−30 (5)	−46 (6)	−53 (5)	−57 (5)
Abortion	15 (9)	13 (4)	20 (8)	21 (3)	7 (−3)
New politics: sociomoral issues					
School prayer	36 (6)	34 (2)	27 (6)	23 (6)	17 (−1)
Homosexuality	63 (6)	62 (5)	61 (4)	63 (2)	51 (−8)
Extramarital sex	72 (2)	75 (3)	74 (−1)	81 (1)	81 (−1)
Foreign policy					
Anticommunism	60 (8)	66 (2)	71 (−2)	65 (−3)	71 (0)
Spending on arms	−14 (2)	18 (0)	−14 (−7)	−34 (−8)	−29 (−5)

Source: General Social Surveys, 1972–91.
Note: The data indicate the conservative bias for selected issue items for the subgroup. The percentage of liberal responses was subtracted from the percentage of conservative responses. (Then the group bias, for the number in parentheses, was subtracted from the national bias shown in table 1. Positive numbers point to a conservative, negative numbers a liberal group bias relative to the national trend.)

cal makeup of the parties in new politics terms whereas in the old politics dimension, they stayed their course. These ideological and issue trends also underline the ongoing ideological differences between party leaders and activists on the one hand, and the rank and file on the other. In particular, the ideological gap between Republican elites and partisans in the mass public widened considerably over the 1970s, to such an extent that in the 1980s they had become as distinct from each other as had Democratic elites and followers.[65] In sum, what has been said earlier is even more true today: "While one would hesitate to suggest that America has become an ideologically polarized society, it is safe to say that the ideological cores of the two

Table 7.3   Ideological and Issue Trends, 1972–1991, Republicans

	Nixon/Ford	Carter	Reagan I	Reagan II	Bush
Ideological self-identification	28 (28)	30 (24)	39 (30)	40 (32)	34 (28)
Old politics: government spending on					
Welfare	49 (18)	60 (13)	50 (24)	41 (19)	34 (16)
Health	−49 (10)	−32 (18)	−36 (17)	−46 (13)	−61 (8)
New politics: law and order					
Spending on crime	63 (0)	58 (−5)	64 (−3)	61 (−3)	63 (−4)
Death penalty	50 (17)	56 (14)	70 (17)	69 (19)	73 (17)
New politics: racial integration					
Spending on blacks	6 (13)	13 (13)	6 (17)	−2 (16)	−7 (14)
School busing	78 (16)	72 (10)	72 (17)	63 (20)	50 (18)
New politics: women's issues					
Equal role	−26 (9)	−29 (6)	−48 (4)	−56 (2)	−63 (−1)
Abortion	1 (−5)	8 (−1)	10 (−2)	20 (2)	17 (7)
New politics: sociomoral issues					
School prayer	37 (7)	43 (11)	23 (2)	21 (4)	22 (4)
Homosexuality	67 (10)	67 (10)	67 (10)	71 (10)	73 (14)
Extramarital sex	80 (10)	82 (9)	83 (8)	85 (5)	87 (5)
Foreign policy					
Anticommunism	60 (8)	74 (10)	80 (7)	76 (8)	78 (6)
Spending on arms	−8 (8)	29 (11)	8 (15)	−10 (16)	−12 (12)

Source: General Social Surveys, 1972–91.
Note: The data indicate the conservative bias for selected issue items for the subgroup. The percentage of liberal responses was subtracted from the percentage of conservative responses. (Then the group bias, for the number in parentheses, was subtracted from the national bias shown in table 1. Positive numbers point to a conservative, negative numbers to a liberal group bias relative to the national trend.)

parties are a great deal more distant and farther apart than at any time before."[66]

The rise of the new politics and the restructuring of the political spectrum in the United States affected the two major parties not only in terms of their ideological profiles but also in terms of voter alignments. Since the early sixties the proportion of voters who rejected both parties and called themselves political independents has risen steadily, and among those who still identified themselves as Democrats or Republicans, party loyalties have been weakening.[67] The decline of partisanship was enhanced by voting behavior. Ticket splitting and issue voting further diminished the function of parties to provide meaningful cues for political orientations and behavior and were interpreted as signs of "party decomposition."[68] The relationship between these developments and the emergence of the new politics has been documented widely. It was the young, better-educated, and postmaterialist new liberals who developed disproportionately weak or nonexisting party attachments (though with a Democratic leaning), made particular use of ticket splitting and issue voting, and exercised unconventional forms of political behavior such as protest marches, sit-ins, and participation in new social movements.[69] But these were not the only population groups that contributed to the dealignment process of recent decades. Among traditional Democratic constituencies, considerable segments of white Protestant southerners, Catholics, and even Jews turned independent or even identified with the Republican Party. In particular, white southerners began to realign with the Republicans in terms of both party identification and voting behavior largely because of the race issue and other "new social issues."[70]

However, in the Reagan-Bush era, some of these trends came to a halt or were even reversed, while others continued. The American electorate of the 1990s is largely defined by these new patterns created in the neoconservative era. Table 7.4 summarizes the trends in party identification and demonstrates that the decline of partisan attachment, that is, the rise of the proportion of independents between 1972 and 1980, was halted when Reagan entered the White House. After his first term the numbers drop and mirror the increase of Republican identifiers who in 1989 outnumber the independents for the first time. The trend suggests that Reagan's first term and the 1984 election had a significant positive impact on Republican Party identification, while the secular decline of identification with the Democratic party continued.

The trends in party identification concerning various subgroups, discussed in the literature on old and new politics, document a continuing deterioration of the New Deal coalition over the last twenty years. Democratic losses were heaviest among the white Anglo-Saxon Protestant (WASP) working class, the white South, and Catholics—that is, those groups that displayed rather conservative views on new politics issues. Among the most liberal groups, Jews and blacks continued to identify largely with the Democratic Party. Some Jews defected in the Carter and early Reagan years, but most returned to the Democratic camp in the late 1980s and early 1990s. As table 7.4 suggests, the disintegration of the New Deal coalition benefited the Republicans among some subgroups. While the WASP middle class has always been more Republican than Democratic, the WASP working class, once a solidly Democratic group, is now almost evenly split into Democrats, independents, and Republicans. In contrast, southern workers, like Cath-

Table 7.4   Trends in the Proportions of Democrats (D), Independents (I) and Republicans (R), Nation and Subgroups

(In Percentages)

	Nixon/Ford			Carter			Reagan I			Reagan II			Bush		
	D	*I*	*R*	*D*	*I*	*R*	*D*	*I*	*R*	*D*	*I*	*R*	*D*	*I*	*R*
Nation	44	33	23	41	36	23	40	36	24	39	33	28	36	31	32
WASPs (white Protestant, non-South)															
Working class	40	32	27	37	38	26	37	37	26	36	35	29	32	33	35
Middle class	25	33	41	27	32	41	20	34	45	23	30	47	24	28	48
White Protestant South															
Working class	47	33	19	44	35	21	45	37	19	41	32	27	40	35	25
Middle class	37	36	27	26	38	26	36	32	32	35	28	37	30	25	45
Catholics															
Working class	58	31	11	55	30	14	48	36	15	49	32	19	43	30	27
Middle class	42	39	19	40	41	19	42	36	22	37	36	27	34	25	41
Jews	60	35	5	57	33	10	50	35	15	57	26	17	67	18	15
Whites, no religious preference	31	56	13	29	59	11	27	62	11	27	52	21	28	53	19
Blacks	73	19	8	67	27	6	68	27	5	70	25	5	67	25	8
College educated	32	41	27	35	39	26	33	36	31	33	34	33	32	30	38
Protest generation	37	47	16	35	48	17	36	43	21	35	39	26	35	36	29
Postprotest generation	—	—	—	—	—	—	36	44	20	29	39	32	25	38	37
College students	35	50	15	36	37	27	30	41	29	36	31	33	28	29	43
Fundamentalists	42	33	25	40	36	24	37	36	27	35	30	35	30	31	39

Source: General Social Surveys, 1972–91.

olic workers, remained Democratic, but the proportion of Republican iden-tifiers rose somewhat over the years. A dramatic conversion took place among the Protestant southern and the Catholic middle classes, which dur-ing the Reagan-Bush years became more Republican than Democratic, while the share of independents among these groups declined steadily from the mid- to late seventies on.

Among the other subgroups similar trends took place. The college-educated were largely independent, with a slight Democratic edge, in the early 1970s but turned more Republican and less independent by the 1990s, while the proportion of Democratic identifiers did not change. Likewise, the protest generation, once also politically rather independent, has be-come more partisan. The share of Democrats among these groups remained rather stable while the proportion of Republicans increased significantly in the Reagan-Bush years. Clearly, the dealignment trend of the sixties and seventies among these groups was stopped in the 1980s, but, as table 7.4 suggests, it was Reagan and the Republicans rather than the Democrats who benefited from increased partisanship. The postprotest generation did not differ from its predecessor generation in the first Reagan term but after Reagan's reelection experienced a growth of Republican identifiers in their ranks who now clearly outnumber the Democrats. College students display even more dramatic shifts in party identification. Whereas half of them were independents in the early 1970s and the rest more Democrat than Republican, most college students of the early 1990s seemed to have found a new political home in the Republican Party. Finally, one of the most striking conversions took place among fundamentalists. During the 1970s, Democratic identifiers in this group clearly outnumbered either independents or Republicans. During the Reagan years the number of Republicans increased while that of Democrats fell, so that in the Bush era Republicans outnumbered Democrats and independents. Thus fundamentalists have become a solid building block of any Republican coalition.

Overall, the trends in table 7.4 demonstrate clear patterns of realignment of various subgroups with the Republican Party, while the dealignment trend, expressed in high or rising numbers of independents, was halted in the 1980s. The Republican Party has not become the new majority party in the electorate, although it is closer than ever before since the New Deal. However, the Republicans have attracted an increasing number of formerly Democratic groups with a conservative profile, as the white South and fundamentalists demonstrate most visibly. Furthermore, the Republicans also gained ground among those groups that, in earlier times, were rather liberal and had a high percentage of independents, such as the postprotest generation or the college students. With these swings toward the Republican Party, the support pattern for the Republicans has become more heterogenous and volatile. One might expect that the steady drift to the right produces tensions among the moderate and the conservative wings of the party (in a similar fashion to the experience of the Democrats) that will ultimately alienate moderate Republicans and weaken their party loyalties.

Post–Cold War Elections? 1992 and 1994 in Perspective

Both the 1992 and 1994 elections stand out for their dramatic deviation from preceding electoral patterns: in 1992 a Democrat captured the White House for the first time since 1976; at the same time, a third-party presidential candidate had the strongest showing since 1912; and in 1994 the Republicans took control of both houses of Congress for the first time since 1952.[71] Taken together, these results, as contradictory as they may seem, indicate a

Table 7.5 Profile of the American Electorate: Selected Presidential (P) and House (H) Elections

% of 1992 total		1980 (P) Reagan	1980 (P) Carter	1980 (P) Anderson	1984 (P) Reagan	1984 (P) Mondale	1988 (P) Bush	1988 (P) Dukakis	1992 (P) Clinton	1992 (P) Bush	1992 (P) Perot	1992 (H) Dem	1992 (H) Rep	1994 (H) Dem	1994 (H) Rep
	Total vote	51	41	7	59	40	53	45	43	38	19	54	46	50	50
87	Whites	56	36	7	64	35	59	40	39	41	20	50	50	42	58
8	Blacks	11	85	3	9	90	12	86	82	11	7	89	11	88	12
3	Hispanics	33	59	6	37	62	30	69	62	25	14	72	28	70	30
22	18–29 years old	43	44	11	59	40	52	47	44	34	22	55	45	54	46
38	30–44 years old	55	36	8	57	42	54	45	42	38	20	53	47	48	52
24	45–59 years old	55	39	5	60	40	57	42	41	40	19	52	48	51	49
16	60 and older	54	41	4	60	40	50	49	50	38	12	56	44	51	49
6	Not a high school graduate	46	51	2	50	50	43	56	55	28	17	67	33	68	32
25	High school graduate	51	43	4	60	39	50	49	43	36	20	58	42	52	48
29	Some college education	55	35	8	61	38	57	42	42	37	21	53	47	47	53
40	College graduate or more	52	35	11	58	41	56	43	44	39	18	50	50	49	51
24	College graduate	—	—	—	—	—	62	37	40	41	19	46	54	45	55
16	Postgraduate education	—	—	—	—	—	50	48	49	36	15	55	45	54	46
49	White Protestant	63	31	6	72	27	66	33	33	46	21	43	57	34	66
27	Catholic	50	42	7	54	45	52	47	44	36	20	57	43	52	48
4	Jewish	39	45	15	31	67	35	64	78	12	10	79	21	78	22
17	White born-again Christian	63	33	3	78	22	81	18	23	61	15	34	66	24	76
19	Union household	44	49	6	46	53	42	57	55	24	21	67	33	63	37
14	Family income under $15,000	42	51	6	45	55	37	62	59	23	18	69	31	62	38
24	$15,000–$29,999	44	47	7	57	42	49	50	45	35	20	57	43	52	48
30	$30,000–$49,999	53	39	7	59	40	56	44	41	38	21	52	48	49	51
20	$50,000–$74,999	59	32	8	66	33	56	42	40	42	18	47	53	46	54
13	$75,000 and over	63	26	10	69	30	62	37	36	48	16	44	56	47	53
24	From the East	47	42	9	53	47	50	49	47	35	18	54	46	52	48
27	From the Midwest	51	41	7	58	41	52	47	42	37	21	46	54	44	56
30	From the South	52	44	3	64	36	58	41	42	43	16	49	51	45	55
20	From the West	53	34	10	61	38	52	46	44	34	22	49	51	59	41

Sources: New York Times, Nov. 5, 1992, Nov. 13, 1994.

THE END OF CONSERVATISM? / 147

shattering of the old electoral order that seems to reflect the global shattering of the old international order and the related sense of disorientation. However, a closer and more differentiated look at these elections suggests that they are less affected by a global warming of international relations than by the decline of domestic temperatures in the increasingly ideological party competition, as outlined above. Thus the 1992 and 1994 elections are complementary expressions of common, underlying trends in the American electorate rather than conflicting messages from voters.

To begin with, the Perot vote in 1992 was clearly economically motivated and had little to do with the awareness of a new international order. Moreover, it was more tied to the voters' personal economic situation than to a concern for the nation's welfare.[72] Inasmuch as Perot voters were driven by a growing alarm with the federal deficit, this was more a reaction to cold war policies, that is, Reagan's massive military buildup, than a reaction to the *end* of the cold war. More generally, the strong showing of Ross Perot indicates more than just a short-term dissatisfaction with the parties and their handling of the issues of the day. Because many Perot voters shared the characteristics of previous Republican voters,[73] one may argue that the ideological polarization between the internally torn Democratic Party and the increasingly religious conservative Republican Party left a significant group of voters looking for an alternative beyond the established parties. Thus the Perot phenomenon, unlike the candidate himself, cannot be reduced to the peculiarities of the election year but must be interpreted in the light of the long-term trends discussed earlier.

The same holds true for the Clinton vote in 1992. It has been suggested that the 1992 election should be interpreted as deviating since it was overshadowed by short-term forces pushing for change while long-term indicators such as economic or foreign policy performance predicted that the incumbent would be reelected.[74] While this is true in terms of the change in party control of the executive branch, one may consider the election as maintaining with regard to the stability of long-term trends in the restructuring of the electorate. The results of the 1992 elections hardly signal the arrival of a new Democratic or even a (neo)liberal era. Instead they demonstrate the continuous decline of the Democrats as the majority party and the ongoing fragmentation of their electoral base. Unlike Jimmy Carter in 1976, Clinton, who with Albert Gore presented an entirely southern ticket, failed to carry the South, as table 7.5 indicates. Except for Jews, he did not manage to improve Democratic candidates' standing among any of the groups, when compared with the Dukakis vote in 1988. Moreover, the Clinton vote did not produce any coattails in the congressional elections; rather, the Democrats lost ten seats in the House and, except for blacks, did not attract new voters among any of the groups vis-à-vis the 1988 and 1990 congressional elections.[75] One might interpret these limited Democratic losses in the context of that year's anti-incumbent mood[76] as a particular version of coattails, but they hardly suggest a mandate for or beginning of major liberal reforms. As indicated by Clinton's failure in his most ambitious reform project, health care reform, and the controversies over some of his liberal initiatives (such as tolerating gays in the military or gun control), there was little ideological direction in the call for change that the 1992 election results seemed to suggest.

In fact, the 1994 congressional and state elections point to another type of change that voters had in mind when they cast their ballots. Table 7.5 suggests that, except for traditionally very liberal constituents such as blacks and Jews, the Democrats lost most heavily among core components of the old New Deal coalition, that is, lower-educated and lower-income voters, southern and even union household voters. In addition, they continue to become increasingly unattractive for white Protestants and for evangelical voters in particular. All in all, the 1994 elections were not so much an anti-incumbent vote as they were an anti-Democratic and antiliberal vote. Whereas Democrats suffered across the board and some liberal icons such as New York Governor Mario Cuomo fell, not a single Republican incumbent lost, and many Republican winners in the 1994 elections reflect the ongoing shift to the right in the Republican Party.

As I have argued, this shift is a domestically generated transformation that, especially in light of the Republican agenda of 1994, seems to ignore the international sea changes after the cold war. Table 7.5 shows that in almost all categories, including college students, support for the Republican presidential candidate dropped in 1992. However, some groups continued to give Bush relatively high support, such as the economically better off and those most sympathetic toward the new right and its positions, white born-again Christians or evangelicals.[77] Like the New Deal Democratic coalition earlier, the Reagan coalition did not survive the 1980s, but its nucleus did. The white South and the religious right now belong to the bedrock of any Republican electoral coalition.[78] Since evangelicals and fundamentalists were traditionally rather apolitical or Democratic, it is no small achievement that the new right has mobilized these groups into the Republican camp.[79]

This development largely shaped the outcome of the 1994 elections, which for the Republicans do not at all contrast with the results of the 1992 elections. The 1992 congressional elections were rather comforting for the Republican party, which had developed particular appeal among white Protestants, especially evangelicals, college graduates, and upper-income strata and had caught up with or bypassed the Democrats in all regions except for the East. By 1994 the Republican advantage among these groups increased, again with the biggest leap among religious conservatives (see table 7.5). The 1994 election results are even more significant when one considers that they benefited a party that at various levels is becoming increasingly conservative.

First, the influence of the Christian right has continuously increased, despite the controversy over its involvement in the 1992 Republican campaign and convention. By reorienting its strategies to the local and state level (see above), the Christian right by 1994 had managed to play a dominant role in eighteen GOP state party organizations, most of which are in the South or West, while having substantial influence in another thirteen cases.[80] In some closely watched races in the 1994 campaigns, far-right candidates failed to get nominated (Paul Quist in Minnesota's gubernatorial elections) or to win the race (Oliver North in Virginia's senatorial elections), but their showing itself demonstrated the massive force of the Christian right in Republican party organizations. More important, there were many less publicized cases in which Republican candidates backed by the Christian right won elections, for example, in South Carolina (governor), Iowa (governor), Oklahoma (Senate), and Minnesota (Senate).[81]

As a result the 104th Congress is dominated by a Republican party in which the new right plays a larger role than ever before. Important Senate committees are chaired by well-known conservative Republicans such as Jesse Helms and Orrin Hatch who rose with the new right in the 1970s, and several of the eleven new senators share the new right's views on law and order, abortion, gun control, and school prayer.[82] The new Speaker of the House, Newt Gingrich, has been a champion of new right issues since he came to Washington in 1978 and, in the 1980s, helped organize the Conservative Opportunity Society with fellow new right Representative Vin Weber. The Republicans' Contract with America reflects the basic political philosophy, if not particular issues, of the new right such as the aim to "reduce crime by building more prisons," toughening law enforcement, and making the death penalty more "effective, able, and timely"; to "strengthen families by giving parents greater control over education" (read: school prayer); and to increase defense spending.[83] The last proposal, which also includes reviving Reagan's Strategic Defense Initiative, appears particularly absurd in the light of the Contract's pledge to introduce a balanced budget amendment and demonstrates that the new international era has had virtually no impact on Republican leaders. Correspondingly, despite a widespread lack of knowledge about the new Republican agenda among the American public and some misgivings about particular proposals, a majority of those who have heard of the Contract favor its general ideas.[84]

In sum, therefore, the 1994 elections cannot be interpreted as a mere protest vote with no ideological direction. They were a selective and directional protest against President Clinton, against Democrats, and, with the exception of some state referenda, against a liberal agenda; that is, they were an expression of a desire for change in a conservative direction.[85] The 1994 elections gave a very conservative Republican Party the power, if not the mandate, to enact policies that seemed more a retreat into the clear-cut ideological antagonisms of the cold war era especially during the Reagan years than an effort to readjust to the end of the cold war.

Summary

This chapter shows that the American public has undergone significant changes over the last two decades. During the 1970s, it entered an era of new politics with a neoconservative response by elites and masses to socio-cultural modernization in general and the protest movements of the sixties and seventies in particular. While the 1980s witnessed the expression of neoconservatism in various policy areas under the Reagan-Bush administrations, some of the trends observed earlier came to a halt or were even reversed. On some issues (government spending on problem areas or groups, women's rights), liberal trends reappeared or prevailed, while in others conservative trends consolidated. This has been interpreted as heralding a new cycle of liberalism in the United States.[86] However, among some politically meaningful groups, such as the white South, Catholic workers, and fundamentalists, the level of conservatism in most issue areas persisted or even increased slightly in the Reagan-Bush years. Thus the early 1990s are characterized by new patterns of ideological conflict and polarization in the new politics dimension while a basic liberal consensus prevailed in old politics terms.[87] The liberalism of the 1990s is a very moderate version of the liberalism of the sixties and early seventies whereas present-day conservatism is more radical than ever before since the New Deal and makes "Mr. Conservative" of 1964, Barry Goldwater, look like a moderate today.

The new politics cleavage has intensified partisan conflict at the level of party leaders and activists and contributed to dealignment and realignment trends among mostly Democratic constituents particularly affected by these changes. The realignment did not occur on a scale that produced dramatic shifts in overall support for the parties. Moreover, the defection of white southern Protestants, workers, fundamentalists, Catholics, and, to some degree, even Jews, was more pronounced at the level of presidential elections than in terms of party identification.[88] Yet trends in party identification reveal a gradual and continuous erosion of the New Deal coalition and significant gains for the Republican Party particularly among those groups that experienced a conservative surge during the 1970s and 1980s. Thus the most significant aspect of the changes in the party system and the contribution of the new politics is the trend toward a realignment of the electorate along liberal-conservative lines, with the American parties becoming more consistent ideologically and leaving more room at the ideological center.

Moreover, the strong alignment of the religiously conservative segments of the electorate with the Republican Party signals a "Europeanization" of the American party system in which the parties become ideologically more homogenous and, with regard to ideology and voter alignments, divide the religious and secular forces along right-left partisan lines.[89]

Overall, the end of the cold war is greeted by an American electorate and party system that seem unprepared and unwilling to take into account the dramatic changes that have occurred at the international level. The ideological and party system changes, as I have discussed in this chapter, suggest a puzzling peculiarity. On the one hand, there has been a significant reconfiguration of domestic politics in the last twenty-five years, yet the dominant international parameters as shaped by the cold war have not changed much for four decades. On the other hand, there is now a significant reconfiguration of international politics while the dominant domestic parameters do not change much. It seems the ripple effects of the global earthquake of 1989 have so far been blocked from American ground by the ongoing aftershocks of an earlier earthquake in the United States—the culture shock of 1968.

Notes

The author wishes to thank Mike Judge and Andrew Rutten (Cornell University) for some deep insights into American politics and culture and for helpful comments on this essay.

1. See, for example, Byron Shafer, ed., *The End of Realignment? Interpreting American Electoral Eras* (Madison: University of Wisconsin Press, 1991).

2. This term refers to what Theodore Lowi labeled "genuine conservatism," mobilized on a national scale. See chap. 1.

3. A subgroup analysis was done as well, but results are not discussed here because of the scope of the chapter. For an earlier subgroup analysis (1972–1984), see Michael Minkenberg, *Neokonservatismus und Neue Rechte in den USA* (Baden-Baden: Nomos, 1990), chap. 5.

4. The coding of the variables and the construction of subgroups follows a procedure developed in an earlier analysis; see Minkenberg, *Neokonservatismus und Neue Rechte,* chap. 5 and app. See also Michael Minkenberg, "Neoconservatism and the American Voter," *Amerikastudien/American Studies* 36 (1992): 407ff. In deviation from those procedures, the protest generation here is defined as those born between 1945 and 1960, the postprotest generation as those born after 1960. In addition, fundamentalists are those who identify themselves as fundamentalist in religious matters and are white and Protestant.

5. See V. O. Key Jr., "A Theory of Critical Elections," *Journal of Politics* 17 (Feb.

1955): 3–18; Walter Dean Burnham, "Party Systems and the Political Process," in W. N. Chambers and W. D. Burnham, eds., *The American Party Systems* (New York: Oxford University Press, 1967), 277–307.

6. Walter D. Burnham, "Critical Realignment: Dead or Alive?" in Shafer, *The End of Realignment*, 125. See also chap. 5.

7. There is almost unanimous agreement about the fact, if not about the nature, of the decline of the American parties; *pars pro toto* see Martin Wattenberg, *The Decline of American Political Parties* (Cambridge: Harvard University Press, 1990).

8. See Arthur M. Schlesinger Jr., *The Cycles of American History* (Boston: Houghton Mifflin Co. 1986). For the concept of old politics and new politics, see Warren Miller and Teresa Levitin, *Leadership and Change: Presidential Elections 1952–1976* (Cambridge: Winthrop, 1976); Samuel Barnes et al., *Political Action* (London: Sage Publications, 1979); Russell Dalton, *Citizen Politics in Western Democracies* (Chatham, N.J.: Chatham House Publishers, 1988).

9. See Seymour M. Lipset and Stein Rokkan, "Cleavage Structures, Party Systems, and Voter Alignments," in S. M. Lipset and S. Rokkan, eds., *Party Systems and Voter Alignments* (New York: Free Press, 1967), 1–64.

10. James Sundquist, *Dynamics of the Party System: Alignment and Realignment of the Political Parties in the United States*, rev. ed. (Washington, D.C.: Brookings Institution, 1983), 14. See also John Petrocik, *Party Coalitions* (Chicago: University of Chicago Press, 1981); Richard G. Niemi and Herbert F. Weisberg, eds., *Controversies in Voting Behavior*, 3d ed. (Washington, D.C.: Congressional Quarterly Press, 1993), 326.

11. See Paul A. Beck, "A Socialization Theory of Partisan Realignment," in Richard G. Niemi and Herbert F. Weisberg, eds., *Controversies in American Voting Behavior* (San Francisco: Freeman & Co., 1976), 396–411; Paul R. Abramson, "Generational Change and the Decline of Party Identification in America, 1952–1974," *American Political Science Review* 70 (1976): 469–78.

12. See Ronald Inglehart, *The Silent Revolution* (Princeton: Princeton University Press, 1978); Inglehart, *Culture Shift* (Princeton: Princeton University Press, 1990).

13. See Dalton, *Citizen Politics*, 82, 133f.; Miller and Levitin, *Leadership and Change*, chap. 2; Minkenberg, *Neokonservatismus und Neue Rechte*, 30–44.

14. See Miller and Levitin, *Leadership and Change*, chaps. 5, 6.

15. See Inglehart, *Culture Shift*, 260.

16. See Ferdinand Müller-Rommel, ed., *New Politics in Western Europe: The Rise and Successes of Green Parties and Alternative Lists* (Boulder, Colo.: Westview Press, 1989).

17. See Benjamin Ginsberg and Martin Shefter, "The New Politics and the Reconstituted Right," in Michael Nelson, ed., *The Elections of 1984* (Washington, D.C.: Congressional Quarterly Press, 1985), 3–21; Minkenberg, "Neoconservatism and the American Voter," 393–97.

18. Karl Mannheim suggests that conservative and progressive thought were established as the two socially based and mutually related *Weltanschauungen* in the modern world as a result of the differentiation of the traditional feudal order into diverse classes, interests, and ideologies, and the emergence of bourgeois society. Only this challenge to the established order and its hitherto unquestioned underlying norms and beliefs could bring about a "conservative" consciousness that "discovered" its interests in defending or even restoring these norms and the order, that is, which transformed them from an unpolitical cosmos of eternal values and institutions into objects of political conflict. See Karl Mannheim, "Das konservative Denken," *Archiv für Sozialwissenschaft und Sozialpolitik* 57 (1927): 68–142, 470–95.

19. See Norman Nie et al., *The Changing American Voter* (Cambridge: Harvard University Press, 1979), 143, 245.

20. See Richard Scammon and Ben J. Wattenberg, *The Real Majority* (New York: Coward-McCann, 1970); Miller and Levitin, *Leadership and Change,* chap. 3.

21. See Michael Harrington, *The Twilight of Capitalism* (New York: Simon & Schuster, 1976); Peter Steinfels, *The Neoconservatives* (New York: Simon & Schuster, 1979).

22. See Minkenberg, *Neokonservatismus und Neue Rechte,* chap. 4; Matthew Moen, *The Transformation of the Christian Right* (Tuscaloosa: University of Alabama Press, 1992), 7, 23f.

23. See Minkenberg, *Neokonservatismus und Neue Rechte,* chap. 4.

24. See Minkenberg, "Neoconservatism and the American Voter," 397–401.

25. Inglehart, *Culture Shift,* chap. 6; Dieter Fuchs and Hans-Dieter Klingemann, "The Left-Right Schema," in M. Kent Jennings et al., eds., *Continuities in Political Action* (Berlin: de Gruyter, 1990), 203–34. See also Byron Shafer, "The Notion of an Electoral Order: The Structure of Electoral Politics at the Accession of George Bush," in Shafer, *The End of Realignment,* 37f., 59f.

26. See Nie et al., *The Changing American Voter,* 112; Hans-Dieter Klingemann, "Measuring Ideological Conceptualizations," in S. Barnes et al., *Political Action,* 225.

27. Miller and Levitin, *Leadership and Change,* 174.

28. See John P. Robinson and John A. Fleishman, "Ideological Trends in American Public Opinion," *Annals of the Academy of Political and Social Science* 472 (1984): 53.

29. Ibid.; see Klingemann, "Measuring Ideological Conceptualizations," 219–22; Pamela J. Conover and Stanley Feldman, "The Origins and Meaning of Liberal/Conservative Self-Identification," *American Journal of Political Science* 25 (1981): 617–45; Jean A. Laponce, *Left and Right: The Topography of Political Perceptions* (Toronto: University of Toronto Press, 1981).

30. See Lloyd A. Free and Hadley Cantril, *The Political Beliefs of Americans* (New York: Simon & Schuster, 1967).

31. See William G. Mayer, *The Changing American Mind: How and Why American Public Opinion Changed between 1960 and 1988* (Ann Arbor: University of Michigan Press, 1992), 325. See also Alan S. Miller, "Are Self-Proclaimed Conservatives Really Conservative? Trends in Attitudes and Self-Identification among the Young," *Social Forces* 71 (Sept. 1992): 196.

32. The GSS contain no data for the years 1979 and 1981; the data analysis for this essay was completed before any post-1991 data were available.

33. See Benjamin Page and Robert Y. Shapiro, *The Rational Public: Fifty Years of Trends in Americans' Policy Preferences* (Chicago: University of Chicago Press, 1992), 127; for an international comparison of welfare state support patterns, see Robert Y. Shapiro and John T. Young, "Public Opinion and the Welfare State: The United States in Comparative Perspective," *Political Science Quarterly* 104, no. 1 (1989): 58–89.

34. See Fay Lomax Cook and Edith Barrett, *Support for the American Welfare State: The Views of Congress and the Public* (New York: Columbia University Press, 1992), 25–27, 61–63.

35. Fay Lomax Cook, *Who Should Be Helped? Public Support for Social Services* (Beverly Hills, Calif.: Sage Publications, 1979).

36. Cook and Barrett, *Support for the American Welfare State,* chap. 4.

37. See Page and Shapiro, *The Rational Public,* 126; Herbert McCloskey and John Zaller, *The American Ethos: Public Attitudes toward Capitalism and Democracy* (Cambridge: Harvard University Press, 1984), 280–84.

38. See Cook and Barrett, *Support for the American Welfare State*, chap. 7.

39. Page and Shapiro, *The Rational Public*, 94.

40. Tom W. Smith, "Liberal and Conservative Trends in the United States since World War II," *Public Opinion Quarterly* 54 (Winter 1990): 490, where race/ethnicity and feminism range very high on a liberal trend score; see also Mayer, *The Changing American Mind*, 23, 39; Page and Shapiro, *The Rational Public*, 68–77, 100f. For a discussion of the ambiguity of trends that are held to document a decline in racism, see Howard Schuman, Charlotte Steeh, and Lawrence Bobo, *Racial Attitudes in America: Trends and Interpretations* (Cambridge: Harvard University Press, 1985).

41. See Smith, "Liberal and Conservative Trends," 490; Page and Shapiro, *The Rational Public*, 110.

42. See Malcom L. Goggin, "Understanding the New Politics of Abortion: A Framework and Agenda for Research," *American Politics Quarterly* (Jan. 1993): 4–30.

43. See Barbara Hinkson Craig and David M. O'Brien, *Abortion and American Politics* (Chatham, N.J.: Chatham House, 1993), chap. 7.

44. See Page and Shapiro, *The Rational Public*, 111–15.

45. See Tom W. Smith, "Report: The Sexual Revolution?" *Public Opinion Quarterly* 54 (Fall 1990): 415–35; Mayer, *The Changing American Mind*, 36–38. Of course, these figures do not cover actual changes in *behavior*. But they indicate what Americans think is right or wrong, and at least in this sense there was no "revolution."

46. See Frank L. Klingberg, "Cyclical Trends in American Foreign Policy Moods and Their Policy Implications," in Charles W. Kegley Jr. and Patrick J. McGrowan, eds., *Challenge to America: United States Foreign Policy in the 1980s* (Beverly Hills: Sage Publications, 1979), 37–55; Arthur M. Schlesinger Jr., "Foreign Policy and the American Character," *Foreign Affairs* 62 (1983): 1–16.

47. See for example, Ole R. Holsti and James N. Rosenau, *American Leadership in World Affairs: Vietnam and the Breakdown of Consensus* (London: Allen & Unwin, 1984); Eugene Wittkopf and Michael A. Maggiotto, "Elites and Masses: A Comparative Analysis of Attitudes toward America's World Role," *Journal of Politics* 45 (1983): 307f.; Michael Mandelbaum and William Schneider, "The New Internationalisms," in Kenneth Oye et al., eds., *Eagle Entangled* (New York: Longmans, 1979); Page and Shapiro, *The Rational Public*, chap. 6; for a critique see Matthew S. Hirshberg, *Perpetuating Patriotic Perceptions: The Cognitive Function of the Cold War* (Westport, Conn.: Praeger, 1993), 70–85.

48. See Mandelbaum and Schneider, "The New Internationalisms," 65.

49. Kurt L. Shell, *Der amerikanische Konservatismus* (Stuttgart: Kohlhammer, 1986), 76; see also Minkenberg, *Neokonservatismus und Neue Rechte*, 66–74.

50. Hirshberg, *Perpetuating Patriotic Perceptions*, 41–44.

51. See Hirshberg, *Perpetuating Patriotic Perceptions*, 90; Alvin Richman, "The Polls: Changing American Attitudes toward the Soviet Union," *Public Opinion Quarterly* 55 (Spring 1991): 135–48.

52. See Bruce Russett, "Doves, Hawks, and U.S. Public Opinion," *Political Science Quarterly* 105 (1990–91): 535–38; Richman, "The Polls," 138f.; Page and Shapiro, *The Rational Public*, 271–75.

53. See Hirshberg, *Perpetuating Patriotic Perceptions*, 94f.

54. See, for example, William J. Wilson, *The Declining Significance of Race*, 2d ed. (Chicago: University of Chicago Press, 1980), 32–36.

55. See Manning Marable, *Black American Politics: From the Washington Marches to Jesse Jackson* (London: Verso, 1985), 34f.

56. See Page and Shapiro, *The Rational Public*, 291, where ten subgroups are defined in terms of largely overlapping characteristics.

57. See B. Farah, M. K. Jennings, and W. E. Miller, "Reports to Respondents: The 1980 Convention Delegate Study," in James L. Lengle and Byron E. Shafer, eds., *Presidential Politics* (New York: St. Martin's Press, 1983), 272f.; see also Ginsberg and Shefter, "New Politics and the Reconstructed Right," 10–17; Warren E. Miller, *Without Consent: Mass-Elite Linkages in Presidential Politics* (Lexington: University Press of Kentucky, 1988).

58. See Steven Bruce, *The Rise and Fall of the New Christian Right* (Oxford: Clarendon Press, 1988), 192.

59. See Moen, *The Transformation of the Christian Right*, 33–64, 130; see also Allen D. Hertzke, *Echoes of Discontent: Jesse Jackson, Pat Robertson, and the Resurgence of Populism* (Washington, D.C.: Congressional Quarterly Press, 1993), chaps. 5, 6.

60. See *New York Times*, Nov. 21, 1992: see also Moen, *The Transformation of the Christian Right*, 107–10.

61. See Gerald Pomper, "The Presidential Nomination," in Pomper, ed., *The Election of 1988* (Chatham, N.J.: Chatham House, 1989), 65; Ronald D. Elving, "GOP Platform: Amplifying the Themes of 1984," *Congressional Quarterly Weekly Report* 46 (Aug. 20, 1988): 2316–17.

62. See *New York Times*, Dec. 11, 1991; Jan. 15, 1992; Mar. 8, 1992; *Congressional Quarterly Weekly Report*, suppl. to 50, no. 32 (Aug. 8, 1992): 31.

63. See Garry Wills, "The Born-Again Republicans," *New York Review of Books* 39 (Sept. 24, 1992), 9–14; Ross Baker, "Sorting Out and Suiting Up: The Presidential Nominations," in Gerald Pomper, ed., *The Election of 1992* (Chatham, N.J.: Chatham House, 1993), 63–68.

64. Garry Wills remarks that "the term 'religious pluralism' was removed from the platform as offensive to the religious right." See Wills, "Sorting Out," 14. See also Beth Donovan, "Abortion: Will the Big Tent Hold All?" *Congressional Quarterly Weekly Report*, suppl. to 50, no. 32 (Aug. 8, 1992): 17–19; George Hager, "Party Avoids Abortion Dispute as Delegates Opt for Harmony," *Congressional Quarterly Weekly Report* 50 (Aug. 22, 1992): 2519–20.

65. See Miller, *Without Consent*, chaps. 3, 5.

66. Theodore J. Lowi, "An Aligning Election, a Presidential Plebiscite," in Nelson, *The Elections of 1984*, 296.

67. See Nie et al., *The Changing American Voter*, 49; Sundquist, *The Dynamics of the Party System*, 396; Wattenberg, *The Decline of American Political Parties*, 36–49.

68. See Walter Dean Burnham, *Critical Elections and the Mainsprings of American Politics* (New York: Norton, 1970); see also Nie et al., *The Changing American Voter*, 164–73.

69. See Miller and Levitin *Leadership and Change;* Barnes et al., *Political Action;* Claus Offe, "New Social Movements: Challenging the Boundaries of Institutional Politics," *Social Research* 52 (Winter 1985): 817–68.

70. See Nie et al., *The Changing American Voter*, 217–34; Sundquist, *The Dynamics of the Party System*, 403–08; Petrocik, *Party Coalitions*, chap. 9.

71. For some details of the 1994 elections, see chap. 1.

72. See Gerald Pomper, "The Presidential Election," in Pomper, *The Election of 1992*, 147; see also Kathleen Frankovic, "Public Opinion in the 1992 Campaign," in ibid., 124f.

73. See Everett C. Ladd, "The 1992 Vote for President Clinton: Another Brittle

Mandate?" *Political Science Quarterly* 108, no. 1, (1993): 22f. Exit polls showed that Perot voters would have split their presidential vote evenly between Bush and Clinton if Perot had not run for office, but in the congressional vote they leaned more toward the Republicans than the Democrats; see e.g., "Portrait of the Electorate," *New York Times*, Nov. 5, 1992.

74. See Ladd, "The 1992 Vote for President Clinton."

75. Data not shown in table 7.5; see *New York Times*, Nov. 13, 1994.

76. See Gary Jacobson, "Congress: Unusual Year, Unusual Elections," in Michael Nelson, ed. *The Elections of 1992* (Washington, D.C.: Congressional Quarterly Press, 1993), 153–82.

77. See also Pomper, "The Presidential Election," 135–40; Paul J. Quirk and Jon K. Dalager, "The Election: A 'New Democrat' and a New Kind of Presidential Campaign," in Nelson, *Elections of 1992*, 75–83.

78. See Bruce Nesmith, *The New Republican Coalition: The Reagan Campaigns and White Evangelicals* (New York: Peter Lang, 1994), esp. chaps. 6, 9.

79. See Corwin Smidt, "Evangelical Voting Patterns, 1976–1988," in Michael Cromartie, ed., *No Longer Exiles: The Religious New Right in American Politics* (Washington, D.C.: Ethics and Public Policy Center, 1993), 97–104.

80. See John F. Persinos, "Has the Christian Right Taken Over the Republican Party?" *Campaigns and Elections*, Sept. 1994, 21–29. In this survey "dominant" was defined as the Christian right having a working majority on major issues in GOP state party organizations, while "substantial" influence means that their strength is above 25% of the organization but short of a majority.

81. See John C. Green et al., "The Christian Right and the 1994 Elections," *PS: Political Science and Politics* 28 (Mar. 1995): 5–23.

82. See Richard E. Cohen, "No More Nice Guys," *National Journal*, Nov. 12, 1994, 2634–47.

83. Quotations are from House Republican Conference, *Contract with America* (Washington, D.C., 1994). For an analysis of the contract, see James Fallows, "The Republican Promise," *New York Review of Books*, Jan. 12, 1995, 3–6.

84. See "Poll Finds Public Doubts Key Parts of G.O.P.'s Agenda," *New York Times*, Feb. 28, 1995: "A New 'Contract with America'?" *Public Perspective* 6 (Feb.–Mar. 1995): 28f.

85. See William Schneider, "Clinton: The Reason Why," *National Journal*, Nov. 12, 1994, 2630–33.

86. See, e.g., James A. Stimson, *Public Opinion in America: Moods, Cycles, and Swings* (Boulder, Colo.: Westview Press, 1991); see also Schlesinger, *The Cycles of American History*, 47, who predicted a new era beginning around 1990.

87. See also Mayer, *The Changing American Mind*, chap. 12.

88. See, for example, William Schneider, "The November 6 Vote for President: What Did It Mean?" in Austin Ranney, ed., *The American Elections of 1984* (Washington, D.C.: AEI Press, 1985), 230–36.

89. See also James L. Guth, in Cromartie, *No Longer Exiles*, 118.

EIGHT

THE AMERICAN PARTIES AFTER
THE COLD WAR

A Comparative Perspective

PETER LÖSCHE

Ever since the Bolshevik Revolution in 1917, but especially after the end of World War II and during the cold war, anticommunism has dominated not only American foreign policy but also the competition and rivalry between the two major American parties, the Democrats and the Republicans. When foreign policy was discussed in election campaigns, the emphasis was frequently on how to react to the communist challenge or how its threat could be effectively countered. In 1952, for example, the Republicans' slogan was "Korea, Communism, and Corruption." In 1960 the Democrats introduced the (alleged) missile gap. In 1976, Gerald Ford provoked a heated discussion over whether Poland was a free nation, because of a verbal blunder during a campaign debate. The Strategic Defense Initiative and the role of the contras in Nicaragua fueled campaigns in the eighties.[1] At this stage anticommunism functioned as a catalyst in various ways: First, it helped to integrate parties at the core, creating a sense of unity and identity while simultaneously providing definite borders. Second, it offered a general consensus for all Americans in confronting the Soviet Union.

The ideological borders and differences between the parties and within the parties themselves have begun to dissolve since the end of the cold war. Concerning the increasingly obsolete conflict between East and West, a differentiation between "hawks" and "doves," at least, has been abandoned. The collapse of the "evil empire" has released the centrifugal forces of American single-issue politics, the politics of particular interests and cultural diversity, and has increasingly weakened the centripetal powers of anticommunism. The demise of the communist threat has encouraged multiple factions and tendencies within the parties to define their respective positions more aggressively. Suddenly neoisolationists emerge, who stand in opposition to the new internationalists, who stand divided from the economic nationalists, who, in turn, stand in contrast to the protectionists. Domestic policy and social and economic questions have advanced into the central focus of American politics, thereby pushing aside issues of foreign policy and national security.

How will American parties and the entire political system generally function and operate without the formerly dominating principle of anti-communism?[2] The most obvious changes can be found in foreign and defense policies, but they also exist in political campaigns where foreign policy and national defense are usually addressed. Alterations in the political institutions (including the parties) themselves, as well as in the actual process of decision making, tend toward long-term modification. An instant, direct influence of the end of the cold war on the organization of parties, on parties in Congress, or in government in general, cannot be observed. But an incipient change of focus from foreign and defense policy to domestic issues can be recognized in electoral behavior, in the "party in the electorate." This partially contributed to Bill Clinton's victory in 1992.

The emphasis of this chapter is thus generally placed on recent developments in American parties and the party system. Yet I shall refrain from primarily or systematically discussing such traditional questions as whether American parties have reached their final days, as in David Broder's words, "the party is over";[3] whether American parties have been suffering erosion over the past two decades or not; whether parties have an essential role in the policy outcome at all. Attempting to take a comparative approach, I would much rather bring new light to these old questions and their covert theses.

My hypothesis claims that over the past two decades an "Americanization" of German parties as well as a "Germanization"[4] of American parties has taken place. This recent form of convergence, affecting diverse aspects of the parties including their general appearance, is rooted in the social and political changes that have taken place in both countries. What is actually occurring is an approach by American parties toward a theoretical model of German parties derived from the history and particularly the historiography of German parties (especially the work of Robert Michels),[5] as well as from the example of contemporary (so-called) people's parties. This model does not necessarily comply with historical or contemporary reality, but rather, it complies with the image of German parties that is popular even with German and American historians and social scientists.

The components of this model are:

1. There is a firm, formalized party membership that is defined by the requirement of regular membership fees as well as each member's basic affiliation with the party's program. Violations of the program potentially result in a member's expulsion.

2. Voluntary party officials serve the party's cause by being responsible for specific, clearly defined tasks.

3. The party represents a relatively stringent hierarchic organization with an executive committee at the top, which is supported by party officials and party bureaucrats.

4. Candidates for legislative bodies and other public offices are nominated "by the party," that is, by the members, responsible officials, or peers.

5. The party's organization and its campaigns are financed by membership fees, but also by donations and federal funding.

6. Although most contemporary critics observe that party platforms are becoming increasingly diversified and tentative, the concept of an original ideological program integrating the party from the inside and lending it a profile toward the outside still survives today. There may be factions and subgroups within the party; nonetheless, all members are clearly affiliated with the same program. Party discipline maintains unity toward the outside; cohesion within the party solidifies party members in the parliaments.

7. Historically, parties were rooted in specific social and moral strata, so-called milieus.

Inversely, German parties are approaching a theoretical model of American parties that also bears historical and contemporary imprints. This model found specific expression in the report of the Committee on Political Parties of the American Political Science Association entitled "Toward a More Responsible Two-Party System," published in 1950.[6] According to this concept, the following elements characterize American parties:

1. Party membership is neither formalized nor institutionalized. A Democrat or Republican is recognized as such when registering to vote in primaries, or simply by verbal allegiance.

2. Although party activists exist, they are comparable to German party officials on the local level, at best.

3. In organization, the two great parties represent little more than a loose union of local, district, or state party organizations. An exception is the so-called party machine, local party organizations fueled by patronage. The national party consists of the respective national committees of Democrats and Republicans, which cannot be compared to the party executive committees of German parties on the basis of large membership numbers (several hundred).

4. Candidates who run for public office or Congress under the label of Democrat or Republican are frequently not nominated "by the party," or by party activists, but by politically motivated and inter-

ested voters in primaries or caucuses. Consequently, American parties are not necessarily "responsible" for "their" candidates.

5. Campaigns and party organization, as far as the latter exists, are financed through private donations and the personal resources of the candidates, but not through membership fees (simply because party membership in the German sense does not exist).

6. The heterogeneous, even diffuse nature of American parties is illustrated by the lack of a real party program in the case of both Republicans and Democrats. The campaign platforms, put together by the national conventions that nominate the respective presidential candidates every four years, are the result of extensive negotiations between the various groups, subgroups, and factions. For the politics and policies of the president, the senators, or representatives, the platform remains without obligations.

7. American social history has been shaped by mobile middle classes, so that parties reflect this upward or downward mobility and do not—as is the case with German parties—represent specific social and moral strata, such as labor.

My thesis states that, in comparison, American parties are more densely organized, have a more cohesive ideology, and by and large have a more profound political role than their image would suggest. German parties, on the other hand, are more decentralized and more loosely organized as well as more diverse in program and ideology than assumed by the Michels tradition, which still dominates political science interpretations.

It is obvious that *Partei* does not indicate the same as *party*. These terms should rather be viewed in their respective historical, cultural, and political contexts. For pragmatic reasons we may initially simplify the comparison by joining the triple-tiered American meaning, namely (1) party organization, (2) party in political institutions especially in Congress, and (3) party as an electoral coalition. The following discussion will focus on the party as an organization.

Party Organization

Fragmentation, decentralization, segmentation, functional differentiation, and division of work all characterize the organizational and political reality of today's German people's parties. The social diversity of their voters and members is demonstrated in various interest groups that have been institutionalized as *Arbeitsgemeinschaften* within the Social Democratic Party (SPD) and *Vereinigungen* within the Christian Democratic Party (CDU). There are groups of women, seniors, young party members (namely the Young Socialist Democrats and the Young Christian Democrats), middle-class entrepreneurs, unionized employees, local and district politicians, lawyers, teachers, and so on. Each of these intraparty interest groups assumes particular tasks within the party while simultaneously addressing the corresponding target groups outside the party. In this they are comparable to the caucuses of the Democratic Party in the United States. The party organization itself is highly decentralized, fragmented, and flexible: the local and regional associations, town associations, and districts in the SPD enjoy considerable autonomy. The same is valid for the medium level, the larger districts, and the state parties. The executive committee, together with the executive board of the party and the party convention, do not stand at the top of a pyramid hierarchy but largely act independently. Aside from the intraparty interest groups of the SPD and the CDU, and the traditional internal factions (left-wing, right-wing, center), single-issue groups form spontaneously. Furthermore, machines of patronage are found in towns and districts where a certain party has been firmly established over decades. All of these intraparty actors cooperate and compete, furthering their candidates and political causes; the forming of coalitions dominates the scene as much among American parties as among German people's parties. The great American parties consist of loosely connected fragments; they represent something like "loosely coupled anarchies."[7] The term *anarchy*, of course, is not used in the prejudiced context of German beer-drinking small talk, where *anarchy* finds its definition in bearded, bomb-toting terrorists. I use the term rather to express an organizational principle that is valid for both American and German parties today, a federation of federations of federations of local organizations.

Summarizing the research of recent years, Leon Epstein notes that, among American parties, organizational structures not only continue to exist but also grow increasingly stronger.[8] This is supposedly especially true of the national parties. According to Epstein, the Democratic National Committee and the Republican National Committee represent highly complex and professional organizations. The Republicans employed 600 regular full-time officers, the Democrats 260.[9] The six national party committees dramatically expanded in the 1970s and 1980s, developing expensive electronic and technological advertising and campaigning methods. A. James Reichley even indicates that because the national party organization is so centralized and ruled by bureaucracy, the parties have grown increasing autonomous and distant from voters.[10] Secondary literature provides the concurring opinion that individual state party organizations have generally gained in strength recently, even if there are still weak organizations in California and New York.[11] And even though political scientists agree that in the twentieth century local party organizations have weakened along with the disintegration of party machines, they still have not lost much power in organizational capabilities over the past two decades.[12] In most states, local party associations are well organized, although there are significant differences between individual states.

Most important to the changes in the American party system, especially concerning the development in organization, is the nationwide establishment of both parties today. The Democrats have lost their former monopoly over the South, which once led political scientists to the thesis that this region was ruled, as was the Eastern bloc, by a single-party system. In the mid-nineties the Republicans have become the majority party in the South.

Without a doubt, American parties have experienced something of an organizational renaissance over the past two decades. Along this line of organizational reform and rejuvenation, the dissolution of the caucuses and the intraparty interest groups within the Democratic Party came about in the mid-eighties. Still, these groups continue to exist informally.

Despite these organizational accomplishments, American parties are still fragmented, segmented, and decentralized. Thus the concept of a "loosely coupled anarchy" applies to both the major German and American parties, although the level of fragmentation differs between parties, states, and the two nations. The anecdote originally pertaining to the Democrats is now transferrable to the Republicans, the Social Democrats, and the Christian Democrats: "Boy, the Democratic Party is in a pathetic condition!" "How pathetic?" "Well, it's so miserable that the party has more factions and wings than candidates."[13]

Primaries and Plebiscites

For approximately five years there has been lively discussion among German parties, including lawyers and political scientists, about introducing direct democratic elements into the process of opinion formation in the inner parties. The rationale behind this debate is simple. This method would counter the increasing apathy among party members and, especially, exercise a positive influence regarding the German public's current exhaustion and disillusionment with politics. Under the former party chairman Björn Engholm, the project group SPD 2000 suggested that nonmembers be included "more vigorously" in party activities and that members be offered more opportunities for collaboration and participation. In connection with this, much thought has been given to petitions and referenda among party members, as well as the formal possibility of a "side entrance" for nonmembers. The latter could be accomplished if each party level's executive board had the right to suggest experts or representatives of certain social groups for two of the first ten slots in the district and state elections of the SPD.[14] In June 1993, Rudolf Scharping was thus elected, de facto by primary vote, formally with a kind of "consultation" of members. The effect on inner party mobilization was surprisingly high, as was indicated by the participation of 56 percent of members. The SPD's convention in Wiesbaden in November 1993 altered the party's statutes, allowing petitions, members' votes (with the exception of questions concerning the finance statute and membership fees), and the nomination of the party's candidate for chancellor.[15] Concerning this aspect, one decisive difference from the situation in the United States is that the nomination of candidates remains in the hands of "the party," specifically, in the hands of party members or party conventions. The CDU and smaller parties have admitted being impressed by the success of this election of the SPD chairmanship and the change of statutes, but they have not yet implemented similar measures themselves.

The possible and (particularly undesirable) consequences that the introduction of direct democratic elements could bring into the organization of German parties have hardly been overtly considered. Elections of personnel by all members creates an advantage for those candidates with sufficient financial resources for campaigning throughout the entire party.[16] In this scenario, candidates might build their personal campaign organizations—further contributing to fragmentation and segmentation of the major German parties. And this is exactly what took place in the United States during the seventies. Here is another parallel for an Americanization of German parties. The Democratic Party may serve as a cautionary example: during the seventies, primaries for nominating the presidential candidate were introduced into so many states that the party organization not only continued to break into fragments; in addition, "the party" and the party activists were no longer responsible for the candidate nominated under their very own party's label. The nomination and election of Jimmy Carter is a prime example of this predicament. Primaries in the United States, which were introduced in the early twentieth century in order to avoid manipulation and corruption in the nomination of candidates, eventually led to a weakening of the parties during the seventies.[17]

Consequently, it is not surprising that all attempts at party reform made in the United States since 1976–1977 (especially among the Democrats) have been aimed at reducing the number and importance of primaries and giving party activists and party members in legislatures greater influence in the nominating process. In other words, attempts are being made to return the process of nomination to "the party"—a kind of Germanization of American parties is taking place.

Party and Campaign Financing

The methods of party and campaign financing in the United States and the Federal Republic of Germany differ in principle, as well as in various small details. In the United States a system centered on candidates prevails in which campaigns and party organizations are financed almost exclusively by private donations. Candidates are basically responsible for financing their own campaigns. By contrast, campaigns in Germany are financed almost exclusively by the party and not the candidates themselves. The parties thrive on membership fees, private donations, and public funding. At the heart of the matter lies a mixed system of party and campaign financing.

Despite these considerable differences between the United States and Germany concerning "political money," one might speak—if only cautiously—of a Germanization on the American side. It is not only the candidates who manage to elicit donations, but also the six national party committees. This has led a number of political scientists to postulate the thesis that national parties in the United States represent little more than gigantic agencies for the collection of donations. What is being ignored is that national parties support their candidates financially as well as with expertise (opinion polls, development of campaign strategies, and financial consultation). This is particularly valid for candidates running in marginal districts. During elections for Congress in recent years, the share of campaign contributions to candidates coming from the national parties was between 15 and 20 percent. U.S. candidates are therefore more obliged to their parties today than they were fifteen or twenty years ago. In addition, national parties have increasingly injected themselves into the recruitment of qualified candidates.

Today, the four congressional campaign committees "are sophisticated operations employing skilled professionals who not only help incumbents but also recruit newcomers and help them build campaign organizations." In 1994 party leaders in the Senate as well as in the House used the committees "as tools for partisan cohesion."[18] That same year the Republican National Committee directed about $13 million to state parties in an elaborate voter identification and get-out-the-vote drive, four times the amount of money spent in 1990. Also in 1994 the Democratic National Committee directed $8 million to state parties for coordinated campaign activities aimed at getting Democratic voters to the polls.[19] In other words: American parties play an essential role in organizing and financing campaigns. In addition, public funding is made available in sixteen states during elections for state offices (governor, state legislature). Some of these states give public funds to the parties, thus lending them influence and power of sanction over their candidates. It remains to be seen whether, with the impending reform of the

Federal Election Campaign Act, public funding will be adopted to elect members of Congress, and whether parties will be strengthened by this. The current tendencies are clear: empowerment of parties and increased public funding of campaigns, a development that, again, may be placed in the category of Germanization.[20]

On the German side, a development in party and campaign financing that could be regarded as Americanization is definitely visible. In this context, three details are noteworthy:

1. There are indicators that, especially considering the recently more strictly enforced obligation to disclose sources of donations to the parties, private donations are more frequently going to candidates personally (and not to the parties).

2. As a result of the decision of the Constitutional Supreme Court in April 1992 and the amendment of the Law on Political Parties in November 1993, public funding for parties has been limited, so that they will be forced to rely more heavily on the income from membership fees and donations.

3. The concept of "matching" has been adopted from the American practice of campaign financing, that is, the addition of public funding to private sources. Essentially, parties will receive fifty pfennigs of federal funding for every mark they earn from membership fees and donations.

Campaign Strategies

Modern campaign strategies were introduced in Germany under the label of Americanization. Quite a variety of elements were perceived as American imports: the use of marketing strategies in campaigns, opinion polls, broadcasting campaign spots on TV that are produced according to American models, the personalization of campaigns, and the adoption of controversial policy issues to mobilize voters and create electoral coalitions.

In this context organizational developments in German parties should be mentioned. The description above—"loosely coupled anarchies"—encompasses disengagement and larger independence of the federal parties from the state and local party organizations. But two important tasks have remained for the national committees of the parties: (1) intraparty communication and, as far as possible, internal integration; and (2) preparation and running of campaigns. To put it bluntly, the federal parties function as service organizations for running campaigns—and in that respect are comparable to the national committees of American parties.

The inverse argument that a Germanization of campaigns has begun on the American side can also be made. The indicators are increased party identification and greater significance of the content of party platforms. Especially regarding marketing strategies, the parties and their platforms are an important factor. It was not a coincidence that the Republicans, led by their candidate Ronald Reagan in 1980, emphasized their slogan "Vote Republican for a Change." Through the example of the Reagan campaign, experts recognized that a clear ideology gave voters and candidates a sense and meaning they could relate to.[21]

Party Program and Campaign Platform

Americanization of German parties—during the Weimar Republic and in the years immediately following World War II—includes replacing originally consistent programs with partially contradicting and superficial campaign platforms. This development should not be exaggerated. Nonetheless, the programmatic profile of the SPD has become more diffused in order to combine and unite socially and politically more heterogeneous groups of voters to form electoral coalitions, while the CDU has lacked a coherent, distinct program from the very beginning. And the two great parties now refuse to assume a position on certain points of conflict, or they even contradict themselves in an attempt not to disappoint any potential groups of voters. This has led Otto Kirchheimer to pass the judgment that the people's parties—the catchall parties, as he calls them—would finally not differ one bit in ideology or program.[22] But this has not happened. Each of the two great parties maintained its own programmatic profile and is easily identified by voters as either left or right of the center: each has a clear reputation for being either the supporter of the "little man" and the welfare state or that of the entrepreneur and the market economy.

The same applies to American parties; their corresponding sociopolitical structures and different social roots are easily recognizable despite certain concurrences. Since the Reagan era, the ideological contours of Republicans and Democrats have become more defined, which has occasionally led to talk of increasing ideological polarization.

Although the major American and German parties originated from entirely different backgrounds and traditions, they resemble each other today in that they combine programmatic pluralism with a specific ideological profile.

Amateur Politicians

German and American parties also bear a growing resemblance in that their party activists are largely amateur politicians. They are not used to professional functionaries who come from specific social and moral strata or attempt to exercise power in party machines. The most distinct example of this change comes from the SPD: the traditional socialist fighter who wanted to form a new model of man and thereby realize socialism does not exist any more. Instead, a new generation of SPD party activists now subscribe to a popular "cult of affection." They are affected by the suffering in Third World countries, by pollution, and by ecological destruction. Or they belong to the "Toscana group," who wish to enjoy life and use the party as a means of self-realization and to meet people. Contrary to Max Weber's assumption, today's major American and German parties are not exclusively bent on attaining and exercising power; to a certain extent they represent a socially supportive organization. Amateur politicians have the opportunity of enjoying both the aspect of power and of socializing. Many amateur politicians frequently work on single-issue politics. For example, they may be interested in cleaning and renaturalizing a local river; or they may be involved in supporting construction plans for a new high school. It is not purely coincidental that the parties' locals are almost exclusively concentrating on local politics, that nearly autistic tendencies become visible in the lower divisions. Amateur politicians frequently combine their single-issue politics with moral rigidity, especially when the topic involves postmaterialist themes. Amateur politicians represent the new middle classes in professions: they are, for example, teachers, attorneys, social workers, and college professors.

Parliamentary Groups

When one compares the role of parties in the legislative and executive branches of government in the United States and Germany, the fundamental differences between the presidential and parliamentary governmental systems become evident. In the presidential system of the United States, there is, notoriously, no party discipline. The legislature and the head of the executive are separately elected by the people. Presidents (or governors in the states) must search for majorities in the legislature for the bills they wish to see passed. They are required to construct coalitions. The situation in Germany's parliamentary government is entirely different: the head of the executive is elected by the majority in the federal parliament. The majority in the parliament and the cabinet, together with the chancellor, form a semi-institutionalized majority stabilized by party cohesion. In other words, Germany has a party parliament whereas the United States maintains a coalition parliament.

To further verify our hypothesis that German and American parties are converging, I will pose the following question: Are there any indications that party cohesion is being weakened in Germany while cohesion of the "parties in parliament" is being strengthened in the United States? As a matter of fact, a number of symptoms do exist. It is an expression of variety and of inner heterogeneous ambiguities within the "loosely coupled anarchies" of the major German parties that party cohesion evidently has decreased in the federal and state parliaments. Several distinct examples may be named:

1. In spring 1993 the CDU/CSU members of the Bundestag rebelled against the cabinet's projected introduction of general toll fees on the autobahn. Although a final vote was never taken in parliament, the government's defeat in the parliamentary party reached public awareness.
2. During a Bundestag vote on limiting Article 16 of the constitution, which covers the rights and privileges of political asylum, the SPD simply split.
3. An increasing number of votes are being declared questions of conscience and have thereby become optional; party discipline is not enforced. Among these votes we find not only the question of abortion but also the question of whether God should be addressed in the preamble of a state's constitution (in this case, Lower Saxony's), or even questions pertaining to party finances.

Party cohesion has decreased especially because the actual party structure has changed through the addition of the five eastern states during the process of German reunification. Many representatives in the Bundestag and state diets from the East are still carried by the momentum of the people's movement and their individualism; as a result few of them agree with the principle of party cohesion, as can be seen in the example of the state of Sachsen-Anhalt.

Conversely, the cohesion of parties in the United States has grown in both houses of Congress and their committees. However, this cannot be strictly defined as party cohesion; rather, it is an advanced level of party unity. This is reached when, during a vote, the majority of representatives of one party stands opposed to the majority of representatives of another. In a normal parliamentary year that has not been characterized by political polarization, party unity would be achieved in one-third of the votes. In 1992 it was 62 percent of the roll call votes in the House of Representatives—an increase of 9 percent as compared to 1991 and the second highest figure since the *Congressional Quarterly* begun measuring party unity thirty-eight years earlier; only in 1987 was higher percentage counted.[23] The same tendency can be observed in the committees, where party affiliation is becoming more significant.[24] The conservative coalition in Congress seems to be vanishing simultaneously; this coalition in the House of Representatives and Senate always appeared whenever a majority of Republicans together with a majority of conservative Democrats from the South voted against a majority of liberal Democrats from the North. Along with the establishment of a nationwide two-party system, conservative Democrats in the South have been dislodged by moderate Democrats or conservative Republicans, just as liberal Republicans in the North have been replaced by liberal Democrats. Parties in Congress have gained in political homogeneity internally, while on the outside they differ more clearly from each other. This is another expression of what many authors have referred to as nationalization of American parties.[25] More recent developments fit our pattern of interpretation. Partisan polarization has dominated the second term of the 103rd Congress (1993–1994). Polarization was across the board, but it was especially dramatic on economic issues. And the change in party leaders of the 104th Congress mirrors the growing polarization in each chamber. Of the top five House Republican leaders, three were among the twenty-three members (all Republican) who had perfect conservative ratings in 1994, while the top two House Democrats were in the most liberal one-fourth of their party's ranks.[26] And Newt Gingrich, the new Speaker of the House, pursued a strategy of nationalizing the issues of the 1994 midterm elections through the Contract with America. The scale of change that Gingrich tries to promote is indicated by his call for a new model to replace the New Deal.[27]

Changes in House rules and procedures, adopted by the House on January 4, 1995, will make the House more open and accountable and will centralize power in the Speaker, thus strengthening party cohesion: there are fewer committees, term limits for committee chairmen, and fewer staff. "Committees will no longer be the power centers they were under the Democrats; seniority will count for little in a system of rotating chairmanships; and more power will be centralized in the hands" of House Speaker Newt Gingrich. James A. Thurber commented: "All of these are centralizing reforms. It is a major shift from the balkanized, decentralized subcommittee government we have had."[28]

Electoral Coalitions

In the social composition of the voters of the major parties in the United States and Germany, convergence becomes visible again. Or, more precisely, in this respect German parties have become more similar to American ones. According to the indicators usually employed in gathering electoral statistics—income, education, ethnicity, gender, religion, and also moral attitudes—Democratic and Republican voters and those of the SPD and CDU have all become more heterogenous. Again, this becomes very evident in the history of the SPD: in comparison to the community of solidarity, which represented social democracy in the Weimar Republic, even through the 1950s,[29] the social composition of voters, members, and also party activists has become more diversified. It is not the unionized, highly skilled worker who dominates the social structure any more; today there is a colorful mixture of blue-, gray-, and white-collar workers, of salaried workers, academics, social workers, entrepreneurs, and even a few farmers. In their campaigns the SPD and CDU, like the Republicans and Democrats, attempt to reach beyond the traditional social barriers of class, ethnicity, and religion. It is their aim to maximize votes, so the gap of cultural and political differences between many groups of voters will be bridged. Ironically, this enterprise of spreading out among the various groups of voters led to an overintegration in the eighties. Support for the parties began to erode. Party identification began to recede, and the share of floating voters and nonvoters began to rise. In Germany small parties started forming on the fringes, successfully challenging the great parties; and just like the Greens or the Republicans or the Deutsche Volksunion (DVU), they managed to clear the 5 percent hurdle in some state elections. In the United States independent candidates have led remarkably successful campaigns. It is interesting that in the United States and in Germany, the attraction of the great parties has diminished at a time when new social movements and citizens' initiatives have gained in popularity.[30]

Nonetheless, the great parties in Germany and the United States have not reached their final days (in Germany they still gain 60–70% of the votes, despite proportional representation, and they are not vanishing in the mist of vagueness). To be specific: even though the social composition of Republican, Democratic, SPD, and CDU voters has converged somewhat, their respective social profiles as individual parties still clearly differ. For example, the conservative parties are still typically chosen by the self-employed with higher incomes, whereas the liberal or social democratic parties are chosen by employees dependent on smaller salaries. For election campaigns and election outcomes, how a party presents itself to the outside is still relevant. And Martin Wattenberg has demonstrated that party cohesion is an important factor in winning presidential campaigns.[31]

Convergence of German and American Parties?

What are the exact reasons for the phenomena we have described as convergence of German and American parties? Initially convergence means nothing more than increasing similarity in organizational structure, content of programs, campaign strategies, party cohesion, and social structure of the voters of the great parties on both sides of the Atlantic—despite other differ-ences still remaining. Some of the reasons are naturally rooted in the re-spective national history and society; others are related to developments that can generally be found in so-called postindustrial service societies, which include:

- Erosion of traditional social and moral strata of milieus, such as the social democratic and Catholic strata in Germany;
- fundamental changes in employment structure: the decline of the secondary sector, the rise of the service and educational industries; the increasing specialization and differentiation in the employment market (there are now several gray-collars (professional groups) be-tween clerical and skilled workers and between white-collar and blue-collar workers);
- development of a complex and differentiated welfare state, by which class division and social contrast are mitigated;
- increasing secularization of society (at least in Germany, but the ten-dency may be found in the United States as well—despite periodi-cally recurring fundamentalist revivals), easing tension and conflict between religious groups;
- the educational revolution of the 1960s and 70s, which assisted up-ward mobility and—as sociologists argue today—contributed to ten-dencies toward the individualization of society and the pluralization of lifestyles;
- increasing role of mass media as a conveyor of political information; and
- social and cultural change that altered attitudes and behavior among voters (postmaterialism) and has also recently begun causing cit-izens to become estranged from political institutions, especially par-ties and interest groups.

When, in conclusion, we revisit the question of whether American parties have reached their final days ("Is the Party Over?"), whether Ameri-can parties are still capable of playing any significant role in the political scene at all, then one may take the comparative perspective and deduce the following tentative answer: Concerning organization, one may speak of a rehabilitation, if not of a renaissance of American parties. And at least in Congress and its committees, parties are acting more cohesively than in the past. As electoral coalitions, however, American parties have lost much of their power of integration. On the other hand, major German parties have become organizationally fragmented, decentralized, and pluralized over the past two decades. They have lost their attraction to voters, and even party cohesion does not appear to be observed as strictly as in the past. German parties have experienced these impairments at a time when American parties have generally gained in cohesion.

In other words, the political and organizational reality of German and American parties does not correspond with the image that can be found even among political scientists and which was elaborated above: Today, German and American parties have become more similar.

Nonetheless, I must caution anybody wishing to overexpand my thesis. The differences between American and German parties are still significant. They are particularly rooted in the fact that parties in parliamentary governmental systems entertain entirely different responsibilities from those in the presidential system of government in the United States. In the parliamentary governmental system, parties represent the cement that bonds the parliamentary majority and the executive branch to build a political unit and guarantee its functioning. Despite the (talk of) party exhaustion and disillusionment, major German parties are still fulfilling their traditional functions: articulation of interests, expression and definition of political direction, political mobilization, and selection of the political elite. In contrast to this, American parties primarily assume the function of selecting the elite ("a party is to elect") while other functions take second place. This is largely due to their marginal position in the presidential governmental system. Even in a phase when there is much complaint about the "crises of the parties" in Germany, the Federal Republic of Germany remains a party state; and the United States remains a "coalition-building state."[32]

But the end of the cold war should have a similar effect on German and American parties, namely the actualization of latent tendencies. Whereas in the past anticommunism integrated parties on the inside and the daily agenda was filled with questions concerning foreign policy and national defense, the collapse of the "evil empire" opened the way for the respective domestic, social, and economic problems to become of primary concern. These problems harbor serious issues of inner conflict. The centrifugal forces of German and American parties, specifically political pluralization, organizational fragmentation, and internal division, are likely to increase.

Notes

1. Norman J. Ornstein, "Foreign Policy and the 1992 Election," *Foreign Affairs* 71, no. 3 (1992): 3.

2. Norman J. Ornstein and Mark Schmitt, "Dateline Campaign '92: Cold War Politics," *Foreign Policy* no. 79 (1990): 169.

3. David Broder, *The Party's Over: The Failure of Politics in America* (New York: Harper and Row, 1971).

4. In this context some political scientists apply the term *Europeanization* of American parties. Since there is too broad a variety of programmatic, organizational,

and political characteristics to European parties to speak of one type of European party, I use the more precise term *Germanization*.

5. Robert Michels, *Zur Soziologie des Parteiwesens in der modernen Demokratie. Untersuchungen über die oligarchischen Tendenzen des Gruppenlebens* (Stuttgart: Kroener, 1925).

6. American Political Science Association, Committee on Political Parties: "Toward a More Responsible Two-Party System," *American Political Science Review* 44 (1950): suppl.

7. Peter Lösche und Franz Walter, *Die SPD. Klassenpartei, Volkspartei, Quotenpartei* (Darmstadt: Wissenschaftliche Buchgesellschaft, 1992), 173ff.; Peter Lösche, *Kleine Geschichte der deutschen Parteien* (Stuttgart: Kohlhammer, 1993), 184ff.; Peter Lösche, " 'Lose verkoppelte Anarchie.' Zur aktuellen Situation von Volksparteien am Beispiel der SPD," *Aus Politik und Zeitgeschichte* 43/93 (1993): 34ff.

8. Leon D. Epstein, "Overview of Research on Party Organizations," in Michael Margolis and John C. Green, eds., *Machine Politics, Sound Bites and Nostalgia: On Studying Political Parties* (Lanham, Md.: University Press of America, 1993), 5.

9. Paul S. Herrnson, "National Party Organizations and the Post Reform Congress," in Roger H. Davidson, ed., *The Postreform Congress* (New York: St. Martin's Press, 1992), 53.

10. A. James Reichley, *The Life of the Parties: A History of American Political Parties* (New York: Free Press, 1992), 380f.

11. Ibid., 394; Kay Lawson, "Questions Raised by Recent Attempts at Local Party Reform," in Margolis and Green, *Machine Politics*, 38.

12. Charles D. Hadley and Lewis Bowman, "The Organizational Strength of Political Parties at the County Level," and Michael Margolis, "The Importance of Local Party Organisation for Democratic Governance," both in Margolis and Green, *Machine Politics*, 20ff., 29ff.

13. William Schneider, "How Democrats Might Win by Losing!" *National Journal*, May 25, 1991, 1266.

14. Informationsdienst der SPD INTERN, no. 5, March 26, 1993.

15. *Frankfurter Allgemeine Zeitung*, Nov. 20, 1993. State party organizations have amended their statutes accordingly. Thus in February 1995 the SPD's candidate for the position of governing mayor of the city-state of Berlin was nominated by a primary vote of all party members.

16. Peter von Oertzen is an exception. See *Vorwärts*, Nov. 1993, 9.

17. Nelson W. Polsby, *Consequences of Party Reform* (Oxford: Oxford University Press, 1983).

18. Richard Cohen: "Deep Pockets," *National Journal*, Oct. 29, 1994, 2512f.

19. James A. Barnes, "Along the Campaign Trail," *National Journal*, Nov. 5, 1994, 2595.

20. Frank J. Sorauf, *Inside Campaign Finance: Myths and Realities* (New Haven: Yale University Press, 1992); Karl-Heinz Nassmacher, *Bürger finanzieren Wahlkämpfe-Anregungen aus Nordamerika für die Parteifinanzierung in Deutschland* (Baden-Baden: Nomos, 1992).

21. Reichley, *The Life of the Parties*, 380.

22. Otto Kirchheimer, "Der Wandel des westeuropäischen Parteiensystems," *Politische Vierteljahresschrift* 6 (1965): 24ff.

23. Holly Idelson, "Signs Point to Greater Loyalty on Both Sides of the Aisle," *Congressional Quarterly Weekly Report* 50 (Dec. 19, 1992): 3849ff.

24. Daniel S. Ward, "The Continuing Search for Party Influence in Congress: A View from the Committees," *Legislative Studies Quarterly* 18 (May 1993).

25. Peter W. Schramm and Bradford P. Wilson, *American Political Parties and Constitutional Politics* (Lanham, Md.: Rowman & Littlefield, 1993), 79ff.; Andrew Taylor, "Southern Democrats May Score if Fading Alliance Dissolves," *Congressional Quarterly Weekly Report* 50 (Dec. 19, 1992): 3845ff.; Alissa J. Rubin, "Influence of Traditional Bloc Clearly on the Decrease," *Congressional Quarterly Weekly Report* 49 (Dec. 28, 1991): 3759; Kitty Dumas, "A Once-Powerful Voting Bloc Loses Some of Its Punch," *Congressional Quarterly Weekly Report* 48 (Dec. 22, 1990): 4192ff.

26. Richard E. Cohen and William Schneider, "Epitaph for an Era," *National Journal*, Jan. 14, 1995, 83f.

27. David S. Cloud, "Speaker Wants His Platform to Rival the Presidency," *Congressional Quarterly Weekly Report* 53 (Feb. 4, 1995): 334; Richard E. Cohen, "Hurricane Newt," *National Journal*, Sept. 24, 1994, 2199.

28. Quoted in Janet Hook and David S. Cloud, "A Republican-Designed House Won't Please All Occupants," *Congressional Quarterly Weekly Report* 52 (Dec. 3, 1994): 3430; David S. Cloud, "GOP to Its Own Delight Enacts House Rules Changes," ibid., 53 (Jan. 7, 1995), 13f.

29. Peter Lösche and Franz Walter, "Zur Organisationskultur der sozialdemokratischen Arbeiterbewegung in der Weimarer Republik. Niedergang der Klassenkultur oder solidargemeinschaftlicher Höhepunkt?" *Geschichte und Gesellschaft* 15 (1989): 511ff.; Peter Lösche and Michael Scholing, "Solidargemeinschaft im Widerstand: Eine Fallstudie über 'Blick in die Zeit,'" *Internationale Wissenschaftliche Korrespondenz zur Geschichte der deutschen Arbeiterbewegung* 19 (1983): 517ff.

30. Marjorie Randon Hershey, "Citizens' Groups and Political Parties in the United States," *Annals of the American Academy of Political and Social Science* 528 (1993): 142ff.

31. Martin P. Wattenberg, *The Rise of Candidate-Centered Politics: Presidential Elections of the 1980s* (Cambridge: Harvard University Press, 1991), 48ff.

32. Peter Lösche, "Parteienstaat Bundesrepublik—Koalitionsbildungsstaat USA. Überlegungen zum Vergleich von Regierungssystemen," *Zeitschrift für Parlamentsfragen* 20 (1989): 283ff.

Part III

POLICIES

CHALLENGES AND RESPONSES

THE DOMESTIC AND INTERNATIONAL SOURCES OF U.S. DEFICITS

PAUL E. PETERSON

The Soviet Union invaded Afghanistan in the fall of 1979. Shortly there-after the United States initiated an arms buildup that continued through the mid-1980s. It also began running budget deficits unprecedented since World War II. Were these events dependent on each other? Or was their juxtaposition quite coincidental?

It is the burden of this essay that budgetary deficits in the United States cannot be blamed on the cold war. On the contrary, if there is any connection between the two events at all, it was the relaxation in tensions between the two great superpowers that induced a politics of deficits in the United States. In the following pages I shall identify 1981 as the critical time when deficit politics became rampant in the United States. I shall show that despite the arms buildup that occurred at this same time, there was only a loose connection between that buildup and subsequent budget deficits. The evidence also casts doubt on the conventional wisdom that fiscal deficits were the product of political decentralization in Congress and/or of divided government. Deficits were instead the product of changing macroeconomic theory, the introduction of new institutional procedures that have stripped elected officials of vitally needed blame-avoidance mechanisms, and the rapid growth of redistributive expenditure in the waning years of the cold war. If my diagnosis is correct, the prognosis for deficit politics cannot be optimistic.

The Rise of Deficit Politics

Figure 9.1 presents the most precise available information on the state of deficit politics in the United States. It presents the gross debt of the federal government as a percentage of the country's gross national product (GNP)

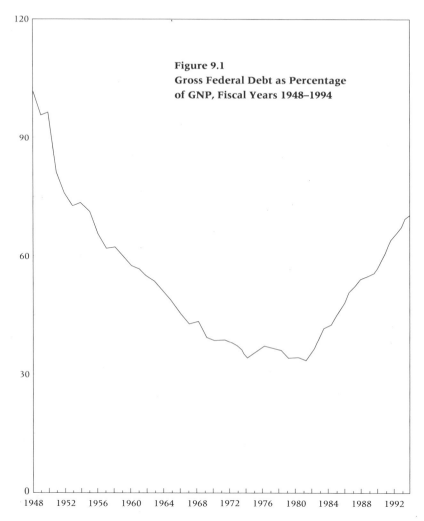

Figure 9.1
Gross Federal Debt as Percentage
of GNP, Fiscal Years 1948–1994

Source: Historical Tables 1990, Budget of the United States Government, Fiscal Years 1990, 1991, 1992, 1993.
Data for 1993–1994 are projected.

for the period between 1948 and 1994 (with estimates for the last two years). When the information is displayed in this manner, the size of the federal debt is adjusted for changes in cost of living and the size of the U.S. economy.[1]

Changes in the size of the public debt, as presented in this figure, are a function of the interaction among three factors: the annual deficits the government is incurring, the rate at which prior debt is being monetized by currency inflation, and the rate at which the economy is growing. Government debt as a percentage of GNP can actually—and often does—fall even when a government is incurring an annual deficit—as long as that annual deficit is not in excess of the amount that past debts are being monetized and/or increasing at a rate faster than the rate of economic growth.

Figure 9.1 shows that deficit politics in the United States begins in 1981, the year when two major pieces of fiscal legislation passed Congress and were signed by President Ronald Reagan: the Economic Recovery and Tax Act and the Omnibus Budget Reconciliation Act, laws that cut taxes by 5 percent of GNP while making no corresponding cuts in public expenditure.

Prior to 1981 the gross public debt of the federal government declined dramatically. As the United States entered into the cold war, it carried a debt burden larger than the size of its annual GNP. Accumulated during the Depression and World War II years, the debt hung heavily over the American economy, an apparent threat to successful adjustment to a peacetime economy. But a combination of fiscal stringency and expansionist monetary policies limited the size of new deficits and monetized old ones. Concomitant economic growth made it seem almost easy. Deficit reduction slowed in the 1970s, as economic growth slowed and annual deficits increased. Monetization, not a very effective deficit reduction tool over the long run, was the only one still available. If the public debt was not increasing in size, neither was it continuing to fall.

In 1981 the government lost all the tools that had helped it reduce the public debt throughout the early cold war period. Over the next decade annual budgetary deficits escalated, economic growth remained sluggish, and inflation slowed, reducing the rate of monetization.

The Cold War and the Deficit

The War of Independence, the Civil War, World War I, and World War II all had profound consequences for the public debt of the United States government.[2] The cold war, continuing over more than four decades, might similarly be expected to have contributed to the government's accumulated debts. Trillions of dollars were spent on armaments; annual defense budgets over the cold war era ran as high as 10 percent of GNP; and some of the larger annual deficits were incurred during the Korean and Vietnam wars, the iciest moments of the cold war. As U.S. troops were drawn from Vietnam in the early 1970s, U.S. defense expenditures fell dramatically from over 9 percent of GNP in 1967 to 5 percent of GNP a decade later (see fig. 9.2). Under the détente umbrella, Nixon, Ford, and Carter together steadily built down U.S. defense capacity. But after the Afghanistan invasion, Carter called for a sizeable increment in U.S. military strength, an increase augmented by Reagan's even more urgent call for a stronger defense. By 1987 defense expenditures had climbed back up two percentage points to about 7

Figure 9.2 Federal Expenditures by Type, Fiscal Years 1962–1990
(as percentage of GNP)

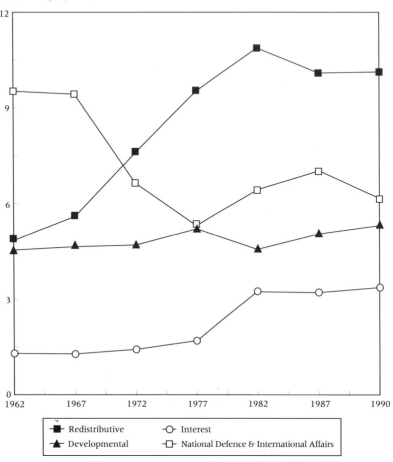

Source: U.S. Bureau of the Census, *U.S. Census of Governments, Compendium of Government Finances, Years, 1962, 1967, 1972, 1977, 1982, 1987; Government Finances in 1989–1990.*

percent of GNP. The increase occurred during the precise period when annual fiscal deficits were peaking.

This explanation for the rise of deficit politics in the 1980s leaves much to be explained, however. Why did the Afghan crisis permanently change the fiscal situation in the United States when the much more severe Korean and Vietnam conflicts did not? Why did the deficit not subside as the Afghan crisis receded and, indeed, when the cold war came to an end? Why were annual deficits in 1992—three years after the end of the cold war—as high as they were in every cold war year but one? The connection between the cold war and deficit politics may in fact be quite the opposite from the hypothesis that we have been considering. Despite the cost of military defense, the cold war may have forestalled the rise of deficit politics in the United States. I shall consider this possibility further after first giving consideration to several possible domestic causes of deficit politics.

Were Deficits Caused by Decentralization in Congress?

A popular explanation for budgetary deficits is the credit-claiming need of reelection-minded members of Congress, who run in first-past-the-post elections held within defined geographical areas. It is argued that representatives and senators have discovered that they can nearly insure their reelection if they hand out observable benefits to the geographic area from which they come—regardless of the fiscal cost to U.S. taxpayers. The political benefits that accrue from expenditures for bridges, dams, tunnels, and space colliders outweigh the political costs of paying for them, which are spread diffusely among taxpayers across time and space.[3]

In the early years of the cold war, this self-serving, reelection-motivated congressional behavior was held in check by conservative appropriation committees and an informal club that kept power in the hands of hardworking insiders. But in the early seventies the increasing power of the Democratic caucus, the "subcommittee bill of rights" (which weakened the power of committee chairs), and the technical changes that shifted more votes to the chamber floors all contributed to the decentralization of political power on Capitol Hill.[4] As power decentralized, more and more pork-barrel schemes were devised, accelerating government expenditures and pushing deficits ever higher.[5] Proponents of this explanation often cite as evidence the ever increasing size of federal expenditures. Federal expenditures increased from about 20.4 percent of GNP in 1972 to 25.4 percent of GNP in 1988.

This is a rather gross test of the congressional decentralization hypothesis, however. A more precise test might differentiate among types of public expenditure. If the congressional decentralization hypothesis is correct, one would expect to find disproportionately large increases in the kinds of domestic expenditure which are particularly popular in local communities—those which facilitate local economic development.[6] Inasmuch as such expenditure usually redounds to the general benefit of local communities as a whole, members of Congress clearly benefit politically from any such expenditure. Redistributive expenditures that help low-income people or other dependent populations such as the old, the sick, and the disabled have less geographic payoff. These redistributive programs have diffuse benefits, which are spread widely across the country. Some people applaud them, others are critical. The local electoral benefits of claiming credit are offset by criticism from those who receive few, if any, benefits from the programs.

To ascertain whether developmental expenditures grew especially rapidly in the wake of congressional decentralization, I classified all domestic government expenditures (other than the interest on the public debt) into two broad categories: redistributive and developmental.[7] If the congressional decentralization hypothesis is correct, one would expect developmental expenditures to have increased more rapidly than redistributive expenditures after decentralization took place.

As can be seen by the triangle studded line in figure 9.2, there is little evidence for this proposition. The percentage of GNP expended for developmental programs has increased only slightly over the decades. It was 4.5 percent in 1962, 4.7 percent in 1972, and 5.4 percent in 1990.

The congressional decentralization explanation also suffers from the fact that power in Congress was recentralizing at about the same time deficits began to escalate. If power was shifting to subcommittees and to the floor of Congress during the seventies, it shifted upward to the congressional party leadership during the 1980s. Especially with regard to fiscal policy, party leaders were called upon to coordinate budget priorities in large "omnibus" pieces of legislation passed under strict time pressures at the close of the fiscal year. Both subcommittees and rank-and-file members lost many of the prerogatives they had enjoyed a decade earlier.[8] But the recentralization of power on Capitol Hill did little to reduce the amount of government expenditure or bring budget deficits under control.

Are Deficits Caused by Divided Government?

Divided government may, if anything, be a more popular political explanation for U.S. fiscal deficits than congressional decentralization. Deficits exploded in the 1980s, it has been said, because a Republican president faced a Democratic Congress and because, for six years, a Democratic House had to contend with a Republican Senate.[9] Republicans wanted to cut domestic spending while cutting taxes and increasing defense spending. Democrats wanted to increase domestic spending while cutting defense and raising taxes. They compromised by both cutting taxes and increasing spending on almost everything. Deficits were the inevitable result.

Proponents of the divided government theory point out that unified governments seldom experienced a rising federal debt/GNP ratio. Truman, Eisenhower, and Carter each presided over a debt-creating unified government for just one year each. Debt creation has been more frequent under divided government. Although the federal debt/GNP ratio fell steadily throughout the six years Eisenhower led a divided government and again for the six years of the Nixon presidency, this ratio rose during the divided governments of the Ford, Reagan, and Bush administrations. So in a statistical sense, one can find an association between divided government and rising debt/GNP ratios.

But correlations are not causes. Most of the increase in the debt/GNP ratio occurred after 1981. To show that divided government was the cause of the deficits of the eighties and nineties, one needs to show that during this period either the executive or legislative branch was prepared to balance the budget, if the other governmental institution had only be willing to tolerate such action.

Did Congress want to balance the budget and did the president refuse to cooperate? Few, if any, have claimed that a majority of Congress systematically tried to raise taxes or cut expenditures but were overruled by a presidential veto. In 1982 and 1984, Congress did eliminate some of the tax cuts it had made in 1981—shortly before these cuts were to go into effect. It may even be argued that even more tax increases would have been voted had President Reagan not remained adamantly opposed. But tax-raising courage is generally in short supply on Capitol Hill. Congress raised taxes in 1993 by only one vote in each chamber and only under strong pressure from the Clinton administration.

Congress also showed a certain amount of fiscal responsibility when it refused to vote Reagan all of the increases in defense expenditure he was calling for. But when it came to domestic expenditure, Congress regularly voted more funding than the president requested. It is difficult to credit the Congresses of the 1980s with deficit reduction commitments in excess of the president's. For one thing, Congress could at any time have balanced the budget simply by reducing its appropriations for the following fiscal year. The president would have had no choice but to acquiesce.

Did the president want to balance the budget and did Congress refuse? Presidents Reagan and Bush repeatedly claimed that they wanted to balance the budget but a tax-and-spend Democratic Congress refused to accommodate their wishes. Both presidents regularly proposed constitutional amendments calling for a balanced budget, and they asked Congress for a line item veto that they said they would use to eliminate unnecessary expenditure. These rhetorical claims can hardly be taken at face value. As part of their obligations under the Budget Act of 1921, Presidents Reagan and Bush each year presented an annual budget to Congress for the following fiscal year. Each year the proposed budget called for deficit spending. Each year Congress kept fairly close to the expenditure targets the president presented.[10] If

Congress did not always spend money on precisely the objects the president preferred, neither did it appropriate total funds far in excess of what the president had asked.

There was little likelihood of Congress passing expenditures greatly in excess of presidential preferences. The president could have at any time vetoed such an appropriation, and Congress, in almost all cases, would have been quite unable to pass the appropriation over the president's veto.

Deficits after 1981 hardly seem to be caused by divided government. The remarkable tax cut (without commensurate expenditure cuts) enacted in 1981 was passed by Congress at the eager urging of the Reagan administration. It passed because the president had a Republican Senate and a conservative majority in the House of Representatives. Once this legislation had put a system of deficit politics in place, neither presidents nor Congresses were willing to make the political sacrifices necessary to bring the deficits under control. Instead, a variety of expedients were attempted, such as the Gramm-Rudman-Hollings Act, which seemed to provide for (but never quite produced) automatic deficit reduction, and the Budget Act of 1990, which slowed expenditure increases and raised revenues slightly. Under unified government, the Clinton proposals, as modified by Congress, have contributed more toward deficit reduction, but deficits are scheduled to rise in the closing years of the 1990s.

Attributing the deficits of the eighties to divided government is making the claim that the distinctive characteristic of the decade was the presence of divided government. But economic theories and blame-avoidance mechanisms also changed during the 1980s. It is a good deal more likely that these changes, not divided government, were the critical factors at work.

Effects of Economic Theory on Deficits

Traditional economic theory treated public debt as analogous to household debt. In the words of Adam Smith, "what is prudence in the conduct of every private family can scarce be folly in that of a great kingdom."[11] Throughout the first 150 years of U.S. history, politicians in peacetime pretty much accepted this dogma and mainly kept the national budget in balance.[12] Although large debts were incurred during the Revolutionary War, the Civil War, and World War I, these were paid off quite steadily during the peacetime years that followed. When Herbert Hoover was elected president in 1928, the debt/GNP ratio was less than 20 percent.[13] When the Depression hit, President Hoover was unwilling to incur fiscal deficits to help unemployed workers, because his economic advisers told him such deficits would only prolong the Depression. No less traditional in outlook, Franklin Delano Roosevelt ran for president on a platform committed to a balanced budget.

Soon after his election, Roosevelt broke his campaign promise by initiating a plethora of New Deal spending programs without calling for any tax increase to pay for them. Advised by Marriner Eccles (a little-known and highly unorthodox Utah businessman whom Roosevelt appointed as chairman of his Federal Reserve Board) that deficit spending would stimulate the economy, Roosevelt, knowing full well that were he to raise taxes, his New Deal programs would never win political acceptability, shifted the debt ratio upward from 25 to 45 percent of GNP in five short years (against the stern admonitions of classic economists at the Brookings Institution).[14] Maynard Keynes soon put forth a general economic theory that gave Roosevelt's policies academic respectability and Keynes a seat in the British House of Lords.

According to Lord Keynes, government deficits could have a positive, stimulative effect on the economy under certain very specific conditions. The macroeconomy was not automatically self-correcting, as classical economists had thought, because wages were sticky on the downside. For a variety of reasons, wages could not be expected to fall far enough—even in a highly depressed economy—to stimulate the investment necessary to reverse the direction of the macroeconomy. Deficit spending by the government was needed to generate new economic demand.

Keynes's ideas became so respectable that James Buchanan and Richard Wagner attribute modern-day deficit spending to Keynesian influence.[15] They point out that economic prosperity following the Kennedy tax cut of 1964 convinced even the most skeptical that government fiscal policy could act as an exogenous shock upon a sluggish economy. Buoyed by this success, neo-Keynesians were willing not just to run deficits in the darkest moments of a deep depression (as was Lord Keynes's original recommendation), but to use red ink whenever the economy fell short of achieving full employment. According to Buchanan and Wagner, government officials were bound to exploit the political potential of this new economic reasoning. Deficit politics is fun politics, as Roosevelt had discovered. Elected leaders can give many people what they want, and the price will have to be paid only by some future generation, long after the existing government has passed into history. Once politicians discovered this new economic myth, deficits became uncontrollable.

Buchanan and Wagner's general line of argumentation has many appealing components. They correctly focus on a propensity on the part of politicians to distribute benefits now and postpone costs until later. They also show how economic theory may have acted as a brake on political irresponsibility in the past. As long as elected leaders believed that immediate and dire economic consequences were a likely concomitant of budgetary deficits, the political inclination to borrow rather than tax was at least partially constrained.

But Buchanan and Wagner's line of argument misrepresents the Keynesian position on deficits, thereby failing to appreciate the constraints on deficit financing that remained in place even after Lord Keynes's ideas became fashionable. Keynes justified deficits only during periods of extreme economic crisis; even modern neo-Keynesians recommended deficits only when the economy was sluggish. And the deficits to be incurred during recessionary periods were to be of modest proportions, only enough to bring the economy back to full employment. These deficits were, moreover, to be offset by budgetary surpluses that accumulated during good times (to reduce inflationary pressures).

Buchanan and Wagner recognize these complexities in Keynesian thought. But they argue that politicians paid only half attention to the economists, listening only to the half of the argument that was music to their election-minded ears. Politicians were told by the neo-Keynesians that deficits were good some of the time; they interpreted that to mean that deficits were good almost all of the time. To politicians, employment was seldom, if ever, "full," and the time to accumulate surpluses virtually never seemed to arrive.

But were U.S. politicians as insensitive to economic advice as Buchanan and Wagner claim? Lord Keynes wrote his general theory in the thirties; after Roosevelt, deficit politics on a massive scale did not reignite until 1981. If politicians were so susceptible to the suggestions of economists, why did it take them so long to construe and misconstrue Keynes's advice? Roosevelt's successful use of deficit politics was a matter of historical record. Why did so many presidents fail to replay it? Why was Ronald Reagan, the least likely of Roosevelt's successors, the first to copy the master politician?

The answer to these questions, ironically enough, is that Roosevelt's example was treated as irrelevant by most neo-Keynesians. Roosevelt's enormous Depression and wartime deficits were attributed to highly exceptional circumstances not reproduced during the cold war. From Truman to Carter (with Eisenhower, Johnson, Nixon, and Ford in between), presidents were warned by their Keynesian advisers to exercise budgetary restraint in order to avoid excessive inflation. These presidents for the most part accepted the economic advice they were given; annual deficits were so modest in size that they were more than offset by economic growth and the monetization of prior debt. For the first thirty-five years of the cold war, the debt/GNP ratio fell from 120 percent of GNP to around 33 percent. As of 1981 the debt/GNP ratio was as low as it had been in the entire cold war era. Far from being condemned for being the cause of deficits, the Keynesians should, if anything, be credited for preventing them.

But, unfortunately for fiscal conservatives, Keynesianism lost its grip on both academic and governmental opinion. In response to the ever intensifying inflationary pressures of the 1970s (which had, among other things, cast doubt on the long-term viability of the Phillips curve, an important emendation to neo-Keynesian theory), many macroeconomists were giving an alternative theory known as monetarism increasing credence.[16] Initially articulated by University of Chicago economist Milton Friedman, monetary theory stressed the indisputable fact that the value of currency was a function of the amount available. If the money supply increased at a more rapid rate than the economy as a whole grew, this could only result in a devaluation of the currency (as long as the rate at which money circulated remained constant, a monetarist assumption that has not always corresponded with reality). To keep inflation under control, monetary authorities (i.e., the Federal Reserve) should ensure that the money supply increased at an invariant pace consistent with the long-term rate of growth in the economy.

Monetarists reject the Keynesian claim that deficits are necessary to stimulate a depressed economy. They reject even more emphatically the neo-Keynesian claim that small variations in government budgets can affect short-term fluctuations in the business cycle, insisting that it makes not a dime's worth of difference to inflation, unemployment, or short-term economic growth whether government spending is paid for by money that is borrowed or money collected through a tax. Most monetarists—as well as most other economists—do agree that a large public debt has unfortunate long-term economic consequences. By sopping up the savings of a society, a large, rapidly growing public debt reduces the amount of money available for private investment, thereby inhibiting a country's rate of economic growth. But these long-term negative effects are unlikely to be given much weight by political leaders who have only a short time horizon.

If monetarism was winning a respectable audience in the academic community during the seventies, it moved to political center stage with the arrival in Washington of the Reagan administration.[17] Even Paul Volker, chairman of the Federal Reserve Board, hitherto a devout Keynesian, said in 1981 that Federal Reserve policies would be dictated by changes in the nation's money supply.

The conversion to monetarism in high government circles had important consequences for deficit politics. As early as 1975, Henry Wallich, both an economist and a member of the Federal Reserve Board, recognized the political problem that monetarism had created. "Increasingly, monetarist prescriptions play a role in political discussions. . . . The elected representatives of the people have discerned the attraction of monetarist doctrine because it plays down the effects of fiscal policy. Deficits can do no major damage so long as the central bank does its job right."[18] If monetarism was a cloud on the horizon when Wallich was expressing his views in the waning days of the Ford administration, it stormed over the fiscal landscape in 1981. Deficits were acceptable because they had no short-term economic consequences. Indeed, the Federal Reserve demonstrated that it could cut inflation in half even as budgetary deficits climbed to heights unseen during the cold war. Reaganites and their Republican supporters on Capitol Hill even went so far as to argue that deficits were beneficial. They felt that increased spending had an even worse effect than fiscal deficits on economic productivity. Big deficits would help slow, perhaps even reverse, the rate of increase in governmental expenditure. Even if Democrats were to regain power, deficits would keep them from new policy experimentation. Under the influence of monetarism, a political party that had bitterly condemned Roosevelt's deficit spending became the promulgator of the largest peacetime debt in the nation's history.

It is often said that Reagan studied and admired Roosevelt the politician if not Roosevelt the policy maker. Had Reagan noticed that spending without taxes was a key to Roosevelt's success? If so, monetarism gave Reagan the economic theory he needed to use a Rooseveltian fiscal strategy for quite different policy purposes. Reagan was not the only politician who saw political opportunities in monetarist theory. Even his moderate, well-meaning successor, George Bush, found deficit politics too attractive to deny, though it must be said that his one attempt at fiscal responsibility, the Budget Act of 1990, may well have cost him his political livelihood. The monetarist word seems also to have spread to Europe. An increasing debt/GNP ratio during the 1980s was more than an American phenomenon. As monetary theory was gaining worldwide respectability, politicians in Europe were learning from their American peers.

Deficits Happen When Blame Cannot Be Avoided

The growing influence of monetarist theory was not the only change in 1981. If changes in economic theory were the only explanation for the rising debt/GNP ratio, then trends in Europe and the United States should have been fairly uniform. But rising deficits, though widespread and general, were unevenly distributed, and the rate of increase in the United States was a good deal steeper than in the average European country. The rapid growth in U.S. deficits was due not just to changes in economic theory but also to critical changes in the blame-avoidance mechanisms available to U.S. politicians.[19]

Indexation

In the early seventies and again in 1981, Congress and the president changed the rules for cutting expenditure and enhancing revenues: The seemingly simple decisions to index federal entitlements and taxes profoundly affected fiscal policy making in the United States. To appreciate the consequences of these policy innovations, one needs first to appreciate the political value of blame-avoidance mechanisms in modern democratic systems.

Politicians need to avoid blame for the harms they must impose as much as they seek credit for the benefits they dispense. Arguably, blame avoidance is even more important to political leaders than claiming credit. When politicians take credit for something that happens, many will remain skeptical. But voters are unlikely to forget a politician whom they blame for a harm they have suffered.

Since political leaders must impose harms, they need devices that help disguise the connections between their actions and the harms that occur. The blame-avoidance mechanisms that members of Congress have devised are legion: voice votes instead of roll-call votes; delegating difficult decisions to presidents, bureaucrats, commissions, or state and local governments; legislation so complex and internally contradictory that few can figure out its impact; and incorporating a vast amount of legislation into a single bill that contains obvious benefits that seem to outweigh the harms imposed.

But few blame-avoidance devices were as effective as the steady, irrevocable processes of inflation that eroded the value of the dollar throughout the cold war years. Inflation cut the value of federal benefits regularly, continuously, almost daily. Unless Congress and the president actively intervened to correct the consequences of currency devaluation, the real value of federal benefits to the old, the poor, and the disabled constantly fell. Congress and the president took benefits away from these needy groups simply by doing nothing.

Congress and the president also raised taxes without lifting a finger. To finance World War II, Congress enacted a tax that contained numerous income brackets, each of which was taxed at a higher rate. After the war, inflation (and increasing economic productivity) regularly shifted taxpayers into higher tax brackets. This inflation-induced bracket creep was a continuous, relentless source of additional government revenue for which political leaders could not easily be blamed.

The president and Congress were sometimes accused of doing nothing to prevent these tax increases and entitlement cuts. But as students of the "other face of power" have often pointed out,[20] it was difficult for political opponents to pinpoint blame for something that did not happen.

Inflation was such an effective blame-avoidance mechanism that Congress hardly ever raised income taxes overtly during the first decades of the cold war. Payroll taxes were increased in order to fund the popular Social Security program. Eisenhower asked for a modest tax on gasoline to pay for the creation of the interstate highway system. And Lyndon Johnson asked for and obtained a temporary 10 percent surtax to pay for the rising costs of the Vietnam War, an unpopular tax that was soon discontinued. But for the most part tax legislation consisted of cuts designed to offset new revenues generated by bracket creep that inflation was inducing. The well-known Kennedy tax cut was just the largest and best known.[21]

Just as taxes were hardly ever overtly increased, so entitlement benefits were seldom, if ever, overtly cut during the first thirty-five years of the cold war. Instead, Congress simply offset inflation by increasing Social Security, welfare, and other benefits whenever an increase in revenue flow made such action permissible.

Farm Price Supports

The chief exception to this pattern—farm price supports—is itself revealing. Under pressure from the farm lobby, Congress and ex-farmer Harry Truman agreed as early as 1949 to guarantee farmers a price for their products which was indexed to changes in the cost of farming. The base period on which the index was constructed, 1909–1914, was one of the most prosperous moments in the history of American agriculture. Farm lobbyists argued that it was then—and only then—that farmers were paid a fair—or parity—price for their crops. According to the lobbyists, government guarantees to farmers should be based on the price farmers received at that time indexed to changes in the cost of farm production in subsequent decades. To rationalize farm policy and to take farm subsidies out of the annual political process, Congress and the Truman administration agreed to guarantee farmers 75–90 percent of this parity price.[22]

As the farm economy fluctuated, so did the cost of maintaining parity programs. Dubious about the efficacy of these attempts to prop up the small family farmer, Ezra Taft Benson, secretary of agriculture during the Eisenhower administration, cut—at great political cost—the parity guarantee from the 90 percent level enjoyed during the Truman administration to 75 percent, the lowest level permitted by law. The parity programs soon became a political football and a bureaucratic morass. By indexing farm subsidies, Congress guaranteed that farm benefits could be cut only through explicit governmental action. Despite the loss by the agricultural sector of more and more workers, the cost of farm programs grew and grew. Above all, Congress denied itself and future presidents the opportunity to avoid blame.

Indexing in the Seventies

What happened to farm price guarantees in 1949 happened to a host of government programs in the seventies. The processes were much the same. In each case, Congress indexed a federal policy to a politically popular base point that was historically unusual. In each case the indexation was proclaimed to be simply the substitution of rational decision making for the complexities of political negotiation. In each case, Congress was stripped of one of the most valuable blame-avoidance negotiating tools. In each case the outcome was deficit-facilitating.

Indexation first appeared in 1962 and 1963 when increases in civil service and military pensions were pegged to the cost of living. Military pay was indexed in 1967, and coal miners' disability insurance was included in 1969. The politics of indexation accelerated in the early seventies. The salaries of white-collar federal employees were indexed to inflation in 1970, food stamp benefits were indexed in 1971, Social Security and Medicare insurance in 1972, Medicaid eligibility in 1973, railroad retirement and supplemental security income in 1974, and veterans' pensions in 1978.[23]

Interest group positions were determined almost exclusively by the base period from which the index was to be derived. Groups representing retirees opposed Social Security indexation in the sixties because they thought the base value of Social Security at the time was inadequate. But after Congress gave retirees an extraordinarily large benefit increase in 1972, the groups enthusiastically endorsed indexation, giving the country a pension system indexed at the highest benefit level the program had ever achieved. It was farm parity prices all over again. The moment a group had achieved its maximum political strength, its policy preferences were frozen into law. Any future legislature could change the policy only by explicit blame-inducing legislation.

If Congress tossed out its blame-avoidance mechanisms on the expenditure side in the seventies, it waited until 1981 before giving up similar capacities on the tax side. Although Ronald Reagan initiated the tax-cutting frenzy of 1981, he cannot be especially blamed (or credited) for indexation per se. His advisers had in fact explicitly decided not to include indexation in the president's proposals. By not including indexation they could fulfill the presidents campaign promise to reduce taxes by 30 percent over the next three years without giving up necessary government revenues. They expected a relatively high rate of inflation-induced bracket creep simply to take away about half of the tax cut as fast as it was being implemented. But Senator Robert Dole, majority leader in the Senate, saw the 1981 tax bill as an opportunity to enact the tax indexation proposals he had long advocated. Even Dole understood the revenue implications of his proposals, so he quite responsibly acquiesced in a delay of indexation for two years so that inflation could induce a fair bit of bracket creep in the meantime.

Little did Dole, Reagan, or anyone else realize that Paul Volker at the Federal Reserve was simultaneously restricting the money supply so sharply that both inflation and the economy would soon plummet. In the two years after the passage of the law but before indexation came into effect, very little inflation-induced bracket creep occurred. As a result, taxes were indexed at the lowest rate they had reached in the entire cold war period. It was the farm parity phenomenon all over again. Indexation took place when taxpayer interests had achieved maximum political power. Any modifications of tax policy would now have to take place through explicit, blame-inducing government action.

The consequences of tax and entitlement indexation for budget deficits became quite apparent almost immediately after the 1981 legislation was passed. Budget deficits ballooned immediately, and there was no automatic process that could bring them under control. Within two years Congress hurriedly rescinded—and Reagan signed—several of the tax cuts included in the 1981 legislation. Since these tax cuts had not yet become effective, the blame that had to be accepted was moderate, not severe. Congress also agreed in 1982 to modest spending cuts and tax increases within the Social Security program. Since most cuts mainly affected future recipients, the blame to be suffered was once again only moderate, not severe. Yet Congress and the president constructed an elaborate, bipartisan, independent commission to help take the heat.[24]

Other schemes to deal with the deficit were less successful. The Gramm-Rudman-Hollings Deficit Reduction Act was expected to reduce the deficit automatically (much as indexation automatically increased entitlements and cut taxes), but automatic deficit reduction (scheduled to become severe in years four and five of the legislation) failed to work in practice. When the Gramm-Rudman-Hollings Act threatened to disrupt government operations, its effect was postponed until it was finally replaced by the budget compromise of 1990. Despite the claim made at the time of its passage that the deficit would be cut by $500 billion over the next five years (mainly in years four and five), the budget compromise also failed to forestall a continued increase in the debt/GNP ratio. The Clinton administration's 1993 proposals once again would have reduced the deficit by $500 billion over the next five years. But just as in the case of the 1990 compromise, most of the deficit reduction was to take place in the fourth and fifth years.

But despite the modesty of the deficit-reduction agendas of the Bush and Clinton administrations, neither was able to escape blame. Instead, both were condemned for cutting vitally necessary entitlement programs and for imposing the steepest taxes ever on the American public. Eisenhower, Kennedy, Johnson, Nixon, Ford, and Carter were able to raise taxes quietly every week simply by doing nothing. Such blame avoidance was no longer possible.

The easiest political solution, perhaps, may be to decide that deficits are not such a problem after all. Given the institutional framework within which the president and members of Congress are now operating, it is increasingly tempting to become a monetarist, a believer in the macroeconomic theory that says deficits are of little short-term import. Indeed, some macroeconomists are now claiming that deficits either do not really exist or have little long-term impact.[25] Their influence in policy-making circles is likely to increase.

The Cold War and the Expansion of the Welfare State

U.S. budget deficits seem to have been more a product of domestic politics than of any changes in the international system. They were not provoked by the cold war, they were only modestly affected by short-term fluctuations in the heat of the cold war, and they were not eased significantly by the cold war's end.

Deficits in fact may have been forestalled by the cold war. The United States may well have decided not to spend money on domestic programs and run fiscal deficits in the immediate postwar period because it faced a harsh international challenge. Only after the United States gained clear superiority over the Soviet Union did it become self-satisfied and self-indulgent. As the cold war dissipated, domestic pressures for an expanding welfare state intensified.

All this began in the early seventies. Although it is conventional to equate the end of the cold war with the fall of the Berlin Wall, the event was only the culmination of changes unfolding for decades. The most intense days of the cold war were in its early decades. Nothing since 1970 can compete with the international crises that occurred immediately following World War II, when Soviet troops marched across Eastern and Central Europe, when the Berlin blockade was broken, when the Soviet Union successfully exploded an atomic bomb, when China fell under communist control, when the Communist Party posed a significant threat in France and Italy, and when the policy of containment was constructed. The competition between the United States and the Soviet Union remained intense through the Prague Spring, the sputnik era, the Cuban revolution, the Cuban missile crisis, the erection of the Berlin Wall, and the most intense years of the Vietnam War.

But even in the waning days of the Vietnam War, détente was being put into place. Strategic arms control discussions were initiated, the People's Republic of China was recognized, and the communist threat in Europe lessened. Striking economic gains in Japan, South Korea, Taiwan, and other parts of Asia undermined the communist threat in the developing world. Within the Eastern bloc, toleration of dissent and a market economy was steadily increasing. The forces supporting Gorbachev were gaining strength for a decade and more before he came to power. The shrinkage of the U.S. defense budget after the end of the Vietnam War provides a quantitative indicator of the gradual relaxation of tensions. Even the brief reversal in U.S. defense policy occasioned by the Soviet invasion of Afghanistan appears to be little more than a short-term deviation from a general pattern of increasingly cooperative relationships.

As cold war tensions relaxed, redistributive pressures in the United States gained momentum. The federal government spent only 5 percent of GNP for redistributive purposes as late as 1962. Despite the New Deal, the Fair Deal, and the Eisenhower acceptance of New Deal institutions, very little of a welfare state had in fact been constructed in the United States seventeen years after the end of World War II, a period when cold war tensions were severe and defense expenditures high. Truman had little success in pushing Fair Deal measures through a do-nothing Congress, Eisenhower ignored domestic issues, and the Kennedy years are better known for tax cuts and future promises than any actual construction of the welfare state.

As cold war tensions relaxed, redistributive pressures climbed. By 1982 redistributive expenditures had more than doubled to over 10 percent of GNP. It is commonly thought that Lyndon Johnson's Great Society brought about this transformation. Johnson is regularly credited (or blamed) for providing both guns *and* butter. But although Johnson did much to initiate the modern welfare state, the steepest upward shift in redistributive expenditure occurred during the Nixon and Ford years, a time when the growth in redistributive expenditure was almost the mirror image of the drop in defense expenditure. Though many an analyst said there was no peace dividend after the Vietnam War, a quick glance at the actual data shows just how swiftly swords were being beaten into plowshares or, more exactly, how quickly guns were being churned into butter. Overall, federal expenditures in the post-Vietnam era remained fairly constant, but the domestic defense ratio of the budget changed dramatically.

Reagan managed to apply a temporary brake to the upward trend in redistributive expenditure, convincing Congress that more resources should be allocated to defense instead. But even before Reagan left office, defense expenditures had begun to decline and redistributive programs reasserted themselves, a trend that continued into the nineties.

These patterns are almost too easily interpreted. When money must be spent on guns, there seems to be little available for butter. When the need for defense lessens, it is tempting to spend the peace dividend on popular social programs. When cold war tensions are high, conservative parties and interests gain influence in domestic politics. When cold war tensions relax, domestic issues come to the fore. During the cold war, Kennedy can defeat Nixon only by decrying a missile gap. But once the Vietnam War is over, Carter can beat Ford for failing to provide jobs for workers. Reagan can call for tax cuts, and Clinton—Clinton, the errant draft dodger—wins office by focusing on the economy. A political outsider such as Ross Perot can win the largest third-party vote since 1912. Republicans can recapture Congress by drawing up a Contract with America that promises tax cuts and deregulation but hardly mentions foreign policy.

But if the connection between the relaxation of the cold war and redistributive politics is easily identified, redistribution is not the same thing as budget deficits. Many countries have built a welfare state without greatly increasing its debt/GNP ratio. Yet it is more difficult to win public consensus for taxes that fund redistribution than for taxes that help defend against foreign aggression. Once economic theory discredits the short-term consequences of deficits, once blame-avoidance institutions are eliminated, it is all the more difficult to impose taxes simply to benefit one social group at the expense of another. Republicans find voters more responsive to calls for tax cuts than balanced budget amendments that might threaten Social Security payments. Deficits are the easy way of financing the welfare state. If the intellectual and institutional order put into place in 1981 continues, and if a "new world order" more peaceful than the old continues to hold, deficits are unlikely to go away.

Notes

I wish to thank Don Lee and Jerome Maddox for research assistance and Allison Kommer and Kristin Skala for staff assistance with the preparation of this paper.

1. For a discussion of the use of debt/GNP ratio as the appropriate measure of governmental deficits, see Robert J. Barro, "Comment," in Alberto Alesina and Geoffrey Carliner, *Politics and Economics in the Eighties* (Chicago: University of Chicago Press, 1991), 111–22.

2. John H. Makin and Norman J. Ornstein, *Debt and Taxes: Politics and Fiscal Policy in America* (Washington, D.C.: American Enterprise Institute, 1993).

3. Major contributions to this interpretation of congressional behavior include the following: David Mayhew, *The Electoral Connection* (New Haven: Yale University Press, 1973); Morris Fiorina, *Congress: The Keystone of the Washington Establishment*, 2d ed. (New Haven: Yale University Press, 1989); Fiorina, *Divided Government* (New York: Macmillan, 1992); John Ferejohn, *Pork Barrel Politics: Rivers and Harbors Legislation, 1947–1968* (Stanford, Calif.: Stanford University Press, 1974); Kenneth Shepsle, *The Giant Jigsaw Puzzle: Democratic Committee Assignments in the Modern House* (Chicago: University of Chicago Press, 1978); Gary C. Jacobson, *The Electoral Origins of Divided Government: Competition in U.S. Elections, 1946–88* (Boulder, Colo.: Westview Press, 1990); Douglas Arnold, "The Local Roots of Domestic Policy," in Thomas Mann and Norman J. Ornstein, eds., *The New Congress* (Washington, D.C.: American Enterprise Institute, 1981), 250–87.

4. See the illuminating essays in Anthony King, ed., *The New American Political System* (Washington, D.C.: American Enterprise Institute, 1973).

5. Allen Schick, *Congress and Money* (Washington, D.C.: Urban Institute, 1980); Makin and Ornstein, *Debt and Taxes*.

6. Paul E. Peterson, Barry Rabe, and Kenneth Wong, *When Federalism Works* (Washington, D.C.: Brookings Institution, 1985).

7. I assume that the ostensible purpose for any domestic governmental expenditure must be either the enhancement of the nation's economy or the redistribution of wealth from the haves to the needy. Whatever less noble motives might be influencing policy makers, expenditure must ultimately be justified as serving either a developmental or a redistributive purpose. For example, police expenditures are necessary to safeguard life and property; otherwise citizens will not be willing or able to engage in productive activity. Or, to give an instance of redistribution, the disabled should receive federal assistance because they cannot care for themselves and society does not wish to see them starve. By analyzing the public purpose of each federal program in this manner, one can classify all expenditures primarily as either developmental or redistributive. This is a simplification of a classification scheme set forth in Paul E. Peterson, *City Limits* (Chicago: University of Chicago Press, 1981).

8. Steve Smith, *Call to Order: Floor Politics in the House and Senate* (Washington, D.C.: Brookings Institution, 1989); Stanley Bach and Steven Smith, *Managing Uncertainty in the House of Representatives: Adaptation and Innovation in Special Rules* (Washington, D.C.: Brookings Institution, 1988); Kenneth Shepsle, "The Changing Textbook Congress," in John E. Chubb and Paul E. Peterson, eds., *Can the Government Govern?* (Washington, D.C.: Brookings Institution, 1989), 238–66; Roger H. Davidson, "The Emergence of the Postreform Congress," in Davidson, ed., *The Postreform Congress* (New York: St. Martin's Press, 1992), 3–24; Paul E. Peterson, "The Rise and Fall of Special Interest Politics," in Marc Petracca, ed., *The Politics of Interests: Interest Groups Transformed* (Boulder, Colo.: Westview, 1992), 326–44.

9. The most explicit statement of this position is provided by Matthew D. McCubbins, "Party Governance and U.S. Budget Deficits: Divided Government and Fiscal Stalemate," in Alesina and Carliner, *Politics and Economics in the Eighties*, 83–111. For a persuasive critique of this statement, see the critical comment by Barro, in ibid., 111–22.

10. Congressional Budget Office, *The Economic and Budget Outlook: 1991–1995*. (Washington, D.C.: Government Printing Office, 1990).

11. As quoted in James Buchanan and Richard E. Wagner, *Democracy in Deficit: The Political Legacy of Lord Keynes* (New York: Academic Press, 1977), 3.

12. Makin and Ornstein, *Debts and Taxes*.

13. McCubbins, "Party Governance," 84.

14. William Greider, *Secrets of the Temple: How the Federal Reserve Runs the Country* (New York: Simon & Schuster, 1987), chap. 10; Donald T. Critchlow, *The Brookings Institution, 1916–1952: Expertise and the Public Interest in a Democratic Society* (Dekalb: Northern Illinois University, 1985), chap. 6.

15. Buchanan and Wagner, *Democracy in Deficit*.

16. The Phillips curve was the hypothesized trade-off between inflation and unemployment. As one went up, the other declined. When both unemployment and inflation escalated in the seventies, rational expectations theory was developed to show that in the long run there was no trade-off.

17. The significance of the triumph of monetarism was overlooked by a mass media that gave exorbitant coverage to the ludicrous Laffer curve, proposed by

Arthur Laffer, who made the far-fetched claim that the government could increase revenues by cutting taxes. Laffer said that tax cuts would so markedly change incentives to work and save that productivity gains would generate more revenues than would be lost by tax cuts. Some Reagan administration officials found it useful to cite Laffer when calling for the largest tax cut of the cold war even while insisting on a need for an arms buildup. But while few respectable economists either inside or outside the Reagan administration agreed with Laffer, many economists influential in Republican circles had been won over to monetarist logic.

18. Buchanan and Wagner, *Democracy in Deficit*, 53.

19. The importance of blame avoidance for policy making has been noticed by an increasing number of political scientists. See, e.g., R. Kent Weaver, *Automatic Government: The Politics of Indexation* (Washington, D.C.: Brookings Institution, 1988); Douglas Arnold, *The Logic of Congressional Action* (New Haven: Yale University Press, 1990); Paul Pierson, *Dismantling the Welfare State? The Politics of Retrenchment in Britain and the United States* (Cambridge: Cambridge University Press, forthcoming); Davidson, "Emergence of the Postreform Congress."

20. Peter Bachrach and Morton S. Baratz, "The Other Face of Power," *American Political Science Review* 56 (1962): 947–52. The authors point out that the power to prevent events from happening can be exercised overtly.

21. Paul E. Peterson, "The Politics of Deficits," in John Chubb and Paul E. Peterson, *The New Direction in American Politics* (Washington, D.C.: Brookings Institution, 1985), 365–98.

22. Wesley McCune, *The Farm Bloc* (Garden City, N.Y.: Doubleday, Doran & Co., 1943; Weaver, *Automatic Government*, chap. 7.

23. This section draws heavily from Weaver, *Automatic Government*.

24. Paul Light, *Artful Work: The Politics of Social Security Reform* (New York: Random House, 1985).

25. According to some economists, some governmental expenditure is for capital investment. Its cost should not be considered part of the operating budget of the federal government. Also, it is argued that the portion of the interest paid on the debt which is a function of inflation expectations should not be considered. One might also exclude the cost of the savings and loan bailout on the grounds that the United States is purchasing assets with these funds. Depending on how these costs are calculated, much of the deficit can be made to disappear.

TEN

SOCIAL WELFARE

Policy Dynamics Emerging from State-Federal Government Interaction

ADRIENNE HÉRITIER

In the past decade social disparities in the United States have deepened. Poverty has increased and problems such as child poverty and homelessness have become more glaring. But less conspicious forms of poverty, too, have multiplied as a result of the stagnation or, in fact, decrease in lower-income earnings. The end of the cold war, so far, has exacerbated the problem because the education of military personnel has closed an important avenue of upward mobility to young underclass blacks.

Also, large-scale layoffs by enterprises producing for the military sector have contributed to the rise of poverty, all while the much-cited peace dividend has not materialized in the domain of social policy. In view of the deepening poverty problems, the questions to be posed in this chapter are: Which social policy measures have been taken in recent years in the United States to come to terms with these poverty problems? Although a variety of factors are at the root of American antipoverty policy such as the belief in the self-sufficiency and independence of the individual, the waning influence of organized labor, and the absence of a social democratic party, to name only a few, I would like to focus on an aspect that is particularly striking to the foreign observer of American domestic policy: the dynamics of social welfare policy making inherent in the federalist structure; dynamics that simultaneously account for progressive innovations in the attempt to fight poverty *and* conservative cutback measures. In contrast to the sixties and seventies, when the federal government set the pace of welfare policy innovation, in the eighties, with a conservative party in power at the White House, domestic policy innovations can be traced back to state experimentation and policy developments, the federal government following suit. The state-initiated policy developments made for progress between 1980–1982 and 1989, but from 1990 on the states—because of the economic recession—

initiated a partial rollback in welfare policy. Both state-initiated developments, in turn, triggered specific responses from the federal government. Important reasons why states function as motors of domestic policy making are: competition between Washington and the state capital in circumstances such as different party majorities; party competition within the state; and the dominance in a state of a party with a tradition of welfare policy. Also, changes are always influenced by the overall economic situation, which is important in shaping the specific direction that policy changes take.

The argument that is presented will proceed in two steps. The first section describes some features of present poverty in the United States; the second analyzes the policy measures developed by the states and the federal government to deal with poverty.

Poverty Problems on the Rise

In U.S. society the gap between rich and poor has deepened. "The concentration of income and wealth during the 1980s . . . [was] unusual."[1] While there was a slight overall growth in median family income—family income went up by 11 percent from 1973 to 1986, with a meaningful percentage increase between 1981 and 1986[2]—the worrisome fact "was the comparative advances or regressions of families in different brackets."[3] Among subgroups, the computation compelling most public attention showed that between 1980 and 1988 the income share of the upper 20 percent of Americans rose from 41.6 percent to 44.0 percent, the highest ratio since the beginning of the official measurements in 1949.[4] In 1991, one-fifth, or the most affluent of all households, accounted for 46.5 percent of all household incomes, while the poorest one-fifth accounted for only 3.8 percent of all household incomes.[5] The increasing disparities in household incomes by subgroups may in part be attributed to the erosion of wages in industrial low-skill sectors. The income of Americans in unskilled positions in the service and manufacturing sectors has dropped; correspondingly, the percentage of the working poor under the poverty threshold ($14,343 for a family of four in 1992) has increased. The number of poor persons went up (in millions) from 25.3 (1970), 25.9 (1975), 29.3 (1980), 33.1 (1985), 31.5 (1989), 33.6 (1990) to 35.7 (1991)[6] and amounted to 14.2 percent of the population in 1992; the number of welfare recipients went up by 21 percent between 1989 and 1991. The average monthly number of families and recipients of cash payments was 4,467,333 families, or 12,930,472 persons (of whom 8,739,493 were children).[7] Vulnerable poverty groups, such as children, have increased in size. Whereas in 1985, 13 million of the U.S. poor or 40 percent were children under age 18 (of whom 5 million were under age 6),[8] in 1991, 9 million out of 13 million welfare dependents were children; or, put differently, 21.8 percent of all children in 1991 were poor.[9] Of the total number of poor (35.7 million) in 1991, 14.2 million were children.[10] Of the households below the official poverty line, a majority of 57 percent have only one parent, and a very high proportion of children were born out of wedlock.[11] Of the 14.2 million poor children, 8.7 million live in a one-parent, female-headed household.[12]

Also, long-term welfare dependency is on the rise: While most women who go on welfare leave it in five years or less,[13] 25 percent of them stay for ten years or longer on welfare, which accounts for 56 percent of the welfare rolls or more than 2 million families at any given time.[14] Long-term welfare recipients are typically young unmarried mothers who often did not finish high school or hold a job before they became mothers. With more children, getting off welfare becomes even more difficult.[15]

In racial terms 10.3 percent of whites, 32.7 percent of blacks and 28.7 percent of Hispanics were poor in 1991.[16] Moreover, the spatial concentration of poverty in urban ghettos has produced new poverty pockets in which a vicious circle of poverty, dropping out of school, unemployment, drug addiction and involvement in the drug trade, teenage pregnancy, and renewed poverty of the children of the poor seems to be feeding upon itself.[17] Inner-city unemployment among teenagers—43.4 percent among black teenagers and 28.6 percent among Hispanic youth—is very high.[18]

In view of these deepening poverty problems, the question arises: What does the government do to lessen the hardship of the poor? How has the interplay between states and the federal government shaped poverty policy in the past decade? To restate the hypothesis: three factors have influenced the development of welfare policy: the interplay between states and the federal government, the background of party political competition, and the general economic context.

The Interplay between States and the Federal Government in Welfare Policy

Federalism in the United States offers the opportunity to create "political energy" and policy outcomes in many arenas. It thereby offers the possibility of policy innovations but also gives social welfare policy, seen in its development over time, a certain volatility and, in its regional heterogeneity, a patchwork character. The innovative but volatile character of welfare policy can be shown by distinguishing for analytic purposes four phases in state-federal government interactions beginning with the Reagan administration and ending in 1992: (1) the states' initiatives to improve welfare policy, (2) the federal government's adoption of policy solutions formulated by the states, (3) a renewed state retrenchment policy in reaction to the economic recession, and (4) the response of the new administration.

The States' Initiatives (1)

The first phase, during the Reagan administration, was characterized by drastic retrenchment measures in social welfare benefits (as opposed to Social Security programs), which, although initiated under Carter, came into full ideological and fiscal swing only under Reagan. Under Reagan's new federalism the states were to assume extensive fiscal responsibility for welfare policy. However, that proposal did not receive either congressional or gubernatorial support.[19] As a consequence, the administration initiated "a program of widespread, long-term experiments in welfare policy through state-sponsored and community-based demonstration projects. . . . Congress should seek . . . legislation that would waive federal welfare rules in order to allow states and communities to experiment."[20]

Given a situation of welfare austerity on the federal level, individual states actively started to develop new welfare initiatives, and the federal government tolerated and supported these initiatives under section 1115 of the Social Security Act by issuing waivers to states that allowed them to experiment with welfare reform measures. Thus, states with a record of liberal policy innovations in social policy such as New York, California, New Jersey, Ohio, and Wisconsin, started programs liberalizing workfare (new style), that is, employment and training programs for welfare recipients, which—since the federal Comprehensive Education and Training Act was repealed by the federal government—seek to integrate the poor permanently into the labor market and to break up the social isolation of single mothers.[21] Although the traditional workfare programs under the Aid for Families with Dependent Children (AFDC) program had been reduced by liberals, the new ones were accepted because they go beyond the old public works measures, emphasizing training and education. More than two-thirds of the states initiated efforts along these lines. Among them were California, Illinois, Massachusetts, West Virginia, Oklahoma, New Jersey, and Arkansas.[22] "The California scheme [GAIN—Greater Avenue for Independence] seems to be most highly developed. An agreement between the Republican governor and Democrats in the legislature led to a fundamental restructuring of the state's welfare system, shifting its orientation from a payment and social service system to one. . . . 'strongly oriented towards training, education, job placement and work—including in some cases the assignment of welfare family heads to obligatory work.'"[23] GAIN requires all eligible recipients to participate in the program until they become employed or go off AFDC. Therefore, mandatory registration is required of all unemployed parents receiving AFDC benefits and AFDC recipients with children of three years or older.[24] The Massachusetts education and training program in addition provided up to one year of child care and health care.[25]

Beyond the reform experiments in workfare, some states such as New York also took important steps in changing Medicaid programs; they extended the benefits to some extent to the children of the working poor even if the parents exceed the state income limits for Medicaid. These measures seem quite significant in view of the "poverty trap" in which the marginally employed and working poor find themselves: in case of illness they easily fall back into welfare dependency since they are not or not sufficiently covered by employers' insurance schemes, let alone private insurance.

The motives underlying the measures taken by single states may be characterized roughly as (party)-political, economic, and cultural. In other words: innovative policies may be spearheaded by liberal Democratic governors, or legislatures controlled by the Democrats in a state with a certain tradition in social welfare policy such as New York State;[26] also, party competition tends work in their favored and, of course, they are to be found in economically prosperous states rather than in poor states. Also "the extent to which low-income citizens are politically mobilized or the liberality of the state's political culture"[27] play an important role.

Thus the specific economic and political conditions in which the two leading states, California and Massachusetts, innovated work programs were characterized by a relative economic prosperity and a liberal Democratic tradition. In both states the per capita income (more than $6,000 in 1983) was among the highest in the nation. The unemployment rate of 3.9 percent (1985) in Massachusetts was the lowest in the nation; in California the unemployment rate was 7.2 percent (1985). The proportion of welfare recipients in the total population in 1985 was 5.9 percent in Massachusetts, compared with 8.7 percent in California, and the average monthly payment per family in 1984 was $389 in Massachusetts and $489 in California. While Massachusetts in 1982 elected a liberal Democratic governor, California reelected a conservative Republican but the Democrats kept a majority in the legislature.[28]

In the case of the Massachusetts program, it became clear that the business community was willing to support it as long as the economy remained robust and political support for it was sustained—and also as long as the AFDC rolls continued to decline and the state's revenues could provide sufficient public funding to maintain the program without facing strong competition from other programs and interest groups.[29]

California's GAIN program, by contrast, presented a compromise among contending ideological perspectives. While California's governor wanted to prolong the old work-for-relief program, the legislature, controlled by Democrats, blocked his proposals. In the ensuing negotiations, under the impact of the continuing increase in the AFDC rolls and public support for tax limitation (Proposition 13), the liberals accepted the strategy of a mandated work program, while the conservatives agreed to the provision of services—education, training, and child care—to help recipients become employable.[30]

The Response of the Federal Government (1)

The cumulative impact of the states' initiatives built up a political momentum that initiated a second phase of policy making in social welfare policy. A new national welfare consensus, "a striking liberal rebound,"[31] emerged, and the federal government, especially Congress, assumed a role of renewed responsibility in welfare policy that led to the 1988–1989 federal welfare reform. The new national welfare consensus may be traced back to the model function of single states and the political pressure exerted by some of these states on the federal government to reach an equalization of financial burdens, such as Medicaid costs, borne by states for welfare services.

However, the new national welfare consensus was also promoted by the sheer pressure of the problem: the fact that the poverty rate of 13.5 percent in 1987 was higher than at any time in the 1970s;[32] the fact that AFDC had become a long-term support program; that so many children were poor; that there are increasing numbers of poor teenage mothers; and that the number of homeless persons is rising. The new national welfare consensus evolved around two legitimizing patterns: to save children from poverty and to integrate the poor into the labor market. Also, a fundamental change in the attitude toward working mothers is at the bottom of the new welfare consensus: since most mothers of young children are now in the paid labor force, many argue that it is only reasonable to expect welfare mothers to do the same[33]—or, put more cynically, "mothers with very young children should now be legislatively classified as a matter of public policy as the 'able-bodied poor.' "[34]

In 1986, four major reports on welfare reform were put forward.[35] They all make a point of disaggregating the poor in their analysis, emphasizing success with some groups and evidence of serious deterioration among others and distinguishing between long-term dependency and short-term dependency. All stress the importance of the family and the view that benefits to the able-bodied must be linked with obligations to work, stressing personal responsibility, self-reliance, and independence.[36] They also underline the need for the federal government to allow greater flexibility for experimentation by states and localities. However, they all point out that the federal government—disposing of a larger revenue base—has the chief funding responsibility.[37] Whereas conservatives have always favored state control over welfare policy, liberals have been more distrustful of the states.[38] Within the new welfare consensus, liberals more readily accept state discretion since there is such a "great variety within and among states as to the range of people on welfare, labor market conditions, educational systems, and bureaucratic capacities; and there is growing agreement that education, training, and employment programs ought to be sensitive to local labor market conditions."[39] However, the reports also reflect a broad consensus concerning the nationwide application of strategies of welfare reform including a new emphasis on training and other services for poor persons, such as have been developed in individual states.[40]

The outcome of the new consensus was the Family Support Act of 1987, the first welfare reform legislation enacted in decades. It reflects the states' recent experiences with work programs and requires all states to integrate AFDC mothers with children under three into "workfare, new style" programs. Further, in order to support the integration of AFDC mothers into the labor market, an extensive federal child care program was enacted providing for day care facilities for working mothers. Aid to two-parent families was extended and child support laws tightened.

The Family Support Act, to some extent, shifted responsibility from the state to the national government. Beyond the definition of categorical eligibility (i.e., the definition of a dependent child), the new federal legislation now required from states, for the first time, that they withhold court-ordered child support payments from the wages of absent parents, that they offer benefits to needy two-person families for at least six months a year, that they establish work and training programs, and that they offer financial assistance for child care facilities.[41] But at the same time the act only partially modified the states' options to include the unemployed father. Financial eligibility and the level of benefits remained state matters, and the definition of work requirements was also allocated to the states.

Implementation of the Family Support Act of 1987–1988 has progressed only in modest steps. When the program is fully in place, the law requires 20 percent of those eligible for assistance payments to join a work or training program; but half of those are exempt either because their children are too young or because they lack either transportation or day care facilities (so far the states have not received the matching funds from the federal government). So in the end only about 10 percent of the eligible will be included.[42]

Complying with the Family Support Act, New York State required all its counties to link training and employment programs with the payment of benefits. Westchester County, for instance, north of New York City, was asked that until 1992 at least 311 of its welfare mothers would have to participate in such a program. On account of the preceding activities of the state, the county had exceeded this number a long time ago: about 3,200 out of 17,000 welfare recipients take part in public works projects, training and educational programs and the county step by step is combing through further thousands of welfare recipients. They are subject to a five-hour test to identify their general educational capability. If they refuse to take part, they lose their benefits. Out of 235 tested recipients 42% were integrated into a college-level education in 1990. The mothers participating in the "Moms on the Move Program" reacted very favorably: "For once, the Department of Social Services is doing something for us. . . . They are giving us the opportunity of a lifetime. You can either stay at home and watch soap operas or you can come to school and get a career. . . . They are always keeping an eye on you. They are behind you, pushing."[43]

Most states oblige their AFDC mothers to achieve a level of "basic education." Systematic evaluation shows that programs emphasizing practical skills—as opposed to those teaching welfare mothers basic education such as reading and mathematics—are more helpful in (re)integrating them into the labor market. "The single mothers there who received the training were no more likely to be employed or to see their earnings rise than a control group of similar women who did not join the program. By contrast, women at the Center of San Jose, Calif. [where practical skills are taught], were 27% more likely to have jobs a year later than those in a similar group who received no training, and their earnings were 47 percent higher. The women in the four programs were members of minorities and all had young children."[44]

However, in spite of some success, experience with state work and training programs and federal welfare reform also suggests that in order to prevent poverty and to integrate welfare dependents into the labor market permanently, more than new-style workfare, transportation, and day care facilities are needed. More comprehensive social policy measures are necessary to include the nondependent working poor who are in danger of falling into poverty in times of recession and in times of illness. Such a comprehensive social policy would have to include measures of school reform, a system of vocational training (combining employment policies with welfare policies),[45] a child allowance program, a more extensive mandatory employers' health insurance scheme, and extensive tax credits for the working poor. In 1990 Congress—against the opposition of the Bush administration—undertook some steps in this direction: In the field of health insurance—again following the examples of several states—Medicaid coverage was extended to children of the working poor (those above the income limit for Medicaid) up to the age of eighteen; these measures are to be introduced on a staggered basis until the year 2000. A coalition of unequal partners including the poor and the welfare establishment, on the one hand, and the health insurance industry and the National Association of Manufacturers, on the other, supported this measure for very different reasons. While the health insurance industry sought to prevent the introduction of a mandatory health insurance scheme, the National Association of Manufacturers argued that the extension of Medicaid makes good business sense because the cost of nonreimbursed medical treatment for the indigent (who have to be treated in community hospitals) constituted an important reason for the increase in private premiums in employers' insurance schemes in the past, since the hospitals shifted the costs of the free treatments to the privately insured.[46] In view of the fact that thirty-three million Americans are not covered by some form of health insurance, by granting Medicaid services to the children of the working poor, the government takes into account, at least to some extent, dangerous linkage between illness and poverty.

Hand in hand with the extension of Medicaid benefits, Congress also enacted a program of substantial tax credits for the working poor which are supposed to function as an incentive to work. The working poor with children and a yearly income between $6,810 and $10,730 (up to $20,262 if both parents are working) are eligible for tax credits of $1,137 for one child and $1,178 for two or more.[47]

Additional measures such as an expansion of the Head Start preschool program, an extension of unemployment benefits, and an increase in the minimum wage may be seen as elements of a more comprehensive social policy on the part of the federal government including the nondependent poor. However, the promising beginnings of a more comprehensive anti-poverty policy were and are jeopardized by the economic downturn.

The States' Initiatives (2): The Impact of the Economic Recession

In the third phase to be distinguished here, it becomes clear that the dynamics of federalism also can set in motion reverse policy initiatives that seek to contain liberal innovations in welfare policy. An important factor in determining whether the state-initiated developments go in a more progressive or conservative direction is the state of the economy. Thus a case study of the "welfare magnet" Wisconsin[48] shows that

> the economy can have an important influence on welfare policy. As Wisconsin became more worried about its ability to compete effectively with other states for economic prosperity, it became more willing to cut back welfare benefits, especially in favor of job training programs. . . . Wisconsin became the site of a major debate over the effect of welfare benefits on the residential choices of the poor. If even a moderately prosperous state with political institutions and cultural traditions that support

welfare ends up reducing benefits to preserve its business climate, to what extent are other states also tempted to cut welfare benefits in order to avoid becoming welfare magnets?[49]

Not surprisingly, the economic recession of 1990–1992, with its strangling effects on state budgets from Massachusetts to California, called into question the national welfare consensus of the late eighties and caused a renewed antiwelfare tide. As a result, states were using only about 60 percent of the federal money available to those who could match it.[50] The recession brought rising unemployment (7.3% in February 1992)[51] and an increase of 13.2 million in the number of welfare recipients, or 21 percent, between 1989 and 1991. Cash assistance to welfare families rose by 15 percent.[52] Medicaid costs went up by 36 percent within the same period. Thus state Medicaid expenditures as a percentage of state general expenditures between 1987 and 1991 increased from 8.6 to 12.1 percent in Connecticut, from 9.7 to 15 percent in Massachusetts, from 9.2 to 10 percent in Maryland, from 17.6 to 19.6 percent in New York State, from 11.7 to 15.9 percent in Pennsylvania, from 10.7 to 13.9 percent in Michigan, from 10.3 to 13.3 percent in Arkansas, from 10.5 to 15 percent in Mississippi, from 13.4 to 20 percent in Tennessee, from 4 to 16.4 percent in Texas, and from 10.1 to 11.4 percent in California.[53] States have started to enact laws that were unthinkable just a few years ago.

As a response to the rising fiscal burdens, two strategies for dealing with welfare programs emerged. One, the so-called carrot-and-stick or punitive strategy, seeks to alter the behavior of the poor through various financial sanctions. Welfare mothers who stay in school get small bonuses in their welfare checks, while those who are frequently absent suffer financial penalties (both amounting to about $50 more or less). Also, welfare mothers who have another child do not receive additional cash assistance.

The other "liberal strategy" consists of two elements: a reinforcement of workfare, new style, as described above that seeks to improve the education and training of families on welfare by providing more funds for this program. The second element clearly goes beyond new-style workfare in that it revives the old Roosevelt ideal of the Works Progress Administration, which put an army of unemployed persons to work to build roads, bridges, stadiums, and other structures during the Great Depression. The new public works projects, also proposed by members of Congress in 1990–1991, put emphasis on the building and repairing of infrastructure ("the government has to come up with an actual job")[54] and requires that 25 percent of the public works jobs be given to the unemployed nondependent—that is, should go beyond welfare recipients. As a strategy it quickly passed on to the federal level.

The first, carrot-and-stick strategy is used, to give a few examples, in Connecticut, where employable welfare recipients are ineligible for general assistance after six months;[55] California cut back payments by 25 percent and pays no further cash assistance for an additional child;[56] Arkansas limits payments to two years,[57] and Maryland decided to cut AFDC payments by 30 percent if children are not sent to school and/or do not get preventive health care.[58] New Jersey has adopted a mixed strategy that legislators hope will encourage family stability by allowing women to keep some benefits if they marry; at the same time it discourages births by denying women the $64 in extra monthly AFDC benefits they previously received for each new child.[59] New York State has been running an experimental program since 1988 which offers mothers only two-thirds of the AFDC benefit and at the same time allows them to keep much more of any money they earn, thereby encouraging work. Under the Child Assistance Program, a mother may keep 90 percent of her earnings up to the official poverty level (instead of giving up a dollar of benefit for every dollar of income).[60]

Response of the Federal Government (2): Party Political Polarization in a Presidential Election Year

It has been claimed that political tradition (liberal or conservative) and party competition in the states, as well as between states and the federal government, within the context of the economic situation, may explain the dynamics of policy developments in the states. Liberal Democratic majorities in the legislatures or liberal Democratic governors (e.g., in California, Massachusetts, and Wisconsin) often set the pace in initiating progressive welfare reforms. During the presidential election year 1992, polarization along party lines, of course, was important in shaping the views on welfare policy.

Welfare as a political issue is part of the liberal Democratic agenda. The label of *liberal* having been stigmatized in the presidential campaign of 1988, Democratic candidates in the 1992 presidential election anxiously avoided declaring themselves liberals, while Republican party leaders eagerly used the label as a political weapon. In early 1992 welfare was picked up by the Republicans as a central campaign issue for three reasons. First, it was envisaged as an opportunity to tap the electorate's discontent with the enduring economic recession; second, welfare issues in the past decade had proved to be useful in keeping alive conflicting opinions among Democratic party members by pitting the poor against the middle class and—to some extent— pitting white against black, thereby creating political cross-pressures for Democratic candidates.[61] Third, the welfare issue is easy to use because welfare recipients are not a powerful target group. "Poor people don't have any power. That's why welfare is such a terrific issue. Who's going to march against you, a 15-year old girl with a baby? She doesn't even get to the polls."[62]

The hypothesis that the welfare issue was used by the Republicans and blown out of proportion may be backed by a look at state budgets. They show that welfare expenditures have to be put into perspective on several grounds: While cash assistance payments to welfare families have increased by 15 percent between 1989 and 1991, total AFDC payments amounted to $20.9 billion in 1991. The federal share was $11.3 billion, the state share $9.6 million.[63] Costs for Medicaid services have gone up by 36 percent; however, much of the growth is driven by the rising expenditures for long-term care for the elderly.[64] Further, cash assistance, far from having kept up with the increases in cost of living, has rather been eroded over the past twenty years by 27 percent—a family of three receiving $402 (if food stamps are included, $623) in monthly payment in 1992.[65]

After the election the welfare objectives of the new administration have to be transformed into policy as yet. During the electoral campaign, the liberal public works strategy was adopted by Bill Clinton as a campaign issue. Simultaneously he supported the punitive strategy, which had been used in Arkansas: payments to welfare recipients were limited to two years to "force" them into the labor market.

In the first two years of the Clinton administration, health care reform, not welfare reform, was at the center of the political stage. Only in the middle of 1994 did the administration put forward its proposal for welfare reform. Based on the welfare consensus of the eighties, which had led to the Family Support Act of 1988, it emphasized the significance of the welfare-to-work programs and called for an increase in education and training programs as well as in child care facilities. However, it also envisaged a limitation of cash assistance to two years. Those who were still unemployed after two years would have to join a work program.[66] Simultaneously a number of welfare reform proposals were put forward by members of Congress, which are now being discussed in the Ways and Means Subcommittee of the House of Representatives.

What can be observed at present is a battle carried on between Democrats and Republicans about the definition of the welfare problem. In this battle, however, both move within the limits of a generally conservative framing of the view of and approach to the problem. Especially the question of a general limit to welfare assistance is perceived to be an issue, one that Clinton snatched from the Republicans and which the Congressional Republicans are currently trying to snatch back from the (more conservative) "New Democrats."

The defeat of the administration's health care reform bill in Congress and the loss of congressional seats and governorships by the Democrats in the midterm elections gave impetus to the Republican welfare reform agenda. During the electoral campaign the Republicans had proposed in their Contract with America that unmarried teenage mothers should be banned from welfare; that unmarried adult mothers should be eligible for welfare, but if they failed to get high school diplomas, their benefits should be reduced by $75 each month; that if welfare mothers had another child, they should receive no additional assistance for this child; and very important, that there should be a lifetime limit of five years on welfare and two consecutive years maximum; that welfare mothers suspected of drug or alcohol abuse must get treatment and submit to testing; and that there should be more funding to build group homes and orphanages.[67]

Seeking to keep the political initiative after the elections, congressional Republicans at the end of 1994 provided fresh details of far-reaching proposals to cut back welfare. They proposed giving states a block grant for AFDC and leaving the question of how to use these funds to the states.[68] Under the plan, federal grants for more than three hundred domestic programs would be consolidated into eight block grants (AFDC, child welfare and child abuse programs, child care, employment and training, social services, food and nutrition, housing, and health care).[69] The proposal would require states to put at least 2 percent of their adult welfare recipients in work programs by 1997 and to have 20 percent in such programs by the year 2003—which would mean an enormous increase from the number in work programs today. Federal officials estimate that no more than 1 percent of the five million adults on welfare are now in programs that require them to work for their cash assistance.[70]

While in principle supporting the objective of devolving welfare activities back to the states and reducing bureaucracy in Washington, as well as using overall limits to payments, the Clinton administration also stresses the importance of tax cuts for low-income groups.

Conclusion

What strikes one as a typical pattern in American policy making is the mutual stimulation of policy developments between single states and the federal government. The multiple political arenas in the states allow for a variety of policy experiments, which—in specific circumstances—may build up a political momentum that bears upon policy making at the federal level. Federal measures, either triggered by state activities or conceived at the federal level in the first place, in their turn shape policy making in the states, of course. As to the political-ideological orientation these innovations take, they may go in either direction: They may either serve liberal social policy objectives or aim at cutting back costs for welfare spending and at applying more punitive strategies with respect to recipients. The direction that the mutually reinforcing policy initiatives between states and the federal government take depends to a large extent on the development of the economy, but also on the specific way they feed into party political conflicts at the state and, of course, the federal level.

Notes

1. See Kevin P. Phillips, *The Politics of Rich and Poor: Wealth and the American Electorate in the Reagan Aftermath* (New York: Random House, 1990), 14.

2. The average gross hourly earnings for production workers in manufacturing between 1980 and 1993 increased (in dollars) as follows: 7.27 (1980), 7.99 (1981), 8.49 (1982), 8.83 (1983), 9.19 (1984), 9.54 (1985), 9.73 (1986), 9.91 (1987), 10.19 (1988), 10.48 (1989), 10.83 (1990), 11.18 (1991), 11.45 (1992), 11.59 (1993). See *Social Security Bulletin*, Annual Statistical Supplement, 1993, 132.

3. See Philips, *The Politics of Rich and Poor,* 16.

4. Ibid., 12.

5. See Robert Pear, "Ranks of U.S. Poor Reach 35.7 Million, the Most Since '64," *New York Times,* Sept. 4, 1992.

6. See *Social Security Bulletin,* Annual Statistical Supplement, 1993, 148.

7. See ibid., 331.

8. See U.S. Department of Labor, *Handbook of Labor Statistics,* 1985, table 18.

9. See Pear, "Ranks."

10. See *Social Security Bulletin,* Annual Statistical Supplement, 1993, 148.

11. See *The New Consensus on Family and Welfare* (Washington, D.C.: American Enterprise Institute for Public Policy Research, 1987), 25.

12. See *Social Security Bulletin,* Annual Statistical Supplement, 1993, 148.

13. See David T. Ellwood, *Poor Support: Poverty in the American Family* (New York: Basic Books, 1988).

14. See Jason deParle *New York Times,* Mar. 1, 1992. According to Ellwood, of the women who go into the AFDC program for the first time, 15.7% will be in it for less than 1 year, 23.5% for 10 years or more, 21.3% for 6–9 years, and 39.5% for 2–5 years. See Ellwood, *Poor Support.*

15. See William Julius Wilson, *The Truly Disadvantaged: The Inner City, the Underclass, and Public Policy* (Chicago: University of Chicago Press, 1987), 10.

16. See Pear, "Ranks."

17. See Wilson, *The Truly Disadvantaged.*

18. See U.S. Department of Labor (Washington, D.C., 1992).

19. See Paul E. Peterson and Mark C. Rom, *Welfare Magnets: A New Case for a National Standard* (Washington, D.C.: Brookings Institution, 1990); see Demetra Smith Nightingale, "Institutional Effects of Reform," Phoebe H. Cottingham & David T. Ellwood, eds., *Welfare Policy for the 1990s* (Cambridge: Harvard University Press, 1989), 211; see also Robert D. Reischauer, "The Welfare Reform Legislation: Directions for the Future," in Cottingham and Ellwood, *Welfare Policy for the 1990s,* 30.

20. Report to the president by the Domestic Policy Council 1986 quoted by Peterson and Rom, *Welfare Magnets,* 3.

21. See Richard P. Nathan, "The Underclass: Will It Always Be with Us?" paper presented at the New School for Social Research, Nov. 14, 1986.

22. Ibid.

23. See Richard P. Nathan, "The Role of the States in American Federalism." paper prepared for the annual meeting of the American Political Science Association, Sept. 4, 1987, Chicago, 20; see also *The New Consensus on Family and Welfare,* 82.

24. See Joel F. Handler and Yeheskel Hasenfeld, *The Moral Construction of Poverty: Welfare Reform in America* (London: Sage Publications, 1991), 191. There are policy contradictions within the program. It places priority on long-term recipients, "yet the contract requirements with the various educational, training, and placement vendors encourage creaming by insisting on payments based on performance (e.g., placement in unsubsidized employment). The program emphasizes job search and placement, but concedes the need for services to those failing to find a job. While the ultimate aim of the program is job placement, there are numerous safeguards, enabling participants to refuse jobs, including net earnings . . . that are less than the monthly A.F.D.C. grant. . . . The program is expected to provide extensive services, but has a built-in disclaimer in case of lack of resources." See ibid., 192.

25. Ibid., 189.

26. See Adrienne Windhoff-Héritier, *City of the Poor, City of the Rich: Politics and Policy in New York City* (Berlin: de Gruyter, 1992).

27. See Peterson and Rom, *Welfare Magnets,* 56.

28. See Handler and Hasenfeld, *The Moral Construction of Poverty,* 187–88.

29. See ibid., 190.

30. See ibid. Implementation of the states' workfare programs, however, shows mixed results: evaluation of the various work programs indicates the following: (a) white recipients tend to benefit more from the employment and training programs than do minority recipients; (b) welfare recipients with little or no work experience benefit substantially more; and (c) the longer and more costly employment training programs seem to have a significant impact on earnings.

31. See R. Y. Shapiro, K. D. Patterson, J. Russell and J. T. Young, "The Polls: Public Assistance," *Public Opinion Quarterly,* 1987, 120.

32. See Reischauer, "Welfare Reform Legislation," 13.

33. See ibid.

34. See Handler and Hasenfeld, *The Moral Construction of Poverty,* 238.

35. These were: American Public Welfare Association and the National Council of State Human Service Administrators, "Investing in Poor Families and Their Children" (1986); Project on the Welfare of Families (cochairmen Gov. Bruce Babbitt of Arizona and Arthur Fleming), "Ladders Out of Poverty" (1986); New York State Task Force on Poverty and Welfare, "A New Social Contract" (Albany, N.Y., 1986); White House Domestic Policy Council, Low Income Opportunity Working Group, "Up From Dependency" (Washington, D.C.: 1986).

36. See *New Consensus on Family and Welfare,* 75.

37. See ibid., 80. If states bear the responsibility for redistributive programs, each state will limit its welfare provision, hoping that some other government will take care of the poor; see Paul E. Peterson, *City Limits* (Chicago: University of Chicago Press, 1981). Therefore, the National Governors' Association and the American Public Welfare Association, consisting of the chief welfare administrators in each state, "while agreeing that states needed flexibility on work requirements and other ad-

ministrative questions, called for clearer national benefit standards, including 'a new cash assistance program based on a national formula reflecting the actual cost of living within each state.' " See Peterson and Rom, *Welfare Magnets*, 4.

38. "We have argued that the allocation of authority coincided with social and political attitudes toward the category of recipients that the particular program served: Those considered deserving were served by a federal program; those underserving, at the local level. As a result of the welfare rights and legal rights activities of the 1960s and 1970s, the states have lost most of their discretion over categorical eligibility, but over the years, they have been given the authority to regulate, sanction, and if necessary, terminate these people from welfare for a variety of other reasons." See Handler and Hasenfeld, *The Moral Construction of Poverty*, 229.

39. See ibid., 202–03.

40. See *The New Consensus on Family and Welfare*, 82. According to Ellwood, the basic philosophical tenets underlying American concerns about poverty are the autonomy of the individual, the assumption that individuals have a significant degree of control over their destinies, the virtue of work ("People ought to work hard not only to provide for their families, but because laziness and idleness are seen as indications of weak moral character"), the primacy of the family, and the sense of community based on religion or neighborhood. See Ellwood, *Poor Support*, 16.

41. See Peterson and Rom, *Welfare Magnets*, 6.

42. See *New York Times*, Oct. 7, 1990.

43. Lisa M. Foderaro, "Leaving Welfare Behind by Degrees," *New York Times*, Sept. 16, 1990.

44. See *New York Times*, Oct. 25, 1990.

45. See Wilson, *The Truly Disadvantaged*, 163.

46. See *New York Times*, Apr. 11, 1990.

47. See *New York Times*, Oct. 31, 1990.

48. See Peterson and Rom, *Welfare Magnets*.

49. Ibid., 49.

50. See Robin Toner, "Politics of Welfare: Focusing on the Problems," *New York Times*, July 5, 1992.

51. See *New York Times*, Mar. 7, 1992.

52. See Kevin Sack, *New York Times*, Mar. 15, 1992.

53. See U.S. Advisory Commission on Intergovernmental Relations, Washington, D.C., A-119 1992:29/30.

54. See Jason deParle, *New York Times*, Mar. 13, 1992.

55. See Kirk Johnson, *New York Times*, June 3, 1992.

56. See Handler and Hasenfeld, *The Moral Construction of Poverty*, 193–94.

57. See Jason deParle, *New York Times*, Mar. 19, 1992.

58. See *New York Times*, Nov. 28, 1992.

59. See *New York Times*, July 6, 1992.

60. See *New York Times*, Nov. 8, 1992.

61. Pitting the poor against the middle class on the assumption that the middle class is hostile to welfare in times of economic recession may turn out to be a dangerous strategy since in public perception the welfare question often is considered as a racial issue. Welfare as an issue has always been high on the black agenda and "playing the racial card" (Moynihan) risks fanning racial conflict.

62. Mario Cuomo, *New York Times*, Mar. 15, 1992.

63. See *Social Security Bulletin*, Annual Statistical Supplement, 1993, 15.

64. See Sack, *New York Times*, Mar. 15, 1992.

65. See Jason deParle, "The Real World of Welfare," *New York Times Magazine,* 1994, 48.

66. Ibid.

67. See Evan Thomas, "Goodbye Welfare State," *Newsweek,* Nov. 21, 1994, 19.

68. See U.S. Congress Report 2/1995, 8.

69. See Pear, *G.O.P.*

70. See ibid.

ELEVEN

IDEOLOGICAL CONTINUITIES AND DISCONTINUITIES IN AMERICAN PUBLIC EDUCATION

Parameters of a New Consensus

HEINZ-DIETER MEYER

There is no nation in the industrialized world, let alone in the developing countries, in which the state of public education is a subject of unequivocal pride or unity. From Japan to Sweden, from France to Britain, and from Germany to Spain, teachers, students, parents, and administrators are entangled in often bitter discussions about flawed policies, teacher burnout, dire financial straits, rigid bureaucracies, outdated curricula, or cutthroat pressures driving students to despair and even suicide. But if the prevailing colors in the imperfect world of mass education are varieties of gray, the system of general education maintained by the richest and most stable democratic power in the world, the United States, is on almost all counts pretty close to black. At the unprecedented "education summit," a conference attended by the U.S. governors in Charlottesville, Virginia, George Bush did not mean to be theatrical when he said: "No modern nation can long afford to allow so many of its sons and daughters to emerge into adulthood ignorant and unskilled. The status is a guarantee of mediocrity, social decay and national decline."[1] At the seat of the University of Virginia, the former president of the United States was echoing the words of the university's founder, Thomas Jefferson: "If a nation expects to be ignorant and free, in a state of civilization, it expects what never was and never will be."[2]

Aroused by reports that found that the poor quality of its general education made the United States a nation at risk, and ever since kept on their toes by successive studies showing American youngsters trailing most of their foreign contemporaries in academic achievement[3] business leaders have joined the chorus for change. They complain that the lack of well-trained and educated employees is quickly becoming a liability in America's struggle for international competitiveness.[4] Parents around the country appear increasingly prepared to contemplate new, sometimes extreme measures to

rescue their schools from the brink of failure—from the radical decentralization scheme of Chicago's "site-based management" project to entrusting the
management of entire school districts to private enterprise.[5] Many observers of public education in the United States maintain that the high-pitched,
even shrill sound of today's educational debate is nothing new in a system
founded on conflicting objectives and interest group tension. Still, a look at
American public education at the end of the cold war registers an anomaly:
In what some saw as liberal democracy's most triumphant hour, its victory
over bureaucratic collectivism, one of the core institutions of liberal democracy—public education—is in deep disarray. While Americans are divided
over what constitutes the main problem of their educational system and
what remedies to prescribe, many agree that some of the core institutions of
schooling in America are in disrepair.

That the nation that introduced the principle of universal, comprehensive, secular, and compulsory education to the democratic world is now failing at it the most dramatically seems a lot of food for thought, indeed. But to
the extent that the recent erosion of once pervasive dichotomies such as
"capitalism versus communism," or "private versus public" prompts social
scientists to attend more closely to the plurality of institutional arrangements to be found beyond the reach of simplistic dichotomies, the end of the
cold war may afford social scientists a unique chance to ask new questions
concerning the future of public education in a liberal democracy. Perhaps
only now does it become possible to ask whether some of the unique features of American public education—local control and funding, ease of private withdrawal from foundering schools into the exclusivity of affluent
suburbs or private schools, and an odd preoccupation of many school administrators with managerialism and efficiency—have something to do
with the nation's difficulties in providing its citizens with a world-class
education.

In this chapter I want to avail myself of the foreigner's privilege and
view from a distance the status quo of education in the United States at this
defining moment of political history. Like others who have engaged in this
sort of exercise before me, I, too, confess confusion over America's chronic
inability to channel qualified teacher talent into the classroom,[6] its propensity to leave crucial policy decisions to lay school boards behaving as "virtually sovereign authorities . . . sometimes arbitrarily and tyrannically,"[7]
and its inclination to leave, until very recently, the setting of standards of
achievement to the accident of time and place.[8] But beyond these "old
world" perplexities (or prejudices?) with the American educational *Sonder-
weg* lie, I contend, deeper issues confronting liberal democracy and its ability
to reconcile the growing aspirations of individuals to control their education
(or that of their children) with the legitimate expectations of local, state,

and national communities to provide their members with an equal chance to acquire the knowledge necessary for responsible citizenship and a productive life in a complex economy. If the American crisis of public education is especially deep and its debate over school reform especially divisive, a review of the current controversies in the context of the historic struggle for democratic education may offer us a unique chance to understand how private individuals in a liberal democracy may best associate to serve their own and the public's needs for education.

Ideological Divisions in American Education at the End of the Cold War

School Reform between Private Choice and Equal Opportunity

One of the most widely noted concomitants of twelve years of Republican rule in the White House has been the emergence of a coalition of school reformers—researchers, practitioners, politicians, and parents—who, if they had their way, would stop before nothing less than the privatization of America's system of public education. Even though couched in a somewhat misleading euphemism, "choice," proponents make no bones about their intention to turn schools into competitive private enterprises and parents into paying customers.[9] From an idea on the ideological fringe of American school politics, the privatization project blossomed, according to many indicators, into a veritable movement, complete with spokespeople, a manifesto, an organization, and influential allies in the Reagan and Bush administrations. The supporters of what only ten years earlier was an intellectually intriguing but politically extremist program of harnessing market forces in order to improve the quality of general education steadily gained force—expressing, if nothing else, the degree of disenchantment with the nation's public schools, which for an increasing number of people had acquired the odious stigma of "beyond repair." As a result of the privatization program, which would provide parents with vouchers entitling them to send their children to schools of their choice, schools would, according to choice advocates, adapt their educational package to the needs of the customers they want to serve or close their doors. The result would be higher achievement rates and an infusion of diversity into general education, as schools as well as parents would be freed from the meddling interference of petty bureaucrats and school board members.

To educators in almost all other countries of the economically developed world, the notion of essentially privatizing a nation's system of primary and secondary education and of reducing the role of the state to that of a licensing board and a voucher-distributing agency is so far outside the ideologically imaginable as to qualify as utopian. In countries as diverse as France, Sweden, Japan, and Germany, general education is an unquestioned prerogative of the state, usually carried out through highly centralized administrative bureaus dominated by officials who, despite their public accountability, enjoy a large latitude of unchecked decision-making power.

But even though advocates of choice, after gathering momentum during the Bush presidency, were denied a crucial second term in which to put some of their germinating ideas into political practice on a larger scale, and despite repeated defeats at the polls,[10] the movement to radically increase the control of parents and schools over the education provided to students has left an indelible mark on American school reform. Programs promoting choice and organizational autonomy—not all of them coupled to the idea of "market control"—are the subject of political controversy in many districts and states.[11] More recently "charter school" models have been introduced in many states on an experimental basis. Entrepreneurial initiatives such as the Minneapolis-based Education Alternatives, Inc., Chris Whittle's Edison Project, or Boston University President John Silber's takeover of the foundering Chelsea, Massachusetts, school district continue to attract some of the most innovative education talent. Perhaps most important, the idea of relying on private initiative to revitalize general education and turning away from discredited forces of government and bureaucracy has, for many, proven ideologically irresistible.[12] And while Republicans, after gaining control of Congress, have so far refrained from announcing radical education policy initiatives (concentrating instead on efforts to "send education home," by reducing the influence of the federal government),[13] it is clear that a new Republican presidency would find the campaign for school privatization poised to launch some new challenges in states and school districts.

Increasing Discontent with Inequality at the Starting Line

If the movement for choice and entrepreneurial initiative is rooted in the feeling that education is ultimately a private affair, a quite different but no less important challenge to the current organization of public education in the United States derives from the opposite sentiment, which holds that a general diffusion of knowledge is a crucial prerequisite for citizenship as well as equal opportunity in a democracy. In this perspective discontent focuses on the often disturbingly large inequalities in funding for public education, which for many students mean irreversible inequalities of opportunity. At the root of this dissatisfaction with the uneven conditions of learning is a uniquely American system of local funding which in other countries would be considered a flagrant violation of equal rights to education.[14] Despite significant increases in state and federal funds, U.S. school budgets until recently still depended on local property taxes for 50 percent or more of their resources. Under this system the funds available per public school child are highly sensitive to socioeconomic differences among local districts, and inequalities easily increase as a result of residential mobility. Widening income gaps have increased incentives for the more affluent to move into the "right" neighborhoods. Racial integration of schools following the 1957 Supreme Court's *Brown v. Board of Education* decision has been another stimulus for a widening gap between inner-city and suburban school quality as many residents left troubled urban districts. As a result, monies spent per schoolchild in different districts have come to differ drastically.[15]

Until quite recently, discontent over differences in public school funding has been checked by the American belief in the principle of local autonomy, which stipulates that local districts are free to use their tax funds on education as they see fit. It has thus come as a political surprise that in the course of the 1980s an increasing number of parents and educators began to challenge the resulting inequalities. In 1993 law suits challenging the unequal funding of schools were pending in twenty-five states. To date, the movement has made some inroads into seemingly unassailable principles. Although the Supreme Court of the United States had ruled as recently as 1973 that education was not a fundamental federal right, some recent opinions offered in state supreme courts uphold such a claim.[16] Under pressure to provide their schools with more equitable funding and to ease the tax load of homeowners already heavily burdened with property taxes, some states such as Michigan have moved to revise their school funding in what the *New York Times* called "the nation's most dramatic shift in a century in the way public schools are financed."[17] Like Michigan, a growing number of states have moved to consider overthrowing the property-tax-based funding in favor of state-tax-based formulas (such as sales or income tax), thereby ending the unequal financial endowments that have characterized American schools for over a century.[18]

Clearly, Americans are deeply divided over the priorities and direction of educational reform at the end of the cold war. Yet these divisions are not new. They have their roots in a political culture that has often exhibited a scarcity of consensus, torn between the pivots of excellence and equality, quality consciousness and equality consciousness. The origin of this conflict can be found in the way Americans have historically tried to reconcile the rival imperatives of individual liberty and community cohesion in education.

Education and Democracy: A Tradition of Conflict

Suspicious of the potential to abuse absolute power, Americans have always believed that making government the nation's educator would be the safest way to enslave a nation. Not by accident did Thomas Jefferson, one of the first ardent promoters of the idea of compulsory and universal education in America, support his proposals by referring to the ease with which central authorities could turn their power into tyrannies when dealing with an ignorant people. The first sentence in Jefferson's draft for a "Bill for the More General Diffusion of Knowledge" reads:

> Whereas it appeareth that however certain forms of government are better calculated than others to protect individuals in the free exercise of their natural rights, and are at the same time themselves better guarded against degeneracy, yet experience hath shewn, that even under the best forms, those entrusted with power have, in time, and by slow operations, perverted it into tyranny; and it is believed that the most effectual means of preventing this would be, to illuminate, as far as practicable, the minds of the people at large.[19]

In a similar vein, Tocqueville, thinking of the state of affairs in continental Europe, wrote a few decades later: "In most countries now education as well as charity has become a national concern. The state receives, and often takes, the child from its mother's arms to hand it over to its functionaries; it takes responsibility for forming the feelings and shaping the ideas of each generation. Uniformity prevails in schoolwork as in everything else; diversity, as well as freedom is daily vanishing."[20] This state of affairs was exactly the opposite of what the young American nation aspired to be. There, locally organized communities had made it their task to provide every child with a minimum of literacy and knowledge to be able to function as a citizen in a democratic republic. The result was a wide diffusion of literacy and general learning observed by almost all European visitors to the new nation. If this result was achieved at the price of a certain administrative inefficiency as the American people "proceed[ed] by sudden impulses and exertions," liberty was, in Tocqueville's eyes, well worth the cost. "What good is it to me, after all, if there is an authority always busy to see to the tranquil enjoyment of my pleasures and going ahead to brush all dangers away from my path without giving me even the trouble to think about it, if that authority, which protects me from the smallest thorn on my journey, is also the absolute master of my liberty and my life?"[21]

The Price of Liberty: Scarcity of Consensus

Having decided from the start against making government the nation's educator, Americans had to rely on more messy and conflict-laden methods to reach educational consensus. While in Europe governments entrusted a corps of civil servants with defining educational objectives and bringing recalcitrant special interests in line,[22] American school administration was left in the hands of local towns, which had in any event developed a more expansive understanding of their rights and responsibilities than their less autonomous European counterparts.[23]

The idea of a universal, secular, comprehensive, and compulsory public education organized in local communities did not meet everywhere with unanimous support. Resistance came from the remnants of aristocratic and patrician families who could afford to pay for tutors privately and send their children abroad. But many of the poorest families who were neither able nor willing to send their children to school and thus keep them from useful employment did not go along easily with the new plan either. Also, some immigrant groups objected to compulsory education because they wanted their own schools to play a role in perpetuating their respective languages and cultures.[24] Even after the 1872 Kalamazoo decision of the Supreme Court, ruling that as public institutions high schools could be publicly funded, the conflict between private interests and community requirements did not cease. Thus the price of Americans' well-founded reluctance to put government in charge of general education was a chronic scarcity of consensus. With each increase in the system's size and complexity, new constituents who entered the scene demanded with the same right as their predecessors that the special interests of their clientele be satisfied. Whereas more government-centered public education systems in Europe or Japan, which incidentally also served a culturally more homogeneous clientele, discouraged direct popular participation, consensus became the main scarce resource in American public education. Under those conditions a single group's prospects of effecting change were quite limited as the diverse interests of different groups checked one another. To overcome stagnation and to effect systemwide change was under those conditions contingent on the ability to identify incontestable ideas or principles beyond the doubt of partisanship. More often than not, however, these principles, while capable of producing consensus in a climate of divisive special interests, turned out to be foreign to the root cause of education: academic learning.

Rationale for Change (1): Efficient Organization

One such presumably unassailable idea to justify systemwide school reform Americans was found early on in the principle of scientific management and organizational efficiency.[25] When the rural school turned out to be ill-adapted to the needs of an exploding urban and largely immigrant population, consensus among the diverse groups was most easily obtained by taking cues from "proven scientific" organizational models that were just then changing America's large-scale industries. Turning illiterate youngsters into literate and numerate students seemed like a simple, unambiguous process that required, above all, order and discipline among students as well as teachers. "Scientific" methods of organization which seemed to be the reason for America's success in building booming industrial organizations thus promised to provide the blueprint for reorganizing the large urban schools as well. The scientific character of these methods made them appear to be above partisan interests. Facilitating order and efficiency, they seemed well equipped to the needs of urban schools in their search for ways to turn crowds of unruly street children into well-behaved pupils.

If scientific methods of management were first imported into the schools to solve discipline and cost problems, widespread graft and corruption in the school districts provided another stimulus to borrow from managerial models of organization. As schooling became an increasingly expensive and complex administrative undertaking that required land, buildings, construction, repairs, equipment, textbooks, and many other resources and that provided employment for a host of workers and staff, from janitors to administrators, decisions over building contracts or textbooks involved increasingly large commercial prospects. Again, school reformers looked to the corporate world for a remedy for the effects of the spoils system in schools. To "keep politics out of schools," the argument went, school districts ought to be run by a "few successful men," just as big corporations such as Sears, DuPont, or the railroads were run by a few men steering highly centralized organizations. The new formula of reform was: small boards consisting of successful men, and managed professionally by the superintendent of schools, the school board's equivalent of the chief executive officer.[26]

Rationale for Change (2): Equality

When the Supreme Court of the United States announced in 1954 its decision in *Brown v. Board of Education of Topeka*, overturning the *Plessy v. Fergusson* doctrine of racially "separate but equal" school facilities, its verdict initiated a reform that changed American public schools perhaps more profoundly than any of the reforms preceding it. It also continued a long tradition of legitimizing change in the name of equality.[27]

Given its pivotal role in the American cultural fabric, the imperative of equality of opportunity is one of the most readily invoked rationales for large-scale social change. In a country that prides itself on its commitment to giving everyone an equal chance at the starting line, the remedy for discrimination is at the same time a powerful rationale for educational reform and change. Employing schools as a vehicle to create equality has a long tradition in the United States. As Horace Eaton, school superintendent in Massachusetts, who described schools as the great "leveling engine," put it in 1850: "Let every child in the land enjoy the advantages of a competent education at his outset in life—and it will do more to secure a general equality of condition than any guarantee of equal rights . . . can give."[28]

The School as a Social Center: From "Created Equal" to "Equally Creative"

With mass immigration and rapid urbanization, the function of public schools expanded drastically. From disseminators of knowledge, schools turned into community centers expected to address social problems from the rootlessness of the immigrant child to the atomization of communities in the new megacities. According to the creed popularized by progressivism, schools were to become social centers replete with public lectures, vacation playgrounds, organized athletics, and civic and social activities. Defining the school as a "center of full and adequate social service"[29] was the result of a large-scale attempt to adapt American towns and cities to the challenges of urbanization. To curb alienation and anomie, educators aimed at a "reorganization of the school so as to give all its activity a social value and in such a way that it will reflect and organize the fundamental principles of community life."[30]

As schools opened their doors to the community, educators celebrated the spirit of the "new school," which "assumes that every child is endowed with the capacity to express himself, and that this innate capacity is immensely worth cultivating. The pupil is placed in an atmosphere conducive to self-expression in every aspect. Some will create with words, others with light. Some will express themselves through the body in the dance; others will model, carve, shape their idea in plastic materials."[31] By lifting the "lid of restraint" from the child to further his or her "self fulfillment," a new generation of educators went to apply the ideas of the *Cardinal Principles* adopted by the National Education Association in 1918, which stipulated that educational objectives be relative, variable, and situation- and child-specific.[32]

Defining the school as a community center expected to fight the social ills of urbanization and atomization severely affected its mission to teach and instruct. Controlled through local boards and committed to openness vis-à-vis the community, the American public school retained little autonomy against a welter of community expectations. One of these expectations was, naturally, parents' expectations concerning their children's advancement. Controlling the reelection of the school board and, indirectly, the appointment of teachers, American parents were, more than the parents of any other nation, able to create normative pressures that made it hard for schools to fail students, especially if they belonged to groups large enough to hold voting power.

To be sure, the resulting equilibrium of low academic expectations was sustained by other mechanisms as well. Observers of the American high school have often commented on the pervasive peer culture stigmatizing achievement-oriented students as "brain geeks," "nerds," "grade grubbers," and such.[33] Another unique feature of American general education, the expansive extracurriculum, has been found to provide "an organizationally legitimate opportunity for the elaboration and activity of academically indifferent student groups"[34] and to contribute to a student culture in which academic achievement and grades rank third behind extracurricular activities (athletics, electing a prom queen, etc.) and peer recognition.[35] In effect, what sociologists have called student society gains a large degree of leverage over the dynamics of everyday American school life. Through its power the student society is often able to "co-opt important segments of the teaching staff," some of whom "respond less to ability variation among their students than to variations in students' social power or personalities."[36]

Strong Pressures, Weak Schools

If public schools in the United States—and not only in the problem-stricken inner cities—have placed American students on the lower rungs of the global educational achievement ladder, this may be in part a result of an equilibrium of expectations shared by parents, communities, students, and teachers in which academic learning has come to take a back seat to community imperatives of social integration and socialization. As the school has expanded its activities to meet the demands and expectations of an increasingly equality-conscious constituency, it has also increased its vulnerability to political criticism. As they are never more than imperfect vehicles to combat the ills of inequality, discrimination, or cultural fragmentation, schools increasingly come under fire for perpetuating the social problems they are committed to fight.[37] The result is that American schools find themselves in an unparalleled dependence on a volatile political process and its ever changing priorities.

Lacking the integrating forces that state bureaucracies provide in other countries and being chronically short of consensus, the American school is forced to look *outside* the educational realm proper for principles and ideas capable of generating consensus. In order to keep the education system free from government control, Americans have drawn on organizational models and political ideals most of which were foreign to the core mission of schools: the diffusion of knowledge. The result is what Michael Walzer calls "weak schools," that is, schools that are not well insulated against social imperatives extrinsic to the purpose of education.[38] Weak schools, in this view, are easily overwhelmed by external demands such as corporate organizations or egalitarian communities. Strong schools, by contrast, buffer both teachers and students from demands that are irrelevant to learning and which they, in any event, cannot promote without producing, by way of unanticipated consequences, large counterproductive effects. Ideals that are necessary or even noble outside the educational realm, such as organizational efficiency or political equality, are blunt instruments at best when harnessed to guide school reform.

Market or Community? Education Between Private and Public Interest

Viewed against this backdrop, the movement for choice which was the centerpiece of both Reagan and Bush educational policies and which promises to come to new prominence under a Republican-controlled Congress, appears as a uniquely American answer to the problems of public education. Shifting control of education from district bureaucrats to individual parents, extending privileges of choice already enjoyed by the well-to-do to all parents, creating room for entrepreneurial initiative and flexibility: these promises made to advance the school choice agenda are deeply rooted in the American ideology of individualism and self-reliance. Yet, as a relentless pursuit of these ideals rarely fails to produce tangible risks to community cohesion and social integration, it inevitably leads the groups threatened by marginalization and exclusion to combine under the banner of equality. Whether American education can, in this see-saw of forces, settle into a new equilibrium seems the key question as the American liberal democratic project enters its post–cold war era.

Education and the Marketplace

To the old European creed that the reach of markets must be curtailed to the bare minimum because of their propensity to stratify people by wealth and to allocate social influence based on property, the idea that general education could be left to the push and pull of market forces is anathema. Leaving education to the imperatives of efficiency and, ultimately, profit making would imply a willingness to hand over the nation's young to a calculus of crude and callous money making at a point when they are most vulnerable. So firmly established is the European consensus on the ineptness of the market to regulate anything beyond the production of steel and TV sets— and even that not without heavy government intervention—that the major features of educational institutions—a centralized system of curriculum planning and recruitment, teachers as civil servants, funding based on a redistributive income tax—have rarely if ever been challenged. The few legally and socially permitted avenues of private education continue to exist on the margins of the public education system.[39]

Ills of an Overgoverned Society?

The rejection of most forms of political-bureaucratic control is at the heart of the choice movement to rebuild America's system of general education. According to the advocates of this program, the problems of American general education are symptomatic of "the sickness of an over-governed society."

> For schooling, this sickness has taken the form of denying many parents control over the kind of schooling their children receive either directly, through choosing and paying for the schools their children attend, or indirectly, through local political activity. Power has instead gravitated to professional educators. The sickness has been aggravated by increasing centralization and bureaucratization of schools, especially in the big cities.[40]

Thus institutions that in other countries are considered essential for an efficient system of general education—professional control exercised through centralized bureaus and ministries—are diagnosed as the main problem of general education in America. Nobel laureate Milton Friedman, one of the most influential spokesmen for market-based school choice, attributes the emergence of government control in schools to the political ambitions of self-interested professional educators. "They expected to enjoy greater certainty of employment, greater assurance that their salaries would be paid, and a greater degree of control if government rather than parents were the immediate paymaster."[41] In his view, the idea of public schooling is closely allied to authoritarian and socialist philosophies. "Aristocratic and authoritarian Prussia and Imperial France were the pioneers in state control of education. Socialistically inclined intellectuals in the United States, Britain, and later Republican France were the major supporters of state control in their countries."

There may have been reasons to employ political means of school control in earlier phases of U.S. history when "close monitoring of the political authorities running the school system by parents was a partial substitute for competition and assured that any widely shared desires of parents were implemented."[42] In those days schools served a legitimate purpose as fire under the melting pot to produce conformity. Today, however, we suffer, according to Friedman, from an excess of conformity; what is needed is diversity.[43]

Markets Without Fail

In a market economy the welfare of the public can be achieved only indirectly: "No one makes decisions for society. All participants make decisions for themselves."[44] As in commodity markets, Mr. Baker's self-interest in making choices about Junior's schooling will lead to better educational outcomes for Mr. Butcher and everyone else. If their suspicions of government are all-pervasive, choice advocates' enthusiasm about the power of markets to produce excellent schools proves equally undifferentiated.

The question whether delivering educational services via markets is susceptible to market failure is seldom, if ever, raised by the advocates of choice—this despite an extensive literature on market failure spelling out in great detail under which conditions markets are unlikely to produce efficient allocations of goods. Thus markets are believed to fail when the know-how of production agents is tied to a particular organizational setting and not easily transferable ("small number problem").[45] Teaching seems to be one of the professions most notoriously subject to this problem of small number idiosyncrasies. Effective teachers know not only their subject matter but also their school, the community, and their students. Much of the know-how that makes them effective comes from their commitment to place. Market-based schools are likely to produce, on average, a much higher degree of teacher turnover, especially in the lower ranks of the prestige hierarchy of schools, as teachers change employers in search of small increments of better pay or working conditions.

Another problem notorious for causing market failure is opportunism resulting from difficulties in monitoring work performance. Markets are efficient to the extent that all information needed for a given transaction is available to all participants. Whereas this is unproblematic when the relevant information comes down to knowledge of price and quality of the product or service, the fact that the work of teachers is difficult to monitor, once they close the classroom door, is part of the folklore of education. This is why strong schools are characterized by strong cultures comprising professional pride, a strong organizational culture, and a high degree of loyalty.[46] Again, that segment of market-based schools which attracts a more heterogeneous student body or which is located in urban problem areas is likely to find it harder, rather than easier, to forge such organizational cultures.

It is quite possible, even likely, that under the privatization scenario some schools may use their freedom to develop specialized curricula and attract a homogeneous group of parent-customers in a way that facilitates student achievement. But if "small number" problems and opportunism make it unlikely that all schools will be among the winners in privatization, the very tenuous rationality of parents and students as players in the education market will increase that probability even further. Historically, compulsory school attendance had to be established against resistance from ignorant and indifferent parents and businesses keen to recruit child labor, as well as from wealthy families who did not need public schools. Parents who would rather have their children work at home or who have lost control of their own lives can obviously not be relied upon to secure for their children that minimum amount of education necessary for responsible citizenship in a democratic society.[47] If parental indifference and irrationality have been a problem in the past, they have, if anything, worsened as drugs have conquered many American inner cities, leaving in their wake addicted or otherwise afflicted parents incapable of guiding their children through the trials of growing up.[48]

At the Core: Diverging Visions of Education in Democratic Society

Whether a society can safeguard the educational needs of its citizens by relying solely on reason and the rationality of its individual members, or whether there are grounds on which a certain amount of paternalism is justified and necessary to ensure that all young people will be furnished with the knowledge needed for responsible citizenship: this is a dispute that goes to the heart of the conflicting ideological currents in American education. The doctrine of market-based choice implies that if individual parents do not act in the best interests of their children, the pressures of market competition will lead them to alter their behavior. If it does not, bureaucratic state intervention would either be lost on them or create unjustifiably large counterproductive effects by unduly interfering with the liberty of individuals.[49] Thus advocates of private educational choice argue much like Tocqueville's individualist, who, "having formed his society of family and friends . . . to his taste, . . . gladly leaves the greater society to look after itself."[50] By contrast, more community-oriented authors argue that community disintegration is an ever present specter of liberal democracy and that even with parents doing their best possible job, "state agents may still have work to do. . . . For the community has an interest in the education of children, and so do the children, which neither parents nor entrepreneurs adequately represent."[51]

Whether the educational community is larger than the sum of the individuals of which it consists, or whether any authority above and beyond that of individual parents is bound to lead to undue constraints on the liberty of individuals is a central question in the struggle over American public education. For communitarians, market failures and the limits of individual rationality suggest that schooling cannot be left exclusively to private interests, not least because any fraction of young people left ignorant, no matter how small, represents an intolerable assault on our democratic values. To guard against the erosion of core democratic values and the very disintegration of community, public authority plays an important role, even at the price of placing certain limitations on individual liberty. For market advocates, by contrast, the gains from state intervention are either so questionable or so positively counterproductive that no sacrifice in individual liberty is justified.

Far from representing temporary positions in a fleeting ideological controversy, individual liberty on the one hand and equality on the other represent, I submit, the two pivots between which American public education oscillates. As the pendulum of change swings toward one or the other of these two extremes, the very limitations of one vision strengthen the arguments of the other.

Post–Cold War Sobriety: Elements of a New Consensus

If the struggle over American public education can be described as a pendulum swinging between the extremes of individual liberty and community welfare, comparing the educational situations at the end of the hot and the cold wars suggests that, stripped of its dogmatic tenets, the movement for choice and diversity coupled with a new sense of educational responsibility of the states may provide the cornerstones for a new consensus that might replace the century-old equilibrium based on local control and private or quasi-private enclaves for the rich.

A Common Sense of Diversity and the Mainstreaming of Choice

At the end of World War II, the education editor of the *New York Times*, Benjamin Fine, went on a six-month tour of American schools. Recording the results of his findings, he wrote, "America's public school system is confronted with the most serious crisis in its history."[52] Fine had seen public schools in great turmoil, with tens of thousands of teachers leaving teaching for better-paying work in industry (the average teacher earning less than a truck driver or garbage collector), one out of seven teachers holding emergency teaching certificates, schools closing because of teacher shortage, "appalling" inequities between schools (some operating on $6,000 per classroom, others on $100). Exacerbating the troubled status of public schools were the glaring inequalities of race. Segregation of schools was firmly established in the South, but not only there. Across the nation, black teachers received a fraction of the pay of white teachers. Access to higher education was in all but a few cases still dependent on the candidate's financial resources and largely out of the question for blacks, Jews, and members of many other minorities.[53]

To right those wrongs, the nation was almost unanimously looking to its capital. Aid to build schoolhouses or to pay outstanding teachers' salaries could in many cases, so it seemed, come only from the federal government, which had the tax base and the political power to support the schools in those many districts in which local communities had already taxed themselves to the limit. Even more troublesome was the complex issue of race, where local communities seemed at a loss to overcome deeply entrenched resistance.

If Americans came out of the victory on the beaches of Normandy with a sense of idealism confirmed, of having fought and won the good fight, of having deployed superior courage, intelligence, and, not least, organization against a despot with designs of world domination, the situation at the end of the cold war could not be more different. Even though today's awareness of educational failure is as acute as it was five decades ago, even though today's list of urgent educational problems is as long as, if not longer than, it was at the end of the hot war, the call for federal intervention is conspicuously absent from today's agenda of educational reform. By contrast, reform plans betting on individual initiative receive an unprecedented hearing. School choice, a program launched from a rather extreme end of the political spectrum, has gained respectability and allies in unlikely political corners.

In fact, a comparison of the United States emerging from the hot and cold wars points to a remarkable shift in zeitgeist and political climate. If the end of World War II marks the beginning of a period of faith in harnessing the forces of the federal government toward social reform, the end of the cold war has clearly brought individual initiative and diversity to the center of public attention. Perhaps the triumph wrought over Hitler's military machine by a well-organized army of American GIs lent itself more easily to spawning idealistic beliefs in "can do" government than the triumph gained by the quiet working of the invisible hand over the tyranny of the iron fist.

In any event, it seems clear that a new consensus on the shape of public education will issue in individuals enjoying more choice and greater diversity than the monolithic, one-size-fits-all school system of old. Which of the many choice schemes will be put into practice in one or another district or state does not matter in this regard, as long as the reform process does not lose sight of the need for community integration and equality of opportunity. Here it should be noted that more pragmatic versions of school choice have become a mainstay on the reform agenda in many states and communities, where even teachers' unions have been ready to contemplate them.[54]

A second element of a new educational consensus may also include a more modest view of schools as social policy instruments. The hopes that schools could be harnessed as a vehicle of social reform, addressing problems ranging from poverty, urbanization, and immigration to racism and multicultural understanding have clearly slackened. Many have come to realize that for any reform goal set, schools inevitably produce complex counterproductive effects, which often all but eradicate the intended improvement.

New Configurations of Power: A Stronger Role for Individuals and the State

While the call for choice and diversity suggests a stronger role for the individual, many recent trends of school reform point to the need for a stronger educational role of state governments, which have traditionally been reluctant to assume such a role. The states' share of school expenditures in the 1980s for the first time surpassed the share of the local districts, and increasing political pressures to equalize financial resources among districts will likely lead to an even further strengthening of the stages' educational tasks and responsibilities.

For several reform objectives that have found majority support over the past decade—improved teacher training and certification, as well as the definition of high school achievement standards—responsibility will have to be assumed by state governments if they are to thrive. Last but not least, there is a growing awareness of education's impact on the economic viability of state economies which is leading the states, as Doyle and Hartle put it, to "take charge."[55] In their survey of the states' new role in education, Doyle and Hartle make a convincing point for a significantly strengthened role of state action in education. They argue that after the recent period where initiative for educational policy has been with the federal government— primarily associated with the Great Society—which in turn was preceded by many decades of local school politics, the time has come for the states to take charge. Lester Thurow's observation that "local governments don't want to pay for first-class schools" because they know that "less than half the population has children in school at any one time, that students will leave home and use their skills in different geographic regions of the country, and that the high taxes necessary to pay for good schools would drive industry away"[56] points in the same direction: local government is overburdened, while federal government is not nimble enough to implement the sort of educational reforms a modern society needs. As state control expands, school boards might change from policy-setting and, often, meddling institutions into agents of quality control and supervision. In fact, that increased individual and state control are, indeed, compatible and potentially mutually reinforcing is perhaps nowhere as clear as in the charter school reform, which, after several years of British experience, has now been adopted in many of the United States.[57]

From "Equality versus Excellence" to "Equality and Excellence": Renewing the American Educational Compromise

As perhaps in no other school system in the world, the conflict between excellence and equality has been a driving force of school reform in the

United States.[58] For much of U.S. history, quality consciousness and equality consciousness appeared to be mutually exclusive concerns of education. If the pendulum in the 1980s, prompted by the Education Commission's *A Nation at Risk* once again moved to emphasize cognitive learning and quality standards, this time the call for excellence has coincided with an equally strong call for equality of opportunity. Perhaps the simultaneity of these two calls signals a growing awareness that effective reforms need to integrate rather than polarize, that equality and excellence are complementary rather than mutually exclusive imperatives of world-class schools.[59]

Beginning with Jefferson's draft for a public education system in Virginia, general education in the United States has at its best been a compromise between the desire to provide knowledge for responsible citizenship and the desire to provide a training ground for the nation's outstanding talent and future leaders. As in all policy domains, the imperatives of excellence and equality cannot coexist in education without tension. But this tension can be productive. Striving for excellence without a concern for the greatest welfare of the greatest number is a recipe for snobbery and callous egoism. Pursuing equality indifferent to the great achievements of human learning invites the rule of mediocrity and a leveling spirit of egalitarianism.

Rather than keeping the tension alive and productive, Americans have, so it seems, allowed it to dissolve. The large urban public school districts—but not only they—have in many instances become a venue of egalitarianism while parents concerned about educational quality and excellence have found refuge in the exclusive schools of suburbia, parochial schools, or elite private institutions. This arrangement, while at first glance easing the tension in the system, has in truth facilitated the weakening of *all* schools and the erosion of academic standards nationwide. Whether and how the conflicting but, in a profound sense, complementary functions of fostering equality as well as academic excellence in general education can be integrated seems uncertain at this point in American educational reform. What is, however, quite certain is that without progress in redefining the American compromise under new conditions, the project of liberal democracy will be once again at risk: this time not from external threats of a hostile superpower but from the inability to reinvent itself in a new and, according to all appearances, more uncertain world.

Notes

Research for this paper was facilitated by a grant from the German Marshall Fund of the United States (Grant No. A-0094-17). I would also like to thank the many teachers and school administrators in school districts throughout the northeastern United States for patiently answering questions and facilitating firsthand observations.

1. Quoted in Chester E. Finn, *We Must Take Charge: Our Schools and Our Future* (New York: Free Press, 1991), 1.

2. Ibid., xiii.

3. For a sample of such studies, see Gallup Organization, Inc., *Geography: An International Gallup Survey: Summary of Findings* (Princeton, July 1988), a study comparing geographical knowledge; for comparisons in mathematical achievement, see National Center for Education Statistics, *Digest of Education Statistics, 1991,* (Washington, D.C.: U.S. Department of Education, 1991), 392–94, 398–400; for science training, see W. Massey, "Science Education in the U.S.: What the Scientific Community Can Do," *Science* 245: 915–21.

4. Lester Thurow, *Head to Head* (New York: Morrow, 1992). See also P. Applebome, "U.S. Business Finds the Work Force Isn't Working," *International Herald Tribune,* Feb. 21, 1995. Prompted by finding that up to 50% of high school graduates could not pass their entrance exams, companies such as Motorola, Xerox, ATT, and many others were forced to spend millions of dollars on remedial education. Motorola reports that 80% of the candidates screened fail entrance tests at the level of seventh-grade English and fifth-grade math. According to an official of the National Association of Manufacturers, "We are where we are today because the American educational system has failed us." See Finn, *We Must Take Charge,* 18–19.

5. For an overview of the results of the first five years of the unprecedented Chicago experiment, see Anthony S. Bryk, "The State of Chicago School Reform," *Phi Delta Kappan,* Sept. 1994, 74–78; for a survey of the host of other reform options, see "The Perfect School," *U.S. News and World Report,* Jan. 11, 1993, 46–61.

6. See Hugo Munsterberg's delightful and surprisingly up-to-date musings on his German *Gymnasium* days contrasted to turn-of-the-century American school reform ideology: "School Reform," in Stewart E. Fraser, ed., *American Education in Foreign Perspectives: Twentieth Century Essays* (New York: Wiley & Sons), 1969, 21–37.

7. Arnold Toynbee, "School Boards," in Fraser, *American Education in Foreign Perspectives,* 221–23.

8. André Maurois, "A Frenchman Appraises United States Schools," in Fraser, *American Education in Foreign Perspectives,* 147–52.

9. For some well-known statements on private choice, see Milton Friedman, *Capitalism and Freedom* (Chicago: University of Chicago Press, 1962); Milton Friedman and Rose Friedman, *Free to Choose* (New York: Avon, 1979); Friedrich A. Hayek, *The Constitution of Liberty* (Chicago: University of Chicago Press, 1960); John E. Coons and Stephen D. Sugarman, *Education by Choice: The Case for Family Control* (Berkeley: University of California Press, 1978); John E. Chubb and Terry M. Moe, *Politics, Markets, and America's Schools* (Washington, D.C.: Brookings Institution, 1990).

10. A recent and highly visible defeat of a voucher plan was that of Proposition 174 in California in November 1993, where a proposal to provide pupils with vouchers worth $2,500 applicable to the cost of attending private school received a 30% yes vote. For an analysis see Myron Lieberman, "The School Choice Fiasco," *Public Interest* no. 114 (Winter 1994): 17–34. Still, proceeding on the assumption that "school choice needs only one clear-cut victory to get off the ground in a big way" (ibid., 25), smaller-scale voucher schemes continue to be tried in several local districts. One is Milwaukee, which has become home for both a private and a publicly

funded voucher experiment. See Patrica Farnan, "A Choice for Etta Wallace: The Private Voucher Revolution in Urban Schools," *Policy Review,* Spring 1993, 24–27. For a discussion of the four-year-old Milwaukee Parental Choice Program, see Daniel McGroarty, "School Choice Slandered," *Public Interest* 113 (Fall 1994): 94–113.

11. Under the heading of "controlled choice," a number of choice schemes have gained prominence which grant parents the right to choose their preferred school from a set of geographically proximate institutions. See, for an example, Charles Glenn, "Controlled Choice in Massachusetts Public Schools," *Public Interest* 103 (Spring 1991).

12. Denis P. Doyle, "Private Management and School Reform," *American Enterprise,* May–June 1994, 12–15.

13. See the statement by Lamar Alexander, William J. Bennett, and Dan Coats, "Local Options: Congress Should Return Control of Education to States, School Boards—and Parents," *National Review,* Dec. 19, 1994.

14. Again, the German case, as laid out in a ruling of the German supreme administrative court, is instructive: "The satisfaction of the educational needs of a community cannot be contingent upon the more generous or narrow attitude of the respective communities. The supra-local interests of the general public and its legitimate desire for a homogeneous discharge of educational tasks weigh so heavily that the state's right of school supervision, whose form is tested in a 150-year-long development, cannot be encroached on by an overemphasis on the self-government of the community, which does justice neither to the history nor to the literal and substantive meaning of article 7, part 1 of *Grundgesetz.*" See Bundesverwaltungsgericht, in a ruling of Mar. 11, 1966, in Sigrid Russig-Kallfass, *Handlungsspielräume kommunaler Schulentwicklungsplanung. Zur Theorie und Praxis dezentraler Schulpolitik* (Weinheim: Beltz Verlag, 1977), 107.

15. Jill Zuckman, "The Next Education Crisis: Equalizing School Funds," *Congressional Quarterly,* Mar. 27, 1993, compares the educational spending per student in the ten richest and ten poorest districts of a state and finds discrepancies of $10,000–$4,000 in New York State; $7,500–$3,000 in New Jersey; $6,500–$3,000 in Massachusetts.

16. Ibid.

17. William Celis III, "Michigan Votes for Revolution in Financing Its Public Schools," *New York Times,* Mar. 17, 1994.

18. Oregon's Measure 5 involves reducing the property tax in annual increments to 5% of total school funds; Kentucky has imposed a property tax ceiling of 15% of school funds. Similar debates are taking place in Arizona, Idaho, and Texas. Information from Horst Dichanz, personal communication, Mar. 1995.

19. Thomas Jefferson, "A Bill for the More General Diffusion of Knowledge," Thomas Jefferson Writings (New York: Library of America, 1984), 365.

20. Alexis de Tocqueville, *Democracy in America* (New York: Anchor Books, 1969), 680–81.

21. Ibid., 92–93.

22. See, e.g., Ernst Kuper, *Demokratisierung von Schule und Verwaltung* (Munich: Ehrenwirth, 1977), 11–18, esp. 25 n. 10.

23. Tocqueville, *Democracy in America,* 67, says of the New England townships that "they have not received their powers [from the state]" but rather have "surrendered a portion of their powers for the benefit of the state. This is an important distinction which the reader should always bear in mind."

24. See David B. Tyack, *The One Best System: A History of American Urban Education*

(Cambridge: Harvard University Press, 1974), 80. One of the best sources on the common school as a contested idea is Charles L. Glenn Jr., *The Myth of the Common School* (Amherst: University of Massachusetts Press, 1987).

25. A good source for the influence of models of scientific management and corporate organization on school reform is Tyack, *One Best System*.

26. Ibid., 95. On the different roles of scientific management in the United States and Germany, see also Heinz-Dieter Meyer, "Organizational Environments and Organizational Discourse: Bureaucracy between Two Worlds," *Organization Science* 6 (Jan.–Feb. 1995).

27. The problems addressed and the problems created through the attempt to overcome racial segregation are authoritatively described in Diane Ravitch, *The Troubled Crusade: American Education, 1945–1980* (New York: Basic Books, 1983), chap. 4. For an account of the social and educational costs of school integration, see Gerald Grant, *The World We Created at Hamilton High* (Cambridge: Harvard University Press, 1988), which chronicles the decline of Hamilton High, a model high school, into racial contentiousness and violence. For criticism of the effects of another Supreme Court decision, *Nichols v. Lau,* designed to provide equal opportunities for students irrespective of their native language, see John Silber, *Straight Shooting: What's Wrong with America and How to Fix It* (New York: Harper Perennial, 1989), 24–33.

28. Quoted in Henry J. Perkins, *The Imperfect Panacea: American Faith in Education, 1865–1965* (New York: Random House, 1968), 12.

29. Perkins, *Imperfect Panacea,* 87.

30. Howerth, quoted in ibid., 82.

31. Harold Rugg and Ann Shumaker, "The Child-Centered School," in ibid., 200.

32. Cf. Finn, *We Must Take Charge,* 130.

33. John Bishop, "Docility and Apathy: Their Cause and Cure," in S. B. Bacharach, ed., *Education Reform: Making Sense of It All* (Boston: Allyn & Bacon, 1990), 234–58.

34. Charles Bidwell, "The School as a Formal Organization," in James March, ed., *Handbook of Organization Theory* (Chicago: Rand McNally, 1965), 990.

35. James S. Coleman, *The Adolescent Society* (New York: Free Press, 1961); Charles W. Gordon, *The Social System of the High School* (Chicago: Free Press, 1957).

36. Bidwell, "School as a Formal Organization," 991.

37. This point is made in Edgar B. Gumbert and Joel H. Spring, *The Superschool and the Superstate: American Education in the Twentieth Century* (New York: Wiley, 1974), 165.

38. Michael Walzer, *Spheres of Justice: In Defense of Pluralism and Equality* (New York: Basic Books, 1983), chap. 8.

39. This was, however, not always so. In the revolution of 1848, liberal ideas held much greater sway in Germany. In the Constitution of 1848, Section 154 read: "Unterrichts- und Erziehungsanstalten zu gründen, zu leiten, und an solchen Unterricht zu erteilen, steht jedem Deutschen frei." [Every German has the right to found and administer schools and to teach there.] How schools became transformed into de facto bureaucratic appendixes of the state is an interesting story in itself. Assuming that the state was a lesser evil than the churches, German liberals obviously did not hesitate to enlist the help of the state in their fight against church control of schools, only to be surprised by the results of their Faustian bargain. Cf. Kuper, *Demokratisierung,* 14–18, 61.

40. Friedman and Friedman, *Free to Choose,* 141–42.

41. Ibid., 143.

42. Ibid., 145.

43. The idea that government cannot solve the problem of general education because government *is* the problem, has been revived by a more recent book on private school choice; see Chubb and Moe, *Politics, Markets, and America's Schools.* The authors hold that the current system's lack of supply-side sensitivity to consumer preferences is a result of over-bureaucratization of school governance and of too little autonomy for the individual school. Private schools in free markets "tend to possess the autonomy, clarity of mission, strong leadership, teacher professionalism, and team cooperation that public schools want but (except under very fortunate circumstances) are unlikely to have." The authors ignore evidence from non-American countries in which "government bureaucracies" play a more positive role in providing general education.

44. Ibid., 29.

45. Oliver E. Williamson, "The Economics of Organization: The Transaction Cost Approach," *American Journal of Sociology* 87, no. 3 (1981): 548–77.

46. Walzer, *Spheres of Justice,* 204.

47. Tocqueville, *Democracy in America,* 45, reports on the situation in postcolonial New England: "The municipal officials are bound to see that parents send their children to the schools, and can impose fines on those who refuse to do so; if the parents remain recalcitrant, society can take over the charge of the children from the family, depriving the parents of those natural rights which they abused."

48. School reformers like John Silber have, for that reason, launched reform programs including a nine-hour-day child care program, not least in order to protect the children from the sometimes destructive influence of their parents. See John Silber, "Speech on Education at McGraw-Hill, Inc.," May 28, 1992, New York (mimeo).

49. On this point supporters of market-based individualism seem to engage in wishful thinking: "Social reformers, and educational reformers in particular, often self-righteously take for granted that parents, especially those who are poor and have little education themselves, have little interest in their children's education and no competence to choose for them. That is a gratuitous insult." See Friedman and Friedman, *Free to Choose,* 150. A look into ethnographic studies of inner-city life reveals a different picture, e.g., Philippe Bourgeois, "Growing Up: Everyday Life in High Risk Neighborhoods," *American Enterprise,* May–June 1991. The author found that "the drug economy, especially retail crack sales, is currently outcompeting the legal, entry-level economy for the 'hearts and minds' of inner-city youth." Left to the choices of their drug-addicted young mothers, the future of the school-age children of these neighborhoods seems a foregone conclusion.

50. Tocqueville, *Democracy in America,* 506.

51. Walzer, *Spheres of Justice,* 219; see also the argument for state control and against private education advanced by Horace Mann and others in Glenn, *The Myth of the Common School,* 219–22.

52. Ravitch, *The Troubled Crusade,* 6.

53. Ibid., 3–43.

54. Bruce S. Cooper, "School Reform in the 1980s: The New Right's Legacy," in Bacharach *Education Reform,* 282–97. Bacharach, *Education Reform,* 425, asserts that on the policy-making level "the stereotype of the left wing advocating centralization and the right wing advocating decentralization quickly falls apart."

55. Denis P. Doyle and Terry W. Hartle, *Excellence in Education: The States Take Charge* (Washington, D.C.: American Enterprise Institute, 1985).

56. Thurow, *Head to Head*, 274. See also Chester E. Finn Jr., "Reinventing Local Control," *Education Week*, Jan. 23, 1991, 40–41.

57. P. Wohlstetter and L. Anderson, "What Can U.S. Charter Schools Learn from England's Grant-Maintained Schools?" *Phi Delta Kappan*, Feb. 1994, 486.

58. Larry Cuban, "Cycles of History: Equity versus Excellence," in Bacharach, *Education Reform*, 135–40.

59. For a similar emphasis, see Bacharach, *Education Reform*, 418–20.

TWELVE

THE FOREIGN POLICY IMPASSE

In Search of a New Doctrine

HERBERT DITTGEN

"I miss it," he says. "The cold war. It gave you a reason to get up
in the morning." —John Updike, *Rabbit at Rest*, 1990

Let mankind endure as long as it may; it shall never be wanting
of impediments to torment it nor of myriad exigencies to
develop its strength. —Goethe to Eckermann, October 23, 1828

Alexis de Tocqueville remarks with some resignation at the end of his book on American democracy that, for contemporary observers, it is difficult to characterize an emerging world. "The world that is rising into existence is still half encumbered by the remains of the world that is waning into decay. . . . I find no parallel to what is occurring before my eyes; as the past has ceased to throw its light upon the future, the mind of man wanders in obscurity."[1] The current observer is similarly vexed in his attempt to identify and describe the distinguishing features of a new world order. The end of the cold war represents an epoch-making change in global politics. The basic constants of the post–World War II period have disappeared. The meaning of the state as a political unit seems to be losing its importance.[2] The common concepts and theories are no longer adequate for a description of world society.

The current system of nation states is a result of the globalization of the European system of states as founded upon the Peace of Westphalia in 1648. Bipolarity during the East-West conflict served to reinforce the global dominance of those norms and rules that the European powers had previously established. The United States emerged from World War II as the preeminent global power. It established a worldwide system of military alliances and successfully institutionalized a political framework for economic and trade liberalism. The United States has authoritatively determined international policy in most world regions for more than forty years. Will it continue to occupy this role following the end of the cold war? European

238

integration, and with it the capability of developing a common foreign policy, is still too weak to realize such a function effectively. This has been further demonstrated and confirmed by the Gulf War and the Balkan crisis. The Europeans were incapable of putting a stop to the killing in Bosnia and looked to the United States to take the initiative for an intervention. The collapse of the Soviet Union has left only one superpower in the world. Charles Krauthammer described this situation as the "unipolar moment," leading to a new Pax Americana under the benevolent hegemony of the United States.[3] The United States is undoubtedly the only remaining superpower; however, the activating opposition based on ideology and power politics has vanished. Furthermore, the end of the cold war has not effected any change in the tripolar order of the world economy. Europe, Japan, and the United States account for two-thirds of the world's products. In economic terms, at least, the United States cannot exercise hegemony.[4]

There is no lack of essays and books on American foreign policy after the end of the cold war.[5] There is agreement that without the challenge presented by an ideological and military rival, there exists no focus for strategic consideration. If one regards strategy as the well-planned adaptation of desired goals to available means, then the American containment strategy has fulfilled, as John Lewis Gaddis observed, this prerequisite perfectly well. "It proved remarkably successful in maintaining the post–World War II balance of power without war and without appeasement until the Soviet Union, confronting the illogic of its own system and its own position in the world, simply gave up."[6] With the end of the cold war, the internal compass and the external geopolitical map have disappeared. As a result of the dissolution of the Soviet threat, one has to come to the realization that U.S. foreign policy has not yet found a suitable replacement for the strategy of containment.[7]

With only a little historical distance from an epoch-making change in world politics, we are well advised to approach the problem step by step in order not to run the risk of making pure speculative assertions about the future. Jacob Burckhardt appropriately noticed that in history the consequences of great upheaval are to be ascertained in their finality only "after the termination of a period of time proportional to the magnitude of the crisis."[8] If the assumption is correct that the significance of the end of the East-West conflict is to be comprehended only gradually, then it is also understandable why as yet there exists no clarity about a foreign policy doctrine commensurate with a new world order.

Another important hypothesis of my arguments is that our analyses of international relations and foreign policy are dependent on prisms, on analytical categories, which we employ for our conceptions. Our formulation of analytical questions—and with it the answers we arrive at—depends on these fundamental preliminary assumptions. This is exemplified demonstratively—and this is the first step in my considerations—in the "idealist" and "realist" interpretations of international politics.

In a second step, the central problems of the new world order after the end of the cold war will be broadly outlined. This is necessary in order to be able to analyze concretely the previous attempts of American foreign policy to confront the new challenges during the transition. The main thesis is that the end of the cold war necessitates a radically changed orientation of American foreign policy. This holds true, of course, not only for setting foreign policy objectives, but—and this is the crucial point—also for the political process, the functioning of the political institutions, and the attainment of political legitimacy for the conduct of foreign policy.[9] Anticommunism was the central organizing principle of the American political system. The cold war made possible the institutionalization of the office of president as commander in chief as well as the establishment of a military apparatus and a "secrecy system" diametrically opposed to the American liberal tradition. The East-West conflict lead to the decline of conservative isolationism during the Eisenhower years and allowed for the rise of internationalism, understood as the leadership of the free world in a global conflict with communism, as the major force. The ideological confrontation between the parties, the distinction between liberal and conservative internationalists was conditioned primarily through the dissent regarding the policies vis-à-vis the Soviet Union.[10] The central questions are as follows: How will the U.S. political system operate without anticommunism as its central organizing principle? Is internationalism, the willingness to accept an international leadership role without the ideological challenge of communism, at all capable of surviving? Is American democracy, again without a direct military threat, in a position to pursue a coherent foreign policy?

The primary difficulty in posing these questions is that the parameters of the discussion concerning the future of American foreign policy stem to a large degree from the cold war era. Therefore, what should first be attempted is to gain an understanding of the new challenges confronting American foreign policy in a radically altered international environment.

Realism and Liberalism and the Post–Cold War World

Realist Theory

The realist theory of international relations was the dominant paradigm for the cold war period.[11] It laid claim to showing timeless political dynamics embodied in human nature. According to this theory, the struggle of states for power was the basic characteristic of international politics. But aside from the validity of realist views is the unmistakably time-bound character of this theory. Morgenthau wrote his classic work *Politics among Nations* with the pedagogical intent of convincing his countrymen of the danger of liberal illusions and the isolationism that had defined American foreign policy between the two world wars. The same holds true for the modifications through the neorealistic structural theories of Kenneth Waltz.[12] The realist interpretation of the consequences of the end of the East-West conflict for American foreign policy can be discussed with the aid of John Mearsheimer's controversial theses.[13]

Mearsheimer's argument is based on the anarchic character of the international system and the subsequent security dilemma. "States seek to survive under anarchy by maximizing their power relative to other states, in order to maintain the means for self-defense. . . . This competitive world is peaceful when it is obvious that the costs and risks of going to war are high, and the benefits of going to war are low."[14] This point of view delivers a compelling explanation of the stability and the absence of war in Europe under the conditions of bipolarity. The balance of power and the system of nuclear deterrence have brought peace to a region that has historically been tormented by war. Mearsheimer concedes that the human costs for those who were subjected to communist rule have been considerable and that the East-West confrontation has led to wars in Third World countries that have claimed a vast number of lives. But his sober review turns out positive: "The net human and economic cost of the Cold War order has been far less than the cost of the European order of 1900–45, with its vast upheaval and suffering."[15]

The dubious nature of such an account will not be further considered here. In the context of our question, the considerations of the consequences of the end of the cold war in the realist view matter most. Since the balance of power is regarded as the most important requirement for containing conflict, the end of bipolarity necessarily leads to instability and with it to a greater probability of crises. The forces of nationalism that were suppressed through the cold war are again becoming virulent following the withdrawal of Soviet and American forces. The recommendation, therefore, is to sustain the system of nuclear deterrence through the U.S. military presence in Europe and also through the controlled proliferation of nuclear weapons. Accordingly, nothing has changed with the end of the cold war with regard to the necessity for a balance-of-power policy except that it has become much more difficult to implement. Domestic factors play a role in these considerations only to the extent that the public must be convinced of America's stake in peace in Europe.[16] Henry Kissinger, the most prominent American practitioner of Realpolitik, also sees only two paths in the new world order leading to stability: domination or equilibrium. The end of bipolarity could not, therefore, signify the invalidity of the old political concepts. "Triumph in the cold war has produced a world requiring adjustment of traditional concepts."[17]

The realist view delivers an explanation for the stability of the cold war order but does not contribute to an interpretation of the failure of Soviet policy. Power is conceived in pure political-military terms; international policy is understood as the relations among states. The definition of the national interest as the self-interest of a state is purely tautological.[18] Transnational relations and norms and the impact of the movement of ideas are largely neglected by the (neo)realist theory of international politics.

Liberal Theory

In the liberal view, the point of reference is entirely different. It is not the balance of power that is the guarantor of order but rather the enforcement of value systems that manifest themselves in liberal democracies and in human rights. Securing and expanding the liberal community and the enforcement of international law via international organizations—for instance, the United Nations—are deemed prerequisites for a peaceful world order. This liberal theory has a long European tradition reaching back to Hugo Grotius, the founder of international law, and Immanuel Kant's *Zum ewigen Frieden*. Nevertheless, it is more at home in the United States, the land of "natural liberalism," than in Europe. Indeed, it served as a rationale for the United States to distance itself from the transatlantic practitioners of Hobbesian power politics.[19]

Woodrow Wilson's efforts to make the world "safe for democracy" were at the core of the Democratic Party's foreign policy vision. Wilson's war message to Congress on April 2, 1917, elucidated this liberal conviction: "Our object now, as then, is to vindicate the principles of peace and justice in the life of the world as against selfish and autocratic power and to set up amongst the really free and self-governed peoples of the world such a concert of purpose and of action as will henceforth ensure the observance of those principles."[20]

The fundamental assumption of the liberal view is that the internal constitution of a political system also determines its external conduct. However, this does not mean that liberal democracies from the outset exhibit a more peaceful behavior. Historical experience is unequivocally at variance with this claim. But historical experience also clearly indicates that constitutional democracies do not wage war against each other but instead establish a separate peace among themselves.[21] Realism cannot offer an explanation for this phenomenon. Immanuel Kant predicted this development. The reason for the propensity that republics have for peace is rooted in the premise that the decision for war requires the consent of its citizens. "Nothing is more natural than that they [the citizens] would think long before beginning such a terrible game, since they would have to call down on themselves all the horrors of war, such as, to fight themselves; to pay the cost of war out of their own pocket; miserably to repair the devastation it leaves behind."[22] It is the commercial spirit that, according to Kant, contradicts the spirit of war and that sooner or later takes hold of all nations.[23] Thomas Jefferson shared the view that citizens of republics are inclined toward peace. He praised the decision to reserve the right to declare war for the Congress as an "effectual check to the dog of war by transferring the power of letting him loose from the Executive to the Legislative body, from those who are to spend to those who are to pay."[24]

The liberal interpretation of the consequences of the end of the cold war is aptly illustrated in the writings of Michael W. Doyle, a follower of the classic liberal tradition.[25] Doyle draws on Kant's argument that foreign policy in republics is dichotomous: "Peaceful relations—a 'pacific union' among similarly liberal states—and a 'state of war' between liberals and nonliberals."[26] The significance of the community of liberal states for world order has not yet been, from this perspective, appropriately considered. For foreign policy strategy, the recognition of the importance of the liberal community would mean that in place of a balanced policy for the defense of interests vis-à-vis adversaries, the development of the liberal community would stand at the center. "Authentically liberal policies should attempt to secure personal and civil rights, to foster democratic government, and to expand the scope and effectiveness of the world market economy as well as to meet those basic human needs that make the exercise of human rights possible."[27] Sufficient for constitutional democracy would be the identification of its allies; its enemies should identify themselves. Crusades for democracy, which are also a component of the liberal tradition, are destabilizing in a world of nuclear weapons and regional conflicts and are beyond the resources of the United States. The key for American foreign policy after the end of the cold war lies in multilateral policies, in human rights diplomacy, and in the support of those countries that satisfy the preconditions for democratic development. Foreign policy, according to the liberal view, requires a "new thinking." The foreign policy of earlier periods in American history, moral isolationism and liberal imperialism, could no longer be regarded as reference points.

Diffusion of Power and Cultural Fragmentation

If one is unbiased in considering the realist and liberal views as they have been presented in the writings of Mearsheimer and Doyle, then it becomes evident that both bring forward a persuasive argument, but that they also contain distinct weaknesses. Mearsheimer's observation that the end of the cold war signifies the end of a long period of stability for Europe is almost incontestable. The end of the cold war represents not the end of history but rather a return of history through the resurrection of ethnic nationalism. We are currently experiencing the dreadful consequences in the former Yugoslavian republics. Also, the religious and ethnic diversity in the former republics of the Soviet Union exhibits a potential for explosive conflict. Mearsheimer is correct inasmuch as he warns against naive hopes for peace that are linked to the end of the East-West conflict. But designating a phenomenon alone does not constitute a good theory. Realism proceeds exclusively from states as actors and units and thereby neglects the role of social forces and the importance of ideas and cultural factors in the analysis of international relations. Conflicts now clearly arise with less frequency from individual states and increasingly from subnational groups; it is less and less possible to describe them as political-military conflicts between states and more and more as ethnic, social, and religious conflicts independent of national borders. A new basic pattern of "strong societies" and "weak states" has formed in underdeveloped countries.[28]

The realist theory is convincing neither in explaining the development of new types of conflict nor in interpreting the end of the cold war. The realists interpret power almost exclusively in political-military categories and define it as the absolute end of foreign policy. The withdrawal of the Soviet Union from Eastern Europe in 1989 and the breakup of the Soviet Union in 1991, a transition effected without military conflict, leaves the heuristic and practical significance of this theory for the post–cold war world in doubt.[29]

The liberal view is compelling in its nearly unshakable observation that liberal democracies do not wage war on one another.[30] The significance for foreign policy strategy is apparent: support of democracy and human rights. The revolutions of 1989 and German unification have demonstrated the attraction and impact of the basic ideas of Western democracies and the meaning they hold for a peaceful transition. President Bush even spoke in the 1992 election campaign of a reversal of the domino theory: "Today the 'dominoes' fall in democracy's way."[31] Francis Fukuyama takes an extreme position in which the victory of liberalism has already been determined.[32] Of liberalism's great foes, fascism was the first to perish as a result of World War II; communism is now following in its footsteps. For Fukuyama it is ideas that are, in the final analysis, decisive. They actually determine what the people regard as their interests.

The assumption that democratic forms of government expand and that democracies tend to ally themselves with one another can claim a certain amount of empirical evidence. But some reservations remain concerning the general applicability of the liberal theory. On the one hand, this involves the dichotomy of liberal and nonliberal states. Democracies are still a minority among the world's regimes. Doyle himself concedes that in relation to the nonliberal states, a balance-of-power policy, based on military strength, is still necessary.[33] Since liberal states have to pursue foreign relations with both liberal and nonliberal states, the realist view has not become fully obsolete; rather, the approaches complement each other.[34] National sovereignty and military power have not become irrelevant after the end of the cold war; however, powerful social changes such as democratic participation, transnational communication, migration, and economic interdependence have contributed to the continual erosion of these concepts. Joseph S. Nye characterizes this new complexity of international power relations as "multilevel interdependence" and as an illustration compares it to a layer cake. "The top military layer is largely unipolar, for there is no other military power comparable to the United States. The economic middle layer is tripolar and has been for two decades. The bottom layer of transnational interdependence shows a diffusion of power."[35] This image illustrates that both the realist and liberal views are justified.

Another important development in the international "anarchic society"[36] is hardly reconcilable with the tenets of either theory. A contrary course of development is to be observed: on the one hand, political and economic processes of globalization and, on the other hand, intensifying cultural fragmentation.[37] The globalization of the economy, technology, and communication fully emerged after World War II. Cultural fragmentation arises from the disintegration of artificial nation-states that were created by the colonial powers and from the politicization of the ethnic conflicts that inherently accompany such a process. The right of national self-determination, which was at the center of decolonization and democratization, is now indisputably leading to the destruction of multiethnic states. The claim to self-determination has launched an almost uncontrollable dynamic that is leading to a proliferation of micronationalisms and encompasses whole regions.[38] Another expression of cultural fragmentation is the upsurge in Islamic fundamentalism. These new developments clearly indicate that the end of the cold war has released antimodern forces that call for a reconsideration of basic assumptions underlying the theory and political strategies of international relations.

The New World (Dis)Order

A World of Regional Conflicts: The Gulf War

On September 11, 1990, President Bush expounded before Congress his goals in the Persian Gulf region, the answer to Iraq's annexation of Kuwait.

Until then, Bush was criticized for failing to formulate a convincing foreign policy concept for a radically changed world—"the vision thing," as he disdainfully called it—in the aftermath of the cold war. However, he could claim that American foreign policy had been very successful in facilitating the transformation processes in Europe, and in particular in orchestrating the international framework for the unification of Germany. The success of American foreign policy in Europe in the two years following the revolutions of 1989 was due not to new ideas but to a skillful diplomacy guided by cautious pragmatism. Confronted with the crisis in the Persian Gulf, intensified in the public eye by a personal clash with the dictator Saddam Hussein, President Bush laid out before Congress his notion of a new world order. "We stand today at a unique and extraordinary moment. . . . Today [a] new world is struggling to be born. A world quite different from the one we've known. A world where the rule of law supplants the rule of the jungle. A world in which nations recognize the shared responsibility for freedom and justice. A world where the strong respect the rights of the weak."[39] Four months later, the war against Iraq began. The first war after the fall of the Iron Curtain was conducted by a coalition of states, supported by the Soviet Union, legitimized by the United Nations and led by the United States. In his State of the Union address, President Bush declared with pride that at this "defining hour" in the nation's history, America was "the only nation on this earth that could assemble the force of peace."[40]

The legitimation invoked by Bush for this military intervention did not differ from the rhetoric employed by Wilson or Roosevelt in justifying the United States' entry into both world wars. Idealistic rhetoric had always been a requisite for the participation of the American nation in a war. The hollowness of the "new world order" slogan became recognizable after the triumphant end of the war. Kuwait was liberated, but Saddam Hussein could not be stripped of his power through the war, and the mass executions of civilians could not be prevented. Only through pressure from the public and Congress could the administration find the resolve to take supportive and protective measures to help the Kurdish and Shiite refugees, who previously had been encouraged by the Bush administration to overthrow the regime. Not until later did it become publicly known that the Bush administration had granted loans to Iraq despite its massive human rights violations and that intensive military and secret service cooperation had existed into 1990.[41]

In the Gulf War, the United States assumed the role of world policeman to which it had become so accustomed under the conditions of the East-West conflict.[42] The Bush administration evoked fears of a return to the old world as the justification for maintaining a role that had been forged in response to the necessities arising from the cold war.[43] This assessment is valid independently of the evaluation of the necessity for military intervention and possible political alternatives. The United States was extremely successful in bringing together an international coalition of allies, as well as former enemies, for the military operation to liberate Kuwait. By the same token, if one considers the important role of the United Nations, then it could be argued that a new American concept of foreign policy had emerged that signaled a departure from the unilateralism of the Reagan years and to be based on respect for international law. However, this is only partly true. The administration, though, continually appealed to the authority granted by the twelve UN resolutions, the last of which authorized the use of "all necessary means" to expel the Iraqis from Kuwait (UN Resolution 678). President Bush declared in his address following the victorious conclusion of the military engagement: "It was not only a victory for Kuwait, but a victory for all the coalition partners. This is a victory for the United Nations, for all mankind, for the rule of law, and for what is right."[44] Despite the legitimation of the allied actions through the UN resolutions, the military command remained in the hands of the United States; the Security Council had no control whatsoever. "Collective leadership" in the Gulf War meant that the United States led and the United States collected—even overfinancing its marginal military costs.[45]

The foreign policy of the Bush administration does not represent a new foreign policy approach to the post–cold war world. The rhetoric of a new world order cannot obscure the fact that the government pursued a power policy in the old style. The formation of a military coalition in the Gulf War was possible because of unique circumstances and is unlikely to occur again.

The conflict with which the United States saw itself confronted in the Gulf conflict, however, threw light upon the new conflict formations that have emerged in the wake of the cold war. Kuwait was the first victim, not the cause, of the new world order.[46] The Soviet Union no longer had any influence over its client Iraq, and Saddam Hussein anticipated that the United States would remain neutral in its conflict with Kuwait.

Europe: In Search of a New Design

The difficulties in formulating a coherent foreign policy without the presence of a Soviet threat is most noticeable in U.S.-European relations. The East-West conflict began in Europe and also ended here. The double containment strategy—prevention of Soviet expansion and restoration of German hegemony—was unexpectedly successful. The division of Europe has been overcome, the communist regimes have been shattered by their own internal contradictions, and a unified Germany is securely anchored in the Western alliance. In 1990 the nations of North America and Europe committed themselves in the Charter of Paris to building and strengthening democracy as the sole political system for all European nations. The full respect for human rights and its consequent political freedoms should form the foundation for a new order of peace in Europe.[47] The task at hand is to create a new security structure in Europe that will integrate Russia and the nations of Eastern Europe, as well as to design instruments for preventing and resolving predominantly ethnic conflicts. Both the Bush and Clinton administrations have held the belief that NATO should serve as the central institution for organizing European security. The question of what role other institutions, such as the Organization for Security and Cooperation in Europe and the Western European Union, should grow into was for the time being answered in a declarative fashion; the foundation of the security architecture in Europe should be a "framework of interlocking and mutually reinforcing institutions."[48]

The problem of a new security organization in Europe became evident when the four "Višegrád nations," Poland, the Czech Republic, Slovakia, and Hungary, pushed for acceptance in NATO. First, the members of the alliance did not want to extend unconditionally the military assistance commitment, the central element in the NATO treaty, to the states of Eastern Europe. Furthermore, the expansion of NATO to the very borders of Russia would be sure to have a provocative effect on that nation. In order to buy time, the "Partnerships for Peace" proposal was offered. Through German and American initiative, the North Atlantic Cooperation Council was also founded. This establishment allows for cooperation between NATO nations and the nations of Eastern Europe. Nevertheless, it is obvious that the military organizations of the West are still relics of the cold war and that the fundamental questions regarding the essence and purpose of the North Atlantic alliance remain unanswered.[49]

The new security organization in Europe also raises the question of how much domestic support the U.S. administration will continue to find for its continued military presence in Europe. The topic of burden sharing remains ever volatile in the United States. The arguments remain just as they were under cold war conditions. Representative Thomas H. Andrews of Maine declared, "Since they do not pay their fair share for their own defense, they invest their dollars in taking our jobs."[50] The Clinton administration rejected one amendment that was brought before the House of Representatives which stipulated that, if the other alliance members would not cover 75 percent of the cost of stationing U.S. troops, U.S. forces would have to be sharply reduced. Similar proposals have in the past had little success in Congress, as the majority of members shared the view that troops stationed in Europe were also important for American security interests outside of Europe. The Gulf War reaffirmed this view. The Clinton administration intends, however, to reduce American troop strength in Europe by 100,000 by 1996.[51]

Under cold war conditions the common external military threat of both the United States and Europeans facilitated compromises within in the alliance over finance and trade disputes. This linkage between security cooperation and economic relations no longer exists. It should then be expected that the resolution of future conflicts between Europeans and Americans over economic issues will become more difficult.

The consequences of the end of the cold war were most dramatically revealed in Yugoslavia. Here the history of national enmity has returned following the collapse of communism and the Soviet retreat from Eastern Europe. The Bush administration originally did not intend to interfere in this European conflict through its own initiative. Even after Croatia and Serbia formally declared their independence, the United States remained firmly committed to the "territorial integrity of Yugoslavia within its present borders."[52] The United States was not prepared to recognize individual republics as long as the fighting continued. For their part, the Europeans could not reach agreement among themselves on a common position. It was Germany that, in disagreement with the United States and the UN General Secretary Perez de Cuéllar, recognized at first Slovenia and then Croatia, and thus determined the path the European Community was to follow. The crucial questions were how Serbian aggression could best be prevented, how the survival of Serbian minorities in Croatia could be ensured, and how a widening of the conflict could be averted. In April 1992 the United States, too, recognized Slovenia, Croatia, and Bosnia-Herzegovina as independent states. However, the recognition of Bosnia-Herzegovina could not alleviate the relentless atrocities of the Serbian militia and the decimation and humiliation of Bosnian Muslims. The United States and Europe were not able to develop a common policy for the Balkan crisis at a time when it might still have been possible to prevent unlimited Serbian aggression. The Europeans were not capable of assembling a concerted effort to protect Bosnian Muslims from Serbian aggression. Until the summer of 1995, the United States, in contrast to its position in the Gulf War, was not willing to provide leadership and intervene. With the end of the cold war in Bosnia, the order and stability of Europe are at stake. Former National Security Adviser Zbigniew Brezinski aptly stated: "Bosnia as a regional conflict thus represents an immediate challenge to the political cohesion of the alliance. The absence of a longer-range design for Europe can deprive the alliance of its historical raison d'être."[53]

Cultural Fragmentation and Globalization: The New Challenges

In the post–cold war world, the United States finds itself confronted no longer with one challenger but with manifold challenges. It is clear that economic competition under the conditions of interdependence does not equate to military power rivalry and would not justify threats and retaliation as reasonable political means. In a highly interdependent world with pluralistic power configurations, multilateral management and internal adjustments are far more essential to meet these economic challenges.

The instruments of American foreign policy during the cold war are no longer adequate to cope with the completely new challenges in the wake of the cold war. The new problems, described above with the notion of "cultural fragmentation," have their sources at the local and regional levels, but their impact generally extends beyond these limits. As a result, the United States is also compelled to take a lead in international efforts for conflict prevention and resolution, respectively, even if its traditional security interests do not at first appear to be affected. The war in the former Yugoslavia demonstrates this unequivocally. The United States may not have any direct strategic interests to defend there, but it most certainly has a vital interest in the stability of Europe.[54]

After the end of the cold war, the complexity of regional conflicts can no longer be neglected. The pattern of cold war bipolarity made it easy for U.S. foreign policy makers to differentiate friend from foe and to shroud the diverse historical, religious, and cultural factors in each region with an analysis of the military situation. Identification of issues and conduct of foreign policy were to a large extent guided by the perspective of the military and civilian military strategists. However, foreign policy beyond the cold war requires a genuine understanding of the nature of regional problems, namely, of the historical and cultural particularities of each area.

In addition to the new challenges associated with cultural fragmentation, globalization poses new problems; not only traditional issues concerning the world economy, trade, and technology but also quite new ones will come to dominate the world political agenda. At the forefront is the need to protect the natural environment, for regulations pertaining to stratospheric ozone depletion, deforestation, and other pressing ecological problems. Other issues include controlling the spread of epidemics (such as AIDS) and containing the international drug trade.[55] Moreover, causal intersections occur between processes of cultural fragmentation and political globalization. Regional civil wars, famines, and ecological catastrophes lead to mass migration on a global scale. International regulation to control this migration is necessary for humanitarian reasons, as well as to avert the risk of new conflicts arising in the countries of destination.

Both political-economic globalization and cultural fragmentation demand multilateral approaches—that is, a reinforcement of institutions at the regional as well as the international level—to conflict resolution. For the United States, this requires a turn away from unilateral policies toward a much more difficult course of cooperation and compromise at the international level. As the only remaining global power, the United States has a crucial role in further developing international law. This effort has to be built around fostering collective responsibility for the observance of human rights and fundamental freedoms based on Articles 55 and 56 of the UN Charter, and in promoting institutionalized international and regional regulations for conflict prevention and environmental protection.

The most difficult task arises from the question of how international law can be enforced in a world of sovereign nation-states. The fact that nearly all states have signed the UN Universal Declaration of Human Rights of 1948 does not mean that it serves as the material basis for the law of all states. Among the most perplexing questions concerning violations of international law is that of whether international intervention is justified or necessary. The principle of self-determination was applied during the cold war only to anticolonial movements. Cultural fragmentation makes necessary a further development of this principle for the protection of minority rights, the support of democracy, and the recognition of successor states.[56]

Agreement can easily be reached regarding the new issues in world politics that need to be addressed and the desirability of enforcing certain goals. An entirely different, but equally important, question is whether the United States will take up the new challenges outlined here and whether it will renew its commitment to multilateral institutions. Can human rights and democracy replace containment as the focus of American foreign policy? Can they provide a basic consensus necessary for an active U.S. role in the world?

American Democracy and Foreign Policy after the Cold War

President and Congress

The militarization of foreign policy and the awareness of a nuclear threat once guaranteed the president the consent of a largely compliant Congress to adopt nearly all foreign policy measures he deemed necessary. Only with the onset of uncertainty regarding U.S. policy in Vietnam and the temporary detente between the superpowers was Congress led to a more active role in foreign policy. In the sixties, Aaron Wildavsky could still speak of the "two presidencies" to illustrate the different authority of the president in making domestic and foreign policy.[57] While domestic policy was marked by a multitude of actors and interests that impeded the successful implementation of programs, the president enjoyed considerable autonomy in foreign policy. Since the early 1970s both domestic and foreign policy-making processes have become very much alike. However, foreign policy always gave the president the opportunity, by dramatizing foreign political crises, to gain support for any actions he deemed necessary, provided that military actions were brief and limited in scale.

The European media likes to depict the president as the most powerful man in the world, who can utilize his instruments of power at will. A similar expectation exists in the United States. In reality, however, the president resides not in a "global office" but in an Oval Office that is wedged among very diverse institutional, bureaucratic, and group interests. Nevertheless, in practice the dominance of security issues has given the president as commander in chief more or less limited prerogatives. Thus he generally used "executive agreements" for military commitments to other countries. The decision to employ military forces was essentially his own. The attempt by Congress to secure its constitutional rights by passing the War Powers Resolution can be considered a failure. President Bush informed Congress of the dispatch of military forces only after the decision had been reached. Congress was not even consulted about the later decision to double the number of troops in the Persian Gulf region.

The dominant issues of the post–cold war world are based no longer on military threats but instead on economic challenges. To these are added issues related to nuclear nonproliferation, the environment, and migration. The president can no longer claim any privilege in these matters. This will make it much more difficult for him to achieve his objectives. Another major problem for presidential decision making arises from the fact that the foreign policy apparatus still conforms to the requirements of the cold war. If President Clinton is truly ready to abandon the unilateralism of the Reagan and Bush era and instead try to implement a multilateral foreign policy, as he promised in the election campaign, then this would also demand a corresponding institutional reorganization in Washington. Comprehensive recommendations for reorganizing the foreign policy making system have been submitted to him in order to structure executive institutions according to the new challenges.[58] A first step, on account of the predominance of economic issues, was the establishment of the National Economic Council. However, sweeping institutional reforms, including the intelligence agencies and the Agency for International Development, are yet to come. Regardless of the necessary institutional adjustments, the multiplicity of issues of equal importance will substantially raise the difficulty of coordinating foreign policy. Since the restrictions imposed on the president will likely increase, it becomes all the more critical for him to set priorities.

Human Rights

In the 1992 presidential election campaign, human rights played a prominent role. Clinton rebuked the Bush administration for its China policy and its passivity in the war in the former Yugoslavia. President Bush used the human rights rhetoric of Wilson and Carter but acted more like Nixon. For Republican administrations, human rights belonged almost exclusively to foreign policy rhetoric; a central dilemma for Democratic administrations that have pursued an active human rights policy, such as the Carter administration, has always been how to bring principles together with foreign policy interests. It remains to be seen whether the Clinton administration can redeem its promise "for a radical change." As early as the 1970s, Congress was partly successful in establishing human rights as a standard for U.S. foreign policy. But during the cold war security objectives and human rights imperatives were always in conflict. With the end of the East-West conflict, the executive cannot, however, reject this claim any longer by referring to geostrategic necessities. The president has lost the most important prerequisite for protecting Realpolitik from moral scrutiny. He has to adopt human rights standards in one way or another in his foreign policy concept. But compelling arguments can be put forward to demonstrate that a realistic human rights policy in the post–cold war world is in the interest of the United States.

Whenever human rights are the guiding principle of foreign policy, two aspects have to be differentiated: on the one hand, the promotion of democracy; on the other hand, the reaction to human rights violations and claims to self-determination in other countries. It is evident that promoting democracy is in the interest of the United States. A more dramatic world would be a safer and a more prosperous world. Thus aid for Russia and Eastern Europe not only serves to ease the transition to democratic forms of government for the people there but moreover coincides with the security interests of the United States. Upholding democracy, as a foreign policy strategy, could also find wide domestic support, synthesizing liberal concerns for human rights, conservative concerns for global order, and the desires of internationalists from both parties to see continued U.S. leadership and engagement in the world.[59] Support for democracy can be successful only by improving the conditions for democratic developments, not by exporting democracy. The means of promoting democracy are comprised of a multitude of economic and political measures that may be controversial in their effect, but not in their general applicability. At the same time, it must not be forgotten that the attractiveness of democracy for other states heavily depends on the political and social condition of American democracy.[60]

In deciding whether to sanction other countries for human rights violations, tying principles and interests together becomes a much more complicated task. America's policy toward China is a case in point. President Bush unconditionally granted China most favored nation (MFN) status for four years. In the election campaign, Clinton declared, "We will link China's trading privileges to its human rights record and its conduct on trade and

weapons sales."[61] Ten months later, as president, he signed an MFN extension to China, albeit with future renewal linked to its stance on human
rights. Neither has the human rights situation improved nor has the concern about weapons transfers been allayed. The problem for the administration was how to create conditions to force Beijing to make changes without
being so tough that the Chinese government dismissed them.[62] In addition
to confronting Realpolitik considerations to best influence China's conduct
of foreign policy, the president had to face domestic pressure in the form of
two sets of competing interests. Congress demanded compliance with human rights principles, while American business pushed ahead with intense
lobbying against withholding MFN status because of the ever increasing
interest in the rapidly growing Chinese market. The decision was presented
by the administration as "a firm, balanced and effective policy" reflecting
both "American values and interests."[63] A realistic human rights policy that
attempts to retain leverage to influence the domestic and foreign policies of
other states will always require a difficult balancing act with domestic policy. But an effective alternate policy that can combine both goals does not
exist. Even more intricate is the task of trying to avoid the impression that
different standards are applied to different countries, depending on the level
of interest. This would undermine the credibility of any U.S. human rights
policy.

The Gulf War demonstrated that only the United States has the capability of organizing a large international military coalition for the purpose
of intervention. However, an international operation of this kind under
American military command is very unlikely to be repeated. Nor is it in
the long-term interest of the United States to play the role of world policeman, since this would fuel anti-American resentment in the non-Western
world. There the question is posed, Why was the West prepared to intervene
militarily when Muslims kill each other in Somalia but remained passive
and hypocritical when Bosnian Muslims were killed by Christian Serbs?[64]
An important task, therefore is to put the Security Council in the position
to deploy troops under UN command for enforcement purposes.[65] This,
however, does not represent a cut-and-dried solution to the problem, for
the international community will hardly be willing or able to intervene in
every regional conflict. Therefore, new means of local and international
conflict prevention must be developed. More improved international coordination is also required with regard to the various demands for national
self-determination that have spread in the aftermath of the cold war. The
war in former Yugoslavia has illustrated the devastating consequences of an
uncoordinated approach. International principles and procedures must be
developed to which any self-determination movement should commit before being granted support or recognition as a newly formed government.[66]

In Search of a New Foreign Policy Doctrine

European observers of the United States have repeatedly described with some astonishment Americans' desire for a higher purpose both in the private and in the political domain. "America," noted Gunnar Myrdal, "is continuously struggling for its soul."[67] This is also evident after the end of the cold war. In the United States the agony of victory reigns: "Winning the Cold War meant that the driving sense of purpose that had pervaded American society and politics since the late 1940s was suddenly gone, leaving a vacuum and uncertainty in its place."[68] In America a continued desire exists for a greater cause that would confirm its special status in the world.

In the 1992 campaign slogans such as "America First," "Come Home, America," and "It's Time to Take Care of Our Own" were espoused by both Republicans (Buchanan) and Democrats (Harkin, Brown). The general conviction that America must put its own house in order does not signify, however, a departure from internationalism. Despite the heightened emphasis on domestic concerns, approximately two-thirds of the public and almost all of the leaders still favor an active role for the United States in world affairs. This degree of endorsement of an active foreign policy has remained relatively consistent since 1986.[69] But this continued support for an active foreign policy would certainly become threatened if the American economy were to become engulfed in a serious crisis.

The confrontation with the Soviet Union had directed the ends and means of American foreign policy for forty-five years. Whereas the debate on the means was moot, that on the ends was not. All other issue areas, including economics, trade, and foreign aid were subordinate to and defined in terms of the policy of containment. The notion of bipartisanship to characterize public and congressional support for the containment policy is perhaps a myth since there was always disagreement, as in the case of the Korean War.[70] It is also true, however, that a coalition of Democrats and Republicans prevented a revitalization of isolationism and that the worldwide military presence of the United States found sufficient public and congressional support. Communism represented the perfect adversary for the self-confirmation of American liberalism. Its ideological challenge likewise provided a foreign policy focus and thereby facilitated the decision-making process.

President Clinton entered the presidency in 1993 with a comprehensive agenda for domestic reform. Clinton only hesitantly devoted himself to the task of developing a foreign policy appropriate for a radically changed international order. He had to learn that foreign policy, despite other priorities, could not be disregarded. The foreign policy challenges facing the Clinton administration are comparable only to those of the Truman administration at the end of World War II.[71] Rather than approaching the new reality with innovative, bold proposals, the Clinton administration gave an impression of being unimaginative and fearful of taking risks. The exceptionally difficult tasks and questions facing the administration can be only briefly summarized here:

- Determination of the role the United States will have in world politics: Which costs and risks is the United States prepared to accept?
- Development of criteria for decisions on military intervention for humanitarian purposes: Is the United States prepared to give up its unilateral policy in favor of military roles under the auspices of the UN?
- Reforming foreign aid: With the end of the East-West conflict, what criteria will guide the composition of foreign aid programs and their regional allocations?[72]
- Development of a new policy toward Europe: Is the extension of NATO into the East desirable and feasible?[73]
- Developing a political strategy for relations with the former Soviet republics aside from Russia.

Through public speeches aimed at clarifying its foreign policy strategy, the Clinton administration has tried to dispel the impression that its foreign policy operates in a conceptional vacuum. National Security Adviser Anthony Lake explained that the policy of containment would be replaced by a "strategy of enlargement."[74] Essentially, this strategy corresponds to the principles of Doyle and other liberal theorists. At the core of the idea is the strengthening and expansion of the community of democracies. In a speech before the UN General Assembly, President Clinton confirmed the preparedness of the United States for international engagement and leadership.[75] However—and this was addressed especially for the American public—Clinton clearly outlined the limits of American international commitments. About the future willingness of the United States to participate in UN peacekeeping missions, he stated, "If the American people are to say yes to UN peacekeeping, the United States must know when to say no."[76] The intended clarification of the U.S. foreign policy strategy was not accomplished through these public addresses; they only confirmed—and this is what the media were almost uniformly critical about—the lack of a foreign policy concept in the Clinton administration.[77] The administration identified a list of ends but was never able to develop a coherent strategy to attain them. Furthermore, a widening gap developed between the rhetoric of promoting democracy and human rights and actual policy.

Not much has been left of the "assertive multilateralism" initially propagated by the Clinton administration. Instead, strict conditions have been formulated for the American participation in UN operations.[78] The new

Republican congressional majority after the elections of 1994 has strengthened the political forces of unilateralism, a propensity that has always been present in U.S. foreign policy. Military interventions for humanitarian purposes have again been subordinated to the "national interest." Stanley Hoffmann suggests that the problem of a foreign policy doctrine based on the theory of liberal internationalism may lie in the predicament of liberal internationalism itself. The plight of the "liberal vision results from the fallacy of believing that all good things can come together."[79] But there is no convincing alternative to liberal internationalism either.

Conclusions

The global bipolar prism of U.S. foreign policy that divided the world into friends and foes during the cold war has become obsolete. The end of the cold war has led not only to a return of history but also to demands for a return of policy. The choreography of foreign policy is no longer predetermined. Instead, a new creativity in formulating foreign policy and the will to prioritize are required. Henceforth, foreign policy cannot be justified to the public on the basis of geostrategic exigencies. Indeed, various political options must be carefully weighed before they can be substantiated. A general focus on human rights and democracy could provide the necessary political legitimacy of foreign policy since they correspond to the American political tradition.

In certain respects, the American political system mirrors the international system. The monism of the cold war and the permanent crisis situation remarkably expanded the executive's latitude for action. Accordingly, the repluralization and regionalization of international relations is leading to a further pluralization, that is, to a greater fragmentation of foreign policy decision making. Just how successful the political institutions of the United States will be in confronting the changes and their consequences as outlined above remains to be seen. The central problem is to develop a consistent foreign policy with clear priorities under the conditions of increasing international and domestic political fragmentation. These priorities have to be set by the president. If, however, he arouses hopes that the United States can provide a panacea for all the world's ills, he will obviously fail.

As far as the intellectual foundation of American foreign policy is concerned, the same conclusion arrived at by Timothy Garton Ash in considering the political situation in Europe is applicable to the United States as well: "The ideas whose time has come are old, familiar and proven. It's the new ideas whose time has passed."[80] With greater historical distance, the cold war will perhaps present itself more as an anomaly than as an analogy[81]—an anomaly that distorted the liberal tradition of the United

States and deformed the republican form of government beyond recognition through worldwide responsibilities and the buildup of an immense military apparatus.

The future of international politics will be characterized less by interstate relationships and more by cultural conflict. Will American liberalism, with its claim to universality, find the wherewithal to tolerate and deal with cultures alien to "the American way"? Coexistence with the Soviet Union was made necessary by the nuclear threat. The coexistence of different cultures in the post–cold war world will not be guaranteed by military coercion; rather, it must be secured and legitimized politically. Integration into the international community of states, respect for international law, and the observance of human rights cannot be forced but can be promoted only by political perseverance. To present the problem as the conflict between civilizations, or as Samuel P. Huntington puts it, "the conflict between the West and the rest," would be a dangerous proposition that could prove to be a self-fulfilling prophecy.[82] Such a perspective leads to new images of antagonism and encourages the ideology of political fundamentalism.

The need for a foreign policy in a world without a direct threat will put American liberalism to a crucial test. The danger of military crusades in the name of democracy is real. The notion of tolerance, which is not to be confused with cultural relativism, is one of the greatest achievements of the Enlightenment. No one formulated the demand for religious and cultural tolerance more fittingly than Gotthold Ephraim Lessing in a parable in his *Nathan der Weise:* "The right ring has the magic power of popularity; before God and man agreeable. This must decide!" These lines are more than two hundred years old, but their call for tolerance is of paramount importance for a post–cold war world marked less by the power interests of states than by the contact and conflict among cultures.

Notes

I wish to thank Manfred Knapp and Tobias Dürr for their helpful comments and Johnny Bonacci for his valuable assistance in preparing this paper.

1. Alexis de Tocqueville, *Democracy in America* (New York: Alfred A. Knopf, 1945), 2:349.

2. Christian Meier, "Vom 'fin de siècle' zum 'end of history'? Zur Lage der Geschichte," *Merkur* 44 (1990): 809–23.

3. Charles Krauthammer, "The Unipolar Moment," in Graham Allison and Gregory F. Treverton, eds., *Rethinking America's Security: Beyond Cold War to New World Order* (New York: Norton, 1992), 295–306.

4. Joseph S. Nye, "What New World Order?" *Foreign Affairs* 71, no. 2 (1992): 83–96.

5. Four excellent collections of essays should be mentioned here: Allison and

Treverton, *Rethinking America's Security;* Michael J. Hogan, ed., *The End of the Cold War: Its Meaning and Implications* (Cambridge: Cambridge University Press, 1992); Kenneth A. Oye, Robert J. Lieber, and Donald Rothchild, eds., *Eagle in a New World: American Grand Strategy in the Post–Cold War Era* (New York: HarperCollins Publishers, 1992); Matthias Dembinski, Peter Rudolf, and Jürgen Wilzewski, eds., *Amerikanische Weltpolitik nach dem Ost-West-Konflikt* (Baden-Baden: Nomos, 1994).

6. John Lewis Gaddis, *The United States and the End of the Cold War: Implications, Reconsiderations, Provocations* (New York: Oxford University Press, 1992), 193.

7. James Schlesinger, "Quest for a Post–Cold War Foreign Policy," *Foreign Affairs* 72, no. 1 (America and the World 1992/93): 17–28.

8. Jacob Burckhardt, *Über das Studium der Geschichte. Der Text der "Weltgeschichtlichen Betrachtungen" auf Grund der Vorarbeiten von Ernst Ziegler nach den Handschriften,* ed. Peter Ganz (Munich: Beck, 1982), 358–59.

9. Regarding the concept of political legitimacy in connection with foreign policy decision making, see Alexander L. George, "Domestic Constraints on Regime Change in U.S. Foreign Policy: The Need for Policy Legitimacy," in John G. Ikenberry, ed., *American Foreign Policy: Theoretical Essays* (Glenview, Ill.: Scott, Foresman, 1989), 583–608.

10. Michael Mandelbaum and William Schneider, "The New Internationalisms: Public Opinion and American Foreign Policy," in K. A. Oye, D. Rothchild, and R. J. Lieber, eds., *Eagle Entangled: U.S. Foreign Policy in a Complex World* (New York: Longmans, 1979), 34–88; Joseph S. Nye, "The Domestic Environment of U.S. Policy Making," in A. L. Horelick, ed., *U.S.-Soviet Relations: The Next Phase* (Ithaca, N.Y.: Cornell University Press, 1988), 111–26.

11. The distinction between the realist and liberal views does not cover all theoretical approaches. However, they do represent the two main strands of theoretical discussion in international relations. For a good overview of the various theoretical models, see Ole R. Holsti, "International Relations Models," in Michael J. Hogan and Thomas G. Paterson, eds., *Explaining the History of American Foreign Relations* (Cambridge: Cambridge University Press, 1991), 57–88.

12. Hans J. Morgenthau, *Politics among Nations,* 5th ed. (New York: Knopf, 1978); Kenneth N. Waltz: *Theory of International Politics* (Reading, Mass.: Addison-Wesley, 1979). See also Joseph S. Nye, Jr., "Neorealism and Neoliberalism," *World Politics* 40 (1988): 235–51.

13. John J. Mearsheimer, "Back to the Future: Instability in Europe after the Cold War," *International Security* 15 (Summer 1990): 5–56.

14. Ibid., 12. See also Kenneth N. Waltz, "The New World Order," *Millennium* 22 (1993): 187–95.

15. Mearsheimer, "Back to the Future," 52.

16. Ibid., 54–56.

17. Henry A. Kissinger, "Balance of Power Sustained," in Allison and Treverton, *Rethinking America's Security,* 238–48.

18. Nye, "Neorealism and Neoliberalism," 239.

19. See Louis Hartz, *The Liberal Tradition in America: An Interpretation of American Political Thought since the Revolution* (San Diego: Harcourt Brace Jovanovich, 1955); Stanley Hoffmann, *Gulliver's Troubles, Or the Setting of American Foreign Policy* (New York: McGraw-Hill, 1968), chap. 5.

20. Quoted in Kendrick A. Clements, *Woodrow Wilson: World Statesman* (Boston: Twayne Publishers, 1987), 170.

21. See Bruce Russett, *Controlling the Sword: The Democratic Governance of National Security* (Cambridge: Harvard University Press, 1990), chap. 5.

22. Immanuel Kant, "Zum ewigen Frieden. Ein philosophischer Entwurf," *Werke,* ed. Wilhelm Weischedel (Darmstadt: Wissenschaftliche Buchgesellschaft, 1975), 9:205–06.

23. Ibid., 226. A similar observation was made by Alexis de Tocqueville, who not without aristocratic melancholy notices that in democratic societies, the "violent and poetical excitement of arms" gets lost. "I think it may be admitted as a general and constant rule that among civilized nations the warlike passions will become more rare and less intense in proportion as social conditions are more equal." See Tocqueville, *Democracy in America,* 2:279. Albert O. Hirschman argued that the internationalization of power over foreign economic relations represents an important prerequisite for peace. See Hirschman, *National Power and the Structure of Foreign Trade* (Berkeley and Los Angeles: University of California Press, 1969), 79–80. Richard Rosecrance argued that an open trading system offers states ways to transform their positions through economic growth rather than through military conquest. See Rosecrance, *The Rise of the Trading State* (New York: Basic Books, 1986). Finally, Francis Fukuyama on the attractiveness of economic liberalism: "This is the ultimate victory of the VCR." See Fukuyama, *The End of History and the Last Man* (New York: Free Press, 1992), 108.

24. Jefferson to Madison, Sept. 6, 1789, *The Papers of Thomas Jefferson,* ed. Julian Boyd, vol. 15 (Princeton: Princeton University Press, 1958), 392–97.

25. Michael W. Doyle, "Liberalism and World Politics," *American Political Science Review* 80 (Dec. 1986): 1151–69; Doyle, "Kant, Liberal Legacies, and Foreign Affairs," *Philosophy and Public Affairs* 12 (Summer 1983): 205–35; Doyle, "An International Liberal Community," in Allison and Treverton, *Rethinking America's Security,* 307–33; Doyle, "Liberalism and the Formulation of U.S. Strategy," in Daniel J. Kaufman, David S. Clark, and Kevin P. Sheehan, eds., *U.S. National Security Strategy for the 1990s* (Baltimore: Johns Hopkins University Press, 1991), 197–213.

26. Doyle, "International Liberal Community," 312.

27. Ibid., 319; see also Max Singer and Aaron Wildavsky's arguments in *The Real World Order: Zones of Peace/Zones of Turmoil* (Chatham, N.J.: Chatham House, 1993).

28. Joel S. Migdal, *Strong Societies and Weak States: State-Society Relations and State Capabilities in the Third World* (Princeton: Princeton University Press, 1988).

29. John Lewis Gaddis, "The Cold War, the Long Peace, and the Future," in Hogan, *The End of the Cold War,* 31.

30. The arguments advanced by Mearsheimer, especially that democracies cannot overcome the basic structural moment of anarchy and, connected to this, the security dilemma, only prove the state-centeredness of the realist theory and does not reflect the importance of transnational relations. See Mearsheimer, "Back to the Future," 48–51.

31. Quoted in Stanley Kober, "Revolutions Gone Bad," *Foreign Policy* 91 (Summer 1993): 63.

32. Francis Fukuyama, "The End of History?" *National Interest* 16 (Summer 1989): 3–18.

33. Doyle, "International Liberal Community," 322.

34. Nye, "Neorealism and Neoliberalism," 238.

35. Nye, "What New World Order?" 88.

36. Hedley Bull, *The Anarchical Society: A Study in World Politics* (London: Macmillan, 1977).

37. Bassam Tibi, *Die fundamentalistische Herausforderung. Der Islam und die Welt-politik* (Munich: Beck, 1992), 20–21.

38. See Peter Coulmas, "Das Problem des Selbstbestimmungsrechts. Mikrona-tionalismen, Anarchie und innere Schwäche der Staaten," *Europa-Archiv* 48 (1993): 85–106; Morton H. Halperin and David J. Scheffer, *Self-Determination in the New World Order* (Washington, D.C.: Carnegie Endowment for International Peace, 1992).

39. President Bush, "Toward a New World Order," address before a joint session of Congress, Sept. 11, 1990, *U.S. Department of State Dispatch* 1, no. 3 (Sept. 17, 1990), 91–94.

40. President Bush, "State of the Union Address," Jan. 29, 1991, *U.S. Department of State Dispatch* 2, no. 5 (Feb. 4, 1991), 65–67.

41. Elaine Sciolino and Michael Wines, "Bush in the Gulf War Fallout," *International Herald Tribune,* June 29, 1992.

42. Anthony H. Cordesman formulated this very soberly: "Like it or not, the U.S. is the only nation that can assemble and project enough power to meet any aggressor. While Americans may not want to be the world's policeman, they must consider what it could be like to live in a world without any policeman at all. See Cordesman, "Why We Need to Police the World," in Micah L. Sifry and Christopher Cerf, eds., *The Gulf War Reader: History, Documents, Opinions,* (New York: Times Books, 1991), 479.

43. Robert W. Tucker and David C. Hendrickson, *The Imperial Temptation: The New World Order and America's Purpose* (New York: Council on Foreign Relations Press, 1992), 26.

44. George Bush, "Kuwait Is Liberated," speech of Feb. 27, 1991, in Sifry and Cert, *The Gulf War Reader,* 449–51.

45. C. Fred Bergsten, "The Primacy of Economics," *Foreign Policy* 87 (Summer 1992): 3–24.

46. Nye, "What New World Order?" 84.

47. "Charter of Paris for a New Europe, November 21, 1990," *Foreign Policy Bulletin* 1, no. 4–5 (1991): 75–80.

48. "Communique of the Ministerial Meeting of the North Atlantic Council, Oslo, June 4, 1992," *Foreign Policy Bulletin* 3, no. 1 (1992): 61.

49. Daniel Hamilton, "USA und Europa: Die neue strategische Partnerschaft," *Aus Politik und Zeitgeschichte,* Mar. 4, 1994, 13–21; Lothar Rühl, "Jenseits der 'Part-nerschaft für den Frieden.' Eine neue Demarkationslinie durch Europa?" *Europa-Archiv* 49 (1994): 101–08.

50. Quoted in Pat Towell, "House Coalition Repels Efforts to Cut Military Fur-ther," *Congressional Quarterly,* May 21, 1994, 1320.

51. Karin E. Dornfried, "Auf dem Weg zu einem neuen Gleichgewicht. Die Vereinigten Staaten, die NATO und die europäische Sicherheit," in Dembinski, Rudolf, and Wilzewski, *Amerikanische Weltpolitik,* 162.

52. Statement of May 24, 1991, *U.S. Department of State Dispatch* 2 (1991): 395.

53. Zbigniew Brzezinski, "A Plan for Europe," *Foreign Affairs* 74, no. 1 (1995): 27. See also Henry Kissinger, "Die Atlantische Gemeinschaft neu begründen," *Internationale Politik* 50, no. 1 (1995): 20–26.

54. Dusko Doder, "Yugoslavia: New War, Old Hatreds," *Foreign Policy* 91 (Summer 1993): 5.

55. See Dieter Senghaas, "Weltinnenpolitik—Ansätze für ein Konzept," *Europa-Archiv* 47 (1992): 643–52.

56. See Halperin and Scheffer, *Self-Determination,* 53–69.

57. Aaron Wildavsky, "The Two Presidencies," *Trans-Action* 4 (Dec. 1966): 7–14.

58. Carnegie Endowment for International Peace/Institute for International Economics, "Special Report: Policymaking for a New Era," *Foreign Affairs* 72 (1992–93): 175–89.

59. Larry Diamond, "Promoting Democracy," *Foreign Policy* 87 (Summer 1992): 25–46.

60. Graham T. Allison Jr. and Robert P. Beschel Jr., "Can the United States Promote Democracy?" *Political Science Quarterly* 107 (Spring 1992): 81–98.

61. President Bill Clinton, Speech at the World Affairs Council, Los Angeles, Aug. 13, 1992, *Foreign Policy Bulletin* 3, no. 3 (1992): 15.

62. Keith Brasher, "China: Clinton's Balancing Act," *International Herald Tribune,* May 24, 1993.

63. Al Sullivan, "Clinton Signs MFN Extension for China," *U.S. Policy Information and Texts* 57 (1993): 35.

64. Ghassan Salamé, "Islam and the West," *Foreign Policy* no. 90 (Spring 1993): 22–37.

65. Secretary General Boutros Boutros-Ghali has proposed the formation of "peace-enforcement units." See Boutros Boutros-Ghali, *An Agenda for Peace* (New York: United Nations, 1992), 26–27.

66. Halperin and Scheffer, *Self-Determination,* 84.

67. Gunnar Myrdal, *An American Dilemma: The Negro Problem and Modern Democracy* (New York: Harper & Brothers, 1944), 4.

68. Norman J. Ornstein, "Foreign Policy and the 1992 Election," *Foreign Affairs* 71, no. 3 (1992): 2.

69. See Daniel Yankelovich, "Foreign Policy after the Election," *Foreign Affairs* 71, no. 2 (1992): 1–12; John E. Rielly, ed., *American Public Opinion and U.S. Foreign Policy, 1995* (Chicago: Chicago Council on Foreign Relations, 1995).

70. Richard E. Neustadt and Ernest R. May, *Thinking in Time: The Uses of History for Decision-Makers* (New York: Free Press, 1986), 258.

71. Henry Kissinger correctly reminded us that the Truman administration needed four years to develop a foreign policy agenda. See Kissinger, "Foreign Policy Is about the National Interests," *International Herald Tribune,* Oct. 25, 1993.

72. See James C. Clad and Roger D. Stone, "New Mission for Foreign Aid," *Foreign Affairs* 72 (1992–93): 196–205.

73. See Ronald D. Asmus, Richard L. Kugler and F. Stephen Larrabee, "Building a New NATO," *Foreign Affairs* 72 (1993): 28–40.

74. Anthony Lake, "Remarks to Johns Hopkins' SAIS, September 21, 1993," *U.S. Policy Information and Texts* 97 (1993): 6–12.

75. President Bill Clinton, "Address to U.N. General Assembly, September 27, 1993," *U.S. Policy Information and Texts* 99 (1993): 3–7.

76. Ibid., 6.

77. See, e.g., Stephen S. Rosenfeld, "The Clinton Foreign Policy: From Discretion to Retreat," *International Herald Tribune,* Oct. 23, 1993; "This Muddled Moment," *New Republic,* Oct. 18, 1993, 7.

78. "Policy on Reforming Multilateral Peace Operations," *U.S. Policy Information and Texts* 47 (1994): 5–6. See also Peter Rudolf, "Kollektive Sicherheit: Politische und ethische Probleme," *International Politics and Society* 4 (1994): 351–63.

79. Stanley Hoffmann, "The Crisis of Liberal Internationalism," *Foreign Policy* 98 (Spring 1995): 167.

80. Timothy Garton Ash, *Ein Jahrhundert wird abgewählt. Aus den Zentren Mitteleuropas 1980–1990* (Munich: Hanser, 1990), 473.

81. Gaddis, *The Cold War,* 31.

82. Samuel P. Huntington, "The Clash of Civilizations?" *Foreign Affairs* 72 (1993): 22–49.

THIRTEEN

AMERICAN TRADE POLICY AFTER
THE END OF THE COLD WAR

ANDREAS FALKE

From Free Trade to Fair Trade

In the 1980s, American trade policy seemed to be headed for a pronounced paradigm shift that can best be characterized by a shift from free trade to fair trade. This shift has been occurring gradually and has not come to an end yet. In everyday political discourse, it is reflected in a rhetoric stressing that trade has to be free as well as fair. At its core, this paradigm change implies that liberal internationalism is not the basic and only point of reference for American trade policy.[1]

During the early nineties, with the advent of the Clinton administration, American trade policy has been characterized by a mix of multilateral, unilateral, and (preferential) regional approaches. The multilateral approach is embodied in the U.S. support for the expansion of the world trading system under the General Agreement on Tariffs and Trade (GATT) and its support for the conclusion of the Uruguay Round; the unilateral approach is most evident in the use of section 301 (in its various versions) of American trade law, which is used to object to unfair trade practices of other nations and force them to open their markets to American goods and services. The regional approach is embodied in the Free Trade Agreement with Canada and in its extension to Mexico under the North American Free Trade Agreement (NAFTA).[2]

It may not be immediately apparent why we can define the shift from "free" to "fair" trade by the rise of unilateral and regional approaches as complements to multilateralism. But the core element of fairness is strict reciprocity, which is much more easily achieved in unilateral or regional contexts. In such context, it is much easier to address certain sectoral or country-specific problems (such as with Japan) in self-initiated moves and bring them to a fair solution than in multilateral negotiations, where goals

264

and results are determined by the interests of a plethora of negotiating partners. Transactions in a unilateral or regional context allow for more fine-tuning and for a head-on challenge to structural trade barriers (for instance, regulatory measures or deeply entrenched business practices), which in today's trade policy environment is the approach favored by sectoral interests, revisionist trade experts, politicians, and part of the executive establishment. The shift toward these approaches is the political response to the populist assessment that the American market is by and large open, while America's trading partners keep their markets closed by virtue of structural trade barriers. This claim finds some backing in the real world of trade: In a world in which, by virtue of the GATT, formal trade barriers such as tariffs and quotas have increasingly lost their punch, more subtle and informal barriers such as restricted public procurement practices, private business restraints such as distribution cartels, industrial norms and standards, regulatory regimes, as well as trade-distorting subsidy and technology support programs, gain in importance. On one level, we can argue that the United States, with the pluralization of its approaches to trade policy, is only reacting to dramatically changed circumstances.

But this is only part of the story. Through diversifying its trade policy approaches, the United States is gaining additional political leverage and expanded room to maneuver. The United States can now choose between or combine various approaches. Above all, it can use the privileged access to the large U.S. market as a lever to open foreign markets. This ability reflects the undiminished superpower status of the United States in the world trading system. No other country can, to the same extent, command such options, even though other actors may have become formidable competitors and are increasingly able to block U.S. initiatives. At the same time, the hegemonic quality of the United States in the world trading system has become more self-centered. With the shift to the fairness doctrine, fulfillment of its own claims has won precedence over maintaining the multilateral world trading system. We should expect less of a willingness to provide unilateral support to maintain the system.

Nevertheless, multilateralism, unilateralism, and (preferential) regionalism are not inherently contradictory approaches. The crucial issue rather is whether multilateralism will have the upper hand over any of the competing approaches or whether it will be relegated to one approach among many. We can posit that the paradigm change has been completed if the latter occurs and multilateralism permanently loses its dominance. For the Bush administration, the competing approaches were subordinated to multilateral goals. The use of unilateral instruments, for instance, was designed to give the GATT negotiations new impetus, and regional arrangements such as NAFTA were to be fully compatible with the GATT and subordinate to the policy strategies associated with it. For the Clinton administration, in the initial stages of formulating its approach to trade the dominance of multilateralism was no foregone conclusion. The Clinton administration sympathized with the idea that all possible approaches had an equal standing. In practice, however, multilateralism quickly became the primary focus of the administration's initiatives as its strong endorsement for a rapid conclusion of the Uruguay Round in 1993 indicated. This suggests that the paradigm shift has not been implemented but kept in abeyance. For the future, a lot will depend on how domestic actors react to the Uruguay Round accord of December 1993 and what effect new trade policy issues such as environmental and labor standards will have on the domestic debate.

The Sources of Paradigm Shift

The end of the cold war is not the only or primary source of a possible paradigm shift. Many of the factors that have been responsible for the shift from free trade to fair trade were present before the collapse of communism and before the end of the cold war threat. Among these sources are:

- the relative decline of the United States, defined by the decreasing relative U.S. share of world GNP, world trade, and global manufacturing output, compared to the eminent position that the United States commanded after the end of World War II;
- specific competitiveness problems of certain older industrial sectors and of some of the more advanced high-tech sectors;
- the rise of competitors in the Asian-Pacific region such as Japan and Korea, who pursued aggressive export promotion schemes coupled with export-oriented industrial policies and protected their own domestic markets;
- serious macroeconomic imbalances that led to an overvaluation of the dollar and to high trade deficits.
- the inadequate willingness of the new competitors of the United States, primarily Japan and the European Union (EU), to carry the hegemonic burden of advancing the multilateral trading order; and
- changes in the domestic basis of American trade policy which can best be characterized by the rise of the U.S. Congress to the position of a coequal player in formulating the basic framework for U.S. trade policy.

The Role of the End of the Cold War

Although the end of the cold war by itself cannot explain the paradigm shift and may not even be one of the major causes, the post–cold war political environment exerts an influence on it. Assessment of this influence can only be preliminary as any shift between the weights assigned to security and trade policies occur gradually and may be reversible with the emergence of a new security threat. Note that the United States is likely to remain an important factor in the construction of the European security order after the end of the cold war and that also with regard to Japan, security concerns will continue to play a major role in Japanese-American relations, even if the disappearance of the communist threat may lead to a quicker adjustment of the security-based elements of the relationship.[3] With respect to Europe, the trade relationship is much more balanced and not burdened by a quasi-permanent structural deficit as it is in the case of Japan, with the consequence that the disappearance of the security-related basis of the relationship is less of a problem.[4] And last but not least, we need to acknowledge that the administrative security and trade policy decision-making systems in the United States are still relatively isolated from each other and that it will take time to reduce the status of the security policy establishment, although the Clinton administration has stated that economic concerns should play a much greater role in foreign policy.

But in whatever direction the relationship between security and foreign economic policy will develop, it remains undisputed that at the height of the cold war, American trade policy was subordinated to a general strategy of strengthening America's alliance partners economically. American trade policy was integrated into an all-embracing security policy based on the concept of containing communism. During the immediate post–World War II years, the United States was willing to tolerate discriminatory practices on the part of Japan and the European Community (EC) or its predecessor, the coal and steel union, and at the same time to open its market unilaterally to exports from allied countries.[5] In Europe, the United States accepted throughout the 1970s a certain economic price for a politically integrated Europe in view of the possible overall gain in political vitality for the Western alliance. While it was evident that the emergence of the common agricultural policy led to a disillusionment and to a greater emphasis on economic self-interests (cf. the "chicken war" of the sixties), until the end of the Tokyo Round in the late seventies, the United States refrained from an all-out attack on the protectionist and increasingly expansionist European agricultural support regime.[6] The contrast to the 1980s, when the Reagan and Bush administrations insisted on the inclusion of agriculture in the GATT and the reduction of subsidized European agricultural exports as a condition for concluding the Uruguay Round is striking.[7]

In view of the Soviet threat, cooperation in security affairs generated a deep-seated solidarity between Western alliance partners, which also served as the basis of cooperation in trade policy. Security policy worked like a safety net that prevented trade policy conflicts from getting out of hand.[8]

The primacy of security policy and the lesser emphasis on narrow economic self-interest did not work in general to the disadvantage of the United States, as some commentators claim today. On the one hand, the United States, through its support for a revitalization of Japan and Europe, created the basis of a global economic system, from which the United States and its multinational companies were first to profit. On the other hand, the primacy of security policy also served as a secondary bargaining chip that could be used to sway America's alliance partners who were dependent on America's security guarantees.[9]

Regardless of the precise effect of the end of the cold war on trade strategies, the end of the cold war and the collapse of the Soviet Union led to a new strategic context for the pursuit of economic and trade objectives. The need to take into account overriding security interests is reduced, and the emergence of more self-centered and mercantile objectives in foreign economic policy became a real possibility. As a result, the primacy of geopolitics is increasingly being replaced by the primacy of economics.[10] This change does not necessarily have to lead to the triumph of economic nationalism, but it indicates a tendency to evaluate economic and trade conflicts on their own terms and not primarily in security and foreign policy terms. The management of economic conflicts will have to be based on the acknowledgment of economic interdependence and pluralistic leadership.[11]

Even though the end of the cold war does not signal the disappearance of security-based global strategies, allowing them to continue to play a prominent role in American strategy in view of the precarious situation in the successor states of the Soviet Union and of the complicated security constellation between East Asian states, it is evident that economic policy objectives gain new weight in American foreign policy. This change is reflected in some of the practices and rhetoric of the Clinton administration. The themes being stressed are:

1. economic security as the basis of America's role in the world;
2. economics as the core of foreign policy; and
3. American foreign policy as a resource to attain economic objectives.[12]

Today, however, it becomes apparent that a greater emphasis on economic self-interest has been a trend that preceded the end of the cold war, which means that other factors have to account for the paradigm shift in American trade policy. But in assessing the effect of the reduced security threat, we can posit that the United States will be able to respond more immediately to these factors and thus accelerate the paradigm shift.

Relative Decline

One of the sources of the fairness paradigm is the relative decline of the United States in the world economy, which can be measured in terms of the shrinking U.S. share of world GNP. The thesis of American decline was first popularized in Paul Kennedy's book, *The Rise and Fall of Great Powers* and has left a significant mark on the consciousness of America's public.[13] His thesis is interesting in the context of trade policy less because of its substantive claims than because of the political effect it had on the public mind from the publication of the book in the heyday of the Reagan era to the presidential election campaign of 1992. On the surface, there is little dispute that the U.S. share of world output since the end of World War II has fallen from 47 percent to roughly 25 percent, but the conclusions drawn from this fact are more ambiguous. These statistics reflect in many ways the state of the devastated economies of Europe and Japan after the war, artificially inflating the preeminence of the United States. As Joseph S. Nye has pointed out, this decline has been a relative one and was caused primarily by the "vanishing World War II effect," which would disappear with the economic revitalization of the former enemies and the industrialization of previously under-developed regions.[14] It was inevitable that with the recovery of Europe and Asia, the United States had to reckon with new competitors, the rise of which cannot be discounted by pointing to the relativity of American decline.

But granted the relativity of the decline diagnosis, the process associated with decline has an important subjective and psychological effect. The United States achieved its superpower status after World War II at a time of enormous, even if artificial economic preponderance. Psychologically, superpower status and economic preeminence were thus closely associated in the consciousness of political elites and the public at large. Given the coincidence of the rise to superpower status and the disproportionate economic weight of the United States, the normalization process in terms of U.S. economic weight in the world almost inevitably had to be interpreted as absolute decline, even though the public debate arose only when the real process had been completed. The political context of this debate was the crucial factor. Its thrust was clearly directed against the Reagan administration's spiraling budget and trade deficits and against its claim that it had revived the United States economically.

The debate's effect on U.S. trade policy should not be discounted. It nourished what Jagdish Bhagwhati has called the "diminished giant syndrome,"[15] which suggests a perception of decline far exceeding reality and extends an invitation to more aggressive and self-centered foreign economic policies. Its political effect consisted in the inducement of self-pity based on an underlying assumption that the United States had become the victim of its own generosity and the unfair trade practices of its trading partners. While the Bush administration tried to contain this syndrome and point to America's economic strengths, in the context of a delayed or not readily apparent economic recovery it was skillfully exploited by the Clinton campaign in 1992 in order to underscore the urgency of a change of administration. However, the Clinton campaign primarily focused on the domestic structural problems associated with decline such as deficiencies in job training and infrastructure development and skillfully avoided putting the emphasis on the external aspects of the decline debate.

Relative decline primarily has psychological-political relevance and has only limited utility in explaining the shift to a new trade policy. Robert O. Keohane has pointed out that despite the United States' fall as the hegemon of the world economic system, cooperation among the major economic powers, including cooperation in trade, has not disappeared. Tensions and continued cooperation simply coexist.[16] This implies that the reason for a possible paradigm shift may have to be found in problems of competitiveness in specific sectors and in structural changes in the U.S. economy.[17]

Diminishing Industrial Competitiveness

The U.S. economy in recent years has experienced challenges in competitiveness in more traditional industrial sectors as well as in high-technology sectors. The real context of these problems was not so much the rather abstract fall in the U.S. share of world GNP as structural problems of the industrial system in the United States, particularly with regard to the organization of the production process. For too long, American industry held on to the system of inflexible mass production, failing to integrate product development and production. It was also deficient in promoting innovation to the production stage and quickly bringing new products to the market. In addition, a short-term orientation of entrepreneurs and investors led to a preference for quick profit over gaining market share in the long run. Weaknesses in vocational training and skill development as well as deficiencies in public school systems highlighted the problem of an unskilled work force. The main symptom of this bundle of problems was a slowdown in productivity as compared to that of America's main commercial rivals.[18] The immediate consequence was an increasing share of the U.S. market in manufacturing goods for foreign suppliers. The share of imports of industrial output rose between 1965 and 1980 from 4.3 percent to 13.5 percent. In sectors such as machine tools, the market share of foreign producers rose until the mid-eighties to almost 50 percent. In consumer electronics, where the United States had market shares for TV sets and phonographs of up to 90 percent in the early 1970s, its share in the mid-eighties had dropped to 10 percent and 1 percent, respectively. The Japanese share of the U.S. auto market reached 30 percent in the eighties.[19]

For a long time many observers and decision makers were not concerned by these developments because they assumed that the United States could leave older, traditional industrial sectors to emerging competitors with lower cost structures. In turn, the United States would concentrate on exploiting its advantages in higher value-added products in the high-tech sectors.[20] But these assumptions did not hold. The United States also experienced serious competitive challenges in high-tech industries. In the critical semiconductor sector, which was dominated by U.S. producers in the 1970s with a worldwide market share of over 70 percent, the Japanese and the Koreans became serious rivals because of government-sponsored catch-up programs. By 1983, for the first time, the two countries had a larger market share than U.S. companies. In 1986 the Japanese share had risen to 65 percent, while the U.S. share had fallen below 30 percent. In memory chip production, Japan held a lead of 73 percent over the United States' 18 percent. In 1986, on a narrow definition of high tech products, the U.S. high-tech trade balance, which in 1980 had a surplus of over $27 billion, had dropped into deficit for the first time ever.[21]

As reasons for these striking developments, we can identify government-sponsored research and technology programs on the part of the Japanese government as well as failings in American industrial strategy. Even the high-tech sector was beset by problems with rapid commercialization and market-based application of research and innovation. Government research supports were concentrated on basic research and military projects and neglected the commercial technology base.[22] The Bush administration responded to these problems by shifting U.S. technology programs toward commercial application and a closer linkup between government and the private sector as embodied in the Semiconductor Manufacturing Technology initiative.[23] The Clinton administration is considering putting such initiatives on a wider basis and thus transforming them into a selective industrial policy with a focus on future technologies.

The Role of Foreign Export-Oriented Strategies and Industrial Policies

The endogenous weaknesses of American industry were exacerbated dramatically by foreign export-oriented industrial- and technology-related policies on the basis of public/private sector coordination. Since the 1950s, Japan has pursued a systematic policy of industrial targeting that aimed to increase sectoral market shares through closely coordinated actions between government and industry. In particular with regard to high-tech production, the free play of market forces and free trade were questioned while the influence of government-directed supports, deliberate steering, and closure of the domestic market increasingly became a factor in international competition. Japan was the pioneer of such policies, but other Asian states such as Korea and Taiwan soon followed suit.[24] Europe and the EU also initiated high-tech industrial policies with mixed success, of which support for a European a civilian aircraft industry under the Airbus program was the most effective and the most controversial in terms of its effects on international trade.[25] The United States, in contrast, restricted its approaches to a quasi-industrial policy related to the defense sector which, because of inefficient commercialization, yielded diminishing marginal returns.[26] There was increasing evidence that government intervention had a greater impact on commercial success than factor endowment or comparative advantage. In the high-tech sector, government intervention did have considerable consequences as factors such as oligopolistic competition, economies of scale, steep learning curves, and high sectoral entry barriers proved to be open to government influence through subsidies, grants, and other forms of support.[27] But direct or indirect supports for the high-tech industries of America's competitors were not the whole story. Market closure through structural barriers to market access played a role as well. In the case of Europe, they could frequently be overcome by direct investment or strategic alliances, but Japanese structural barriers to access were much more of a serious problem because of the many obstacles to foreign investment.[28] U.S.-Japanese investment relations are asymmetrical, and at a time when intraindustry trade as well as production and distribution through subsidiaries abroad comes to play an increasing role, informal restrictions on foreign investment in Japan can be identified as one of the major reasons for the low market penetration by foreign suppliers.[29]

The Growth of Structural Barriers to Market Access and the Role of Differing Regulatory Regimes

After the extensive lowering of tariffs through successive multilateral liberalization, nontariff barriers have become the main obstacle to market access. Among them, structural barriers assumed a greater importance than formal or explicit ones such as voluntary export restraints. Structural barriers can be defined as those which have not been explicitly sanctioned by government action (although they may be tolerated) but have been established by private actors through informal consent or practice. Among them are restrictive practices such as cartels or monopolies, closed distribution and supplier relationships, and informal interlocking relationships between banks and corporations, as with the Japanese *Keiretsu* system.[30] Similar arrangements can be found in Europe in the close relationship between banks and large corporations in Germany and the network of state-run companies and banks in France.

Differing national regulatory standards play an important part in such arrangements. Indeed, they can define differential market access opportunities. Examples are the different ways in which the United States and the EU regulate their banking and insurance sectors and their public procurement practices. In both areas, the United States leaves substantial autonomy to the state and local level, whereas the EU, under the single market program, is striving to establish uniform systems. The processes for setting standards and industrial norms also differ substantially between the EU and the United States in the EU they are undertaken by government bodies and in the United States by voluntary private bodies.[31] Industrial countries have different ways of regulating their domestic markets, and these differences create reciprocally different access opportunities for foreigners.

The problem of structural access barriers and of different regulatory approaches indicates that market access depends increasingly on the characteristics of each nation's economic system, including its domestic regulatory regime. This situation is compounded by another asymmetry, which defines an important difference between the United States, Japan, and Europe: In the United States, access barriers on the basis of explicit laws and legal regulations play a larger role than in Japan or in the EU, where structural or informal barriers are more prevalent. This asymmetry has an important impact on assessing the effectiveness of GATT. Multilateral rules are more effective with regard to market access barriers based on explicit laws, whereas they frequently remain ineffective with regard to structural barriers. This may explain a certain disappointment with GATT in the United States.[32] Any attempt to advance the harmonization of national regulatory regimes is faced with the problem that national regulations are largely determined by domestic interests and standards of domestic stability, which may represent a precarious political bargain immune to foreign pressure. Domestic political structures have inevitably been on the agenda of international trade policy, but they militate against their international or multilateral transformation because all too frequently, basic economic and political structures of a nation are at stake.[33]

The Role of Macroeconomic Imbalances

The major constraint on American competitiveness and American trade policy in the 1980s, however, was unfavorable macroeconomic policies. The expansive fiscal policies of the Reagan administration caused budget deficits to rise dramatically. The federal government's borrowing requirements and the low domestic savings rate, coupled with highly restrictive monetary policies of the Federal Reserve Board under Paul Volcker in the early 1980s, led to massive capital imports and to rapid appreciation of the dollar. The overvaluation of the dollar caused imports to rise rapidly and was responsible for very slow export growth.[34] Until 1987 the American trade deficit reached unprecedented heights. Between 1980 and 1986, it rose from $24 billion to $160 billion.[35] The situation worsened as the Reagan administration, under its polices of "benign neglect," refused to cooperate on exchange rate policies.[36] The impact of these macroeconomic imbalances on trade policies was disastrous. They touched off a wave of protectionist demands from import-competing firms that were hit by the high dollar. Congress and interest groups attributed the high trade deficit to unfair foreign trade practices. The interconnection between the "twin deficits" was not evident to these critics. Budget deficits were caused not by unfair policies of America's major trading partners but by a failure of the macroeconomic management of national economic policies. One of the main reasons was the inadequate coordination of fiscal and monetary policies between the Federal Reserve Board and the Reagan administration.

Insufficient Interest of America's Trading Partners in Expanding the GATT System

The waning U.S. interest in maintaining multilateralism and the search for other forms of trade liberalization can be attributed to the hesitation on the part of America's leading trading partners to join the United States in expanding the GATT system. The thrust for starting the Uruguay Round and for the inclusion of new issues such as services, intellectual property rights, trade-related investment measures, agriculture, and textile trade came from the United States, while the EC, particularly France, and Japan remained recalcitrant or passive.[37] While there can be no question that there were domestic motives behind the U.S. approach,[38] it was nevertheless a U.S. achievement to have defined the playing field and to have induced other countries to join in the game. By including textiles and agriculture on the one hand and intellectual property rights and services on the other, the United States managed to achieve a trade-off between industrial and developing countries which created a multipolar coalition of interests that would eventually lead to a quantum leap to a new world trading order.[39]

When it came to the conclusion of the GATT talks, it was the EC, on France's insistence, that acted as a brake. The EC's refusal to make any concession on agricultural export subsides led to the failure of the Brussels GATT ministerial meeting in 1990. The compromise on agricultural export subsidies between the United States and the EC, the so-called Blair House agreement, which was accomplished only after a threat of sanctions, was rejected by the socialist as well as the ensuing conservative government in France.[40] By mid-May 1993, France demanded far-reaching exceptions from multilateral rules and from further liberalization and nondiscrimination between sectors and demanded special treatment for agriculture, civil aircraft, and audiovisual services. France, in contradiction to the Treaty of Rome, abused the trade policy of the EC to an unusual degree for national and domestic policy purposes. In the domestic debate, the GATT was declared the main enemy.[41] In the end, it was the threat of complete isolation and the prospect of a major crisis in the EC which led France to agree to a conclusion of the Uruguay Round. France's consent required U.S. concessions on agriculture and audiovisual services and EU acceptance of French demands regarding EU trade-remedy procedures.[42] Despite the successful conclusion of the round, the negotiations left a bitter aftertaste because one EC member state had been able to hold the entire negotiations hostage. This weakened the position of the EC as a serious partner in maintaining the world trading system.

Changes in the Domestic Base of American Trade Policy

The heated debate about the NAFTA agreement must be taken as an indication that there is considerable discontent among the American public about the status quo in trade policy which is shared by significant segments of the political elite, of the U.S. Congress, and of the Democratic Party. Just as in France, positions that reject unrestricted trade with nations having low labor and environmental standards as inherently unfair gain respectability. Even though the causes of such attitudes may be found primarily in domestic changes and anxieties, the opposition to NAFTA managed, for the first time in American trade policy since 1934, to forge a broad political coalition against a trade agreement.[43] The American public views the increasing integration of the United States into the world economy with distrust. Opinion polls indicate that even before the fall of the Berlin Wall, Japan's power and commercial success were seen as a greater threat than the military potential of the Soviet Union.[44] In post–cold war America, national security is increasingly defined in terms of economic variables. The same trend is evident in an elite media and academic circles that influence the public debate. Some critics argue that integration of the United States into the global economic system under multilateral rules works to the disadvantage of the United States and that it would be more beneficial for the United States to give up its leadership position in the world trading system to pursue more unilateral strategies for more narrowly defined interests.[45] Trade policy has been politicized for domestic consumption.

Increased congressional involvement in trade policy had an enormous impact on domestic policy formulation. In many ways, Congress could claim for itself a coequal role in formulating trade policy. Congress reacted much more rapidly to the changes in American trade policies in the 1980s than did the executive and was one of the moving forces in pushing the concept of fairness on the political agenda. For the first time since the Great Depression of the 1930s, Congress originated major trade policy initiatives. Sector-specific measures such as restrictive textile laws and local content legislation for automobiles failed, but with the Omnibus Trade and Competitiveness Act of 1988, the Congress initiated for the first time a comprehensive trade bill and became the champion of unilateral actions against "unfair" trading practices of other nations.[46] With NAFTA, Congress reacted to a public groundswell and threatened to let a trade agreement fail for the first time. It required President Clinton's unconditional involvement to push the agreement through the Congress.[47]

Institutional changes in Congress gave it an enhanced role in trade policy. The decentralizing reforms of the 1970s weakened those committees (such as the Ways and Means Committee in the House and the Finance Committee in the Senate) which had prime responsibility for trade policy and led to a proliferation of actors claiming a piece of the pie in trade policy. In the 1980s centralizing trends in congressional decision making did not restore the role of committees but enhanced the position of the party leadership, which increasingly became involved in trade policy issues. Until the election of President Clinton, divided government highlighted even further the divisions between a Republican administration and a Democratic Congress.[48] The executive had to invest more energy to pull diverging forces together and display a willingness to compromise in order to remain at the helm of trade policy making. But it proved unable to prevent the Congress from becoming an agenda setter and having a decisive influence on trade policy. For some analysts, the U.S. Congress became a destructive force in the world trading system.[49] Part of the reason for congressional activism in trade policy was that the domestic lineup of interest groups was changing. The dividing line between protectionists (old industries) and free traders (multinational corporations in high technology and services) became blurred as formerly free-trade-oriented multinationals began to view favorably the use of protectionist levers to open markets abroad and coalitions with protectionist industries became a real possibility.[50]

Political analysts such as Robert Pastor have argued that the U.S. Congress, with its increased activism in trade policy, has played precisely the role reserved for it by the separation of powers in the U.S. political system. It functions as a corrective for an executive that is frequently detached from the real needs of American businesses, and it is thus a better guardian of America's trading interests. Congress reacted much faster and much more directly to the symptoms of America's decline; because it does not have to exercise diplomatic restraint, it was the crucial factor in forcing America's trading partners to open their markets. Congress is an important lever in asserting America's trading interests and as such a unique asset for the conduct of American trade policy.[51]

Other authors have argued that there are few good reasons for congressional activism. The high trade deficit, which can be attributed to the high dollar and a low savings rate and not to unfair trading practices of other nations, is by and large the United States' own fault. During the 1980s many developing nations did not become more protectionist but scrapped their trade barriers unilaterally. Although there may be several cases where aggressive actions were necessary, congressional initiatives were a form of neomercantilism to secure benefits for clients when budgetary constraints precluded the provision of any other benefits. The fairness doctrine only served to legitimate this objective.[52] There is probably a kernel of truth in both positions. The fairness doctrine served as a good cover for initiatives that were motivated by narrow material interest, but many of these did not come to fruition as the executive managed to keep the worst abuses under control without losing sight of the multilateral goals of American trade policy.[53]

The Future of American Trade Policy: The Clinton Administration and the Unlikely Triumph of Multilateralism

In the 1980s prospects for the United States to maintain its traditional role in the world trading system worsened. The Soviet threat (and with it all trade policy assumptions based on that threat), long taken for granted, disappeared, and it remains unclear whether it will be replaced by another. Regardless of the global changes in world politics touched off by the end of the cold war, American trade policy underwent a fundamental transformation. The factors that we have identified here—relative decline (and its psychological impact), sectoral competitiveness problems, the aggressive export push combined with market closure pursued by East Asian countries, structural barriers to market access, the lack of support from America's trading partners in expanding the GATT-based trading system, and a domestic base for U.S. trade policy that was much harder to control—all suggested the emergence of a trade policy that would emphasize national and sectoral interest. In particular, one could expect American trade policy to assume a more unilateral character and stress elements of sectoral and country-specific reciprocity. This tendency was dramatically enhanced by the high value of the dollar during the mid-eighties.

As expected, under the prodding of the U.S. Congress, the United States introduced the Super-301 measure, contained in the 1988 trade bill, as an effective instrument against the "unfair" trading practices of its trading partners that met with their outright opposition. Countries such as Japan, India, and Brazil were declared to be unfair traders. The pressure of that instrument brought about a series of bilateral negotiations on the reduction of barriers to market access and unfair trade practices, such as the Structural Impediment Initiatives with Japan.[54] The frequent invocation of the fairness doctrine served primarily to claim legitimacy, because it implied that markets at home were open and thus avoided any taint of protectionism. The push of concerned industries for countermeasures was even more effective if one could support one's demands with fairness arguments. This, for instance, also explains why many industries resorted to countervailing duty procedures.[55] Sectoral reciprocity became a major concern of high-tech sectors such as the telecommunications, computer, satellite, and aircraft industries, which, because of high research and learning costs, were all dependent on economies of scale and large global market shares.

Given the reluctance of American trading partners to expand the multilateral system, the idea of limited liberalization through regional integration was a promising alternative. Between 1985 and 1992, the United States concluded free trade agreements with Israel, Canada, and Mexico.[56] NAFTA, involving the United States, Mexico and Canada, created an economic block that surpassed the EC-12 in terms of GNP and population. The attractiveness of regional arrangements such as NAFTA led not only to the creation of a large, integrated market but also to opportunities for trade policy makers to address needs of sectoral and country-specific reciprocity. The negotiation of free trade agreements offered better ways to arrive at "fair" solutions in all sectors instead of watering them down in complex multilateral trade-offs. Special U.S. demands with regard to services, investment, and intellectual property rights could be asserted with a greater prospect of success in cases where access to the large U.S. market was a greater bargaining chip than access to much smaller markets of other negotiating partners. Free trade agreements were also pursued to exert pressure on those trading partners that refused to follow America's strategies in the GATT negotiations.

In the wake of the meeting of the heads of state of the Asian Pacific Economic Cooperation area in November 1993, shortly before the deadline for the Uruguay Round, Fred Bergsten, a leading international economist, advised the EU to leave the multilateral negotiations if Europe was unable to sign on to the Uruguay Round. Bergsten suggested that further liberalization could be pursued between the United States and the Asian-Pacific states without the Europeans, who could join in the agreements later, after stabilizing their economies and settling their internal differences. Also, some U.S. government officials indicated that closer regional cooperation in the Asian-Pacific area could be an alternative to the GATT, if the Europeans blocked further progress.[57]

The Paradigm Shift Postponed

Unilateralism and regionalism thus became elements that had a determining influence on American trade policy; however, the anticipated paradigm shift did not take place. One answer can be found in the change of the macroeconomic contexts and of the economic fundamentals affecting U.S. trade policy, such as the drop of the dollar from its peak in the mid-eighties.[58] The U.S. trade deficit fell from a peak of $152 billion in 1987 to $66.8 billion in 1991. The average export growth during this period was 12.5 percent annually. The trade balance with the EC shifted from a deficit of $20 billion in 1987 to a surplus of $17 billion in 1991. And even the trade deficit with Japan reacted to the trend and fell during the same period from $55 billion to $40 billion. The improvement in American trade performance was mostly due to increased exports of industrial goods, with capital goods taking the lead.[59]

American industry, on the basis of a lower dollar, massive restructuring, and low labor costs, displayed renewed competitiveness and regained about half the market share it had lost since the mid-eighties.[60] A marked improvement was evident with regard to high-tech goods. In the view of some observers, the deficit recorded for 1986 was primarily due to a too narrow definition of high-tech goods. There was indeed an exchange-rate-induced drop in 1986, but according to a wider definition of high-tech (including biotechnology and high-tech chemicals), the high-tech balance remained positive throughout the 1980s. Between 1982 and 1992 high-tech exports grew by an average of 10 percent annually, and the balance between 1990 and 1992 reached surpluses between $33 and $37 billion. Japan was the only country with which the United States recorded a deficit in high-tech goods. There can be no question that absolute market shares declined in the 1980s, but these were relative declines, as other countries made inroads in international high-tech markets. The absolute levels of American high-tech production and trade remains impressive, particularly in comparison with Europe. The United States remains the global market leader in microprocessors, supercomputers, high-definition TV, software, and telecommunications. American firms have expanded their position in high-tech goods since 1990.[61] In semiconductors, the United States, for the first time since 1985, surpassed the Japanese.[62] Despite the contention of tightly held oligopolistic markets in high-tech products and alarmist views of some pundits, U.S. industries reacted to the competitive challenge and intensified competition in its favor.[63]

But even on the policy side, developments were not as dramatic as was anticipated by many critics. Unilateral instruments such as the Super-301 section of the trade act, which had been passed by Congress to force the

Reagan administration to assume a tougher stance in trade policy, were used by the Bush administration with circumspection. In the first year of the applicability of the law, U.S. Trade Representative Carla Hills named only Japan, India, and Brazil as priority countries and started negotiations with them. The agricultural policies of the EC were not targeted under Super-301 for political reasons. The negotiations with Japan led to some Japanese concessions (in supercomputers and satellites) and were finally transferred to the Structural Impediment Initiative. Brazil unilaterally liberalized its trade policy, in a general shift of its foreign economic policies, and India refused to enter into any negotiations with the United States. Carla Hills could point to the GATT as a possible solution of the problems with India. Taiwan and Korea liberalized some of their trading practices without having been formally named under Super-301.

The Bush administration's strategy consisted of defusing potentially vicious trade disputes, which could have had an adverse effect on concluding the Uruguay Round. In no case did the administration introduce sanctions or retaliatory measures. The areas most affected by Super-301 such as services and intellectual property rights were all issues under negotiation in the Uruguay Round. The use of the "simple"-301 procedure (which leaves considerable room for discretion to the administration) as well as the special-301 for intellectual property rights, played an important role in bringing countries such as Brazil and India to accept the agenda of the Uruguay Round. By and large, the administration pursued a strategy of damage control by using the Super-301 instrument in ways compatible with the goals of the Uruguay Round. In the second and last year of its applicability,[64] the Bush administration refused to name offending countries under Super-301 and declared the conclusion of the Uruguay Round to be the main goal of American market-opening initiatives under the 301 law.[65] Although the imposition of a unilateral arsenal by Congress on the executive represented a burden for American trade policy makers and for the relations between the United States and its main trading partners, it did not have the explosive consequences anticipated and did not lead the United States to stray from its GATT course. In terms of domestic policy, it was a belated response to the distortions wrought by the macroeconomic imbalances and the strong dollar. I. M. Destler termed the use of Super-301 "constructive," as it became the equivalent of the "bargaining tariff" at a time when the administration, under intense domestic pressure, could not avail itself of any other market-opening instruments and was faced with the need to deflect protectionist legislation in the Congress.[66]

The widely shared assumption that the United States was going to retreat to "fortress North-America" with the conclusion of NAFTA was also premature. It is true that GATT pessimists in the early 1980s, in view of the many obstacles to starting a new GATT round, were considering limited liberalization in bilateral and regional frameworks as a alternative to the GATT. Such considerations, however, served to deflect domestic pressure, to exert some pressure on those GATT partners resisting a new GATT round, and to come up with models to deal with new issues such as intellectual property rights and services.[67] The free trade agreements with Canada and Mexico ratified intensive existing economic integration, and the agreement with Israel had primarily political importance. The bottom line is that the United States conducts almost 70 percent of its trade outside North America and thus cannot afford to retreat to "fortress North America" and to relegate the multilateral system to a back seat. The countries of the Western Hemisphere conduct a larger percentage of their trade outside their region than Europe.[68] This is why waving the regional card is an empty threat.[69] There may be serious problems if regional preferences are extended to high-tariff states such as Argentina and Brazil, but this is not a realistic option yet.

In the heated domestic debate about NAFTA, which was driven by populist demagogy, the issue of job losses has been blown out of reasonable proportion. Even though a large, integrated domestic market is attractive to the United States, the economic impact of NAFTA on the U.S. economy is probably quite small. Mexico's GNP is about 5 percent of the GNP of the United States, and average American tariffs before NAFTA amounted to only 4 percent. Massive losses of jobs should have occurred already under those tariff rates. The highest estimate of job losses in all serious econometric studies amounts to 500,000 in the next few years, about one-half of 1 percent of total American employment. Given this dimension, variables such as the strategy of the Federal Reserve Board and future interest rates should have a much greater impact on employment and job creation. Despite the inflated rhetoric from all sides of the debate, we can expect that NAFTA's impact on U.S. employment and growth will be negligible as opposed to its impact on Mexico, whose industrial sector faces massive restructuring under NAFTA. The domestic debate ignored economic reality.[70]

This fact, however, brings us closer to the core of NAFTA, which is political rather than economic. It has been frequently overlooked that NAFTA was first proposed by Mexico and that the United States initially responded only reluctantly to Mexico's initiative, as there was a clear preference among trade policy makers to conclude the Uruguay Round first.[71] For Mexico's President Salinas, NAFTA was a lever to safeguard Mexico's economic modernization and liberalization that was the hallmark of his tenure and to bolster the trust of foreign investors at a time of a perceived worldwide capital shortage. For the United States, Mexico's initiative was an opportunity to improve bilateral relations that had been troubled by frequent tensions and historical misunderstandings. The U.S. objective was to stabilize a country that, because of its economic crisis and severe social dislocation in the early and mid-eighties, appeared to pose a greater security threat to the United States than continued in-migration.[72] NAFTA was to stabilize Mexico politically and economically. In conjunction with the "Enterprise of the Americas," NAFTA was a political overture to a new departure in U.S. policies toward Latin America. Even taking the long-term economic benefits of regional integration into account, a failure of NAFTA would have been a greater blow to America's foreign policy interests in the Western Hemisphere that to its immediate trading interests.

NAFTA does not abrogate U.S. GATT commitments. The agreement is compatible with Article 24 of GATT, or at least as compatible as most other customs unions and free trade areas, and the trade-diverting effects are small even for Caribbean and other Latin American states. In fact, NAFTA is complementary to the Uruguay Round, as the multilateral liberalization of American tariffs and quotas actually discounts all NAFTA preferences and has a dampening effect on any trade-diverting and discriminatory features of the agreement. If trade barriers are dismantled multilaterally, the value of preferences accorded to participating nations in free trade areas will be diminished accordingly.[73] This is why the United States aimed at concluding NAFTA and the Uruguay Round in tandem, even though the initial assumption was that the Uruguay Round would be finished before NAFTA. The close political connection between NAFTA and the Uruguay Round became apparent during the NAFTA ratification debate, when a possible failure by Congress to ratify NAFTA would probably have doomed the Uruguay Round, as countries such as France, which resisted a conclusion, would have had their case strengthened with the argument that even in the United States the political base for a trade agreement is not given. President Clinton's success in pushing NAFTA through the U.S. Congress provided the necessary impetus for concluding the Uruguay Round.[74]

Finally, the multilateral approach through GATT netted a number of benefits for American trade policy. Contrary to arguments used by American critics of GATT that it is not the appropriate forum for trade liberalization, the course of the negotiations opened opportunities for the United States to tackle difficult sectoral and bilateral issues, achieving some of the fine-tuning that is so desirable to some American trade policy makers as well as sectoral interests. Problems with the EC regarding civil aircraft subsidies were first addressed in a bilateral context and will be extended through multilateralization to future competitors such as China, Taiwan, and Japan. The market access package was first negotiated in a bilateral framework with the EC and then later transferred to a broader context in the so-called quad group (United States, EC, Japan, and Canada). The results of these negotiations were the basis for the final market access agreement. The central axis of the negotiation was the relationship between the EC and the United States. With the core issue of agriculture threatening to block a consensus, this demonstrated that the GATT could be an effective lever for managing relations between the two.

The Clinton Administration and the Conclusion of the Uruguay Round

When the Clinton administration assumed office, there was considerable uncertainty about the future course of American trade policy. On the one hand, the administration indicated that the focus of all its economic initiatives would be on domestic economic reform and on shoring up the domestic base of American competitiveness. On the other hand, there were clear signals that the administration would not assign the same priority to GATT and would thus implement the paradigm shift from free to fair trade in its programmatic policy approaches.[75] President Clinton and his trade representative declared that multilateralism was no longer the primary "philosophical" point of reference for trade policy but that all approaches such as unilateralism and regionalism would have co-equal status, the only distinguishing criterion being how much they would help in opening markets. Trade needed to be free and fair at the same time.[76]

A tougher approach was apparent in the first trade policy initiatives of the new administration. The first target was surprisingly the EC rather than Japan. In February 1993, beginning with remarks by President Clinton on the harmful effects of European civil aircraft subsidies, the administration threatened to terminate the agreement regulating them. In March 1993, U.S. Trade Representative Mickey Kantor threatened the EC with sanctions unless it opened its public procurement markets for telecommunications and utilities to American suppliers. A serious trade war was not out of the question.[77] An imminent row in the spring of 1993 about Airbus subsidies was played down quickly, and a solution with regard to electrical utilities was reached in the public procurement dispute. In telecommunications, the United States instituted limited sanctions, which affected only a volume of $30 million and thus had mostly symbolic value. But the message seemed to be clear: American trade policy would become unilateral and sectoral and thus would execute the paradigm change.

The initiatives vis-à-vis Japan were to support this interpretation. In view of a sharply rising Japanese current account surplus, the thrust of American policy toward Japan was in the form of managed trade, which could best be captured by the concept of voluntary import expansions. The so-called framework agreement of 1993 does not anticipate numerical targets for imports but refers to vaguely interpreted "objective criteria." These criteria were to be applied to the automotive sector (cars and parts) and the public procurement of supercomputers, satellites, and telecommunications equipment. Other provisions covered financial services, intellectual property rights, and access to technology. There was no agreement on whether the United States had the right to resort to sanctions if it decided that Japan had violated the terms of the agreement or what impact the agreement would have on third parties. The "framework agreement" was unequivocal proof that economic aspects had assumed the central role in U.S.-Japanese relations.[78] Leading American economists criticized the agreement because that the GATT had been excluded as a possible avenue for the settlement of disputes with Japan.[79]

In his first speech on trade policy, however, President Clinton used a different tack. He expressly acknowledged the deep integration of the American economy in the world economic system, pointed to the increasing dependence of American growth on exports, and emphasized the necessity for the United States to adjust to increasing interdependence in the world economy. "To Compete, Not to Retreat" was the slogan. The president underlined the necessity of bringing the Uruguay Round to a rapid conclusion.[80] The Clinton administration undertook the decisive step in reaching its goal by requesting a negotiating mandate and "fast-track" authority from Congress, which assures that once an agreement is reached it will be passed by Congress without changes and undue delay. The administration forwent any linkage with a renewal of Super-301 as an instrument. It was now clear that, together with NAFTA, the conclusion of the Uruguay Round was the top priority of American trade policy.[81]

One of the reasons for the successful conclusion of the Uruguay Round was the administration's willingness to retain the Blair House agreement[82] and allow certain modifications, given strong French pressure. This agreement, originally negotiated by the Bush administration in 1992 under the threat of sanctions,[83] regulates the level of permissible export and other subsidies. Another element was a market access package that settled all major tariff changes. Even sharp disagreements over guaranteed access to the European audiovisual market, a major concern to the influential Hollywood film lobby, could not stop the conclusion of the negotiations.[84] In the final stages of negotiation, the administration's engagement was characterized by an almost unconditional willingness to come to a successful conclusion. In close cooperation with Germany, which was careful not to offend France, its closest ally in the EC, the United States helped to avoid a difficult conflict between Germany and France. American willingness to compromise allowed France to leave its self-imposed isolation. At the end of the negotiating process, narrow mercantile consideration did not carry the day, as the American ambassador to the EC, Stuart Eizenstat, emphasized: "The United States negotiated with more than the specific interests of its corporations and farmers in mind. We have a second consideration. That is as the only remaining superpower, as the strongest economy in the world and the world economic leader, we also have to take into account the potential impact of a failure."[85]

Particularly with regard to some of the central conflicts with the EC, the agreement did not fulfill all American expectations. But it did reach major American goals such as the inclusion of services, intellectual property rights, agriculture, greater discipline in subsidies, improved access to public procurement, and more effective dispute settlement procedures.[86] The market access agreements are expected to have a positive effect on the United States: According to an analysis by the Institute of International Economics, American exports by the year 2000 will show a net growth of more than $20 billion, and the U.S. GNP by 2004 will be 1 percent higher than without Uruguay Round liberalization. Its effect on the U.S. labor market will be slightly positive.[87] The United States insisted on exceptions for financial services and the audiovisual sector. It remained unclear, however, whether unilateral instruments were still permissible in the excepted areas.[88] With its active engagement for the conclusion of the Uruguay Round, the United States, at least for the time being, removed all doubts about its willingness to support a multilateral trading system and gave proof of its support of a rule-based trading system, the core of which would be a newly created World Trade Organization (WTO).

This result leaves us with a certain paradox: The administration that had put domestic reform and renewal at the top of its political priorities and wanted to take a self-defined standard of fairness as the yardstick of its trade policy counts among its major achievements to date the conclusion of two trade agreements. The two are mutually complementary and will lead to a liberalization of trading relationships and less conflictual development of their pursuit. Under American leadership, multilateralism won the day, despite a drastically changed global political constellation,[89] relatively weak global economic growth and growing protectionism in some countries. The United States was willing to make a contribution to the maintenance of a multilateral world trading system and relegate its narrower economic self-interest to a secondary position. Was the paradigm shift prevented at the last minute?

It is noteworthy that the Clinton administration, in the final phases of the GATT negotiations, did not differ dramatically from the Bush administration. In the executive branch we can testify to a far-reaching continuity in trade policy. The maintenance and expansion of the multilateral world trading system had a high priority for both administrations. The first four months of the Clinton administration created a different impression, but with hindsight, it becomes clear that these deviations were supposed to demonstrate to the U.S. Congress and to America's trading partners a new assertiveness. The administration had to meet the expectations raised during the election campaign that it would fight harder for American interests than its predecessor. The greatest deviation can be found in the policy toward Japan, with the attempt to use quantitative market access criteria, although the basic goal of greater access to the Japanese market is not different from that of the Bush administration.[90]

The fact of continuity underscores the insight that the executive is capable of resisting the pressure for a unilateral and sectoral policy emanating from the Congress and interest groups, and that it takes into account wider consideration of the global economic system. In this context we have to point to the increasing interdependence and commercial integration on the level of firms and corporations through direct foreign investment, global alliances, joint ventures, and established supplier relationships. Even with respect to Japan, sanctions are ever harder to apply because they would hit American companies dependent on the supply of vital Japanese inputs as much as those for which they were intended for.[91] This suggests that increasing interdependence in the world economy may take over the function of the "escalation brake" from the security policy "net" of the cold war period. This is one of the factors that allow the executive to remain capable of integrating multilateralism with unilateral approaches toward market opening.

From these observations alone, we cannot put the issue of a paradigm shift to rest; the paradigm shift has, rather, been left pending. The return to the unchallenged dominance of multilateralism is impossible, but so is its complete replacement by unilateralism and regionalism. The conclusion of the Uruguay Round does not point to the reestablishment of multilateralism as the lone reference point for American trade policy. The political conditions (the U.S. Congress) and structural conditions (the way international markets are structured) which led to the retreat from unconditional multilateralism continue to exist. It is more likely, in the future, that all three approaches will be closely intertwined, and it will require good management on the part of the executive to assure an integration between the conflicting goals in order to prevent destructive unilateral approaches from gaining an upper hand.

The conclusion of the Uruguay Round will not grant the executive any reprieve from this task. There are still a number of loose ends in the Uruguay Round. Under the services agreement, liberalization commitments for financial and maritime services and telecommunications have to be negotiated. There remain a number of unresolved and potentially contentious issues in audiovisual services, public procurement, and the banana trade.[92] The negotiators also failed to reach a multilateral steel agreement as part of the Uruguay Round package. In addition, major decisions on setting up the

WTO, the successor to GATT, must be made.[93] There still remains plenty of room for conflict, and any gap not covered by multilateral discipline creates an incentive for unilateral action.

In March 1994, President Clinton reactivated the Super-301 provision of the 1988 trade act by executive order, that is, without having been prompted by Congress. While highly symbolic, the action may exacerbate the tensions between Japan and the United States because initiating a Super-301 motion always raises the specter of sanctions.[94]

Of great concern also is the deterioration in the U.S. trade and current account balance since 1992. The current account deficit rose from $66 billion in 1992 to $109 billion in 1993. Between 1992 and 1994, the merchandise trade deficit rose from $96 billion to $166 billion and surpassed the 1987 record by 4 percent. Between 1991 and 1994, the U.S. trade deficit with Japan grew from $38.4 billion to almost $60 billion.[95] Even though these numbers reflect the uneven development of the major world economies, with the United States coming out of the recession much earlier than Germany and Japan, such data have an unsettling effect on trade policy making and may push Congress to some unwarranted actions. In late July 1994 the administration announced sanctions against Japan because Japan failed to open its government procurement process for medical and telecommunications equipment. The crucial issue was the adoption of benchmarks to measure market penetration.[96] A partial settlement of the long-running trade dispute was achieved in October 1994 covering glass, insurance, and government procurement, but not cars and car parts. The immediate threat of a trade war was averted.[97] A certain dampening effect on trade activism was likely to occur from the drastic fall of the dollar against the yen and the deutsche Mark, which made American exports more competitive than Japanese and German products but which also signaled a lack of credibility in U.S. economic and monetary policies. The United States is paying for improved competitiveness with a lowering of its terms of trade.

The congressional implementation of the Uruguay Round results was not characterized by the same polarization and mobilization as was NAFTA. The political costs and benefits were spread more widely and could not be exploited as easily for populist political gains.[98] Environmental and labor issues could not be framed as existential issues, as they had been in the case of Mexico, to underscore deep-seated domestic anxieties. But the large margins by which the implementing legislation was passed—288 to 146 in the House and 76 to 24 in the Senate—papered over the heated disputes that trade policy is subject to in the post–cold war world. The congressional debate was not immune to partisan tactical calculations, which were exacerbated after the Republican victory in the congressional elections; nor was it immune to a populist onslaught, amounting to general challenge to the merits of a multilateral trading order. GATT was seen as a "must do" establishment issue, which was attacked by both the populist left and the populist right as benefiting only Wall Street, transnational companies, and the financial elite.[99] The populist onslaught as well as tactical considerations by the triumphant Republicans articulated strong reservations against the new WTO and its procedures.

On the left, the same groups of environmentalists and unions as in the NAFTA debate fought against congressional consent to the Uruguay Round, with Ralph Nader's Public Citizens being the most outspoken. On the populist right, Ross Perot and Pat Buchanan stirred up public sentiment against the GATT/WTO agreement. Before the election, Newt Gingrich, the Republican leader, seemed to share the critics' concern but after the election went on to support GATT/WTO.[100] This time it was not the issues of labor and environmental standards that dominated the debate but the perception of those opposing the accord that the WTO mechanism for settling disputes and the restraint on American unilateral actions would amount to a loss of sovereignty.[101] The WTO critics charged that the organization was an unelected bureaucracy for invalidating U.S. laws. These critics were joined by some of the U.S. governors, who feared that trade-restricting state law and regulations would be the target of complaints by WTO signatories.[102] Critics of GATT from both ends of the political spectrum saw the WTO as an instrument for other nations to undercut U.S. economic, environmental, labor, and consumer regulations.[103]

Another obstacle to congressional consent was the issue of how to compensate for the revenue losses (roughly $12 billion over a five-year period) that were incurred as a result of the tariff cuts. As the Republicans objected to raising taxes and no appropriate cuts could be agreed on, a sixty-vote majority was necessary in the Senate in order to waive the rules of the budget law. GATT opponents were joined by fiscal conservatives, and the threshold for passing GATT/WTO was raised even higher.[104] To top things off, Senator Ernest Hollings (D., S.C.) managed to exploit parliamentary procedure under fast-track rules to force a postponement of the vote until after the congressional election, which led to additional uncertainty after the Republican triumph at the polls.[105] In mid-November the administration was no longer sure that it could pass GATT. GATT critics charged that lame-duck congress members would decide the future of U.S. trade policy.[106] The mounting congressional opposition to GATT was an indication that the domestic basis of trade policy had undergone a dramatic transformation after the end of the cold war.

The first victim of this politically complicated situation was the extension of the fast track provision that President Clinton had requested for negotiations with Chile on extending NAFTA. The failure of the extension was due to the administration's wish to include the environment and labor standards as priority goals of the negotiations under the fast track provision while the Republicans in the Senate objected to their inclusion. As no agreement could be reached, the administration dropped the request in order not to endanger the passage of the Uruguay Round.[107] A much more serious issue was the Republican embrace of the sovereignty issue, which, after pressure by Ross Perot and right-wing populist radio hosts, was picked up by Senator Bob Dole. Dole spearheaded the effort of the Republican opposition to GATT and pushed through an ostensible weakening of the American commitment to the multilateral trading system.[108] In exchange for Dole's support of the Uruguay Round results, the Clinton administration agreed to establish a panel of federal judges that would review any decision on the part of the WTO settling a dispute in which the United States was involved. Should this panel three times in a row reach the conclusion that the United States had been treated unfairly, the Congress by a joint resolution can require the president to withdraw from the WTO.[109] Another provision of the implementing legislation requires Congress to review American membership in the WTO every five years. With the solution of the sovereignty question, the budget waiver found the necessary majority.[110] Unresolved is the issue of the extent to which unilateral instruments such as section 301 can still be used. With the implementing legislation, Congress reauthorized the Super-301 provision for unilateral actions.[111]

The large majorities that were finally achieved for the Uruguay Round somehow covered up the heated political debate on the merits of U.S. participation in a multilateral trading system. Regardless of what impact the panel of federal judges and its review of dispute settlement rulings will have on the debate on trade policy, by implementing the Uruguay Round, Congress has asserted a basic vote of no confidence against one of the tenets of the multilateral trading system, the dispute settlement mechanism. Congress succeeded in this, although the implementing legislation was subject to the fast track provision, and as such not amendable. It is highly unlikely that the United States will ever withdraw from the WTO, but the mere operation of the review mechanisms will put the pros and cons of America's participation in the multilateral trading system constantly on the political agenda. Congressional implementation of the Uruguay Round has revealed considerable domestic discontent over the direction of U.S. trade policy. The same can be said of the cool reception that the Mexican financial aid package received on the Hill, which forced the Clinton administration to seek a solution that did not require congressional involvement.[112]

For the future course of American trade policy, it will be crucial whether the challenge to multilateralism by significant number of members of Congress is merely a tactical device or more of a matter of principle. If the former is the case, multilateralism has emerged reinvigorated from the Uruguay Round, at least for the time being. It would thus be premature to talk of the completion of a paradigm shift. It probably makes more sense to speak of a new complexity of American trade policies that will render it also less predictable.[113] Short-term national interests will clash more frequently with the American interest in maintaining a multilateral world trading system. Unilateralism and regional approaches will thus not disappear.[114] Regulation of the trading relationship with Japan and with China—as the dispute about the protection of intellectual property rights has shown—will continue to be the object of exclusive negotiations and pressure politics. Unilateral approaches are a temptation for the United States to tailor market access packages to the needs of its own industry without taking the consequences for multilateralism into account.[115]

American trade policy will be freed of the rigid constraints of the cold war, but it will still take place within the general constraints of American foreign policy objectives. The interdependence of global economic linkages will play a more important role in preventing a regress to trade wars and escalating conflicts. But interdependence is not benign but leads to friction (particularly with regard to the effects of domestic regulations and to dealing with structural barriers), which makes it a source of conflict.

In the long run, the multilateral trading order will also assume more complexity as new issues such as environmental standards, labor standards, and policy on competition find their way onto the agenda. These are issues that are all rooted in the domestic regulatory regimes of modern industrial states and that will define new areas of conflict and a new alignment of interests in the world trading system. During his consultations with the EU commission in Brussels in early 1994, President Clinton stated that the United States will focus on these new issues in future talks on the world trading system. At this point, it remains uncertain whether inclusion of these issues will bolster the multilateral trading system or whether they will distract from its central task of maintaining the free flow of trade by pandering to new domestic constituencies that have little stake in upholding this system. For these reasons, we can foresee a continuous shift of emphasis and vacillation between the major approaches to trade policy that we have identified. All this will lead to an increasingly tension-ridden and differentiated U.S. trade policy, but for an effective management of world trade, the multilateral approach will remain an indispensable, even though not the only, approach.[116]

Notes

1. Jagdish Bhagwati, *The World Trading System at Risk* (Princeton, 1991), 13–23.
2. Andreas Falke, "Die USA und das Welthandelssystem: Auf dem Weg zu einer

neuen Handelspolitik," in Matthias Dembinski, Peter Rudolf, and Jürgen Wilzewski, eds., *Amerikanische Weltpolitik nach dem Ost-West-Konflikt* (Baden-Baden, 1994), 280–83. As in other industrial and newly industrializing countries, there remain protectionist tendencies in American trade policy, particularly in the area of dumping and countervailing duty actions. In general, such practices are covered under GATT and proliferate in other nations. In the same category fall negotiated voluntary export restraints, which are usually termed "gray area measures," and their legality has not been tested under GATT.

3. See I. M. Destler and Michael Nacht, "U.S. Policy toward Japan," in Robert J. Art and Seyom Brown, eds. *U.S. Foreign Policy: The Search for a New Role* (New York, 1993), 289–314.

4. This is also the argument made by Joseph S. Nye and Robert O. Keohane, "The United States and International Institutions in Europe after the Cold War," in Joseph S. Nye, Robert O. Keohane, and Stanley Hoffmann, eds., *After the Cold War: International Institutions and State Strategies in Europe, 1989–1991* (Cambridge, Mass., 1993), 122–26. From a European perspective, see Elke Thiel, *Die USA und die EG: Wirtschaftkooperation in einem "neuen" Atlantizismus* (Ebenhausen, 1992), 41f.

5. Alfred E. Eckes, "Trading American Interests," *Foreign Affairs*, Fall 1992, 136ff. Note that the European Community changed its name to the European Union (EU) when the Maastricht treaty took effect in 1994.

6. Rene Schwok, *U.S.-E.C. Relations in the Post-Cold War Era: Conflict or Partnership* (Boulder, Colo. 1991), 7–42.

7. See Robert L. Paarlberg, "Agricultural Policy," in Art and Brown, *U.S. Foreign Policy*, 205.

8. Robert J. Art, "Defense Policy," in Art and Brown, *U.S. Foreign Policy*, 108–10. Art points out that thorough investigation of the interrelationship between security policy and the pursuit of economic interests for the period of the cold war is still missing. For the beginning of the cold war, see Robert Pollard, *Economic Security and the Origins of the Cold War, 1945–1950* (New York, 1985).

9. See I. M. Destler, *American Trade Politics* (Washington, D.C., 1992), 91.

10. See the pointed remarks by Fred Bergsten, "The World Economy after the Cold War," *Foreign Affairs*, Summer 1990, 98–101; Bergsten, "The Primacy of Economics," *Foreign Policy*, Summer 1992, 3–24. From a European point of view, see Thiel, *Die USA und die EG*, 39f.

11. Art, "Defense Policy," 112–14; Robert Gilpin, *The Political Economy of International Relations* (Princeton, 1987), 366–78.

12. See, for instance, "The New Centrality of Economics in U.S. Foreign Policy," speech by Undersecretary of State for Economic and Agricultural Affairs Joan Spero to the American Chamber of Commerce in Brussels, reprinted in *Wireless File*, Nov. 5, 1993, 17ff.

13. Paul Kennedy, *The Rise and Fall of Great Powers* (New York, 1989), 432–37. Kennedy talks not only of relative decline but also of decline cause by undue burden on the economic resources of a country through high defense expenditures and external commitments. See ibid., xi, 514–21.

14. The fall in the U.S. share of world GNP occurred primarily between 1950 and 1973, when the United States was considered the undisputed economic superpower. Even the U.S. share of world manufacturing output did not drop more dramatically. For both indicators, the figures in 1980 were approximately at the same level as for 1938 before the outbreak of World War II, which indicates that the process of decline

resulted in normalization. See Joseph S. Nye, *Bound to Lead: The Changing Nature of American Power* (New York, 1990), 72–78. For a sophisticated analysis of the decline debate, see Aaron L. Friedberg, "The Strategic Implications of Relative Economic Decline," *Political Science Quarterly* 104 (1989): 402–06.

15. Jagdish Bhagwati, "The Diminished Giant Syndrome: How Declinism Drives Trade Policy," *Foreign Policy,* Spring 1993, 22–26.

16. Robert O. Keohane, *After Hegemony: Cooperation and Discord in the World Political Economy* (Princeton, 1984), 182–216.

17. Ibid., 213.

18. These arguments are summarized in Michael L. Dertouzos, Richard K. Lester, and Robert M. Solow, *Made in America: Regaining the Productive Edge* (Cambridge, Mass., 1989); U.S. Office of Technology Assessment, *Making Things Better: Competing in Manufacturing* (Washington, D.C., 1990).

19. See B. R. Inman and Daniel F. Burton, "Technology and Competitiveness: The New Policy Frontier," *Foreign Affairs,* spring 1990, 117 f.; Friedberg, "Strategic Implications," 405.

20. See David B. Yoffie, "American Trade Policy: An Obsolete Bargain?," in John E. Chubb and Paul E. Peterson, eds., *Can the Government Govern?* (Washington, D.C., 1989), 119.

21. Council on Competitiveness, *Picking Up the Pace: The Commercial Challenge to American Innovation* (Washington, D.C., 1988), 13–17.

22. See Inman and Burton "Technology," 120f.

23. Ibid., 121, 128–33.

24. For the origins and structure of Japanese industrial policy, see Chalmers Johnson, *MITI and the Japanese Miracle: The Growth of Industrial Policy, 1925–1975* (Stanford, Calif., 1982), esp. chaps. 8, 9 for strategies of industrial targeting. Also Inman and Burton, "Technology," 119f.

25. Laura Tyson, *Who Is Bashing Whom: Trade Conflict in High-Technology Industries* (Washington, D.C., 1992), 155–216.

26. See Kenneth Flamm and Thomas M. McNaugher, "Rationalizing Technology Investment," in John D. Steinbrunner, ed., *Restructuring American Foreign Policy* (Washington, D.C., 1989), 119–57.

27. See Tyson, *Bashing,* 3f.; Robert Z. Lawrence, "Innovation and Trade: Meeting the Foreign Challenge," in Henry J. Aaron, ed., *Setting National Priorities: Policy for the Nineties* (Washington, D.C., 1990), 162.

28. See Tyson, *Bashing,* 6–9.

29. This point is emphasized by Dennis J. Encarnation, *Rivals beyond Trade: America versus Japan in Global Competition* (Princeton, 1993).

30. Their effect on trade with the United States is analyzed in C. Fred Bergsten and Marcus Noland, *Reconcilable Differences? United States–Japan Economic Conflict* (Washington, D.C., 1994), 74–82.

31. Stephen Woolcock, *Market Access in EC-US Relations: Trading Partners or Trading Blows?* (London, 1991), 7–26.

32. See Falke, "Die USA und das Welthandelssytem," 292–98.

33. See Andreas Falke, "The Impact of the International System on Domestic Structure: The Case of American Federalism," *Amerikastudien* 39,3 (1994): 371–86.

34. See Fred C. Bergsten, *America in the World Economy: A Strategy for the 1990s* (Washington, D.C., 1989), 33–42.

35. U.S. Bureau of the Census, *Highlights of U.S. Export and Import Trade*, FT-900 (Washington, D.C., 1987), A-3.

36. Bergsten, *America in the World Economy,* 109–13.

37. Barbara Fliess, *Die Vereinigten Staaten zwischen Protektionismus und Liberal- isierung. Handelsdiplomatie im Vorfeld der Uruguay-Runde* (Ebenhausen, 1991), 60–79.

38. The United States tried to engage the high-tech and service sectors for the Uruguay Round to counterbalance the pressure of traditional manufacturing indus- tries that were not as interested in trade liberalization.

39. Andreas Falke, "Die Einstellung und Strategie der USA in der Uruguay- Runde," in Benno Engels, ed., *Weiterentwicklung des GATT durch die Uruguay-Runde?* (Hamburg, 1992). On Japan, see, Manfred Pohl, "Japan und die GATT-Runden," in ibid., 79–82.

40. See "France Demands Changes to the EC-US Farm Trade Agreement," *Fi- nancial Times,* Sept. 7, 1993.

41. See Rolf J. Langhammer, *Die Handelspolitik der EG nach 1992* (Kiel, 1993), 16– 18. See also "Frankreichs Unternehmer wollen GATT kippen," *Süddeutsche Zeitung,* July 7, 1993; "Tarnangriff gegen das GATT," *Süddeutsche Zeitung,* Aug. 8, 1993; "Bal- ladur's Bravura Balancing Act," *Financial Times,* Sept. 11, 1993.

42. "Zweck-Allianz gegen Frankreich," *Süddeutsche Zeitung,* Dec. 12, 1993; "Amerika musste doch nachgeben," ibid., Dec. 7, 1993.

43. See "NAFTA Debate Reveals Americans' Antipathy to Trade Is Rising," *Wall Street Journal,* Nov. 17, 1993. With regard to NAFTA, see the arguments in Gary Clyde Hufbauer and Jeffrey J. Schott, *NAFTA: An Assessment,* rev. ed. (Washington, D.C.: 1993), 11–14.

44. See Destler and Nacht, "U.S. Policy toward Japan," 289.

45. See, for instance, Clyde V. Prestowitz, Alan Tonelson, and Robert W. Jerome, "The Last Gasp of GATTism," *Harvard Business Review,* Mar.–Apr. 1991, 130–38; Robert Kuttner, "Another Great Victory of Ideology over Prosperity: What the Bush Administration Should Learn from the Instructive Failure of the Uruguay Round Trade Talks," *Atlantic Monthly,* Oct. 1991, 32–39.

46. On the role of Congress in the 1980s, see Destler, *American Trade Politics,* 65– 103.

47. After a long struggle, the House of Representatives approved NAFTA by a margin of 234 to 200 on Nov. 18, 1993, with a majority of Democrats voting against the agreement. See "Jubilant Clinton Pledges to Liberalise World Trade," *Finan- cial Times,* Nov. 19, 1993. For the position of congressional critics of NAFTA, see "Gephardt Sees Major NAFTA Deficiencies," *International Herald Tribune,* Nov. 15, 1993; Robert Kuttner, "Seeing through NAFTA's Clothes," *Business Week,* Sept. 20, 1993, 9.

48. Destler, *American Trade Politics,* 67–71, 79–84.

49. For instance, Jagdish Bhagwati and Douglas Irwin, "The Return of Re- ciprotarians: U.S. Trade Policy Today," *World Economy* 10 (1987): 109–30.

50. Pietro Nivola, *Regulating Unfair Trade* (Washington, D.C., 1993), 62f.

51. Robert A. Pastor, "The President versus Congress," in Art and Brown, *U.S. Foreign Policy,* 11–31, esp. 16ff., 21ff.

52. This position is argued by Nivola, *Regulating Unfair Trade,* xi–xv, and esp. 19. Nivola, "Trade Policy: Refereeing the Playing Field," in Thomas A. Mann, ed., *A Question of Balance: The President, the Congress, and Foreign Policy* (Washington, D.C., 1990), 200–53.

53. See Destler, *American Trade Politics,* 91–103.

54. A good survey of these actions is given by Nivola, *Regulating Unfair Trade,* 69– 90.

55. Ibid., 51, 61.

56. On the impact of free trade areas on American trade policy, see Jeffrey J. Schott, ed., *Free Trade Areas and U.S. Trade Policy* (Washington, D.C., 1989).

57. "U.S. Waves the Asia Card in Stalled Trade Game," *International Herald Tribune,* Nov. 17, 1993.

58. Barry P. Bosworth and Robert Z. Lawrence, "America's Global Role: From Dominance to Interdependence," in Steinbrunner, *Restructuring American Foreign Policy,* 14f.

59. See National Association of Manufacturers, *Can the U.S. Export Drive Continue? An Analysis,* by Stephen Cooney (Washington, D.C., 1991), 19ff.

60. Ibid., 11ff.

61. See Ernest Preeg, "Who Is Benefitting Whom? A Trade Agenda for High-Technology Industries," *Washington Quarterly* 16 (1993): 19–25.

62. "Japan wurde erstmals seit 1985 wieder überrundet," *Handelsblatt,* Dec. 21, 1993, 16.

63. Ibid., 24.

64. The Super-301 section expired in 1990 and was not reenacted by Congress in the following years, very much to the pleasure of the Bush administration. The Clinton administration, in the initial stages of its tenure, did consider requesting reenactment but subsequently, despite expressed sympathy for its use, decided to hold back in order not to endanger the outcome of the Uruguay Round. In March 1994, after negotiations with Japan failed again, it reenacted the procedure through executive order.

65. See Destler, *American Trade Politics,* 126f., 131–33; and Bergsten and Noland, *Reconcilable Differences?* 228–32 on Super-301 with reference to Japan.

66. Destler, *American Trade Politics,* 211.

67. See Fliess, *Die Vereinigten Staaten,* 56–60.

68. "Uruguay-Round May Be Gatt's Last Hurrah," *Financial Times,* Dec. 13, 1993.

69. See Bhagwati, "Jumpstarting the GATT," *Foreign Policy* 83 (1991): 109.

70. This argument is convincingly made by Paul Krugman, "The Uncomfortable Truth about NAFTA," *Foreign Affairs,* Nov.–Dec., 1993: 13–19.

71. See Destler, *American Trade Politics,* 134; M. Dalal Baer, "North-American Free Trade," *Foreign Affairs,* fall 1991, 130–49.

72. Baer, "North-American Free Trade," 18–19.

73. See Gary Clyde Hufbauer and Jeffrey J. Schott, *North American Free Trade: Issues and Recommendations* (Washington, D.C., 1992), 42f., 342ff. George D. Holliday, "GATT and Regional Free Trade Agreements," *CRS Report for Congress,* 93–989 E (Washington, D.C., 1993).

74. See "Fresh Dose of Political Will," *Financial Times,* Nov. 20, 1993.

75. For a more detailed analysis, see Andreas Falke, "Geht Amerika neue Wege in der Handelspolitik," *Politische Studien* 329 (1993): 75–89.

76. Ibid., 76f.; "Clinton erläutert seine internationale Wirtschaftspolitik," *Amerikadienst,* Nr. 9, Mar. 3, 1993, 1–9; Patrick Low, *Trading Free: The GATT and US Trade Policy* (New York, 1993), 3.

77. See "Not an Open and Shut Case," *Financial Times,* Mar. 24, 1993; "Risk Grows of EC-US Tit-for-Tat Trade War," ibid., Mar. 15, 1993; "Airbus Flap: Washington Says What It Wants," *International Herald Tribune,* Feb. 24, 1993.

78. See "Clinton Sees New Dawn in Relations," and "Tokyo Claims Advantage

in Numerical Targets Battle," *Financial Times,* July 12, 1993; "Price of Victory: Trouble Seen in U.S.-Japan Trade," *International Herald Tribune,* July 12, 1993.

79. "US Economists Attack 'Myopic' Trade Calls," *Financial Times,* Oct. 7, 1993.

80. "Clinton erläutert."

81. Falke, "Geht Amerika neue Wege," 83–85.

82. On the Blair House agreement see Elske Mohr, "Uruguay-Runde, Blair-House-Abkommen, Reform der EG-Agrarpolitik—wo liegen die Probleme?" *IFO Schnelldienst* 32 (1993): 3–13.

83. The sanctions, however, did not relate to the immediate agricultural subsidy issues but to an unresolved GATT dispute settlement case relating to the arcane issue of oilseed.

84. "US Deal Paves Way for Trade Pact," *Financial Times,* Dec. 6, 1993; "Time to Square the Quad for the Round," ibid., Oct. 13, 1993.

85. See "Paris Perceived That U.S. Wanted Pact at All Costs," *International Herald Tribune,* Dec. 12, 1993.

86. Jeffrey J. Schott, assisted by Johanna W. Buurmann, *The Uruguay Round: An Assessment* (Washington, D.C., 1994), 3–39.

87. Ibid., 30–33.

88. See "Confusion over Section 301 Powers on Services," *Financial Times,* Dec. 17, 1993.

89. Another interpretation would argue that multilateralism prevailed because of this changed constellation, i.e., a failure of the GATT talks would have induced an unwelcome instability into the relationship among Western partners, which were under strong pressure to cooperate with regard to the instability created by the collapse of the Soviet Union.

90. Falke, "Geht Amerika neue Wege," 86. See the criticism with regard to numerical targets by former U.S. Trade Representative Carla Hills, "Targets Won't Open Japanese Markets," *Wall Street Journal,* June 14, 1993.

91. For examples see Bergsten and Noland, *Reconcilable Differences?,* 230.

92. Schott, *Uruguay Round,* 33f.

93. See "Trade Negotiators Face Hectic Three Months," *Financial Times,* Jan. 10, 1994; "US, EU in Procurement Talks," ibid., Jan. 11, 1994.

94. See "Wall Street's High Anxiety over Reviving Super-301," *Washington Post,* Mar. 27, 1994.

95. See "U.S. Current Account Deficit Increases Four Quarters in Row," and "U.S. Goods, Services Trade Deficit Widens Sharply in April," *Wireless File,* June 22, 1994; "1994 U.S. Trade Deficit in Goods Hits Record, Up 25%," ibid., Feb. 21, 1995.

96. See "Japan Unmoved and Immovable," *Financial Times,* Aug. 2, 1994.

97. See "US and Japan Both Claim Victory in Trade Dispute," ibid., Oct. 3, 1994.

98. See "Where NAFTA Divided, GATT Finds Unity," *Congressional Quarterly,* Oct. 29, 1994, 3118.

99. See William Schneider, "The Populist Takeover of Congress," *National Journal,* Feb. 11, 1995, 394; "The New Populism," *Business Week,* Mar. 13, 1995. William Schneider called the GATT vote "the dying gesture of an old political order" and suggested that "measures such as GATT and NAFTA probably could not get through Congress today."

100. See "Critics Fear GATT May Declare Open Season on U.S. Laws," *Congressional Quarterly,* July 23, 1994, 2005–10.

101. "GATT Caught in U.S. Crossfire," *Financial Times,* July 14, 1994. Under the

new mechanism for the settlement of disputes, the WTO signatories are unable to block the adoption of a panel report. If the defendant country refuses to follow the decision of a panel, the plaintiff country is authorized to demand compensation or withdraw concessions, i.e., to retaliate. See Schott, *Uruguay Round,* 120–32.

102. "Critics Fear GATT," 2009f.

103. "Free Trade Carries the day," 3450.

104. "In GATT Vote, Clinton Hopes to Avoid Another Nail-Biter," *Congressional Quarterly,* Nov. 19, 1994, 3348f.

105. Hollings's opposition to GATT/WTO is primarily motivated by his concern for the textile industry in his state, but beyond this sectoral issue, he has begun to question the benefits of an open world trading system for the United States. See "GATT Pact Lurches Off Course as Hollings Hits the Brake," *Congressional Quarterly,* Oct. 1, 1994, 2761–64.

106. "In GATT Vote."

107. See "Removal of 'Fast-track' May Put GATT in the Fast Lane," *Congressional Quarterly,* Sept. 17, 1994, 2561f. Clinton planned to resubmit his request for fast track in early 1995, but by March the administration had not acted yet. The conflict between Republicans and Democrats over labor and environmental standards had not been resolved yet. See "The Price of 'Fast-Track,'" *Financial Times,* Dec. 14, 1994.

108. See "In GATT Vote."

109. Since a joint resolution by both houses is subject to the presidential veto, Congress effectively needs a two-thirds majority to force the president to withdraw from the WTO, which is a formidable barrier for such an action. The question is also whether this provision makes a real difference, as any nation can withdraw from the WTO on six months' notice. However, the mere existence of this review mechanism puts political pressure on multilateralism.

110. However, Senator Dole failed in his bid to link his vote for the Uruguay Round with the administration's support for reducing the capital gains tax. "Dole, Clinton Compromise Greases Wheels for GATT," *Congressional Quarterly,* Nov. 26, 1994, 3405.

111. According to most experts, the United States will have to forgo unilateral procedures in those cases that are subject to the dispute settlement mechanism of the WTO and, with regard to the use of sanctions or retaliation, will have to follow the responses authorized by the WTO. The open question is whether Section 301 and related sections can still be used in areas not covered by GATT and whether among these areas are those service sectors in which countries have not submitted any liberalization commitments. See Schott, *Uruguay Round,* 130f., 196f.

112. "Mexican Aid Prospects Remain Precarious," *Congressional Quarterly,* Jan. 28, 1995, 293.

113. See Michael Mastanduno, "Trade Policy," in Art and Brown, *U.S. Foreign Policy,* 136–65, esp. 150ff.

114. See Jagdish Bhagwati, "Beyond NAFTA: Clinton's Trading Choices," *Foreign Policy,* winter 1993–94, 155–62.

115. It is not only the American preference for going it alone that is at work here. Europe, for instance, would not be such a good partner since it is less interested in market opening and more interested in protecting its own markets from Japanese imports. That the EU fails to achieve the same results may be due not only to American unilateralism but also to the EU's divisiveness and its lack of a consistent trade strategy. However, in Europe doubts persist that the market access and intellectual property rights provision of the U.S.-China acccord also effectively apply to third

countries. If this were the case, however, one could argue that the United States did the Europeans' dirty work. See "US-China Piracy Deal Yields Bonus on Market Access," *Financial Times*, Feb. 27, 1995; "Europa muß um seine Interessen kämpfen," *Handelsblatt*, Feb. 28, 1995; "PolyGram Attacks Chinese Piracy," *Financial Times*, Feb. 22, 1995.

116. See "Trade Round Like This May Never Be Seen Again," *Financial Times*, Dec. 12, 1993; "Environment Is Top of Clinton's Agenda," ibid., Jan. 1, 1994. For some basic thoughts on the role of environmental issues in trade policy, see Jagdish Bhagwati, "Trade and the Environment," *American Enterprise*, May– June 1993, 43–49; Daniel C. Esty, "GATTing the Greens," *Foreign Affairs*, Nov.–Dec. 1993, 32–36.

FOURTEEN

U.S. IMMIGRATION POLICY
AFTER THE COLD WAR

DEMETRIOS G. PAPADEMETRIOU

In terms of concrete outcomes, measured in terms of legislative changes designed to respond to or otherwise reflecting the changed international politicoeconomic environment, the U.S. immigration system seems to have made few adjustments directly as a response to the end of the cold war. However, the United States is indeed in the midst of a battle royal about its immigration policies. The focus of that battle has been and is likely to remain on the ineffectiveness of U.S. immigration control policies and on the costs to the social infrastructure of certain immigrant categories, especially the undocumented,[1] but also elderly immigrants and refugees. Both of these strands of the debate have been driven largely by the situation in California—now, as it has for much of the past century and a half—simultaneously one of the states that has benefited most from immigration[2] and the source of a disproportionate amount of both invective and action against it.[3]

As this chapter is written, the precise outcome of that battle is difficult to predict. Certain inferences about the general layout of the U.S. immigration landscape when the dust settles, however, are possible. First, the United States will be investing much more physical and political capital in both border and interior enforcement initiatives than it ever has in the past. Second, it will continue to seek out and experiment with new unilateral and multilateral methodologies for dissuading fraudulent asylum applicants from attempting to file a claim in U.S. territory. Third, it will be far less willing to play by the old rules in the refugee area, by increasingly deemphasizing resettlement, experimenting with different concepts of protection—such as enforceable temporary protection statuses, safe havens, and protection in place—and retreating from the special categorical treatment that it has offered to such groups as Cubans and Jews fleeing the former Soviet Union. Finally, it will have made immigration policy more responsive to a narrower definition of U.S. interests by reforming its legal immigration system. In this last regard, the most likely candidates for "reform" would be overall immigration numbers and the services to which immigrants are now entitled. These changes, if and when enacted, will require that the arguments and analysis of this chapter be revisited.

For the time being, however, virtually all legislative and administrative measures that have been implemented address two broad issues: first, what have been deemed as crises at the U.S. border with Mexico and second, emergency responses to mass migration flows. The responses to the first set of issues have focused on tightening border enforcement in certain areas of high illegal immigration traffic—a strategy that has met with some success, although the jury is still out on whether it might largely relocate the problem—and on measures to limit access to state and federal disaster relief in the aftermath of the 1994 earthquake in California (primarily as a means of addressing also the growing sense that immigrants are a significant drain on limited public resources).

The responses to "immigration emergencies" have tested the concept of safe havens, but with two slightly different twists. In the Haitian case, following a tortuous series of decisions at the highest levels, the interception of Haitians on the high seas was stopped and those fleeing Haiti were "rescued" and taken to the U.S. military base at Guantanamo, Cuba.[4] In the Cuban case, and in response to Floridians' fears of a repetition of the mass outflow of Cubans of nearly fifteen years ago, fleeing Cubans were also taken to Guantanamo and, temporarily, Panama, while the United States negotiated an agreement with the Cuban government. The agreement committed the Cuban government to prevent additional departures *and* to accept back some of those who had fled, in return for a U.S. commitment that gave unprecedented special treatment to immigrants from Cuba. This set of events may suggest to some that in this instance, the United States took the first step toward coming to terms with the changed post–cold war realities—which at some vague level it was. The more appropriate lesson to take from it, however, is that domestic politics—and particularly the dark side of the politics of immigration—was truly at the bottom of these decisions and that, in another sense, continuing to fight the cold war has in fact prevented the Clinton administration from treating Haitians and Cubans with full equality.

Overall, however, not only has U.S. immigration policy retained the conceptual framework and overall configuration of categories that existed during the cold war, but also it has not yet responded in any systematic way—in either a forward-looking or defensive manner—to the changing immigration and refugee challenges ushered in by the cold war's end. In effect, policy makers have continued to regard immigration much as they always have: through the lens of domestic politics and as a tool for advancing U.S. economic interests. Not surprisingly, then, many of the immigration-related difficulties currently confronting the United States can be traced, if only in part, to this narrow focus.

The abruptness with which the post–World War II political order collapsed left the United States and much of the West without a new policy paradigm interpreting the events in the East properly and without the ability to respond in the vigilant and coordinated manner they had shown during most of the cold war period. However unsettling, the East-West competition had served to focus the West's collective mind on a single preeminent threat, while the broader ideology of containment had allowed governments considerable latitude in policy matters beyond those strictly concerned with security and security-related issues.

Strangely, the East's collapse has created a paradigmatic, if not ideological, void in international relations which foreign policy elites have yet to fill. This conceptual vacuum has led to ad hoc, poorly organized, and ineffective responses to many of the new post–cold war challenges. The resulting sense of impotence in shaping, or simply managing, important processes and events is contributing to a sense of public and private sector malaise, made worse by a pronounced feeling of vulnerability to myriad seemingly intractable crises.

Migration Systems and Economic Interdependence

Almost no crisis in the cold war's aftermath looks more intractable than migration.[5] At its root are a number of factors, the strongest of which stem from the harsh social and economic restructuring brought about by global economic integration. Economic interdependence places countries within and across geographic regions in the grasp of an increasingly global migration system[6] in which economic and sociopolitical events increasingly flow from and result in direct migration consequences. This emerging global migration system now includes virtually all open democratic countries.[7] It incorporates traditional *inter*regional migration subsystems such as those between Western Europe and countries along the Mediterranean littoral; North America[8] and countries in and abutting the Caribbean Basin; and Australia and several of the world's regions. In addition, its de facto reach has expanded to such by now mature *intra*regional migration flows as those in Western Europe, the Middle East,[9] sub-Saharan Africa, North America, and South America. It also includes South and East Asia (and increasingly, Japan), and the entire area formerly controlled by the Soviet Union.

As a principal cause of the current migrations, economic restructuring has also fueled anxieties among receiving countries' publics concerned about their future economic security. The correlation and interaction of these two events makes immigration one of the most politically potent issues in the post–cold war era.

Migration and Advanced Industrial Societies

For many societies, immigration policy is about nothing less than who they have been, who they are, and most crucially, who they will become—a link to their past, a reflection of deeply diverse ethnic, racial, and cultural presents, and a bridge to increasingly shared futures. It is not surprising, then, that immigration policy is both the product and the cause of tension[10] as policy makers navigate between the Scylla of the global market (with its rhetoric of openness and expansiveness and its attendant cultural idiom of internationalism and inclusion), and the Charybdis of economic nationalism (with *its* credo, and attendant cultural idiom, of inwardness, isolation, and exclusion). In its extreme form, the former sees in the free movement of all classic production factors (including labor) an opportunity not only for immense profits but also for enormous improvements in human development and prosperity. The latter, in turn, uses the nation-state as its exclusive reference point and, with neomercantilistic fervor, extols the virtues of giving priority to domestic considerations in all economic decisions—the very essence of protectionism.

The clash between these two political, economic, and cultural[11] worldviews poses a significant challenge to the political navigational skills of leaders throughout the advanced industrial world. The crux of that challenge is to devise legal, tax, and regulatory policies that will encourage businesses to balance their profit goals with "socially responsible" investment decisions. In other words, the task for policy makers lies in formulating an appropriate mix of economic incentives and disincentives that will motivate firms to weigh short-term economic advantage against the domestic social and political costs associated with undue reliance on a global labor market.

Conceptual Issues

Increasing and accelerating movements of persons across state boundaries in virtually every region of the globe have made migration one of the unavoidable issues of our time. These movements are fueled by such forces as officially perpetrated or countenanced intolerance, entrenched conflict, natural and manmade catastrophes, growing economic disparities, and high rates of population growth in much of the less developed world (the South). They are also stimulated by various decisions and "nondecisions"[12] in the more developed world (the West or North), which explicitly invite, or simply encourage, the migration of various groups of immigrants. The movements are facilitated by a communications revolution that makes people in the South aware of opportunities in the North, as well as by economic and noneconomic gains that are perceived to outweigh probable costs.

Most people who migrate fall into one of three broad categories: (1) those who are encouraged to move by the immigration policies, or lack of policies, and labor needs of receiving societies; (2) those who are inspired to move by the social, political, and economic rhetoric of the North, as well as by overall commercial propaganda; (3) those who are "forced" to move by conditions at home. The first group will continue to migrate, primarily along channels—legal and illegal—created, or simply made possible, by the North. The second group is likely to continue to increase in importance and may become a critical policy challenge for the 1990s. It is the third group, however, that poses the truest long-term challenge, as the North gropes to find durable responses to its causes.

The expanding and intensifying character of international migration flows necessitates the development of a new conceptual prism if social science is to help policy makers understand and develop policy tools for managing the process more effectively. The current conceptual framework was conceived of and shaped in an era when the overwhelming majority of countries behaved in their international migration relations as ideal constructs. At that time, essentially binary analytical models classified states as sending or receiving; people as either permanent settlers or temporary residents (or as political or economic migrants); the study of internal migration as an analytic subfield distinct from that of international migration; and borders as instruments controlling both the entry and exit of people.

Legal distinctions among different types of flows were also much more than social science heurisms. "Legal" migration was the dominant type of migration, and the West's rhetoric of protection from group-based political and ethnoreligious persecution largely matched the opportunities for resettlement that it offered the victims of such persecution. The non-refugee-related migration system was consequently narrow and included a handful of "traditional" settlement countries, as well as a small group of countries interested in temporary foreign labor.

Increasingly, however, such traditional classifications are no longer accurate for confronting current realities of migration, and they fail to reflect the multiple ways in which most countries currently participate in the migration system. Analytical differentiations between sending and receiving societies, for instance, emphasize an artificial distinction that frequently confounds both analyst and policy maker.[13] Similarly, it is less useful to think of flows along permanent and temporary lines, for the economic, social, and increasingly, political behavior of participants in each flow become less discrete. Furthermore, in many existing and emerging examples of intraregional migration, the distinction between internal and international migration is (or is becoming) blurred. Although such classifications never accurately captured the migratory patterns of some regions,[14] the internal-international dichotomy is increasingly losing its meaning in regions where groupings of states are organizing, or are planning to organize, themselves into regional integration and free trade associations.[15] Additionally, though perhaps less frequently, border controls have been eased or virtually eliminated as a result of special agreements between and among states.[16]

Finally, it has become increasingly difficult to distinguish clearly between economic migrants on the one hand and refugees and asylum seekers on the other. The current conceptual framework for the protection of refugees was conceived of and shaped more than forty years ago. At that time the need for resettlement was geographically narrow and time-specific, confined to Europe in the aftermath of World War II. Not surprisingly, the legal doctrine of protection and the national and international assistance mechanisms and institutions that grew out of this era are no longer able to address adequately many of today's refugee and refugeelike crises. More important, genuine refugees and purely economic migrants have become ideal constructs infrequently found in real life. As the distinction between bona fide refugees and those who flee both oppression and poverty (the gray area where most asylum seekers likely fall) becomes more ambiguous, public support for generous responses has begun to erode.[17] Ironically, at the very time when the need for protection is exploding, outmoded and inflexible instruments for refugee assistance and waning public compassion and tolerance are resulting in the denial of humanitarian protection to many who are otherwise worthy of temporary protection.[18]

Policy Issues

A number of additional factors also interfere with the formulation of effective post–cold war immigration policy. The divergent and sometimes conflicting priorities of key actors on this issue have polarized the policy debate, reducing opportunities for effective dialogue just as migration and refugee issues have become more salient. Many immigrant advocates find that their perspectives are seen as too parochial or inflexible to contribute to constructive policy discussions. International agencies engaged in the protection end of the migration "business" are typically too overextended—and too involved in their programmatic and operational priorities—to have the necessary energy or inclination to challenge the status quo seriously. The same is true of domestic agencies, which must contend with policy and programmatic mandates that diffuse responsibility for challenging existing policy. Finally, researchers and analysts too often appear distant from the practical concerns that motivate policy makers to seek to change policies.

Two other factors impede the rethinking of immigration policy in the post–cold war era. The first is a sense that with the diminished ideological conflict—and the resulting de-emphasis on foreign policy considerations in each country's calculus about which displacements are "worthy" of humanitarian intervention—policy makers may in fact be less motivated in displaying generosity toward refugees.[19] Second, as generosity toward refugees is being stripped down to its basic humanitarian garb, the public is more likely to select self-interest over compassion in judging government decisions about accepting refugees.[20]

The interaction of multiplying conflicts, increasing displacements, tight budgets, and growing domestic intolerance toward migrants and refugees pose enormous challenges for policy makers seeking to manage immigration influxes effectively. Among the obstacles to open dialogue and novel approaches to the challenge are a short policy attention span, the escalating number and seriousness of emergencies, an increasingly shared perception of immigration as a problem rather than a balance of costs and benefits, deepening public impatience, a focus on short-term policy results, and a tendency to hide behind the shield of control policies. For the past decade the United States has exhibited all of these attributes as it agonized over changes to its immigration system.

U.S. Immigration Policy

Migration policies are rarely at the cutting edge of economic and political realities, except during crises. Rather, by their very nature, they are defensive adaptations to changing circumstances and usually lag far behind other policy decisions. Even in instances where an immigration regime is bold or progressive enough to exploit the economic opportunities that immigration can offer, it often merely codifies existing international business practice.[21]

The discussion of immigration in the United States has always been driven by domestic considerations. In fact, one would be hard pressed to find more than an occasional change in immigration policy that was a response to external forces or events. Moreover, those which have occurred have been largely insignificant both in the number of visas involved and in their effect on the overall immigration system. These include various responses to refugee situations; unavoidable adjustments in law to accommodate obligations incurred through trade negotiations;[22] narrow immigration programs that respond to specific foreign and security policy concerns;[23] or changes that provide nationals of specific countries access to U.S. visas.[24]

Otherwise, the U.S. immigration debate has reflected little concern over the changed East-West political equation. Except for a few individuals in the foreign policy community, few have grasped the potential significance that the end of the cold war has for U.S. immigration and refugee policy. In fact, despite wide fluctuations in both U.S. official and public attitudes about immigration in the 1980s, outside political and military events never played more than a background role.

The early part of the 1980s was a period of scrutiny and soul-searching about immigration, whereas the latter part exhibited a resounding reaffirmation of the value of immigration. This confirmation culminated in decisions resulting in a nearly 40 percent boost in the number of available U.S. visas—reflecting a fundamental belief in the value of immigration as both an element of a continuing process of nation building and as an important positive economic force. It also reasserted a strongly held, if often politically motivated, commitment toward humanitarian and compassionate ideals.

Legislative Initiatives

On October 27, 1990, the U.S. Congress passed the Immigration Act of 1990 (PL 101–649), completing the round of significant reforms to the U.S. immigration system which it had started more than a decade earlier. In addition to the Immigration Act, other major legislative reforms of the U.S. immigration system were the passage of the Immigration Reform and Control Act of 1986 (PL 99–603) and the Immigration Nursing Relief Act of 1989 (PL 101–238).

The Immigration Reform and Control Act (IRCA)

Public Law 99–603 focused primarily on the issue of illegal or undocumented immigration. Having failed to pass a comprehensive immigration reform package (one that addressed legal, illegal, and temporary migration) in both the 97th (1981–1982) and 98th (1982–1983) Congresses,[25] U.S. legislators began to recognize that more modest proposals that confronted the perceived crisis of the moment—illegal immigration—clearly stood a much better chance of success. Therein lies the genesis of IRCA.

The key provisions of IRCA included the following: (a) legalization programs for several types of illegal aliens; (b) the requirement that employers hire only individuals who could establish evidence of their right to work in the United States, or risk substantial civil and criminal penalties known as employer sanctions; (c) a program guaranteeing a supply of legal foreign workers to growers of perishable crops between fiscal years 1990 and 1993;[26] and (d) significantly enhanced border controls.[27]

The Immigration Nursing Relief Act (INRA)

The Immigration Nursing Relief Act had two major provisions. The first offered permanent U.S. residence to those temporary foreign registered nurses (RNs) with a minimum of three years of service in the U.S. health delivery system.[28] The second—and in many ways more significant provision—set up a rather complex regulatory system that, while facilitating employers' access to foreign RNs, conditioned such access on evidence that employers were instituting policies designed to increase the supply of U.S. nurses.

INRA responded to a widely acknowledged nursing shortage that was thought to be threatening the United States' ability to deliver adequate health care. The new law created a new temporary visa subcategory (H-1A) explicitly for foreign RNs that streamlined their entry.[29] In an effort to expand the supply of U.S. nurses and thus control the growth in the U.S. health care providers' dependence on foreign nurses, INRA also required employers actively to develop, recruit, and retain U.S. workers in the nursing profession.[30]

The 1990 Immigration Act (IA)

The most comprehensive overhaul of U.S. immigration laws since the last round of significant reforms in 1965, however, was left to the Immigration Act of 1990. The act represented an attempt to achieve a finer—if still tentative and fluid—balance between promoting national economic interests in an unforgiving global economy and protecting the interests of U.S. workers. In pursuing that balance, policy makers relied heavily on assessments of the country's human resources needs and overall economic strengths and weaknesses—including an evaluation of the skills and qualifications of its work force—and on appraisals of the preparedness of its workers to help the United States compete in the ever changing international economic environment. In many respects, the resulting changes to U.S. immigration laws reflect the preliminary conclusions of these calculations—tempered primarily by two factors: (a) the political reality that U.S. workers must be protected at some level from undue competition from foreign workers; and (b) something of an appreciation that long-term economic competitiveness ultimately rests with a nation's ability to prepare its own workers to meet the challenges of global competition.

Two factors were most influential in this round of the immigration debate. The first, and probably most influential, was the recognition that the goods producing sector's share of the U.S. labor force was continuing to decline in significance while that of the service employment sector was growing. This signaled an important shift in the U.S. economy that favored nonproduction over production workers.[31] Since the literacy and reasoning and problem-solving skills required of many of the service workers—and increasingly, the remaining production workers—were widely thought to be in short supply in the United States, many began to view immigration as a potential source of such workers. The second factor grew out of concerns over the economic implications of the long-term decline in U.S. fertility rates. Persistent below-replacement fertility rates and an aging population sensitized policy makers to the fact that immigration would play increasingly important roles in both population[32] and economic growth.[33]

It was the intersection of these issues with the debate over U.S. global competitiveness, however, that brought them to center stage in the national debate over immigration. The concern that the United States faced serious educational and skill deficits and, to a lesser degree, even a shortage of entry-level workers, was fueled by a series of high-level and widely disseminated reports.[34] These reports lent legitimacy and urgency to calls for fundamental reforms, including the notion (though usually within carefully laid parameters) that immigration should be relied upon to compensate for these deficits.

The demographic issue lost momentum as the debate evolved, however, as conflicting claims by population control advocates and environmentalists, on the one hand, and immigration advocates,[35] on the other, effectively canceled each other out.[36] A much more potent, though not necessarily clearer, strand of the debate was the notion that structural changes in the U.S. labor force might adversely affect U.S. economic growth.[37] Despite some, if largely weak, appreciation of the fact that projections about skill and general labor force surpluses and deficits are unreliable in the best of circumstances—especially in market economies where the interplay of market forces constantly shapes the forces of labor supply and demand[38]—immigration was nonetheless seen as the answer to this structural economic dilemma.

Finally, as I mentioned previously, much of the debate leading to the passage of the IA had to maneuver between this issue of "international competitiveness" and the notion that immigration policy could have a critical impact on the formulation of U.S. policies on the development of human resources. This required some degree of coordination of immigration policy with overall national employment goals. In other words, it required weighing the economic role that immigrants could play in enhancing the competitive posture of the United States against immigration's possibly adverse effect on policies that sought to enhance the skills of and opportunities for U.S. workers.[39] Underlying the necessary calculations was some recognition that larger employment-based visa numbers were inextricably tied—philosophically and politically—to both an analytical and a regulatory issue. The analytical issue pointed to the need for a reliable formula for making key decisions about labor market immigration more consonant with an area's human resources needs.[40] The regulatory issue concerned the mechanism that conditions U.S. employers' initial access to foreign workers on credible evidence of the unavailability of U.S. workers; and—within certain parame-

Table 14.1   Legal Immigration Levels under Current Law, S. 358, H.R. 4300, and the Immigration Act of 1990 Projected to Fiscal Years 1992 and 1995

Preference System	Current Law	S.358	H.R. 4300	1990 Immigration Act 1992–1994	1995 on
Family stream	480,000	480,000	564,000	465,000	543,000
Immediate relatives of U.S. citizens[a]	264,000[†]	264,000[†]	264,000[†]	264,000[†]	317,000[†]
Family preferences	216,000	216,000[b]	300,000	226,000	226,000
1st preference	54,000	19,440*	55,500	23,400	23,400
2nd preference	70,200*	123,120*	150,150*[c]	114,200	114,200
4th preference	27,000*	19,440*	29,600*	23,400	23,400
5th preference	64,800*	51,840*	64,750*	65,000	65,000
Independent stream	54,000	150,000	158,500	140,000	140,000
Special immigrants[a]	Unlimited	4,050	Unlimited	10,000	10,000
Medical workers	—	4,950	—	—	—
Employment-based workers	54,000	80,400	158,500[ef]	120,000	120,000
High-level professionals	(27,000)[g]	(40,200)	—	(80,000)	(80,000)
Entry-level professionals and skilled and unskilled workers	(27,000)[h]	(40,200)*[i]	—	(40,000)[j]	(40,000)[j]
Investors	—[k]	6,750	—	10,000	10,000
Point system immigrants	—	53,850*	—	—	—
Diversity (begins in 1995)	—	—	55,000[l]	—	55,000
Transitional visas[m]	—	—	146,000	107,000	—
Adversely affected countries (1992–1994)	—	—	25,000	40,000	—
Displaced aliens (East Europe & Tibet) (1991–1993)	—	—	15,000	—	—
Africa (1991–1993)	—	—	15,000	—	—
Preference backlog reductions[n]	—	—	76,000	—	—
Employees of U.S. businesses operating in Hong Kong (1992–1994)	—	—	15,000	12,000	—
Spouses and children of aliens legalized under IRCA (1992–1994)	—	—	—	55,000[o]	—
Miscellaneous	—	—	—	2,000[p]	—
Grand Total (excluding refugees)	534,000	630,000	868,500	714,000	738,000

Source: The first column is based on the Immigration and Nationality Act; the next two columns on proposed legislation; and the last two on the 1990 Immigration Act.

*Plus unused numbers from preferences above.

[†]These projections use a straight linear extrapolation of an annual increase in the category of about 6%. The baseline figure is the 218,000 visas issued to immediate relatives in FY 1989. The General Accounting Office (1989) projects the category to increase by 6.2% annually beginning with FY 1990. This is also the rate at which the category has grown for the past decade.

a. Immediate relatives remain unlimited in all scenarios.

b. 216,000 is the minimum for family preferences. For at least two years, when visa use by immediate relatives falls below 264,000, unused visas would be provided to this group.

ters—conditions their continued access to additional foreign workers on efforts to prepare, attract, and retain U.S. workers for such jobs.[41]

Obtaining satisfactory answers to these two questions required reflection on two other antecedent issues that were equally elusive. First, how to establish that a U.S. employer's need for a foreign worker was of such a nature that the entry of the worker would neither displace an American worker nor adversely affect the wages and working conditions of those similarly employed. And second—and of perhaps even more consequence—how to be reasonably certain that the de facto intervention in the labor market (which is what employment-based immigration amounts to was not so substantial that it interfered significantly with the market's natural propensity to adjust to a tighter labor supply or contributed to a growing dependence on foreign workers by U.S. business.

Even a cursory look at the two legislative proposals shown in table 14.1

---

c. The bill would split the category into (1) spouses and minor children (115,000 visas) and (2) other children (35,150 visas).

d. The current system and H.R. 4300 exempt "special immigrants" from numerical limitations. This category includes certain former employees of the U.S. government abroad, babies born abroad to legal permanent residents, and aliens who have continuously resided in the United States since 1972. An annual average of approximately 3,500 immigrants has entered the United States through these exempted categories during the 1980s.

e. For 1992–1996 employment-based immigration would be set at 65,000 principal workers per year. On the basis of recent data, it is estimated that an additional 93,500 accompanying spouses and children would be admitted. In 1997 the ceiling would be raised to 75,000 principal workers with an estimated accompanying 104,250 spouses and children.

f. Employment-based preference immigrants under H.R. 4300 include "priority workers" and "other employment-based aliens." Priority workers comprise: (1) aliens with extraordinary ability, (2) outstanding professors and researchers, (3) certain executives and managers of multinational corporations, and (4) aliens with business expertise. (This last category is limited to 2,000.) Any visas not used by priority workers become available for "other employment-based aliens", i.e., immigrants "performing specified labor, not of a temporary or seasonal nature, for which a shortage of employable and willing persons exists in the U.S." Both skilled and unskilled labor would qualify the alien.

g. Current law does not really differentiate among different types of professionals.

h. Current law provides only for the entry of skilled and unskilled workers in this category.

i. S. 358 would have eliminated access to U.S. independent immigrant visas by unskilled aliens.

j. The IA of 1990 limits unskilled workers to 10,000 visas.

k. Theoretically available under the current nonpreference category.

l. This number is not used to calculate the total for FY 1992 because it starts in 1994. At that time, the first three transitional visa programs will have lapsed, for a total of 55,000 in visa "savings."

m. The dates in parentheses denote the years during which each set of visas would be available.

n. H.R. 4300 proposed backlog reduction programs of 76,000 visas for each year between 1991 and 1995. These visas would have been distributed as follows: 10,250 for the 2nd preference; 40,750 for the 5th preference; and 25,000 for the employment-based categories.

o. The 1992–1994 visa numbers are capped at 714,000. In order to accommodate the growth in the immediate relative categories without disadvantaging family preference immigrants, a floor of 226,000 visas was agreed to for the family preference immigrants. Any additional visas required to maintain this floor during 1992–1994 would be subtracted from the 55,000 allocated annually to the spouses and children of those aliens legalized under IRCA.

p. Half on these visas would go to displaced Tibetans over a three-year period; the other half to aliens selected by the IRCA "adversely affected" country lottery for whom no visas were available because of a bureaucratic miscalculation.

Table 14.2   Overall Immigration Levels of the Immigration Act of 1990

A. The total number of immigrants entering the United States annually in fiscal years 1992–1994 under the IA is 714,000.[a] This figure cannot be exceeded.

The visas are distributed as follows:

- 465,000 for family immigrants;
- 55,000 for the spouses and children of aliens legalized under IRCA;
- 140,000 for employment-based immigrants;
- 40,000 for nationals from "adversely affected" countries;
- 12,000 for Hong Kong nationals who are high-level employees of large U.S. multinationals having a subsidiary in Hong Kong;[b]
- 1,000 for displaced Tibetans;
- 1,000 for aliens who were notified that they had "won" a U.S. visa under the IRCA lottery system for nationals of "adversely affected" countries (NP-5), but for whom no visas where actually available.

B. Beginning in fiscal year 1995, the number drops to a minimum of 675,000. That figure can be exceeded to accommodate growth in the size of the "immediate relatives of U.S. citizens" class.[c]

The visas would be distributed as follows:

- 480,000 for family immigrants;
- 140,000 for employment-based immigrants;
- 55,000 for "diversity immigrants."

Source: Immigration Act of 1990, PL 101-649.

a. This figure excludes refugees, whose admission numbers are announced annually.

b. Visas issued to certain employees of U.S. government entities who are nationals of Hong Kong will be valid until Jan. 1, 2002; employees of the U.S. consulate in Hong Kong can also obtain "special immigrant" status until Jan. 1, 2002, with up to 500 of them being able to enter the United States outside any numerical limitations.

c. This refers to spouses, parents, and minor children of U.S. citizens.

suggests that the law's three-year deliberation by Congress was often acrimonious. Columns 2 and 3 show how the two competing proposals reflected significantly different approaches to immigration reform. These differences stemmed both from profoundly different philosophies about immigration by each proposal's authors[42] and from sharply different levels of ambition about how deep reform should be. Considering the timing of final passage of the act (the serious reconciliation of the two bills did not really begin until the 101st Congress was already past its originally scheduled date of adjournment) and the difficulty the Congress has in enacting complex pieces of social legislation, it should come as no surprise that the Immigration Act of 1990 was primarily a product of compromise.

The IA's admission totals fell midway between the Senate (table 14.1, column 2) and House (column 3) proposals. Though it postponed consideration of some of the tough decisions about immigrant families for another day,[43] it did make a number of unambiguous statements.

- The 1965 Immigration Act's principles of nondiscrimination and neutrality with regard to the ethnicity, race, and national origin of immigrants were strictly maintained.
- In response to concerns that the U.S. immigration selection system's internal dynamics might have inadvertently disadvantaged certain countries, the IA provided both a transitional (3-year) and, beginning in 1995, a permanent program intended to diversify the immigration flow.
- The IA gave family immigration a resounding reaffirmation as the defining feature of U.S. immigration policy through an allocation of about four-fifths of total visas.[44]
- The IA nearly tripled employment-based immigration's share of overall immigration from 54,000 to 140,000 visas. In addition, and in the first explicit affirmation of immigration's significant role in spurring economic growth in recent years, it set the educational and occupational qualifications of prospective immigrants decidedly higher than those under the former system.
- In line with this affirmation, the IA streamlined the decision-making process on employers' petitions to import foreign workers. At the same time, however, and with an eye toward balancing the interests of employers with those of U.S. workers vis-à-vis immigration, the IA established additional safeguards against immigration's potentially adverse effects on the wages, working conditions, and job opportunities of U.S. workers—particularly in the temporary foreign worker system.
- In further opting for the middle road between these two interests, the IA required the testing of several new mechanisms in search of the one method that might eventually allow a reliable assessment of an employer's claim of the unavailability of qualified U.S. workers and thus the need for a foreign worker.
- The IA also linked permanent and temporary legal immigration reforms.[45] In a similar approach, though neither as stringent nor as intrusive as that devised under INRA (1989), the IA changed the way foreigners entering the United States for temporary work could gain access to the labor market.
- In that regard, the IA added two new elements of control: (a) it restricted the number of such workers in certain key employment-based visa categories;[46] and (b) it took certain tentative steps[47] to-

ward extending to additional temporary work categories the principle that qualified U.S. workers should be given some preference in employment.

- To prevent employers from paying temporary foreign workers lower wages—which could lead to the erosion in wages of similarly employed U.S. workers—the IA required that employers in additional visa categories[48] compensate foreign workers at the higher of the rates for the job classification that prevail at the place of employment or in the recruitment area.

- Finally, the IA formally interposed the U.S. Department of Labor as the resolver of disputes arising from the terms and conditions of the employment of temporary foreign workers.[49] However, the law attempted to do so relatively nonintrusively. While mandating that employers attest to these terms and conditions in advance of obtaining access to a foreign worker in several temporary visa categories, the IA simultaneously limited the government's investigative authority.

Conclusion

IRCA, on the one hand, and INRA and the IA, on the other, were conceived in and thus reflect fundamentally different socioeconomic and political perceptions. The passage of IRCA was in many respects the Congress's immigration response to an ideology of limits. The 1970s and early 1980s had given rise to, and had subsequently fueled, perceptions of extreme U.S. vulnerability to foreign political and economic events. Such perceptions had reinforced U.S. fears of an eroding ability to control its own fate. This self-image was translated into a fundamentally defensive approach to immigration policy reform that highlighted law-and-order initiatives offset only partially by a legalization program.[50]

In contrast, both INRA and especially the IA were expressions of a different set of perceptions and overall environment. This environment exhibited a more economically and politically confident United States, with a sense of itself and of its ability to control its destiny, seen only rarely in the previous twenty years.[51]

No other issue, however, played as critical a role in the shaping and final passage of the IA than "international competitiveness," that is, the notion that immigrants could play an important role in enhancing U.S. competitiveness in the global economy. Although evidence of the importance of this theme was neither always compelling nor obvious to the uninitiated—and despite the fact that numerous other issues were very much the leading themes during different (especially the earlier) phases of the debate[52]—the competitiveness argument was never far from the center of the discussion. And global economic competition was the deciding factor both in the legislation's passage and in its signing by President Bush.

The first U.S. immigration legislation in the post–cold war period was thus exclusively a reflection of domestic politics and economic imperatives. Although the cold war's end may have enabled the United States to focus more fully on economic competition in the global market, it was the latter, and not the former, that dictated changes to the immigration system.

This trend is likely to continue to define the United States' overall approach to immigration. It is also clear that recurring headline-capturing events in countries with which the United States has had long-standing complex relationships (including immigration ones) will continue to have specific, if at times indirect, implications for primarily illegal, or simply unwanted, immigration to the United States. These events are likely to continue to be treated as highly idiosyncratic phenomena, at least for the time being. Most recently, for instance, the Mexican economic crisis and the subsequent U.S. bailout of the Mexican currency presented yet another scenario to which the United States responded in an idiosyncratic manner. Indeed, the Clinton administration's response was anchored to a significant degree to concerns that Mexico's worsening economic situation would result in a substantial increase in illegal immigration pressures, thus signaling a new and more nuanced appreciation of the complexity of the U.S. relationship—and interdependence—with Mexico. As with so many of the themes explored in this chapter, and this book more generally, however, this is another area in which the policy response has not yet been fully defined.

Notes

1. Public and private sector accounting exercises have shown state and local fiscal costs associated with illegal immigration to be between $4 and $5 billion. Three categories account for virtually all such costs: education, emergency medical services, and incarceration of criminal aliens. See, for example, Rebecca L. Clark, Jeffrey S. Passel, Wendy N. Zimmermann, and Michael E. Fix, *Fiscal Impacts of Undocumented Immigrants: Selected Estimates for Seven States* (Washington, D.C.: Urban Institute, 1994).

2. California's economy has benefited from both the brawn and brains of generations of immigrants. Chinese workers helped develop California's physical infrastructure, and more broadly, Asians and Mexicans have served the needs of the economy—and the wants of middle-class Californians—well throughout the state's history. Almost half of the state's $20-billion-a-year agricultural sector owes its survival during the two world wars and its vitality, profitability, and growth throughout this century to Mexican workers. See Commission on Agricultural Workers, *Report of the Commission on Agricultural Workers* (Washington, D.C.: Government Printing Of-

fice, 1992). And talented and hard-working Asians have made extraordinary contributions to the state's national and global leadership in such intellectual endeavors as university education and high-technology research and development and to the opening and nurturing of vast economic opportunities in the Far East.

3. California's dubious "distinctions" in this last regard in fact include many of the immigration restrictionist movement's most aggressive manifestations. These have ranged from the anti-Asian agitation and the systematic local and state legislative discrimination against Chinese and Japanese immigrants throughout the second half of the nineteenth century and the early part of the twentieth to the mass expulsions of illegal Mexican workers of the early 1930s and again the early 1950s. Proposition 187, the most recent California initiative targeting illegal immigration (also known as the "Save Our State" initiative of 1994), tracks that tradition by placing the political burden for a period's economic malaise squarely on the shoulders of a population that has few means of defending itself politically. No judgment is intended here about the legitimacy of some of the concerns that led Californians to vote by a nearly two-to-one margin for the initiative. Such judgments would require their own analysis and are beyond this paper's scope.

4. This was the second time in two years that the base was used for that purpose. This time, however, it was made clear that it would become a holding tank until circumstances changed in Haiti rather than being a way station to resettlement in the United States. As a result, the outflow from Haiti came to a virtual halt.

5. Calling people on the move "one of the most complex and volatile issues of the post–Cold War era," a Carnegie Endowment report acknowledges immigration's dual role in both "enriching" and inflicting "serious problems of adjustment, social tensions and financial costs" upon their receiving countries. The report calls for a "comprehensive multilateral agenda" to address the issue and is an extraordinary admission by foreign policy elites of the "threat" to global stability posed by a migration system that is, or is perceived to be, "out-of-control." See Carnegie Endowment for International Peace, "Changing Our Ways: America and the New World," Report of the National Commission on America and the New World (Washington, D.C., 1992), 46, 48–49.

6. The term *migration system* refers here to migration processes that may or may not be under state control. As such, it includes population movements across state boundaries that are both systematic and unsystematic, organized and spontaneous, legal and illegal. Understood in this broad context, a migration system includes both movements responding to the market mechanism (economically motivated migration) and flows of refugees and asylum seekers. A migration system is a much broader concept than an *"imm*igration *regime"* or *"policy,"* to which it has a genus/species relationship. An immigration regime or policy refers to the attempt by receiving societies (sometimes in cooperation with sending societies) to institutionalize, regulate, and generally manage movements of people across state boundaries. This involves the establishment of numerical, procedural, and qualitative terms and conditions for a foreigner's entry and stay in that society.

7. Even such "closed" societies as Cuba, the Peoples' Republic of China, and North Korea participate in this system, albeit in a relatively limited way and under closely regulated conditions.

8. The migration systems of the United States and Canada have been global in character for most of these countries' existence as independent states.

9. This subsystem also includes an interregional component since it has received massive flows from several South Asian countries during the last twenty years.

10. This refers to responses to humanitarian emergencies or certain foreign policy quandaries by offering resettlement opportunities (viz. Great Britain and Hong Kong, the United States and Vietnam, or Germany and ethnic Germans); affirmative responses to the principle of family reunification; or the engaging in negotiations for trade liberalization which are constantly pushing against the limits of what is considered possible at a given time in terms of "international labor mobility."

11. A fundamental fissure is developing in the political culture of most advanced industrial societies. While political and intellectual elites have largely become strongly inclusionist and internationalist in their thinking, the mass publics—excited by demagogues and political opportunists and buffeted by an unrelenting economic downturn—are becoming increasingly exclusionist and nationalistic. Immigration, and also ethnicity, race, and class issues, are used to exploit tensions born of de facto changing national identities. While the idea that national identities are inherently dynamic, and thus fundamentally mutable, may be largely accepted in states where the process of nation building has never really stopped (as in the "new" countries of the Americas and in Australia), or in the abstract, it is strongly resisted by most intellectuals and publics in Europe and Japan.

12. In terms of their consequences, nondecisions (such as the failure to address illegal immigration before it becomes entrenched) can and routinely do have enormous impact.

13. This is the case with several countries in the South that both serve as magnets for immigrants from less prosperous countries and at the same time send national emigrants to more prosperous countries. Some southern European countries have been simultaneously attracting immigrants from the South in addition to re-emigrants. Many in this latter category are the children and grandchildren of earlier emigrants with often only a tentative cultural attachment to the country of their forebears.

14. That distinction has always had little meaning in much of sub-Saharan Africa. There, borders are often arbitrary, and population movements occur regularly among family members who may live in adjacent state jurisdictions, or among people who follow patterns of movement for economic survival and mobility which predate the formation of the current independent states. See Aderanti Adepoju, "Binational Communities and Labor Circulation in Sub-Saharan Africa," in Demetrios G. Papademetriou and Philip L. Martin, eds., *The Unsettled Relationship: Labor Migration and Economic Development* (New York: Greenwood Press, 1991), 45–64.

15. These may take various forms, such as that of the federalist-leaning European Union (EU); or the more purely trade-based European Free Trade Association, North American Free Trade Agreement (NAFTA), and several nascent or emerging trading groups in Southeast Asia, Central and South America, the Caribbean, and elsewhere; or they may adopt the hybrid character of the European Economic Area.

16. Among those one can point to are intermittent agreements between and among certain Middle Eastern countries; the essentially open access to the United States for citizens of Canada (and to a lesser degree, for some Mexicans who live along the U.S. border) or that between Colombia and Venezuela; and the still likely elimination of internal frontiers in the EU.

17. Increasingly, domestic considerations are also beginning to impinge significantly on decisions about refugees and asylum seekers in a syndrome some people have called "compassion fatigue." Most important among such considerations are the financial costs associated with adjudicating claims and resettling those found to meet the appropriate standards and a state's perception of its "national interest"—a

vague construct that can be and is routinely used to mean virtually whatever the day's government wishes it to mean.

18. The resulting ad hoc responses to the many new types of humanitarian "crises" threaten to undermine the legal foundation for all such actions. In Iraq, for instance, we see the emergence of a new "principle" whereby intervention for humanitarian purposes, or the creation of "safety zones" within a country's territory, may supersede national sovereignty and present pragmatic alternatives to first asylum. Cambodia, Central America, and several African examples are serving as testing grounds for the successful repatriation of refugees while highlighting the need to link repatriation with effective efforts at relief, reintegration, and development. New legal and institutional frameworks for protecting and assisting internally displaced people are also being tested in the former Yugoslav republic. Finally, Haiti is "permitting" one of the first experiments with "in-country processing," a near non sequitur in both principle and practice. See Doris M. Meissner, R. D. Hormats, A. G. Walker, and S. Ogata, *International Migration Challenges in the New Era,* Report to the Trilateral Commission, (New York: Trilateral Commission Publications, 1993); Kathleen Newland, "Refugees: The Rising Flood," *World Watch* 7, no. 3 (May–June 1994).

19. In other words, the end of the superpower rivalry has diminished the foreign policy and domestic political value of refugee issues in the eyes of many policy makers.

20. The reasoning here is that the importance of protecting those "fleeing communism" had become almost a U.S. national mantra, leading to reflex actions in policy which were accepted by most Americans. Far fewer, however, are likely to be well informed enough about the conditions in specific countries that make the citizens of these countries "worthy" of protection—and particularly, of resettlement to the United States. Hence a new national consensus about refugee protection policies will have to be carefully crafted. This, of course, offers both opportunities and challenges to the refugee policy-making community.

21. Such as with the U.S. establishment in 1990 of a new permanent visa category to accommodate, with a minimum of regulatory interference, the migration of very talented individuals—a class of persons who had already become de facto global citizens.

22. Such as the implementation of the General Agreement in Tariffs and Trade, the free trade agreements with Israel and Canada, and the North American Free Trade Agreement with Mexico and Canada.

23. Such as changes facilitating the immigration of certain scientists from the former Soviet Union or accommodating various defense coproduction agreements involving U.S. allies.

24. This includes several special programs since 1986 which offered citizens from thirty-six "adversely affected" countries (countries whose nationals were adversely affected in terms of access to U.S. visas as a result of various changes in U.S. immigration law) the opportunity to compete by lottery for small numbers of visas. Beginning with fiscal year 1995, 55,000 visas will be distributed annually by lottery to nationals of certain countries in inverse proportion to a region's and a country's overall use of U.S. immigrant visas during the previous year.

25. In 1978, Congress impaneled the Select Commission on Immigration and Refugee Policy to make comprehensive recommendations on immigration policy. The commission issued its final report in 1981. Both legislative chambers introduced immigration reform legislation and held extensive hearings based on the commission's recommendations, but neither chamber was able to obtain passage of new

legislation. The legislation introduced was almost identical to that introduced into the 97th Congress.

26. This provision corresponded to that sector's fears that the new law would lead to shortages of workers, and it thus sought to wean the growers gradually from their historical dependence on an illegal foreign work force. The law has failed totally in that regard.

27. See D. M. Meissner, and D. G. Papademetriou, "The Legalization Countdown: A Third-Quarter Assessment" (Washington, D.C.: Carnegie Endowment for International Peace, Feb. 1988) both for a discussion of IRCA's major provisions and its underlying assumptions. For an evaluation of the effectiveness of the law's implementation, see D. G. Papademetriou, R. L. Bach, D. A. Cobb-Clark, R. G. Kramer, B. L. Lowell, S. J. Smith, and M. Shea, *Employer Sanctions and U.S. Labor Markets: First Report* (Washington, D.C.: U.S. Department of Labor, 1991); Demetrios G. Papademetriou, "The New U.S. Immigration Law: Continuity in Change," paper prepared for the International Migration Meetings of the Institute of Sociology of the Soviet Academy of Sciences, Moscow, June 17–21, 1991.

28. Ordinarily, foreign temporary workers can stay in the United States for up to five years. A sixth year is possible only in "extraordinary" circumstances. Many of the nurses in question were at, or had already exhausted, that legal limit.

29. Under INRA, U.S. employers of foreign RNs were required to file an "attestation" with the U.S. Department of Labor prior to obtaining a foreign RN. Employers had to certify that: (1) a substantial disruption would ensue in the petitioning facility's delivery of health care services without the services of such aliens; (2) the employment of foreign nurses would not affect adversely the wages and working conditions of similarly employed U.S. workers; (3) foreign nurses would be paid wages equal to those for other similarly employed RNs; and (4) the petitioning facility was taking a series of steps designed to recruit and retain U.S. workers who were RNs in order to remove as quickly as reasonably possible the facility's dependence on immigrant RNs.

30. Five steps were required. The employer must (1) operate a training program for RNs at the facility or finance (or participate in) one elsewhere; (2) make available career development programs for other health care workers to enter the nursing profession; (3) offer RNs in their facility higher wages than those being paid to RNs similarly employed in the geographic area; (4) provide adequate support services to RNs in order to free them from administrative and other non-nursing duties; (5) provide reasonable opportunities for meaningful salary advancement by RNs.

31. Occupational projections by the U.S. Bureau of Labor Statistics indicated that in the 1988–2000 period, the greatest absolute job growth was expected to be in service (4.2 million), professional (3.5 million), and executive, administrative, and managerial (2.7 million) occupations. Similarly, the largest percentage increases were projected for technical and related support (31.6), professional (24.0), service (22.6), and executive, administrative, and managerial (22.0) professions. The bureau's employment data and projections by industry for the same period were largely consistent with the occupational projections. Employment in goods-producing industries (composed of manufacturing, construction, agriculture, forestry, fisheries, and mining) was projected to grow by only 0.1% annually (1.7% over the entire 1988–2000 period), while manufacturing, of both durable and nondurable goods, and the mining sectors were projected to experience job declines. In contrast, service industries (such as general services, retail trade, and financial services, insurance, and real estate), were projected to grow by 1.6% annually (20.9% over the entire

1988–2000 period). See G. Silvestri, and J. Lukasiewicz, "A Look at Occupational Employment Trends to the Year 2000," *Monthly Labor Review* 110, no. 9 (1987): 47–63; R. Kutscher, "Overview and Implications of the Projections to 2000," ibid., 3–9; R. Kutscher, "Projections Summary and Emerging Issues," ibid. 112, no. 11, (1989): 66–74. For a full discussion of these projections and their meaning for immigration policy, see Demetrios G. Papademetriou, "Immigration Reform: Key Issues for the Department of Labor," keynote address at the U.S. Department of Labor Conference on Legal Immigration and Early Impacts of IRCA, Washington, D.C., May 1990.

32. Immigration currently accounts for about 30% of total U.S. population growth, as compared to almost 50% during the 1900–1910 period. Using a different measure, in 1980, the census determined that 6.2% of the U.S. population was foreign-born, a figure that approached 8% in 1990. These figures include both permanent and temporary legal immigrants, as well as partial estimates of the illegal population.

33. Immigrants (permanent and temporary legal immigrants, but also refugees, asylum seekers, and illegals) may make up as much as two-fifths of new entrants into the labor force. This figure is up from roughly one-quarter only a few years earlier. See D. G. Papademetriou, R. L. Bach, K. Johnson, R. G. Kramer, B. L. Lowell, and S. J. Smith, *The Effects of Immigration on the U.S. Economy and Labor Market*, Division of Immigration Policy and Research, report 1, (Washington, D.C.: U.S. Department of Labor, 1989); Papademetriou, Bach, Cobb-Clark, Kramer, Lowell, Smith, and Shea, *Employer Sanctions*.

34. For instance, Hudson Institute, *Workforce 2000: Work and Workers for the Twenty-first Century* (Indianapolis: Hudson Institute, 1987); Perrin Towers and the Hudson Institute, *Workforce 2000: Competing in a Seller's Market: Is Corporate America Prepared? A Survey Report* (Indianapolis: Hudson Institute, 1990); Commission on Workforce Quality and Labor Market Efficiency, *Investing in People: A Strategy to Address America's Workforce Crisis* (Washington, D.C.: U.S. Department of Labor, 1989); National Center on Education and the Economy, *America's Choice: High Skills or Low Wages*, report of the Commission on the Skills of the American Workforce (Rochester, N.Y., June 1990); Carnegie Forum on Education and the Economy, *A Nation Prepared: Teachers for the Twenty-first Century*, report of the Task Force for Teaching as a Profession (Washington, D.C., May 1986); and Carnegie Council on Adolescent Development, *Turning Points: Preparing American Youth for the Twenty-first Century*, report of the Task Force on Education of Adolescents (Washington, D.C., June 1989). For a full discussion of this issue, see D. G. Papademetriou, "Contending Approaches to Reforming the U.S. Legal Immigration System," paper presented at the New York University–Rockefeller Foundation Conference on Migration, Ethnicity, and the City, New York Nov. 1990.

35. Projections on the likely future demand for labor in the United States were seized upon by immigration advocates in a remarkable coalition that saw the business lobby, the immigration bar, church and ethnic groups, human rights advocates, and a cluster of less central proimmigration players parlay the economic competitiveness argument into a significant increase in immigration levels.

36. The complex link between immigration and population dynamics is frequently lost in such discussions. The Organization for Economic Cooperation and Development recently studied that link and reached the following conclusions: First, most of the advanced industrial societies' perceived demographic challenges cannot be effectively remedied through immigration unless extreme immigration measures

are implemented. This would include admitting many more immigrants than are currently allowed and making age a principal criterion of admission (i.e., admitting primarily very young immigrants). Second, sustained labor force growth in the face of continuing low fertility *can* be ensured by sustaining regular flows of immigration. (The effects of immigration on fertility are usually modest, however, because in many cases the fertility of immigrants does not exceed the rate of generational replacement. And in virtually all cases, higher initial fertility of immigrants is transient. In other words, immigrant fertility rates tend quickly to approach those of the indigenous population.) And third, ensuring a fairly stable ratio of retirees to working persons (as a means of shoring up retirement systems) will require not only major and sustained compensatory immigration flows but concomitant changes in such factors as retirement age, further rationalization of the work force, etc. See Organization for Economic Cooperation and Development, *Migration: The Demographic Aspects* (Paris: Organization for Economic Cooperation and Development, 1991).

37. Projections about the labor market by the U.S. Bureau of Labor Statistics were repeatedly cited to support arguments in favor of changes in immigration. Among the most influential were: (1) that the labor force would continue to grow until the year 2000 (albeit at a less rapid pace)—from the 2.6% annual growth between 1970 and 1980, and the 1.6% between 1980 and 1988—to 1.2% between 1988 and 2000 (see H. Fullerton Jr., "New Labor Force Projections, Spanning 1988 to 2000," *Monthly Labor Review* 112, no. 11 [1989]: 7; R. Kutsher, "Projections Summary," 67); and (2) that the age composition of the labor force would shift slightly during the 1988–2000 period as workers between the ages of 25 and 54 made up a slightly larger proportion of the labor force, while the youth labor force (persons 16–24) contributed to a slightly lower proportion of the total (though remaining the same size in absolute numbers). Such projections helped win passage of the immigration reform package. The immigration debate, however, largely ignored other important projections by the Bureau of Labor Statistics. Among them were (1) that by the year 2000 the U.S. labor market would be much "looser" than at present, as increasing numbers of teenagers and persons in their early twenties (the "echo" of the postwar baby boom generation) entered the market; and (2) that total rates of participation in the labor force would subsequently increase from the current 65.9% to 69.0% as the baby boom generation reached its prime working years. See Fullerton, "New Labor Force Projections," 5, 11; and H. Fullerton Jr., "Labor Force Projections: 1986 to 2000," *Monthly Labor Review* 110, no. 9 (1987): 19–29; Kutscher, "Overview and Implications"; Kutscher, "Projections Summary."

38. See Papademetriou, "Immigration Reform."

39. Clearly, beyond a certain threshold, access to immigrant labor would interfere with these opportunities.

40. Among those decisions were how many employment-based immigrants should be admitted, what their qualifications should be, and under what immigration status they should enter (i.e., permanent or temporary).

41. This second condition was a central component of the version of the immigration bill put forth by the House of Representatives (see table 14.1 col. 3). After considering extending requirements similar to those for employers of temporary foreign nurses to virtually all categories of labor market immigration, the House settled on a set of fees to be imposed on those employers wishing to import and employ foreign workers. These fees were to be distributed to state and local public sector employment agencies, where they would be used to train U.S. workers for jobs

thought to be in short supply. The scheme was abandoned when it became apparent that neither the Senate nor the administration would support what was quickly branded a tax on employers—and therefore anticompetitive.

42. See Papademetriou, "Contending Approaches."

43. Principal among these decisions were whether to change the distribution of visas for relatives and how to deal with the extensive waiting lists (known as backlogs) in these categories. In January 1989 there were 2,328,000 persons on these lists. See U.S. Department of State, Bureau of Consular Affairs, "Report of the Visa Office 1990," Department of State Publication 9823, Oct. 1991, 128.

44. In addition, the IA included a particularly hard-fought provision known as "family unity." This provision offered to spouses and unmarried children of aliens legalized under IRCA who were in the United States illegally as of May 5, 1988 relief from deportation and immediate work authorization until they became eligible for full immigration benefits as members of reunified families. This status, though a lesser one than the full legalization offered to illegal aliens in 1986 under IRCA, was won primarily on the philosophical and humanitarian principle of family unity. This was also true of another provision of the IA, which granted up to 165,000 visas over three years for the reunification of the immediate families of this same cohort of legalized immigrants.

45. See Papademetriou, "Contending Approaches"; Papademetriou, "New U.S. Immigration Law."

46. See D. G. Papademetriou, "Temporary Migration to the United States: Composition, Issues, and Policies," paper presented at the East-West Center–University Research Center of Nihon University Conference on International Manpower Flows and Foreign Investment in the Asia/Pacific Region, Tokyo, Sept. 8–13, 1991.

47. At this juncture these steps are indirect and derivative (through regulation) rather than statutory in nature.

48. Employers seeking to employ foreign workers temporarily in the agricultural and other low-wage sectors (H-2A and B visas) have always had to pay special wage rates.

49. This enforcement role was first enshrined in statute in IRCA's reforms of the temporary foreign worker program for agriculture (H-2A). The permanent immigration program provides neither for attestations nor for challenges to a decision.

50. Offering legal immigrant status to nearly 3 million persons was certainly an act of extreme generosity. It was also, however, an act of simple pragmatism. The government sought to avoid both the economic/labor market and the social and political disruptions that a massive exercise in removing the illegally resident population would entail. Furthermore, everything the government knew about the effectiveness—and the excesses—of police operations (including the United States' two previous similar experiences in the 1930s and 1950s, the latter the infamous "operation wetback") gave everyone pause both about the feasibility and the legal and civil rights implications of such vast operations. See Nicholas DiMarzio and Demetrios G. Papademetriou, "Legalization: The Right Thing to Do," MRS Issue Analysis Series Paper no. 1, Migration and Refugee Services, U.S. Catholic Conference, August 1986; Meissner and Papademetriou, "Legalization Countdown." Nonetheless, the main legalization program's eligibility date of January 1, 1982, years removed from the date of the law's passage, may have been set without adequate thought, though it reflects what proponents of legalization considered politically viable at the time. Little thought was given, for instance, to the implications of that distant date for the government's ability to control illegal immigration further, absent draconian control

measures. (None of the principal architects of IRCA advocated such measures.) Legalization programs in other countries had chosen eligibility dates much closer to or concurrent with such laws' passage. See D. Meissner, D. G. Papademetriou, and D. North, "Legalization of Undocumented Aliens: Lessons from Other Countries," report on a consultation held at the Carnegie Endowment for International Peace (Washington, D.C.: Carnegie Endowment for International Peace, 1987).

51. Both Congress and the administration ignored the fact that, by the time the IA became law, the U.S. economy was already in a phase of uncertainty as they moved to enact legal immigration legislation. (It was, however, a critical part of the calculus of proimmigration lobbies, which had not been fully enamored of the proposed legislation's provisions but saw in the changing economic environment the makings of a far less generous immigration package if enactment were postponed until the next legislative session. Consequently, these groups managed to put their differences and reservations aside at the last minute and worked extraordinarily hard for the passage of a compromise bill). This reflects the difficulty for the U.S. Congress, and undoubtedly other legislative bodies, of finding the will necessary to change complex pieces of social and economic legislation that have developed their own momentum, simply because some of the circumstances that had made the legislation appear compelling may no longer exist. IRCA also became law well after the era of limits in which it was conceived had given way to relative political and economic confidence.

52. For instance, the issue of restricting the admission of more distant relatives of U.S. citizens was one of two centerpieces in the early rounds of the reform debate, dominated by the initially discrete, and later, joint proposals of Senators Kennedy and Simpson. (The other centerpiece was a point system for selecting independent immigrants.) Soon after the House entered the reform debate in full, however, it became clear that restrictions on family immigration were of no interest to the legislative leaders of that chamber, and thus labor market issues came to dominate the discussions. As is clear from table 14.1, the resulting legislation bears the unmistakable imprint of the House's version of reform. For a full discussion of the legislative and political history of the 1990 act, see Papademetriou, "Contending Approaches."

CONTRIBUTORS

Joel D. Aberbach is a professor of political science and policy studies and director of the Center for American Politics and Public Policy at the University of California, Los Angeles. He is the author of *Keeping a Watchful Eye: The Politics of Congressional Oversight* (1990); *Bureaucrats and Politicians in Western Democracies* (1981) with Robert D. Putnam and Bert A. Rockman; and numerous other publications on executive and legislative politics in the United States and abroad.

Herbert Dittgen is a visiting scholar at the Center for U.S.-Mexican Studies, University of California, San Diego. He was previously a visiting scholar at the Center for International Affairs, Harvard University, an assistant professor at the Center for European and North American Studies at the University of Göttingen and has been a guest scholar at the Brookings Institution and the Carnegie Endowment for International Peace. He has written on the political theory of Marx and de Tocqueville and on U.S. foreign policy, and is the author of *Deutsch-amerikanische Sicherheitsbeziehungen in der Ära Helmut Schmidt* (1991); and *Aussenpolitik in der amerikanischen Demokratie* (1996).

Tobias Dürr works at the Center for European and North American Studies at the University of Göttingen. He is author of *Die SPD in Sachsen und Thüringen zwischen Hochburg und Diaspora* (1993), with Franz Walter.

Andreas Falke is a German national who works as an economic specialist at the American embassy in Bonn. He has written extensively on American trade policy and is currently completing a project on U.S. foreign trade. He also teaches in the American Studies Program at Bonn University. The views expressed in his chapter are his own and are not to be attributed to the American Embassy or any other U.S. government agency.

Adrienne Héritier is a professor of political science and public policy at the European University Institute, Florence. Her main fields of research are policy analysis, European policy making, and social and environmental policy.

Peter Lösche is a professor of political science at the University of Göttingen and director of the Center for European and North American Studies at the University of Göttingen. He has written extensively on German political parties and on American government and is the author of *Amerika in Perspektive* (1990); *Die SPD. Klassenpartei—Volkspartei—Quotenpartei* (1992) with Franz Walter; and *Kleine Geschichte der deutschen Parteien* (1994).

Theodore J. Lowi is John L. Senior Professor of American Institutions at Cornell University. He has written on various aspects of American government, such as the presidency, the welfare state, and federalism, and is the author of *The End of Liberalism: The Second Republic of the United States* (2d ed., 1979); and *The End of the Republican Era* (1995).

Heinz-Dieter Meyer is an assistant professor at the Center for European and North American Studies at the University of Göttingen. He has written on organization, culture, and comparative education and is currently completing a research project on the crisis of the American high school.

Michael Minkenberg is an assistant professor at the Center for European and North American Studies at the University of Göttingen. He was a visiting assistant professor at Cornell University from 1991 to 1995. He is the author of *Neokonservatismus und Neue Rechte in den USA* (1990); *The New Right in Comparative Perspective: The USA and Germany* (1993); and other publications on the radical right in Western democracies.

Demetrios G. Papademetriou is a senior associate and director of the International Migration Policy Program at the Carnegie Endowment for International Peace and serves as chair of the Migration Committee of the Paris-based Organization for Economic Cooperation and Development. He is currently completing two books, *At the Precipice? Europe and Migration;* and *Reluctant Promised Lands: Immigration and Advanced Industrial Societies.*

Paul E. Peterson is the Henry Lee Shattuck Professor of Government and director of the Center for American Political Studies at Harvard University. He is the author of *The Price of Federalism* (1995); and editor of *The President, Congress, and the Making of Foreign Policy* (1994) as well as *Classifying by Race* (1995).

Bert A. Rockman is University Professor of Political Science at the University of Pittsburgh. He is also Research Professor in the university's Center for International Studies and Director of the Center for American Politics and Society. He is the author of *Bureaucrats and Politicians in Western Democracies* (1981); with Joel D. Aberbach and Robert D. Putnam, *The Leadership Question: The Presidency and the American System* (1985); and many other publications on U.S. executive and administrative politics.

James Thurber is a professor of government at the American University in Washington, D.C., where he is director of the Center for Congressional and Presidential Studies and the Campaign Management and Lobbying Institutes. He is the author of *Divided Democracy: Cooperation and Conflict Between Presidents and Congress* (1991), *Rivals for Power: Congressional-Presidential Relations* (1995), and coauthor of *Setting Course: A Congressional Management Guide* (1994). With Candice Nelson, he is coeditor of *Campaigns and Elections: American Style* (1995) and, with Roger Davidson, coeditor of *Remaking Congress: The Politics of Congressional Stability and Change* (1995).

David B. Walker is a professor of political science at the University of Connecticut and former director of the University of Connecticut's Institution of Public and Urban Affairs and master of public affairs program. He has served for many years in Washington as assistant director for government structure and function with the Advisory Commission on Intergovernmental Relations and has published extensively on problems of American federalism, most recently *The Rebirth of Federalism: Slouching toward Washington* (1995).

INDEX

Abortion, 135–36, 138
Aid to Families with Dependent Children (AFDC), 116, 118, 120, 201–02, 204–05, 208–10
Amateur politicians, 166–67
Anticommunism, 137, 157–58, 172, 240
Arms control, 137

Balanced Budget Amendment, 2, 69–70, 117, 119, 149, 195
Brazil, 278, 280–81
Buchanan, Pat, 139–40
Budget: Balanced Budget Amendment, 2, 69–70, 117, 119, 149, 195; Budget Enforcement Act (1990), 69–70, 83, 184, 188; and the deficit, 34–35, 81–83, 99, 111, 177–97, 269, 273–74, 277, 279, 287; and federal spending, 34, 97–100, 111–12; legislation regarding, 35, 69–70, 74, 82–84, 99–100, 183–84, 188, 191–92; and the national debt, 34–35, 99, 111, 178–79
Bush, George: appointments of, 43, 46–47; budget policy of, 99, 183, 188; educational policy of, 225; foreign policy of, 22, 25–28, 30, 49, 245–49, 252; and the Gulf War (1991), 245–47; immigration policy of, 313; legislative action of, 81, 83, 111–12; and the New Right, 139–40; as politician, 25–28; and the 1992 presidential election, 148–49; trade policy of, 265–66, 270–71, 280, 285–86; welfare policy of, 111–13

Campaign financing, 164–65
Campaign platforms, 160, 166
Campaign strategies, 165–66
Carter, Jimmy, 2, 19, 25, 49, 81, 86–87, 97, 105, 108, 129–30, 163, 253
China, 253–54

Christian Right, 10, 131, 139–40, 145, 148–49
Civil service: appointments of Bush to, 43, 46–47; appointments of Clinton to, 49–52, 114; appointments of Nixon to, 35–37; appointments of Reagan to, 36–43; and civil servants, 37–47; Civil Service Reform Act, 39–44; congressional oversight of, 43–44; ideological orientation of, 35–46; reform of, 39–46, 52–53, 114–17
Clinton, Bill: appointments of, 49–52, 114; budget policy of, 70, 99, 192; and civil service reform, 52–56, 114–17; foreign policy of, 16, 18–20, 22, 25–28, 30–31, 48–49, 53–55, 248, 252–53, 255–56; immigration policy of, 299, 313; legislative action of, 2, 18, 25–28, 51–53, 89–90, 99–100, 114–18, 120; and the 1992 presidential election, 18, 89, 113, 147–48, 158; political goals of, 25–28, 47–49, 113; as politician, 25–28, 87, 113; trade policy of, 53, 266, 267–68, 271, 283–90; welfare policy of, 113–20; 209
Clinton, Hillary Rodham, 50, 92
Competitiveness, 270–74, 279, 307
Congress: Appropriations Committees, 62, 66, 70; Armed Services Committee, 24; and budget legislation, 69–70; committees of, 62, 65–67; congressional oversight, 43–44; in the Constitution, 59–60; and the filibuster, 61, 88; and federalism, 108–09; Foreign Affairs Committee, 24; and foreign policy, 16, 24, 30, 33–34, 72–73, 251–52, 254; House Democratic Caucus, 65, 68, 161–62; members of, 61–62, 64–65, 88–89; organization of, 60–63; and partisanship, 81, 84, 87–88, 159, 167–69; public opinion of, 5, 64, 72–73; and reforms, 63–

Congress (*cont.*)
72, 87, 181–82, 276; Rules Committee, 61–62, 66, 71; and seniority, 65, 67; speaker, 67–68, 121; staff and support services for, 68–69; Steering and Policy Committee, 66–68; and Sunshine Reforms, 66, 70–71; trade policy of, 275–76, 279–80, 287–89; Ways and Means Committee, 62,66; and welfare legislation, 203

Congressional election of 1994, 3, 54–55, 63–64, 66–68, 113–14, 145–50

Conservatism, 4–7, 125–26, 132–33, 136, 140, 150–51

Contract with America, 16, 22, 27, 54–56, 58, 61, 64, 66–68, 72–74, 92, 117–19, 149, 195, 210

Crime control, 120, 135, 140

Cultural fragmentation, 243–45, 249–51

Dealignment, 127–28, 138, 142–45, 150

Deficit, 34–35, 81–83, 99, 111, 177–97, 269, 273–74, 277, 279, 287; and divided government, 182–84; and economic theory, 184–88; and Gramm-Rudman-Hollings Deficit Reduction Act (1985), 69–70, 82–83, 184, 192; and indexation, 188–93; and inflation, 187–92; and Keynesianism, 185–87; and monetarism, 187–88, 193; and taxation, 189–92, 195. *See also* Budget

Democratic Party, 129–30, 138–39, 163; electorate of, 142–45, 147–48, 162, 169–170; ideological orientation of, 4, 6–7, 140–42, 166; and welfare policy, 209–210

Divided government, 2, 76–95, 182–84, 276

Dole, Robert, 29, 88, 99, 191, 289

Domestic programs, 100–21

Duke, David, 139–40

Elections. *See* Congressional election of 1994; Presidential election of 1992; Voting

Ethnicity, 8–10

Executive, 33–57

Europe, 247–49, 266–69, 272–75, 279–85, 290

Family Support Act (1987/88), 204–05, 209

Federalism, 96–122, 200, 206

Foreign policy: and Congress, 16, 24, 30, 33–34, 72–73, 251–52, 254; and cultural fragmentation, 243–45, 249–51; decision-making processes for, 24–25, 257; and human rights, 252–54, 257–58; and liberal

theory, 242–45, 256; and the president, 17, 26, 251–52, 257; and realist theory, 240–45; and trade policy, 19, 21–22

Fundamentalists, 10, 131, 139–40, 145, 148

General Agreement on Tariffs and Trade (GATT), 22, 264–65, 267; 273–75, 277–78, 280–85, 287–89

Gingrich, Newt, 92, 114, 117, 119, 121, 149, 169, 288

Globalization, 8–9, 245–50, 300–01, 307–13

Government expenditures, 97–120

Gridlock, 1–3, 7–8, 58, 64, 73–74, 76–95, 99, 121

Gulf War (1991), 17, 21, 24–25, 27, 245–49; 252, 254

Haiti, 23, 27, 29, 299

Hart, Gary, 130

Health care, 134, 140, 206–07, 209

Helms, Jesse, 149

Homosexuality, 136, 140

Human rights, 252–54, 257–58

Immigration, 8–10, 23; and employment, 307–12; and globalization, 307–12;

Immigration Act (1990), 305–12

Immigration Nursing Relief Act (1989), 305–06, 312; and Clinton immigration policy, 299, 313; Immigration Reform and Control Act (1986), 305, 312

Indexation, 188–93

India, 277, 280, 290

Inflation, 187–92

Interest groups, 103, 109, 276

Jackson, Jesse, 130

Japan, 266–290

Johnson, Lyndon B., 97, 100, 103–05, 190, 194

Kennedy, John F., 2

Kennedy, Ted, 130

Keynesianism, 185–87

Kissinger, Henry, 22

Lake, Anthony, 19–20

Liberal democracy, 9–11

Liberalism, 4–7, 125–26, 131–33, 136, 140, 150–51

Liberal theory of international relations, 242–45, 256

McGovern, George, 129
Medicaid, 111–12, 116, 120, 206–07, 209
Mexico, 22, 24, 281–82, 287, 289, 299, 313
Military, 21, 24–25, 53–54; and military interventions, 16, 18–21, 24–25, 27–29, 53–54, 97–99, 245–47, 252, 256–57; spending for, 17, 21, 24–25, 27, 34, 53–54, 70, 96–101, 118, 137, 177–81, 194
Minorities, 8–10; public opinion of, 135, 138, 140
Monetarism, 187–88, 193
Moral Majority, 7, 131

National Performance Review, 52–53, 114–17
Nationhood, 8–11
NATO, 248
Neoconservatism, 125–26, 130–31, 137, 150
New Deal, 4–7, 33, 102–03, 126–27, 131–32, 135, 137, 169, 185, 194
New Deal Coalition, 4, 7, 138, 143–44, 150
New Left, 126, 129–31, 138
New Politics, 127–29, 132, 137–38, 141–43, 150–51
New Right, 126, 131, 136–37, 139–40, 148–49
New World Order, 21, 53, 195, 238–41, 245–51
Nixon, Richard, 35–43, 105, 108
North American Free Trade Agreement (NAFTA), 22, 24, 49, 53, 90, 264–65, 275–76, 278, 280–82, 284, 287–88

Old Left, 129–30
Old Politics, 129–33, 137–38, 141, 150

Party financing, 164–65
Party identification, 127, 142–45, 150, 170–71
Party membership, 158
Perot, Ross, 51, 73, 147, 195, 288–289
Political parties: and campaign financing, 164–65; and campaign strategies, 165–66; and candidate nomination, 163; in Congress, 67–68, 81, 84, 87–88, 167–69; financing of, 164–65; membership of, 158; and national party committees, 159, 161, 164–65; organization of, 103–04, 109, 159, 160–62; and partisanship, 81, 84, 87–88, 159, 167–69; platforms of, 159–60, 166. *See also* individual parties
Postmaterialism, 129–31

Poverty, 198–200
President, and foreign policy, 17, 26, 251–52, 257
Presidential election of 1992, 79, 83, 89, 113, 145–49, 158
Primaries, 162–63
Public education, 215–237; administration of, 220–21; and school choice movement, 217–18, 225–231; and equality, 218, 222–23, 231–32; funding of, 218–19; privatization of, 217; state activism in, 231; and social integration, 219, 224–25; and teachers, 229
Public opinion, 125–56; on abortion, 135–36, 138; on anticommunism, 137; on arms control, 137; on Congress, 5, 64; on crime control, 135, 140; on death penalty, 135, 140; on distrust of Congress, 2, 5, 64, 71–74; on foreign policy, 255; on health care spending, 134, 140; on homosexuality, 136, 140; on military spending, 137; on racial issues, 135, 138, 140; on school prayer, 136; on sexuality, 136; on trade policy, 275; on welfare spending, 134–35, 140; on women's issues, 135–36, 140–42

Quayle, Dan, 139

Reagan, Ronald: appointments of, 36–43; budget policy of, 35, 99, 179, 183–84, 188, 191–92; educational policy of, 225; foreign policy of, 252; legislative action of, 81, 97–99; 110–12; and liberalism, 4–5; and the New Right, 131, 139–40; trade policy of, 269, 273–74; welfare policy of, 110–12; 200
Reagan coalition, 7
Realignment, 4, 79, 126–28, 138, 143, 145, 150–51
Realist theory of international relations, 240–45
Religiosity, 10
Republican Party: electorate of, 142–45, 148–50, 162, 169–70; campaign platforms of, 139–40; and foreign policy, 17, 26; ideological orientation of, 4, 6–7, 140–42, 160; and the New Right, 131, 139–40, 148–49; political goals after 1994 of, 17, 54–55, 100, 114, 117–21, 149, 210, 257; and trade policy, 288–89; and welfare policy, 208–10

Scandals, 64, 71–72

School prayer, 136

Sexuality, 136

Social welfare, 110–20, 134–35, 140, 198–213

Somalia, 19, 23, 99, 254

Super-301–Measure, 264, 277, 279–80, 284, 287, 289

Supreme Court, 102, 104–05, 113

Tarnoff doctrine, 28, 31, 53

Taxation, 189–92, 195

Term limits, 2, 73

Trade policy, 19, 21–22, 53, 264–97

Uruguay Round, 264, 266–67, 274–75, 278, 280–90

Value change, 128–29

Vietnam War, 16, 18, 21, 24–26, 29, 34, 104, 136–37, 179–80, 190, 193–95, 251

Volcker Commission, 44–46

Voting: and electoral coalitions, 142–50, 169–71; in 1992 presidential election, 146–49; in 1994 congressional election, 146–50; and voting behavior, 142–45

Weinberger doctrine, 24–25

Welfare spending, 108–20, 134–35, 140

Women's issues, 135–36, 140–42

World Trade Organization (WTO), 285–89

Yugoslavia, 9, 16, 21, 23, 27–28, 99, 248–49, 252, 254